2014

MICHAEL SCOTT

PRINCETON UNIVERSITY PRESS   *Princeton and Oxford*

DELPHI

DELPHI

A History of the Center of the Ancient World

Copyright © 2014 by Michael Scott
Requests for permission to reproduce material from this work
should be sent to Permissions, Princeton University Press
Published by Princeton University Press, 41 William Street,
Princeton, New Jersey 08540
In the United Kingdom: Princeton University Press, 6 Oxford Street,
Woodstock, Oxfordshire OX20 1TW

press.princeton.edu

Cover image: Detail of Albert Tounaire, *Sanctuary of Apollo at Delphi*, watercolor, 1894, Ecole des
Beaux-Arts Paris. Photo Credit: CCI / The Art Archive at Art Resource, NY

ISBN 978-0-691-15081-9

Library of Congress Control Number: 201393891

British Library Cataloging-in-Publication Data is available

This book has been composed in Garamond Premier Pro

Printed on acid-free paper. ∞

Printed in the United States of America

10 9 8 7 6 5 4 3 2 1

For my friends, mentors, and colleagues in Cambridge, to whom I will always owe a great debt for their support, comradeship, and encouragement.

The investigation of the remains at Delphi is the most interesting and important work now remaining to be accomplished in the field of Classical archaeology. The part which Delphi played in the history of Greece is too well known to need recounting. The imagination of every man who recognises what modern civilisation owes to ancient Greece is stirred by the name of Delphi as by no other names except that of Athens. . . . Delphi will be forever one of the sacred seats of the life of the human race.

Circular of the Archaeological Institute of America, 11 May 1889

CONTENTS

Acknowledgments   *xi*

Maps   *xiii*

Prologue: *Why Delphi?*   *1*

PART I: *Some are born great*

    1:   Oracle   *9*

    2:   Beginnings   *31*

    3:   Transformation   *51*

    4:   Rebirth   *71*

PART II: *Some achieve greatness*

    5:   Fire   *93*

    6:   Domination   *119*

    7:   Renewal   *139*

    8:   Transition   *163*

PART III: *Some have greatness thrust upon them*

    9:   A New World   *183*

   10:   Renaissance   *203*

   11:   Final Glory?   *223*

   12:   The Journey Continues   *245*

    Epilogue: *Unearthing Delphi*   *269*

    Conclusion   *285*

    Guide: *A Brief Tour of the Delphi Site and Museum*   *291*

    Abbreviations   *303*

    Notes   *309*

    Bibliography   *375*

    Index   *401*

ACKNOWLEDGMENTS

This book would not have been born without the enthusiastic interest of my agent, Patrick Walsh, and of my editor, Rob Tempio, at Princeton University Press. Its development would not have been possible without the resources of the Classics Faculty in Cambridge, the British School at Athens, and the École française d'Athènes. Its story builds on the work of many scholars who have helped unravel Delphi's history, and who have in many cases kindly given their time and expertise to help me. Most importantly, this book's completion was secured thanks to the constant support I have been privileged to receive from the friends and loved ones I am lucky to have in my life.

MAPS

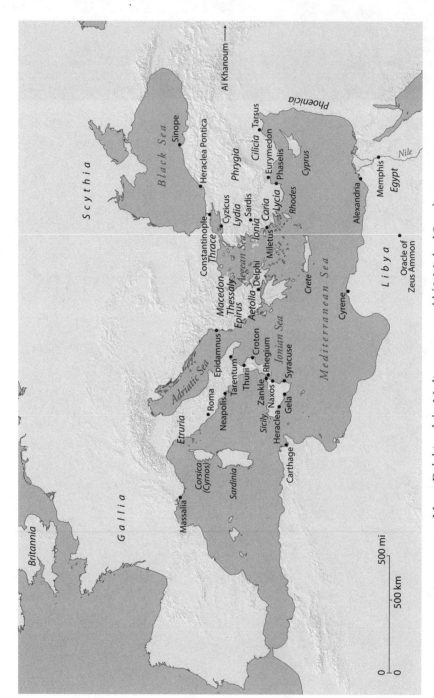

Map 1: Delphi and the Mediterranean world (© Michael Scott)

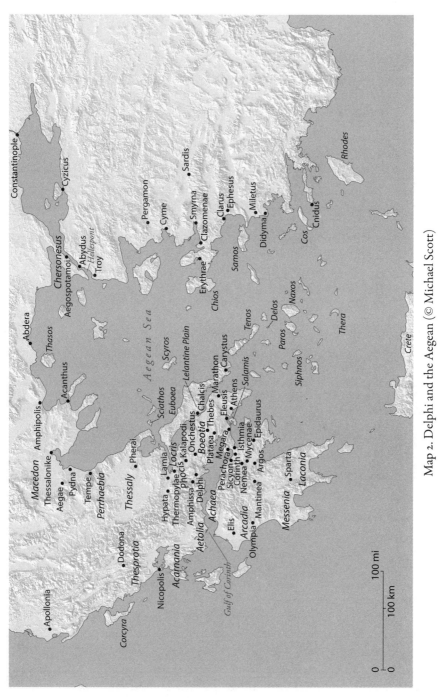

Map 2. Delphi and the Aegean (© Michael Scott)

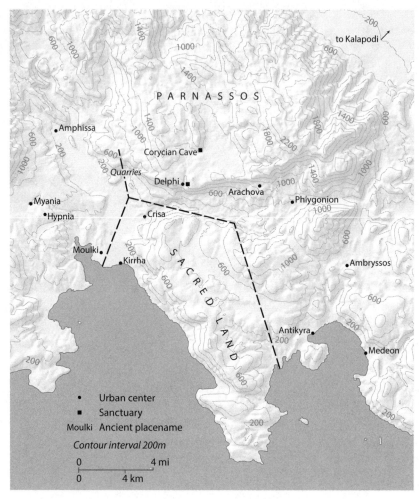

Map 3. Delphi and its immediate surroundings (© Michael Scott)

The following text labels appear on the map:

to Kalapodi

PARNASSOS

Amphissa

Corycian Cave ■

Quarries

Delphi ■

600 Arachova

Myania

Hypnia

Crisa

Phlygonion

Moulki

Kirrha

Ambryssos

S A C R E D   L A N D

Antikyra

Medeon

•   Urban center
■   Sanctuary
Moulki   Ancient placename

Contour interval 200m

0 —————— 4 mi
0 —————— 4 km

DELPHI

One of the enduring missions of Delphi is to bring
together men and women who otherwise remain divided
by material interests.

—Memorandum of Justification[1]

PROLOGUE: *Why Delphi?*

The love affair began, it was said, during the sacrifices in honor of the
hero Neoptolemus. It was conducted in secret: the woman was already
promised in marriage to someone else within the community. Eventually, the two young lovers decided to flee. They were helped to escape by
a priest, and traveled to the farthest reaches of the Mediterranean world,
where, after facing numerous trials and tribulations, they emerged triumphant and together.

This is the plot of an ancient Greek novel written by a man called Heliodorus.[2] The two lovers came from Delphi, a small city and religious
sanctuary clinging to the Parnassian mountains of central Greece, but
which was also known throughout antiquity as the very center, the omphalos, the "belly-button," of the ancient world. It is from this omphalos
that these two lovers escaped, aided by a priest, not of Apollo who ruled
at Delphi, but of the Egyptian god Isis. And it was to Memphis in Egypt,
to the extremes of the ancient Greek world that the two lovers traveled,
where, eventually, the couple themselves became priest and priestess of the
god of the Sun, *Helios*, and of the Moon, *Selene*.

Heliodorus's fictional novel creates a picture of a vast and yet connected world with Delphi at its center, to which the priests of Egyptian

Figure 0.1. The ancient sanctuary of Apollo at Delphi in its immediate land-scape, hidden from the Itean plain below within the folds of the Parnassian mountains (© EFA/P. Amandry [Aupert FD II Stade fig. 23]) 1 Gulf of Itea. 2 Itean plain. 3 Museum of Delphi. 4 Sanctuary of Delphi. 5 Zig-zag 'sacred way' path through Apollo sanctuary.

deities were welcomed and feted, and in which inhabitants of Delphi could become priests of deities worshiped at the boundaries of the ancient Mediterranean world. In the novel, Delphi is praised as a place ruled by Apollo, but where a plethora of other gods are honored; it is hailed as a place to which philosophers flock from all over the ancient world to perfect their wisdom secluded from the maddening crowds; and it is described by the priest of Isis, as he approached Delphi for the first time, as a divine location, resembling a fortress that Nature herself had chosen to take care of.[3]

Anyone who has visited Delphi will recognize the reality behind the priest's description, and particularly the way in which any sight of Delphi is denied to the visitor until the very last moment of their journey, as if the mountains themselves were protecting the city and sanctuary from view (see figs. 0.1, 0.2).[4] It is only as the road sweeps you around the final jutting crag of Parnassian rock, that there, hidden, protected in the womb of the mountains, Delphi is suddenly revealed. Marble glistens in the morning sunlight and glows golden at dusk. Ornate, carefully

Figure 0.2. The modern town of Delphi and its ancient counterpart on separate sides of a fold of the Parnassian mountains (© Michael Scott) 1 Corycian cave. 2 Ancient path leading from Delphi to Corycian cave. 3 Stadium. 4 Apollo sanctuary. 5 Castalian fountain. 6 Modern town of Delphi.

choreographed temple columns contrast with the gray wildness of the Parnassian rock face behind. The sound of mountain spring water making its way down to the plain below reaches your ears. And you are overcome by a stillness and a sense of otherworldliness as this hidden treasure finally reveals itself to you and beckons you in. There is a magic in the air, unlike that of any other place I have visited on earth.

It is no accident that Heliodorus chose Delphi as the location for some of the key events in his novel, as it was not just a spectacular setting, but a linchpin in the framework of the ancient world for centuries, well known to the majority of that world's inhabitants. At the heart of Delphi was the temple dedicated to the god Apollo, in which sat an oracular priestess, to which people from cities and dynasties all over the Mediterranean world flocked to hear her responses to their questions about the future. Surrounding the temple of Apollo was a religious sanctuary in which a number of different divinities were worshiped and which was full of stunning artistic and architectural offerings in bronze, silver, gold, ivory, and marble dedicated to the gods by these endless visitors. And surrounding the sanctuary of Apollo was the city and community of Delphi, as well as a number of other smaller sanctuaries and the facilities in which to hold massive athletic and musical competitions (which were considered on a par with the Olympics by the ancient Greeks), and to which, for centuries, competitors traveled to compete for glory in the eyes of men and of the gods (see plates 1, 2, 3).

This book tells the story of this extraordinary place, and of its significance in the history of the ancient world. How did its famous oracle work, and why did it capture the attention of the ancient world for so long? What were the crucial factors in securing Delphi's emergence as the predominant oracular site in a world teeming with oracles? How did the opportunities provided by offering rich dedications and taking part in athletic competitions contribute to Delphi's importance and its role within ancient society? What, in an ancient world almost constantly beset by tectonic changes in politics and war, enabled Delphi, a small city and sanctuary clinging to the Parnassian mountains, to survive it all? What eventually caused its demise? Why was the modern world of the nineteenth and twentieth centuries so fascinated by this ancient site, and what, if anything, can it still hold of value for us today?

The following pages tackle these questions and, in so doing, put forward a manifesto for how we should study this (and indeed other) crucial locations from the ancient world. Too often, past study of Delphi has been subdivided into its respective activities: its oracle, its dedications, its games; or into particular chronological periods of its activity, particularly its so-called golden age, that of the archaic and classical periods (650–300 BC); or into particular kinds of evidence for its role and importance (literary, epigraphic, or archaeological). These studies—while without doubt providing important, detailed, and scholarly insights into the sanctuary's history—have often treated each of these particular activities, time periods and sources in isolation from their wider contexts, fuller histories, and complementary viewpoints. But this is not how such activities, time periods, and sources existed in the ancient world, nor indeed how they, or the site itself, were perceived in the ancient world. To see Delphi as the ancient saw it and understood it, we need to consider these multiple activities together across the sanctuary's entire history and through the viewpoint of all the different historical sources available to us. This book seeks to offer such a perspective. It seeks to offer a global, fully rounded, view of the wide spectrum of activity that went on at Delphi across its entire lifespan, in total almost fifteen hundred years, as put forward through the complete range of source material available.

Thus, this book will highlight not only how each of Delphi's activities had its own trajectory of highs and lows over time, but also how Delphi's different activities impacted upon one another, as well as how Delphi's representation varied in the different source materials. And by bringing the study of these different activities, time periods, and sources together, this linked approach will enable us to understand better than ever both how Delphi's role and importance in the ancient world was perceived, shaped, and changed, and how and why Delphi survived for so long. We will, finally, begin to see Delphi—the omphalos of the ancient world—in full and brilliant Technicolor.

In viewing Delphi through this kind of lens, three main phases in its history become apparent, which have, in turn, become the three parts of this book. To my mind, these phases correspond to Shakespeare's famous line in *Twelfth Night*: "some are born great, some achieve greatness, and some have greatness thrust upon them." In part I, "Some are born great," we examine Delphi's oracle and earliest history, the ways in which the ancients sought to understand Delphi's emergence as a place born great and blessed by the gods, and the ways in which the archaeological evidence highlights a much more uncertain and difficult path to prominence. In part II, "Some achieve greatness," we learn about the golden age of Delphi's influence and the multiple ways in which it achieved greatness by becoming central to the ancient world. In part III, "Some have greatness thrust upon them," we see how Delphi was heroized, as well as used, abused, and misinterpreted, and indeed how Delphi actively played up to its developing reputation, from the Hellenistic period until the time of its rediscovery in the nineteenth century, in order to understand how Delphi secured its permanent reputation as one of the great centers of the ancient world. In the epilogue and conclusion, Delphi's story is brought to the present day, asking what value the sanctuary still holds for us and where our investigation of its extraordinary life will go next.

It is a testament to Delphi's unparalleled tenacity and ability to survive that Heliodorus wrote his novel about the love affair at Delphi and about Delphi's crucial place at the center of a connected Mediterranean society not in the hey-day of the classical world, but in the third or fourth centuries AD, on the cusp of the Mediterranean world's gradual conversion to Christianity and the end of pagan sanctuaries like the one at Delphi.[5] And yet, even in this twilight, Delphi's description glows bright. More tellingly, Heliodorus's description echoes that of another ancient writer, the geographer Strabo, who labeled Delphi, above all, as a *theatron*: a theater.[6] It was a space in which most of the moments that mattered in the history of the ancient world were played out, reflected on, or altered. As a result, an understanding of the ancient world and, I would argue, of humankind itself, is incomplete without an understanding of Delphi.

PART I
Some are born great

The oracle neither conceals, nor reveals, but indicates.

—Heraclitus in Plutarch, *Moralia* 404D

I

ORACLE

The appointed day had come. Having journeyed up the winding mountain paths to the sanctuary hidden within the folds of the Parnassian mountains, individuals from near and far, representatives from cities and states, dynasties and kingdoms across the Mediterranean had gathered in Apollo's sanctuary. As dawn broke, the word spread that it would soon be known whether the god Apollo was willing to respond to their questions. Sunlight reflected off the temple's marble frontage, the oracular priestess entered its inner sanctum, and the crowd of consultants moved forward, waiting their turn to know better what the gods had in store. The gods were considered all powerful, all controlling, and all knowing; their decisions, time and again, had proven to be final. The consultants had waited perhaps months, traveled perhaps thousands of miles. Now they waited patiently for their turn, each likely entering the home of the god with a great deal of trepidation as to what he might be told. Some left content. Others disappointed. Most thoughtful. With dusk, the god's priestess fell silent. The crowds dispersed, heading to every corner of the ancient world, bringing with them the prophetic words of the oracle at Delphi.

Without doubt, what fascinates us most about Delphi are the stories surrounding its oracle and the women who, for centuries, acted as the

Figure 1.1. Tondo of an Athenian red-figure cup c. 440–30 BC, found in Vulci, Etruria, showing Aegeus consulting Themis/the Pythia (© Bildarchiv Preussicher Kulturbesitz [Staatliche Museum, Berlin])

priestesses and mouthpieces of the god Apollo at the center of a Delphic oracular consultation (see fig. 1.1). But just how did the oracle at Delphi work, and why did it work for the ancient Greek world for so long?

These are difficult questions to answer for two central reasons. First, because, incredibly for an institution so central to the Greek world for so long, there has survived no straightforward, complete account about exactly how a consultation with the oracle at Delphi took place, or about how the process of bestowing divine inspiration upon the Pythian priestess worked. Of the sources we have, those from the classical period (sixth through fourth centuries BC) treat the process of consultation as common knowledge, to the extent that it does not need explaining, and indeed the consultations at Delphi often act as shorthand for descriptions of other oracular sanctuaries ("it happens here just like at Delphi . . ."). Many of the sources interested in discussing how the oracle worked in any detail are actually from Roman times (first century BC to fourth century AD), and thus at best can tell us only what the people in this later period thought (and often they offer conflicting stories) about a process that, as all of those writers agreed, was by then past its heyday. Also, while the archaeological evidence is of some use both in helping us understand the environment in which the consultation took place and in revealing possible scenarios about the process by which the Pythia was inspired during the classical, Hellenistic, and Roman periods, it comes up short in helping us understand the first centuries of the oracle's existence (the late eighth and seventh centuries BC), during which the oracle was, according to the literary sources, astoundingly active.[1]

The second difficulty surrounding the oracle is in analyzing the literary evidence for what questions were put to her and the responses she gave.[2] This is not only because many of the responses are recorded for us by ancient authors writing long after the response was supposedly uttered, and sometimes by those hostile to pagan religious practices, like the Christian writer Eusebius. And it is not only because these writers themselves often were relying on other sources for their information, with the result that even if two or more describe the same oracular consultation, their records of it are often different. It is also because these writers tend not to record oracular consultations as "straight" history, but rather employ these stories to perform a particular function within their own narratives.[3] As a result, some scholars have sought to label as ahistorical nearly everything the oracle from Delphi is said to have pronounced before the fifth century BC. Others have thought it almost impossible to write a history of the Delphic oracle after the fourth century BC because of difficulties with the sources. Still others have tried to steer a middle path in a spectrum of more likely to less likely, albeit with the understanding, as the scholars Herbert Parke and Donald Wormell put it in their still-authoritative catalog of Delphic oracular responses in 1956, that "there are thus practically no oracles to which we can point with complete confidence in their authenticity."[4]

As several scholars have remarked, it is thus one of Delphi's many ironies that the Pythian priestesses—the women central to a process that was supposed to give clarity to difficult decisions in the ancient world—have taken the secret of that process to their graves and left us instead with such an opaque view of this crucial ancient institution. In such a situation, the only option is to produce a fairly static snapshot of what we know was a changing oracular process at Delphi over its more than one thousand–year history; a snapshot that is both a compilation of sources from different times and places (with all the accompanying difficulties such an account brings) and one that inevitably takes a particular stance on a number of conflicting and unresolvable issues.

The oracle at Delphi was a priestess, known as the Pythia. We know relatively little about individual Pythias, or about how and why they were chosen.[5] Most of our information comes from Plutarch, a Greek writing in the first century AD, who came from a city not far from Delphi and served as one of the priests in the temple of Apollo (there was an oracular Pythian priestess at the temple of Apollo, but also priests—more on the latter later). The Pythia had to be a Delphian, and Plutarch tells us that in his day the woman was chosen from one of the "soundest and most respected families to be found in Delphi." Yet this did not mean a noble family; in fact, Plutarch's Pythia had "always led an irreproachable life, although, having been brought up in the homes of poor peasants, when she fulfils her prophetic role she does so quite artlessly and without any special knowledge or talent."[6] Once chosen, the Pythia served Apollo for life and committed herself to strenuous exercise and chastity. At some point in the oracle's history, possibly by the fourth century BC and certainly by AD 100, she was given a house to live in, which was paid for by the sanctuary. Plutarch laments that while in previous centuries the sanctuary was so busy that they had to use three Pythias at any one time (two regular and one understudy), in his day one Pythia was enough to cope with the dwindling number of consultants.[7]

Diodorus Siculus (Diodorus "of Sicily"), who lived in the first century BC, tells us that originally the woman picked had also to be a young virgin. But this changed with Echecrates of Thessaly, who, coming to consult the Pythia, fell in love with her, carried her off, and raped her; thus the Delphians decreed that in the future the Pythia should be a woman of fifty years or older, but that she should continue, as Pythia, to wear the dress of a maiden in memory of the original virgin prophetess. Thus, it is thought not uncommon for women to have been married and to have been mothers before being selected as the Pythia, and, as a result, withdrawing from husbands and families to perform their role.[8]

The Pythia was available for consultation only one day per month, thought to be the seventh day of each month because the seventh day of the month of Bysios—the beginning of spring (our March/April)—was considered Apollo's birthday. Moreover, she was only available nine months of the year, since during the three winter months Apollo was considered absent from Delphi, and instead living with the Hyperboreans (a mythical people who lived at the very edges of the world). During this time, Delphi may have been oracle-less but was not god-less; instead the god Dionysus was thought to rule the sanctuary.[9]

Despite this rather narrow window of opportunity for consultation—only nine days per year—there has been much discussion of the availability (and, indeed, popularity) of alternative forms of divination on offer at Delphi. In particular, scholars have debated the existence of a "lot" oracle: a system whereby a sanctuary official, perhaps the Pythia, would perform a consultation using a set of randomized ("lottery") objects, which would be "read" to give a response to a particular question.[10] Such a system of alternative consultation may also have been supplemented by a "dice" oracle performed at the Corycian cave high above Delphi (see figs. 0.2, 1.2), which from the sixth century BC onward, was an increasingly popular cult location for the god Pan and the Muses, and a firmly linked part of the "Delphic" itinerary and landscape.[11]

On the nine days a year set aside for full oracular consultation, the day seems to have progressed as follows. The Pythia would head at dawn to bathe in the Castalian spring near the sanctuary (see fig. 0.2). Once

Figure 1.2. The Corycian cave from the outside (*top*) and inside (*bottom*), high above Delphi on a plateau of the Parnassian mountains (© Michael Scott)

purified, she would return to the sanctuary, probably accompanied by her retinue, and enter into the temple, where she would burn an offering of laurel leaves and barley meal to Apollo, possibly accompanied by a spoken homage to all the local deities (akin to that dramatized in the opening scene of the ancient Greek tragedy *Eumenides* by the playwright Aeschylus).[12] Around the same time, however, the priests of the temple were responsible for verifying that even these rare days of consultation could go ahead. The procedure was to sprinkle cold water on a goat (which itself had to be pure and without defect), probably at the sacred hearth within the temple. If the goat shuddered, it indicated that Apollo was happy to be consulted. The goat would then be sacrificed on the great altar to Apollo outside the temple as a sign to all that the day was auspicious and the consultation would go ahead.[13]

The consultants, who would have had to arrive probably some days before the appointed consultation day, would now play their part. They first had to purify themselves with water from the springs of Delphi. Next, they had to organize themselves according to the strict rules governing the order of consultation. Local Delphians always had first rights of audience. What followed them was a system of queuing that prioritized first Greeks whose city or tribe was part of Delphi's supreme governing council (called the Amphictyony), then all other Greeks, and finally non-Greeks. But within each "section" (e.g., Amphictyonic Greeks), there was also a way to skip to the front, a system known as *promanteia*. Promanteia, the right "to consult the oracle [*manteion*] before [*pro*] others," could be awarded to individuals or cities by the city of Delphi as an expression of the close relationship between them or as thanks for particular actions. Most famously, the island of Chios was awarded promanteia following its dedication of a new giant altar in the Apollo sanctuary (see fig. 1.3), on which they later inscribed, in a rather public way given that the queue very likely went past their altar, the fact that they had been awarded promanteia. If there were several consultants with promanteia within a particular section, their order was decided by lot, as was the order for everyone else within a particular section.[14]

Figure 1.3. A reconstruction of the temple terrace, the area in front of the temple of Apollo in the Apollo sanctuary of Delphi, with main structures marked (© Michael Scott) 1 Delphi charioteer. 2 Fourth century BC column with omphalos and tripod. 3 Stoa of Attalus. 4 Apollo temple. 5 Athenian palm tree dedication. 6 Statue and columns of Sicilian rulers. 7 Column and statue of Aemilius Paullus. 8 Altar of Chians. 9 Salamis Apollo. 10 Rhodian statue of Helios. 11 Statues of Attalus II and Eumenes II of Pergamon. 12 Direction of approach for those coming from lower half of Apollo sanctuary. 13 Plataean serpent column.

Once the order was decided, the money had to be paid. Each consultant had to offer the *pelanos*, literally a small sacrificial cake that was burned on the altar, but that they had to buy from the Delphians for an additional amount (the "price" of consultation, and the source of a regular and bountiful income for Delphi). We don't know a lot about the prices charged, except that they varied. One inscription, which has survived to us, recounts an agreement between Delphi and Phaselis, a city in Asia Minor, in 402 BC. The price for a "state" inquiry (i.e., by the city) was seven Aeginetan drachmas and two obols. The price for a "private" inquiry by individual Phaselites was four obols.[15] The interesting points here are not only the difference in price for official and personal business (ten times more for official business), but also that such individual agreements could be made (the thinking being perhaps that the cost was related to city wealth, and richer cities like Athens should pay more). But it's clear that, even at the cheaper end, the price would ensure that thought was given to the necessity of consultation. The price for an individual Phaselite to consult the oracle was the equivalent of about two days pay for an Athenian juryman in the fifth century BC, so combined with the costs of return travel to Delphi, and loss of income while away, this was a real investment. Another inscription, from 370 BC, between Sciathus, an island in the Aegean, and Delphi, records a lower cost: only two drachma for a state inquiry and one sixth of that for a private one. But we don't know for sure whether this was a difference in agreement between Delphi and Phaselis and Delphi and Sciathus, or whether Delphi had dropped its prices in the fourth century BC (as scholars who argue for the decline of the popularity of the oracle in this period like to think).[16] As well, some people were awarded the honor of not paying at all. King Croesus of Lydia in Asia Minor was one of these, but so were the Asclepiads (the worshipers of the healing god Asclepius) from the island of Cos in later times.[17]

All this would take time, and consultants would be obliged to wait for long periods (the surviving inscriptions speak of a *chresmographeion*—a sort of shelter built against the north retaining wall of the temple terrace—as their "waiting area" in the shade). When it was his turn, however, the consultant would enter the temple, where he (no women except the Pythia were allowed into the inner part of the temple) was required to perform another sacrifice on the inner hearth. If not a Delphian, he had to be accompanied in this process by a Delphian who acted as *proxenos*, the "local representative."[18] The sacrifice, often of an animal (which the consultant would also pay for), was burned, part offered to the gods, part given to the Delphians, and part used "for the knife" (meaning most probably that it was given as a tip to the man actually conducting the sacrifice).[19] Once this was completed, the consultant moved forward to where the Pythia was waiting and was encouraged by the priests of the temple to "think pure thoughts and speak well-omened words," and finally the consultation could begin.[20]

It is at this point that the sources become even more difficult to reconcile. The first difficulty is over the arrangement of the inner sanctum of the temple. The Pythia was said to prophesize from the adyton, a special restricted access area within the temple. Several different sources tell us the adyton was a fairly packed environment, containing the omphalos (the stone representing the center of the world), two statues of Apollo (one in wood and one in gold), Apollo's lyre and sacred armor, the tomb of Dionysus (although this may have also been the omphalos), as well as the Pythia sitting on her tripod alongside a laurel tree.[21] But scholars have bitterly disputed where and how this adyton was situated within the temple, some arguing it was sunk into the floor at the back of the *cella* (the main part), others that it was a completely underground space, and others that it was simply part of the inner cella.[22] The initial excavations of the temple found no obvious architectural evidence for such a sunken space, although the latest plan of the (fourth century BC) temple now shows a square room walled off within the cella, which may or may not have been the adyton (see fig. 1.4).[23]

Where did the consultant stand? The issue becomes even more difficult. The famous vase painting of the Pythia on her tripod facing a consultant has traditionally been interpreted as demonstrating that the consultant was in the room, facing the Pythia, delivering his question directly to her and thus hearing her response directly as well (fig. 1.1).[24] But Herodotus and Plutarch also indicate that there was some sort of other structure within the cella of the temple in which the inquirers sat at the moment of consultation. This room, named the *megaron* by Herodotus (7.140) and the *oikos* by Plutarch (*Mor.* 437C), has not been identified archaeologically.

Who else was present? Again the sources give us an unclear answer. We know that there were the priests of the temple of Apollo, who

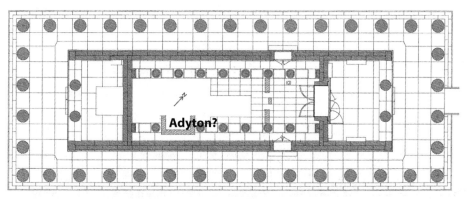

Figure 1.4. The latest plan of the fourth century BC temple of Apollo in the Apollo sanctuary at Delphi, indicating the possible location of the adyton where consultations took place (© EFA [Amandry and Hansen FD II Temple du IVième siècle fig. 18.19])

had conducted the ceremony involving the goat.[25] Yet the sources also mention individuals named *prophetes*, and, in later sources, individuals called *hosioi*, as well as a group of women who were in charge of keeping the flame burning on the (laurel-wood-only) inner sacred hearth.[26] Part of the problem in understanding this collection of people and their roles is that the terms may overlap (e.g., "prophetes" is used in literature but not recorded as an actual title in Delphic inscriptions), and that the numbers as well as groups of people present changed over time.[27] If, as Plutarch says, the consultants stayed in a separate room, then the likelihood is their question was given orally, or in writing, to one of the priests of Apollo, who, in later times perhaps along with the hosioi, accompanied the Pythia into the adyton and put the question to her. Did they write down/interpret/versify/make up her response? None of the ancient sources give us a clear answer, although it does seem to have been possible for the consultant not only to have (at least partially) heard the Pythia's response while sitting in a separate room, but also to receive either an oral or written form of the response in turn from the priests.[28] But just what role the priests had in forming that response depends on what kind of response we understand the Pythia to have given, which, in turn, depends on just how we understand her to have been "inspired."

No issue has been more hotly debated than the process by which the Pythia was inspired to give her response. First, the ancient sources. Before the fourth century BC, there is no source that discusses how the Pythia was inspired, but all say that she sat on her tripod, from which she uttered "*boai*" "cries/songs" (e.g., Eur. *Ion* 91). From the fourth century BC, some sources mention her shaking a laurel branch, but perhaps as a gesture of purification rather than of inspiration.[29] We have to wait until Diodorus Siculus in the first century BC for the first mention of a "chasm" below the Pythia.[30] Some subsequent writers agree with this, but others describe it is a space she physically descends into and prophesizes from.[31] In Diodorus's narrative, it was this chasm, and the powerful vapor that emerged from it, that led to the initial discovery and installation of an oracle at Delphi. He recounts the story of how a goatherd noticed that his goats, approaching a particular hole on the mountainside, started to shriek and leap around. Goatherds began to do the same when they approached, and also began to prophesize. The news of the spot spread and many people started leaping into the hole, so "to eliminate the danger, the locals appointed one woman as prophetess for all. They built her an apparatus [the tripod] on which she could be safe during her trances."[32]

Plutarch, in the first century AD, mentions the *pneuma* (translated as "wind," "air," "breeze," "breath," or "inspiration"), and that occasionally the oikos was filled with a "delightful fragrance" as a result of the pneuma, but he does not describe its exact nature. Instead he relays a long-running argument among his friends about why the oracle is less active now than it was in the past. The arguments include less pneuma; the moral degeneration of mankind leading to its abandonment by the gods; the depopulation of Greece and the departure of the *daimones* (spirits) responsible for divination. But Plutarch also insists that the Pythia did not at any point rant or rave. Instead, he comments that, after a consultation session, the Pythia "feels calm and peaceful." In fact, the only time the Pythia is said to have sounded odd was on the occasion when the entire process of consultation had been forced (the goat was deluged in cold water to ensure that it shivered to provide the right signs for the consultation to go ahead). The result was that the Pythia's voice sounded odd. "It was at once plain from the harshness of her voice that she was not responding properly; she was like a labouring ship and was filled with a mighty and baleful spirit," which suggests that, in normal circumstances, the Pythia responded in a normal-sounding voice and manner.[33]

Strabo, a geographer of the ancient world writing in the first century AD, represents the Pythia as sitting on the tripod, receiving the pneuma, speaking oracles in both prose and verse. Another writer, Lucan, however, still in the first century AD, gives a very different impression of the Pythia, in which the her body is taken over by the god through the inhalation of the vapor, and she raves as a result. In the writings of Pausanias, a Greek travel writer from the second century AD, the Pythia also drinks from the Cassotis spring (the one that runs by and under the temple at Delphi) for inspiration. In the writings of Lucian, a rhetorician from the second century AD, the Pythia chews laurel leaves for inspiration and drinks not from the Cassotis, but from the Castalian spring. In the Christian writers, for example John Crysostom, the picture focuses again on the effects of the pneuma: the Pythia's "madness" is caused by the "evil" pneuma rising upward from beneath her, entering through her genitals as she sits on the tripod.[34]

Thus the most well-known modern picture of a Pythia, inspired/sent "mad" by breathing in/being taken over by "vapors" from a chasm below the tripod, and giving as a result raving and insensible answers (which then have to be made sense of by the priests around her) is a composite one, from mostly late Roman and indeed several anti-pagan sources. Scholars have long pointed out that in particular the Roman assumption of the Pythia's madness, and search for an explanation for it (via the chasm and its vapors), could well have emerged from the mistranslation of Plato's description of her divine inspiration as *mania* (linked in Greek to *mantike*—"divination"), which became the Latin *insania* ("insanity"). To a Roman audience, used to divination carried out through a series of taught, more scientific "arts" (e.g., the reading of livers from sacrificed animals), understanding her mania, her madness, as a result of intoxication by gas from a subterranean chasm rendered the Delphic oracular process "intelligible and satisfying."[35]

Yet despite this understanding of the raving Pythia as a consequence of cultural mistranslation and subsequent elaboration, and despite the fact that no source mentions it before the first century BC, the picture of the Pythia breathing in vapors from a chasm below her tripod has always been the dominant model for understanding how the oracle at Delphi functioned. To such an extent that finding the mechanism of the vapors was originally regarded as the litmus test for successful archaeological investigation at Delphi. The original excavators of the site were extremely disappointed not to find a chasm below the temple—they felt almost cheated by the "deception" of the literary sources.[36] The stakes were understandably high: at the time of Delphi's excavation in the 1890s, interest in the oracle, and in psychic research more generally, could not have been stronger. In 1891 the burlesque opera *Apollo*, or *The Oracle at Delphi* played to great acclaim on Broadway. In the same year, John Collier painted his famous *Priestess of Delphi* in which a sensual priestess breathes in vapors from her tripod over a chasm (see plate 4), and the Society of Psychical Research was started by Cambridge academics and published its first volume examining the oracle at Delphi. In the wake of the disappointing excavations, thus, there was a feeling that the ancient sources had lied. The scholar A. P. Oppé in 1904 in the *Journal of Hellenic Studies* argued that the entire practice at Delphi was a farce, a sham, put on by the priests of Apollo, tricking the ancient world.[37] Others sought different explanations for the Pythia's madness: they focused on the laurel leaves, and suggested the Pythia had been high from eating laurel. One German scholar, Professor Oesterreich, even ate laurel leaves to test the theory, remarking disappointedly that he felt no different.[38] Others opined that the answer relied not in some form of drug, but in psychology. Herbert Parke and Donald Wormell argued in the 1950s that the Pythia, in the heat of the moment after so much preparation on the particular day of consultation, and after so many years perhaps involved with the temple as one of the women guarding the sacred flame, would have found herself in an emotionally intense relationship with the god, and could easily have fallen victim to self-induced hypnosis.[39] More recently, scholars have employed a series of anthropological approaches to understand belief in spirit possession, and applied these to how the Pythia may have functioned.[40]

The chasm idea, however, was hard to forget. The Rev. T. Dempsey in the early twentieth century argued that perhaps, just as Plutarch had suggested the oracle worked less in his day thanks to less pneuma, the chasm had, in modern times, completely closed up.[41] Others sought even more ingenious explanations for how the vapors had been created without a chasm, including one in which the Pythia herself descended to a room below her tripod to light a fire that produced the smoke (possibly from the hemp plant) she then breathed in, as if it were vapors from the god.[42] This explanation, coupled with the analysis of a particular stone block filled with mysterious holes and grooves, thought to be that on which the tripod and omphalos were positioned and through which the vapors arose (still on view at Delphi but now recognized as a stone later recut as an olive press), crystallized the sense that the ancients had "bought" a hoax for more than a thousand years at Delphi.[43]

More recently, the debate over the presence of inspiring vapors at Delphi has re-emerged, thanks to a reassessment of Delphi's geology.[44] Analysis by the geologist Jelle De Boer and the archaeologist John Hale through the 1980s and 1990s led, in the first decade of the twenty-first century, to their publishing evidence for two major geological fault lines crossing at Delphi (one running east-west, the other north-south) directly underneath the temple of Apollo (see plates 1, 2; figs. 0.1, 0.2). At the same time, they argued that the bedrock beneath the temple was fissured, which would allow for small amounts of gas to rise up through the rock, despite the absence of a chasm. This gas originated from the bituminous (full of hydrocarbons) limestone naturally occurring in this area, which would have been stimulated to release its gas by shifts in the active fault lines beneath. Testing both the travertine (itself a product found only in active fault areas) and the water beneath the temple at Delphi, they found ethane, methane, and ethylene, which had been used as an anaesthesia in the 1920s, thanks to its ability to produce a pleasant, disembodied, trancelike state. They postulated that the geology of Delphi could thus have produced enough of these potent gases to, within an enclosed space like the adyton, put the Pythia into a trancelike state.[45] The ancients may not have been lying after all.

This research created huge excitement in public and academic circles, but in reality, while fascinating, it still did not really solve the problem. Even if intoxicating gases were produced in the temple at Delphi, and these gases did "inspire" the Pythia (despite that none of the sources before the first century BC point to this as the method of inspiration), how did the answers she gave, even if massaged and shaped by the priests of Apollo, remain suitable, useful, right enough for the oracle to continue as a valid institution for over one thousand years? Or as Simon Price, a scholar with a reputation for pushing straight to the heart of a problem, put it: "Why was it that the sane, rational Greeks wanted to hear the rantings of an old woman up in the hills of central Greece?"[46] To understand this, we must put the process of oracular consultation at Delphi in its wider religious context, and think more carefully about the way in which the oracle was perceived.

Oracles were an essential, and respected, part of the Greek world. They were also everywhere you looked. Scholarship has demonstrated the vast array of oracular sanctuaries on offer, which varied from the Pythian priestess at Delphi to the consultation of the rustling of leaves of Zeus's sacred tree at Dodona in northern Greece, to consultation with spirits of the dead, like at Heracleia Pontice on the Black Sea (see map 1).[47] Sometimes even the same god could have very different forms of oracular consultation at his different sanctuaries: so while Apollo *Pythios* (as Apollo was worshiped at Delphi) had the Pythia at Delphi, at the sanctuary of Apollo *Pythaios* in Argos, his priestess took part in nocturnal sacrifices and drank the blood of the sacrificial victims as part of her inspiration to prophesize.[48] But this form of divination (putting a question to a god through a priestly representative) was also just one of the forms of divination available in ancient Greece. Another was the reading of signs from particular natural events and actions and interpreting them in relation to a particular question. Just about everything could be read: the flight of birds (although not the movement of fish), patterns of words, sneezing, entrails, fire, vegetables, ripples on water, reflections in mirrors, trees, atmospheric phenomena, stars, as well as randomized dice, beans and other forms of "lot" oracle. In addition, there was a host of wandering *chresmologoi* or *manteis* ("oracle-tellers" or "seers") who could be engaged on the street in any major Greek city for consultations, which could be conducted in a variety of ways, from the reading of appropriate oracle responses in books of oracles to connecting with dead spirits.[49]

Key here is that the Greek world was filled with a "constant hum" of divine communication.[50] It was a system used by all levels of Greek society, and as well, it was a system in which everyone had their "preferred" form of communication, which could alter depending on the type and importance of the question to be asked. The Athenian general Nicias in the fifth century BC had his own personal seer as did many other military commanders. In the sixth century BC, Peisistratus, the Athenian tyrant, never consulted Delphi, but liked using chresmologoi. Alexander the Great in the fourth century BC liked his manteis to come from Asia Minor. Such seers could be incredibly well respected: Lampon was a seer in the fifth century BC but also a friend of the famous general and statesman Pericles and responsible for the foundation of Thurii in South Italy. Nicias's chief seer, Stilbides, was also one of his top soldiers.

The importance of divination does not mean, however, that the oracular system was never mocked in Greek culture. The consultation of oracles was lampooned in Greek comedy: in Aristophanes' *Knights* and *Birds*, for example, oracle sellers are figures of fun. The strength of their connection with the divine too could be questioned. Euripides, in a fragment of an otherwise lost play (Frag. 973N), wrote "the best seer is the one who guessed right." Sometimes too their usefulness could be questioned. Xenophon, in the fourth century BC, argued that divination became useful only when human capacity ended.[51] We shall see in the coming chapters instances wherein even the oracle of Apollo at Delphi was said to have been bribed and to have become biased, or was treated with circumspection by even its most loyal consultants. But all these instances represent an aberration from the norm, an aberration that did not in the long term shake belief in the system as a whole, a system that continued to speak of divination as a useful and real connection to the gods.

It is difficult for us to understand this kind of mindset today. In the 1930s, the anthropologist Sir Edward Evans-Pritchard tried to understand the Greeks' acceptance of oracles by observing the Azande community in Central Africa, who used a form of poison-chicken oracle to resolve disputes and make difficult community, as well as individual, decisions. His research showed that within the framework of a particular culture and life in which everyone agreed that the poison-chicken oracle was a proper and respected way to choose a solution, it was as good a means as any to help run a community.[52] But where does this leave us with the Pythia? On the one hand, we have to imagine ourselves into a society in which oracular connection with the divine was a commonly accepted cultural activity into a world that was believed to be controlled by the gods. Those gods could be for you or against you, and so it made sense to make every effort not only to appease them with offerings, but to use a variety of methods of divination to find out what they had in mind for the future. At the same time, the gathering of tradition about the power and importance of an oracle like the Pythia at Delphi, coupled with the prolonged rituals encountered before the consultation, would have helped to ensure belief in the process and its outcome. This does not mean people had to *know* exactly how the Pythia connected with the god: even Plutarch, himself (as indicated above) a priest at Delphi in the first century AD, was content to relate the argument and debate among his friends, who each had their own ideas about how the inspiration took place and why it happened less frequently in their time. Key is that—however it happened—there was a belief in a connection between the divine and human world through the Pythia.

At the same time, a number of other factors must be taken into consideration to understand how the Pythia retained her reputation for over one thousand years. The first is the kind of information sought from the Pythia. The questioning of the Pythia in the sixth century BC by King Croesus of Lydia in Asia Minor is often thought, because it is so well known, to be typical of how consultants put their questions to the oracle. But one of the things Herodotus, our major source for this encounter, is likely indicating is that Croesus's encounter with Delphi shows how little this "non-Greek" understood about Greek culture. As we shall see in later chapters, Croesus's direct question to oracles all around the Mediterranean in order to find out which was the "best" (the "what am I doing at this moment?" question) was, in fact, a very unusual type of question to ask an oracle. Not because it was a test of present knowledge, but because it involved such a direct request for information. Very rarely, it seems, did consultants ask the oracle direct questions about the future (so Croesus's second question about whether he would win the war against King Cyrus of Persia was again an odd form of question).[53] Instead, most questions put to the oracle seem to have been in the form of "would it be better and more profitable for me to do X or Y?" or else, "to which god shall I pray before I do X?"[54] This is to say, consultants presented problems to the Pythia in the form of options, or rather sought guidance for how their goals might come about, rather than asking directly what would happen in the future.

Such a process, focused around guidance rather than revelation, underlines the kind of occasions on which people chose to consult the oracle at Delphi, particularly instances in which individuals, or a community, were having trouble reaching a consensus over which of a particular set of potential actions to take. It is this usefulness of an oracle at moments of community indecision that has been, as we shall explore in the following chapters, thought critical in turning the Delphic oracle into such a well-known and important institution in the Greek world in the late eighth and seventh centuries BC, the period that bore witness to the tectonic forces of community creation that laid the bedrock for the landscape of the classical world.

Second to be considered is the question of the Pythia's response. Scholars have long remarked on the perfect hexameter verse responses reported in the literary sources as coming straight from the Pythia. There has been substantial doubt cast over her ability to utter directly such poetry, and instead scholars have pointed the finger at her priests as the ones who constructed the responses. At the same time, scholars have pointed to Delphi as a developing "information center," since it was one of the few places in the ancient world people were going to from all over on a regular basis, and bringing with them information about their home-lands. As a result, a picture has formed of priests who were "plugged in" to the information "hub" at Delphi and thus able to give better-informed guesses about which options were better and outcomes more likely (and have more ability to put those responses into verse). I have some sympa-thy with elements of this picture: no doubt Delphi was, especially in the sixth through fourth centuries BC, something of an information center. We can only imagine the exchange of information going on during the nine days of the year that consultants from all over the Greek world could turn up (not to mention the days either side they had to wait, or at the Pythian games, or while constructing monuments or while visiting the sanctuary to see it in all its splendor), and the degree to which this infor-mation fed back into the consultation system. But at the same time, this can only at best explain the success of Delphi once it had become a suc-cess. When Delphi's oracle first began to be consulted, there was precious little more information going to Delphi than elsewhere.

More fundamental in understanding the Pythia's success from the out-set is the in-built ambiguity of her responses, in part as a direct result of the nature of the questions asked. As we saw above, questions normally came in the form of "is it better and more profitable that I do X or Y" or "which gods should I pray to before I do X." As a result, if the Pythia replied "do X" or "it is better and more profitable to do X," and X proved disastrous, people would still never know how bad option Y might have been in comparison. As well, even if the oracle replied telling you to pray to a particular god, this indicated only a prerequisite action to ensure a chance of success; it did not guarantee a good result: praying to a god came with the understanding that there was no guarantee the god would listen in return. The comparative form of the question, and the unequal nature of the relationship between human and divine, ensured that it was impossible for the oracle to be categorically wrong in its response.

Sometimes that ambiguity seems to have been taken a step further in the form of a more complex answer, which in turn demanded a process of further interpretation from the consultant. King Croesus's inappropri-ate question about waging war, for example, received a very ambiguous

Delphic answer: "Croesus, having crossed the river Halys, will destroy a great empire." The response doesn't make clear whether it will be Croesus's empire or that of his enemies. In Herodotus's narrative, Croesus took it to mean his enemies', but it turned out to be his own (Croesus lost his kingdom as a result of losing the battle). Once again, the oracle, thanks to the ambiguity of the response could not be argued to have been wrong: it was Croesus who had chosen to misinterpret the Pythia's response.[55]

Plutarch, in the first century AD, commented on this well-known ambiguity in oracular responses of the past, noting that, in his day, responses tended to be more direct, but that in olden times, ambiguous replies were necessary because they protected the Pythia from the powerful people who came to consult her: "Apollo, though not prepared to conceal the truth, manifests it in roundabout ways: by clothing it in poetic form he rids it of what is harsh or offensive, as one does with brilliant light by reflecting it and thus splitting it into several rays."[56] Not for nothing was the god Apollo often known as Apollo Loxias, Apollo "the ambiguous one."

Moreover, and crucially, an ambiguous response demanded further debate and deliberation from the consultant and his city. What often began as an issue the community could not decide on, was referred to the Delphic oracle for further enlightenment, and was thus often sent back to the community for continued deliberation about the problem, but with the fresh information/indication and momentum toward making a decision in the form of the god's response. As classicist Sarah I. Johnston puts it, consulting the oracle at Delphi "extends [consultants'] agency; it puts new reins in their hands."[57] Consulting the Pythia thus did not always provide a quick answer to a straightforward question, but rather paved the path for a process of deliberation that allowed the community to come to its own decision.[58] Indeed the very process of deciding to consult Delphi, sending representatives to ask the question, waiting for one of the rare consultation days and potentially more than one if it was a very busy time, and then returning with a response that became part of a further debate meant a decision to consult Delphi substantially slowed down the decision process and gave the community much longer to mull over the issue.

All this means that we need to understand the Pythia at Delphi not as providing a "fortune-telling service," but rather as a "sense-making mechanism" for the individuals, cities, and communities of ancient Greece. Or as Heraclitus said in the quote that opens this chapter, "the oracle neither conceals, nor reveals, but indicates." Delphi was, as one businessman once remarked to me, something of an ancient management consultant. It was an adviser, albeit one with powerful authority.[59] In a world that never seriously doubted the power and omnipresence of the gods, a complex and widespread system for consultation on what the gods had in store made perfect sense. Within that network of different levels and types of consultation, the Pythian priestess at Delphi had emerged, by the end of seventh century BC, preeminent, and would continue to be consulted right through until the fourth century AD. What a consultation at Delphi offered was a chance to air a difficult decision in fresh light, receive extra (divine-inspired) information and direction, which, while itself necessitating further discussion, brought with it powerful authority and thus a significant push toward consensus in regard to community decisions, and contentment that one was following the will of the gods in individual decisions. At the same time, the processes by which the Pythia was consulted—the form of the questions and the form of her responses—insulated the oracle at Delphi so that even Croesus's exasperated attempts to show the oracle as having lied to him failed to dent its reputation. It gave Delphi a Teflon coating, a resistance to failure that, while challenged on particular occasions, would ensure that the oracle survived for over a millennium.

But, how, when, and why did it all begin? Just how did the city and sanctuary of Delphi, with its oracle at its center, emerge to such preeminence by the end of the seventh century BC? What can we know about the earliest development of this institution and its surrounding community that would come to be known as the center of the ancient world, and how did the ancients themselves seek to explain the importance and origins of Delphi and its oracle? These questions are the focus of the next two chapters.

"The names have strength, the shadows have authority."

—George Daux, one of the early Delphic scholars
    (quoted in Mulliez 2007, p. 156)

2

BEGINNINGS

How, when, why did it all begin?

At some time between the late seventh and mid-sixth century BC, the earliest origins of Delphi were explained in the form of the *Homeric Hymn to Apollo*. This hymn, which forms part of a larger collection of hymns—attributed at different times to the authorship of Homer, Hesiod, Cynatheus of Chios and, as a result normally left anonymous— praising the different Olympian gods, charts Apollo's life from his birth on the island of Delos through to his search for a suitable place to set up his oracle:

> And thence you went speeding swiftly to the mountain ridge, and came to Crisa beneath snowy Parnassus, a foothill turned towards the west: a cliff hangs over it from above, and a hollow, rugged glade runs under. There the lord Pheobus Apollo resolved to make his lovely temple, and thus he said "In this place I am minded to build a glorious temple to be an oracle for men, and here they will always bring perfect offerings, both they who dwell in rich Peloponnesus and the men of Europe and from all the wave-washed

isles, coming to question me. And I will deliver to them all counsel that cannot fail, answering them in my rich temple."[1]

Apollo's journey did not take him directly from Delos to the Parnassian mountains. Before eventually settling upon Crisa, he had passed through, and rejected, a number of sites throughout Greece: the Lelantine plain in Euboea, Thebes, Onchestus, Telphusa, and the city of the Phlegyians. After finally arriving at Crisa and establishing the foundations for his temple—completed by the legendary architects Trophonius and Agamedes—Apollo, according to the Hymn, had to do battle with a monster living nearby:

> But near by was a sweet flowing spring, and there with his strong
> bow the lord, the son of Zeus, killed the bloated great she-dragon,
> a fierce monster wont to do great mischief to men upon earth. . . .
> She was a very bloody plague.[2]

There, the *Hymn* continues (lines 356–73), the dragon, in agony, died under the onslaught of Apollo's arrows. The mountainside was filled with an awful sound as she writhed this way and that, her life ebbing away as the blood flowed from her wounds. The power of the sun slowly rotted her body, and this, according to the *Hymn*, is why the place is now called Pytho instead of Crisa, and why "men call the lord Apollo by another name, Pythian; because on that spot the power of the sun made the monster rot away [the Greek verb to rot is *puthein*]."

The *Homeric Hymn* also sets out what happened next. Apollo turned his attention to selecting the priests to run his new temple. He spied a boat full of Cretan sailors, and, having turned himself into a dolphin (in Greek *delphis*), he enticed the boat to go off course and brought it to the port of Cirrha (modern-day Itea—see map 3; fig. 0.1) on the plain below Crisa/Pytho/Delphi (lines 388–450). At which point, he revealed himself and commanded them to beach their ship, build an altar, worship him as Apollo Delphinios, then follow him, singing in his honor, up to the site at Pytho (lines 450–512). But once there, seeing the rocky landscape that would hardly sustain their community, the Cretans cried out in dismay, asking the god how they could possibly survive in this barren land. Apollo replied that they would survive thanks to the unstinting generosity of all those who came to worship and consult his oracle. But, he continued, such a privileged position came with a price: if they ever committed the kind of hubris ("arrogant folly") common among men, they would become servants to the rest of mankind for all time (lines 513–44).

A complex tale thus sets out the story of Delphi's beginnings, but it does not provide answers to all our questions, in particular how the site Pytho eventually became known as Delphi. Yet, in reality, the picture is even more complicated than this. For the *Homeric Hymn* is not our only source for Delphi's origins. Around the same time, another lyric poet, Alcaeus, whose work survives only in fragments, recounts a slightly different tale in which Apollo is ordered by Zeus to set up his oracle at Delphi, but instead flies to live with the Hyperboreans. A year later, Apollo is convinced by enterprising Delphians to come back to Delphi (always known as Delphi) and is encouraged to set up his oracle there.[3] Gone is the serpent, gone is Pytho, gone are the Cretans, and Apollo appears not so much the savior of Delphi, but more a naughty schoolchild eventually persuaded to do what his father ordered him to do in the first place.

The story becomes much more complex in the fifth century BC. The great tragedian Aeschylus, in his famous trilogy *Oresteia*, recounts the gruesome workings of the fated house of Atreus ending eventually with Orestes who comes to Delphi seeking salvation for having murdered his mother (Clytemnestra, who had murdered his father Agamemnon, who had sacrificed their daughter Iphigeneia to get a fair wind to sail to Troy). In the final play, *Eumenides* (lines 1–19), the oracular priestess of Apollo herself tells the story of Delphi's beginnings:

First, in this my prayer, I give the place of chief honour among the gods to the first prophet, Earth (Gaia), and after her to Themis; for she, as is told, took second this oracular seat of her mother. And third in succession, with Themis' consent, and by constraint of

none, another Titan, Phoebe, child of Earth, took her seat. She be-
stowed it, as birth-gift, upon Phoebus Apollo, who had his name
from Phoebe. . . . With prophetic art, Zeus inspired his soul, and
stabilised him upon this throne as fourth and present seer.

Aeschylus's version not only offers a much longer history of the oracle
at Delphi—stretching back to Gaia (also known as Ge), the "Mother
Earth" goddess, and thus to the gods who ruled over the earth long
before the Olympian deities (Zeus, Apollo, and the rest)—but also
says nothing about Apollo having had to slay a she-dragon at the site.[4]
Instead the succession from Gaia to Themis to Phoebe to Apollo is a
peaceful one. Later that same century, however, the famous tragedian
Euripides, in his play *Iphigenia at Tauris* (lines 1234–58), offers yet another picture:

From the spot famed for their birth [Delos], she [Apollo's mother
Leto] brought them [Apollo and his sister Artemis] to Mount
Parnassus, mother of surging streams, whose slopes ring with revels of Dionysus. There the dragon with wine-red eyes, with body
of bronze and coloured scales, as fierce a monster as land or sea
can show, lay in the leafy laurel-shade guarding the ancient oracle
of the Earth [Gaia]. Though you were still a little child, Phoebus
Apollo . . . yet you killed the dragon, and became successor to the
sacred oracle.

Euripides' tale eliminates the peaceful transition and reintroduces the
slaying of the dragon, who is now guardian of Gaia's oracle. But Gaia
does not take kindly, in Euripides' version, to this coup, for she sends
dreams that reveal the future into the minds of men, thus stealing the
oracle's preeminence. Apollo, in turn, complains to almighty Zeus, who,
amused, favors Apollo and his oracle and stops the dreams. In yet another version of the story, by an unknown author and seemingly prevalent by this time, Apollo did not get off so easily for slaying the dragon,
but was forced by Zeus to pay atonement by suffering nine years' exile
from Delphi, at Tempe in Thessaly (in remembrance of which, at least in

the third through first centuries BC, there was a special festival practiced every nine years at Delphi).[5]

The plot thickens. But the *Homeric Hymn*, Alcaeus, Aeschylus, and Euripides are not the only ancient sources to offer versions of a Delphic beginning involving Gaia, Themis, Apollo, a serpent, and exile. For Ephorus, the fourth century BC historian, Themis and Apollo held the oracular site together.[6] For an ancient scholiast of Pindar, the divine personification of Gaia is replaced with that of the Night.[7] Simonides, the lyric poet, thought the dragon was male, not female.[8] Another interpretation, this by the first century BC geographer Strabo, has the Corycian cave, eight hundred meters higher up the Parnassian mountains from Delphi (see map 3, figs. 0.2, 1.2), as the home of the serpent and the area of the first Delphic community.[9] Others thought it was not a dragon that Apollo fought but a fearsome warrior, and not at Delphi, but at Panopeus.[10] Pindar related that Gaia did not respond with dreams to Apollo's usurpation of her oracle, but with a request that Apollo be sent to Tartarus.[11] Pausanias said the Cretans argued that they had purified Apollo, and not the Thessalians at Tempe, after the murder of the dragon, and also that the Argives and Sicyonians claimed they had been responsible for Apollo's purification.[12]

For the ancient Greeks there were thus various ways in which to answer the questions how, when, and why the oracle at Delphi began, as well as how the site became known as Delphi and why Apollo here was worshiped as Apollo Pythios. Nor do the different versions simply tinker with details. Some intimate that additional gods were involved—for instance, Poseidon who may have had a home at Delphi in association with Gaia long before Apollo, and who may have given Delphi to Apollo in exchange for a sanctuary at Tainaron in the modern-day Mani area of southern Greece.[13] Other sources cite Dionysus not only as being involved at Delphi alongside Apollo, but in fact predating him.[14] Later sources evoke a second prophetess, a Sibyl, perhaps a daughter of Poseidon, operating at Delphi before Apollo.[15] Pliny and Pausanias report the involvement of Parnassus, the eponymous hero of the mountains, as well as Delphus, both sons of Poseidon, in the invention of divination.[16]

Other ancient stories go even further and offer us an entirely different set of stories about why Delphi became important and how it got its name. Some report that Delphi was discovered by Zeus as the center of the world after he let loose two eagles from opposite ends of the world and they met at Delphi.[17] Others believed that Delphi's name was derived from the Greek word for "hollow," "cavern," or even "womb," evoking its place as the center of the earth.[18]

In fact, pretty much every detail of Delphi's beginnings comes in different forms in the ancient literature. And nor is it only Delphi's origins that thus vary. The ancient sources also offer multiple interpretations for the history, and meaning, of particular parts of the Delphic sanctuary. For some, the omphalos stone (see fig. 2.1), supposed to be housed (somewhere) inside the heart of the temple of Apollo, was the marker of the center of the earth (with images of Zeus's eagles inscribed on either side of it). For others it was the stone Cronus was tricked by his wife Rhea into swallowing (instead of the baby Zeus) so as to protect Zeus from being eaten, and that Zeus later, after he had killed his father and achieved world sovereignty, set up as a sign of his power. For others still the omphalos was a symbol of the "voice" of the gods. For others it was the tomb of the serpent Pytho, or even of Dionysus.[19] Moreover, the lineage of the temple of Apollo at Delphi itself was contested. Pausanias (10.5.9–13) insists on four consecutive temples—the first made of laurel, the second of birds' feathers and beeswax, the third of bronze, and the fourth of stone—the last of which was burned down in 548 BC. Pindar's fragmentary eighth *Paean*, in contrast, attributes the bronze temple to different builders, and disagrees with Pausanias over the manner of its disappearance (for Pindar, it was swallowed up by the ground after a lightning strike).[20]

With so many varying stories, how should we understand Delphi's beginnings, let alone the stories about crucial elements of its later sanctuary (for instance, the temple and the omphalos) and the nature of the gods worshiped there? Earliest scholarship worked hard to sort the different myths, to weigh their authenticity and come up with a single, synergized, "credible" story of Delphi's foundation. Later scholarship

Figure 2.1. A Hellenistic/Roman version of the omphalos stone found at Delphi (Museum at Delphi).

has sought, instead of trying to collapse the different versions, to understand the narrative roles of these stories in their respective literary genres. As well, broader comparisons with the myth cycles of other ancient cultures have been undertaken in order to see whether different myths from different cultures at different times have influenced the Greek tradition.[21]

What all these later approaches prompt us to keep in mind is the date of the sources themselves. The earliest, the *Homeric Hymn*, sits somewhere in the late seventh to mid-sixth century BC, the latest at the very tale end of the ancient world. None of them are contemporary with Delphi's origins, nor, of course, would we expect them to be. But as a result, we need to understand that these different tales of Delphic beginnings tell us little about the reality of Delphic origins, and, rather, about how different eras, authors, and places in the ancient world sought, or rather chose, to perceive those beginnings. In response, our question has to change. Not how, when, why did Delphi begin, but how and why did Greek society, at a time when Delphi was already a successful and key part of their world, seek to explain its origins, development, and the nature of the gods worshiped there?

One of the key tenets of the story in the *Homeric Hymn* is how the geographical range of Apollo's journey links him, and thus Delphi, to a wide range of places covering a vast swathe of the ancient world, that same ancient world to which, by the time of the *Hymn*'s first known appearance (seventh–sixth century BC), Delphi was becoming increasingly central (see maps 1, 2). The *Hymn* thus portrays Apollo as forecasting what has now, demonstrably, come true.[22] But the *Hymn* also delves into Delphi's curious geographical position, which is, after all, precarious in the way it clings to the mountain slopes of Parnassus. As the Cretan sailors point out to Apollo, it is not an obvious choice for the founding of a community. Apollo's rejection of the many sites he examines prior to Delphi cites three requirements for his oracular site: tranquillity, accessibility, and poverty of natural resources. Apollo's priority list in the *Homeric Hymn* thus acts to justify the particularity of Delphi's position, and, by assuring the Cretan sailors that they would always be provided for, reaffirms the gods' will for the continuing success of Delphi as a place to which the world will come.[23] It has further been suggested that the foundation of Delphi by Apollo as laid out in the *Homeric Hymn* also mirrors one of the activities Delphi was (seen to be) heavily involved in during the late eighth–sixth centuries BC: colonization. Its foundation story thus becomes a reflection of the oracle's contemporary role in the Greek world.[24]

The emergence of myths that push the origins of Delphi much farther back, to the time of the pre-Olympian gods, and make the succession a fraught one, has been associated with the development in Greek thought of a clearer genealogy of the divine (following Hesiod's

Theogony), and subsequently of that genealogy describing a move from darker primordial forces toward a more civilized order, which Apollo's battle with the serpent comes to represent.[25] In so doing, at a time when Delphi's position in Greek society has come, as we shall see in later chapters, to be associated with the establishment of law, order, and good relations between human and divine, the myths surrounding its origins come to mold that role as one for which Delphi was predestined and has been performing since its inception; indeed the very act of its inception enabled Apollo to establish order over chaos. Similarly, the myths surrounding the lineage of Apollo's temple (built of laurel, then of beeswax, then of bronze by gods, then of stone by heroes, and finally by men) have been argued to articulate a continuing transition from the work of Nature, to that of the gods, of the heroes, and then of man, underscoring both Delphi's key position in the traditional framework of the mythic history of the Greek world's development, and also, as a result, justifying Delphi's later central role in the ancient Greek world.[26]

At the same time, the emergence of stories that prioritize the longevity of Delphi and the tendency for there to be conflict over its ownership have also been argued to reflect the fact that Delphi was the subject of numerous conflicts during its archaic, classical, and Hellenistic existence. Conflict about the origins of Delphi and about the violent seizure of its sanctuary by Apollo mirror a series of fights for Delphi both in myth and history over its ancient lifetime, as it came time and time again to be the subject of hostile takeover.[27] Equally, the importance of longevity and conflict in Delphi's origins has been attributed to the developing competition for authority between different oracular sites in the ancient Greek world during the archaic and classical periods.[28] The emergence and dominance of origin myths, which push Delphi's origins back to the gods before Zeus and the Olympians, like Gaia, could be seen as part of the later propaganda game between oracular sanctuaries competing for business through a stress on longevity and thus importance.[29] Pausanias (5.25.13), in the second century AD, informs us that Delphi was not the only oracle to play this game; the oracle of Zeus at Olympia also claimed descent from Gaia.

It is not only the hotly contested hierarchy of oracles (and their gods) that the varying stories surrounding Delphi's origins illuminate, but also the more particular nature of Apollo as he was worshiped at Delphi (Apollo Pythios). How the site became known as Delphi, the oracle as the Pythia, and Apollo at Delphi as Apollo Pythios are all issues to which the many origin stories give conflicting answers.[30] Yet despite the difference in detail, these stories all construct Apollo as the god who brought knowledge to mankind, as well as the one who imposed order over chaos. In the *Homeric Hymn to Apollo*, as soon as Apollo is born on Delos, he announces his interest in music, shooting with a bow, and divination. His privileged position among the gods as the only one who knows Zeus's mind is underscored in the *Homeric Hymn to Hermes*, when Hermes tries to trick his brother into giving him the gift of divination (*Hom. Hymn Hermes* 533–38). It is this position of power and the responsibility entailed in knowing the future, along with his interests in "cultural" activities like music, that associate Apollo, and particularly his worship at Delphi as Apollo Pythios, with the forces of order and lawful action.[31] These qualities are also reflected in several other epithets under which he was worshiped at different sanctuaries around the Greek world: Apollo Prostaterios (protector); Delphinios (protecting and mediating the relationship between seafarers and the oceans, but also in terms of relations between cities especially in Asia Minor); Epikourios (protector of mercenaries); and Maleatas (associated with healing).[32]

Yet his warlike activities (particularly his brutal slaying of the serpent and his forceful taking of the oracular site from Gaia/Themis), his love of the bow, and perhaps even the etymology of the name Apollo, also call attention to a darker side to his character, as one who punishes those who cross the line he guards (see his threat to punish the Cretan priests if they commit hubris in the *Homeric Hymn to Apollo*).[33] This duality of order and violence in the character of Apollo Pythios at Delphi, as expressed through the sources relating to Delphi's origins, is an important feature of the way the Greeks conceptualized the role of Delphi and Apollo Pythios in their world, and it mirrors the duality of centrality and conflict that is the mainstay of Delphi's story in ancient history.[34]

As such, the different emerging stories surrounding Delphi's origins all seem to have been oriented toward explaining, justifying, and mirroring its later, central position in the Greek world, the dual nature of the site and its god, and even perhaps toward defending and buttressing that position in the face of increasing competition from other oracular shrines. It is even more fascinating that this process does not seem to have occurred only in ancient literature, but also on the ground at Delphi itself. The emergence of the importance of a lineage dating back to Gaia, particularly in literature from the fifth century BC onward, is evidenced in the archaeological development of the sanctuary at that time. In fact, our earliest solid datable evidence for an actual cult of Gaia at Delphi comes from the fifth century BC; statues to Gaia and Themis dating from the period have been found, not in the Apollo sanctuary, but near the Castalian fountain (see plate 1, fig. o.2).[35] However, we also know from the accounts of the Apollo temple reconstruction in the mid-fourth century BC that there was a sanctuary of Gaia inside the main Apollo sanctuary at Delphi by this time, and its continued presence in the first century AD is confirmed for us by Plutarch.[36] Is this archaeological evidence of a cult beginning only in the fifth century BC (by the Castalian fountain and later being transferred into the Apollo sanctuary), or is it simply that evidence for a much older cult survives only from the fifth century BC onward? We can't be sure. But it is an intriguing coincidence that, just as Gaia's presence at Delphi in the ancient literature emerges from the fifth century BC onward, so too, in the physical space of the sanctuary and the local landscape, does Gaia's worship at Delphi come into focus.

The many, often conflicting, stories regarding Delphi's beginnings have in the past been taken as a way of filling in the blank canvas of the site's early history and, by the first archaeologists of Delphi, as a guide to the identification of its earliest structures (see the following chapter). Few scholars would be prepared to use these myths in the same way today. Instead, the myths are considered products of their own time, a time by which Delphi was already an incredibly successful phenomenon (late seventh–fifth centuries BC) that required an origin to match, an origin that could in turn be used not only to reinforce the natural order and succession of the cosmos, but also the particular importance of Delphi in comparison to other oracular sanctuaries, the details of its location, the dual nature of Apollo Pythios, and conflicting notions of Delphi's history. The gods, which were supposed to be its earliest masters, may well have become the object of worship in its sanctuaries from only the fifth century BC onward, because, by the later periods of Delphic history, particularly of Plutarch and Pausanias in the first–second centuries AD, all these tales were part of the rich tapestry of stories that could be used to evoke, realign, and even reframe the place of Delphi, and indeed of Greece, in the ancient world.

So if the literary representations of Delphic beginnings tell us rather more about the mindset, needs, and desires of the periods in which they were developed than about Delphi's origins, what can we know about how, when, and why Delphi developed? For this, we must turn to the archaeological investigation of Delphi and the surrounding landscape, which has transformed our understanding of Delphi's early years.

Delphi's earliest history was, however, by no means the prime focus of its initial excavators. During the first major excavation of the sanctuary, known as the "big dig" (1892–1901; see the final chapter), the landscape was rarely excavated to below archaic period levels, and most of the original excavation was focused on exposing the sanctuary as the Greco-Roman tour guide Pausanias had seen it during his visit in the second century AD. It is ironic that the oldest object to have so far been found in the sanctuary of Apollo was discovered during the big dig, but aroused no interest from the excavators at the time. It is now recognized as a lion's muzzle, which formed the lower decorated edge of a Minoan rhyton drinking vessel, dated to between 1600 and 1450 BC.[37] It bears signs of being repaired in antiquity, but, given the lack of context for its discovery, there is no way of knowing whether it came to the site shortly after its creation, or indeed many centuries later.

It was only during subsequent excavation seasons from the 1920s on-ward, spurred by an increasing awareness and interest in the possibility of finding significant material from much earlier cultures (cf. to Sir Ar-thur Evans's excavation at the Minoan palace of Knossos beginning in 1900) that the French excavators actively sought to excavate lower levels at the site. Since that time, as the focus has expanded from the main sanctuary site to the wider Delphic landscape, a much more complex picture of Delphi's earliest origins has begun to appear.

In the Corycian cave, 1,400 meters above sea level, and 800 meters above Delphi, traces of Neolithic occupation have been discovered dat-ing to 4300–3000 BC. This cave (see map 3; figs. 0.2, 1.2), which will in later times be closely linked with the Delphic sanctuary by a proces-sional path that still today can be followed as it clings to the sheers cliffs of Parnassus, seems to have been used for occasional habitation. The pottery remains have been argued to be similar to Thessalian ceramic from the same period.[38] This is interesting because of the links that many scholars have claimed between the Delphic region and that of Thessaly to the north during the ninth and early eighth centuries BC. The similar-ity in the Neolithic ceramic may suggest a much longer-term connection between these two areas.

Throughout the early and middle Helladic periods (c. 2800–1550 BC), there is material evidence for the development of settlement in dif-ferent parts of the (modern-day) Itean plain below Delphi. Yet, despite the lion-muzzle rhyton find, there is no evidence for consistent settle-ment in the actual region of the Delphic sanctuary until a period known as late Helladic III (part of a system of chronology based on pottery styles), which equates to c. 1400–1060 BC. At this time, the Corycian cave seems to have been out of fashion (very few finds dating to this pe-riod have been discovered there), in contrast to the plethora of objects discovered among the nascent community at Delphi.[39] Most of the set-tlement from this early period covers the later Apollo sanctuary's eastern side, stretching up the hillside from the area of the temple of Apollo to the lesche of the Cnidians. The impression is of a lot of poor housing and a particular fondness for terra-cotta animal figurines. Yet we also know of at least one rich dromos tomb in the area, along the later road leading from Delphi to Arachova, which contained a large number of vases and even a bronze sword (see map 3).[40]

None of this is evidence for cult practice, for an actual practicing sanctuary. Indeed, archaeologists have a hard time agreeing what, if any, archaeological material can definitively be declared as votive (that is, associated with cult practice) prior to the latter parts of the seventh century BC. But this has not stopped many from becoming very excited by Mycenaean period finds in the later Athena sanctuary (see plates 1, 3). For here, in the 1920s excavations, groups of female figurines (so called *Phi* and *Psi* figurines because their stance echoes those Greek letters of the alphabet) were unearthed. Coupled with the facts that no traces of habitation could be found in this area and that the later literary stories associated with Delphi claimed the site was held originally by the female Earth goddess Gaia, many scholars advocated that the later Athena sanctuary was the earliest site of cult worship of Gaia at Delphi, confirming the historicity of the literary myths. Today, it has been recognized that the collection, and burial, of these Psi and Phi figurines happened at a later time, perhaps associated with later reconstructions of the Athena sanctuary in the archaic period.[41] But does this mean they should not still be associated with an early cult of a female divinity (perhaps Gaia-like) at the site? The debate remains open, although it has also been suggested, following comparison between these figurines and Mycenaean cult figurines from other sites, that the Delphic ones should be associated with funerary, rather than cult use.[42]

The traditional narrative of Delphic history based on the archaeology, up to the last years of the twentieth century, claimed a slow decline in the size and vitality of its habitation (and perhaps cult practice) toward the end of the Mycenaean period (c. 1100–1000 BC), with a complete abandonment of the site until the early ninth century BC.[43] That picture has been radically changed in the last decade, thanks to the most recent excavations at the Apollo sanctuary. Now, almost continuous habitation can be demonstrated in the area of the Apollo sanctuary between the eleventh and ninth centuries BC. The pottery associated with this period is distinctly local, mixed with a degree of contact with northern Phocis. Yet by the ninth century BC, there is evidence for an increased amount of contact between the Delphic region and areas farther north, in particular Thessaly.[44]

Through the ninth century BC, settlement in the area of the later Apollo sanctuary continued to expand, often building on (and reusing) the foundations and material associated with earlier Mycenaean structures. But at the beginning of the eighth century BC, there is substantial change, both in terms of style of building at the site and in influence on the styles of material culture found in and around the settlement. The most recent excavations have shown how, in the region of the later "pillar of the Rhodians" dedication to the east of the temple of Apollo (see fig. 1.3), the existing habitation, which seems to have existed on the natural incline of the mountain, was reorganized substantially by the construction of leveled terraces at that time. On one of these terraces, the remains of a house, known to the French excavators as the *maison noire* (the "black house"), have been uncovered. Gradually over the course of the eighth century, this house seems to have become part of an increasingly regularized pattern of what are known as row houses, with the wider settlement split into two main camps and an open spine, which seems to have served as the main access route for the settlement, running north-south up the mountainside.[45] The decision to invest in the landscape and create a more organized, leveled building space was matched at the time by a decisive shift in the nature and style of objects brought to the site. Soon after 800 BC, the predominant Thessalian-influenced pottery is replaced by imported high-quality Corinthian pottery, although Thessalian influence continues for both metalwork and low-quality pottery. At around the same time, the first monumental objects that can be definitively associated with cult use (the three-legged bronze tripods) appear at Delphi.[46]

The beginning of the eighth century BC thus seems to have borne witness to much change at Delphi, which evolved from being a settlement connected to Thessaly and the north—with little contact to the sea and communities to the south, or with any powerful regional role—into a newly reorganized community strongly connected to the sea and the powerful settlements to the south (particularly Corinth), and with an increasingly important regional role.[47] Nor was it the only place in the Greek world to undergo such transformation. The eighth century BC is often cited as *the* critical period of change for the emergence of archaic and classical Greece, in part thanks to the influence of increasingly dense contact with the world outside. As the historian Robin Osborne has put it: "in 800 BC, the Greek world was poor, small, and lacking in general organisation. Its communities were small, and hard-pressed to survive in a hostile natural environment. Greeks had few contacts in the wider world and no special advantages."[48] During the eighth century BC, all this changed. The number of sites of habitation increased dramatically; the amount of resources available increased; the social and political organization of settlements seems to have been more open and flexible to question and change; the investment by communities in their tombs and sanctuaries increased substantially; and, on a larger scale, the influence of different cultures (e.g., the Phoenicians in the western Mediterranean, and the Greeks in Italy, Sicily, and the eastern Mediterranean) bear witness to a greater social mobility and international interaction. Places of cult worship seem to have been major beneficiaries of these changes in part because they were able to provide useful locations in which to conduct and display a material culture associated with these changing social priorities, attitudes, and interests. At the sanctuary of Kalapodi, for example, in the region of Phocis (see maps 2, 3), not far from Delphi, there are the remnants of construction for a more monumental cult structure at the end of the ninth century. On the island of Samos, the later sanctuary of Hera received its first temple c. 800 BC, as did the sanctuary of Hera at Perachora near Corinth. At Perachora, too, there is evidence for a vast range of international material culture being dedicated at the site (including no less than 273 Phoenician scarabs), while at Samos there is evidence for contact with Egypt, Cyprus, North Syria, Phoenicia, Phrygia, and Assyria.[49]

Yet, as has often been pointed out by scholars, this investment, particularly in cult spaces, was by no means uniform. Though Delphi clearly sees a change and increase in investment from the beginning of the eighth century BC, it is by no means on the scale of other sanctuaries such as at Samos or Perachora, or even nearby Kalapodi.[50] The sanctuaries that benefited most in the first part of the eighth century seem to have been those tied more closely to growing political communities (the eighth century is also often known as the time of the "rise of the polis"). Conversely, sanctuaries like Delphi and Olympia, which would eventually become known as the great Panhellenic sanctuaries, are significantly less monumentalized than their counterparts more firmly attached to particular communities probably because they lie in this period outside the sphere of control of particular poleis. At the same time, as we shall see in later chapters, it is ironic that this very absence of attachment to a community in this early period would become in turn an important factor in the eventual successful development of these sanctuaries as places with Panhellenic significance.[51]

So just what is going on at Delphi during the eighth century BC, and how, if at all, can we understand the development of its sanctuary, cult activity, and oracular practice? It is clear that by the beginning of the century, there was an important settlement at Delphi. Yet it is unclear to what extent any of this space was considered sacred, unclear to what degree a religious cult had developed, and unclear whether any oracle was functioning. The arrival at the site in c. 800 BC of Corinthian fine-wear pottery and of more monumental votive offerings, and the increased investment in construction at the site mark our first clear indication of both wider interest in Delphi and a more insistent investment in cult practice. Delphi, it seems, had become part of Corinth's broadening interest in the region, and part of its expanding trading network (a particular type of Corinthian pottery, known as Thapsos ware, which was reserved for export by Corinth, is found at Delphi from the middle of the eighth century BC onward). This interest of Corinth in Delphi may have been occasioned by Delphi's longer-standing connections with Thessaly to the north, which Corinth may in turn have hoped to exploit for its own trading network (and this link to the north will become increasingly important toward the end of the eighth century).

Yet we should not overemphasize Delphi's newfound trading or cult importance in the first seventy years of the eighth century BC. Other sanctuaries with which Corinth was heavily involved, like Perachora, or even nearby sites like Kalapodi, have provided much richer material records for this period.[52]

As far as cult activity at Delphi goes, our evidence is based entirely on the contents of several later deposits (effectively rubbish heaps) of material found buried in different parts of the later Apollo sanctuary, which were used as packing to create a more solid floor level for building in the sixth century BC. What has been found proves cult practice at the site—pottery, charred bone, fragments of bronze tripods—but it is unlikely that this originated from any significant separate cult area. The origin of this material (particularly the pottery and tripods) reflects Corinthian interest in cult activity at the site, but also a significant Argive presence, some Thessalian, and a certain amount of (perhaps) locally made material for dedication. As for the oracle, no material find proves that it was in operation for the better part of the eighth century BC, or indeed during any time before that. Some scholars argue that the oracle was not instituted until the late eighth century, others that it may have had a much longer existence dating back into the second millennium, which is what motivated the continuation of settlement in this otherwise rather difficult physical habitat clinging to the mountainside.[53]

Whenever the oracle began, however, it is crucial that, in regard to that nascent phase of Delphic development, we distinguish between a real Delphi and the early Delphi described in later literary and historical sources. The literary sources, whichever story you choose to follow, paint a picture of a Delphi born for success and international prestige. Yet the archaeology reveals a different story. A tiny, isolated community with a connection to northern Greece slowly refocused its attention south and was drawn into the trading network of Corinth, and, in turn, benefited from the more general social and political processes of eighth century development, which, at the same time, left Delphi much less elaborated than many sanctuaries more closely tied to particular political communities. Many scholars, encouraged by the literary and historical sources for Delphi's divine origins, have taken the traditional picture of later Delphic international and Panhellenic success and transposed it back onto the site's early history.[54] In reality, Delphi, through to the last quarter of the eighth century BC, did not play anything like such a role. It was not born into success as the center of the Greek world, but struggled, for centuries, to be anything more than a small and isolated community clinging to the Parnassian mountains.

And yet, in this formative phase of Delphic development, there are signs of the forces that will propel Delphi over the next century and a half to the forefront of the Greek political and religious world. One is the occasional glimpse of dedicated objects at Delphi that originate from much farther afield: eighth-century amber from Scandinavia, probably arriving with traders from Etruria; a Villanovian helmet from 800 BC; Italian spearheads from the mid-eighth century; tripods not only from Corinth and Argos, but also from Crete by the middle of the century.[55] Another sign is not dedication, but destruction. The maison noire was burned down (hence its name "the black house"!) during the first seventy years of the eighth century BC, and rebuilt, suggesting a consistent desire for habitation at Delphi.[56] A further sign comes from the references to Delphi in Homer's *Iliad* (9.401) and *Odyssey* (8.79–81). Both these epics are thought to have coalesced into their near final forms during the course of the eighth century BC, and, while they do not refer to the oracular importance of Delphi (the references to Apollo Pythios are thought to be later interpolations in the text), they do give a sense of an acknowledgment that Delphi was (already by this time) a recognized place of wealth and importance.[57] Yet perhaps the most interesting sign is that though other sanctuary sites, like Perachora, may have been showered with a far greater number of dedications than Delphi during the first half of the eighth century, the nature of most of those objects was personal and/ or trade related.[58] Perachora never received the kind of monumental offerings that Delphi was beginning to receive, seemingly (given their expense) from state elites.[59] Delphi, which around 800 BC, had been a local and isolated settlement, was, by the last quarter of the eighth century (725–700 BC), seemingly (also) becoming a location serving the demands of (particular) emerging states and their elites. And it was thanks to the pressures, needs, and desires of those emerging communities that Delphi, from the last quarter of the eighth century BC, was to burst forth onto the international stage.

Apollo is the god who sits in the centre, on the navel of the earth, and he is the interpreter of religion for all mankind.

—Plato *Republic* 427B

3
TRANSFORMATION

Fire is all consuming. So easily started, so often uncontrollable in the dry, hot conditions of Greece. In the late eighth century BC, c. 730, fire took hold of Delphi. It spread through the small community clinging to the Parnassian hillside, leaving destruction in its wake. As the smoke ebbed away, as the charred timbers finally began to cool, and as Delphi's inhabitants began to come to terms with the extent of their loss, Delphi's precarious position in the Greek world must have felt even more fragile.

We know that the maison noire—the house recently discovered by excavators just to the east of the later temple of Apollo at Delphi—burned to the ground a second time (it definitely earned its name) in this fire.[1] The French archaeologist Jean-Marc Luce, who conducted the excavation of the maison noire, ties this destruction to the accounts in later ancient sources of a raid on Delphi by the Phlegyians, whom, according to the *Homeric Hymn to Apollo* (lines 277–80), were people from one of the places Apollo had visited as a potential home for his oracle, and were said in later sources not only to have raided but to have set fire to the temple of Apollo at Delphi (their name comes from the Greek verb "to burn").[2]

Even if we are not willing to make such a close link between the literature and the archaeology, it is clear that the last thirty years or so of the eighth century BC were a dynamic time in Delphi's history, quite apart from its fiery destruction. The settlement during the eighth century had grown considerably, covering most of the area of the later Apollo sanctuary. By Iron Age standards, Delphi was, at century's end, a large and important site in its own right. But it was not the only settlement that developed in the area at this time. In fact, in the last quarter of the eighth century BC, a number of new sites seem to have been established across the Itean plain, helping to connect Delphi—somewhat isolated high up on the mountainside—to the other old settlements along the coast (such as Medeon; see map 3).[3] One of these new sites—now the modern town of Amphissa—was founded at the foot of the most easily accessible corridor through the mountains to the north. A northern presence has been noted at Delphi since its earliest history, and its links to Thessaly may have been part of the reason for Corinth's expansion into the area at the beginning of the eighth century as it sought to exploit these connections for trading purposes. Now, in the last quarter of the eighth century, the tables were turned. The increasingly strong trading network with Thessaly and the North, fueled by Corinthian interest and facilitated by the development of new settlements along the route, acted as a catalyst for Delphic growth. Whereas Corinth may have originally come to Delphi to feed off its northern contacts, now Delphi was feeding off the increasingly strong north-south trading network. This whole area of the Phocian coast was increasingly drawn into a pattern of trading traffic, extending from across the Gulf of Corinth, through the Itean plain, north to Thessaly, and even into the Balkans (see maps 1, 2). And Delphi seems to have benefited most. By the beginning of the seventh century BC, other, previously more affluent settlements on the coast, such as Medeon, were suffering thanks to Delphic expansion. Delphi had begun to warp the local landscape, a process that would eventually lead to the total decline of its local competitors.[4]

Yet Delphi was expanding not only thanks to its place in an increasingly affluent and important trading network. The excavations have

revealed a vast increase in objects in the last quarter of the eighth century BC that can be securely tied to cult activity. This expansion was
both in terms of type (new kinds of tripod dedications) and also origin.
Attic and Cretan metalwork, for example, began to arrive at the site, and
pottery, which had been overwhelmingly Corinthian, was now coming
from Achaia, Attica, and Boeotia as well as from Euboea, Thessaly, and
Argos. It was also in the last quarter of the eighth century BC that the
Corycian cave, seemingly abandoned since the fourteenth century BC,
received material again, which was increasingly votive in character, suggesting the establishment of the cave as a rural shrine.[5]

Delphi at the end of the eighth century BC thus seems to have taken a
quantum leap, both as a settlement on an increasingly affluent trade network, and as a place of cult activity that attracted an increasing variety
of rich offerings associated with a widening number of important civic
centers themselves in the throes of ever-rapid social and political change.
How these two aspects affected one another, we may never know in detail. Did Delphi's position in a trade network help bring the settlement
to the attention of more long-distance civic centers that in turn began to
deposit increasingly rich offerings at the sanctuary's hitherto local (and
still very much unelaborated) cult center? Or should we see the two as
relatively independent, with Delphi's increasingly international cult activity more the result of the growing fame of, and need for, its (perhaps
long-established or perhaps only recently instituted) oracle?

No archaeological evidence exists to prove there was a functioning
oracle at Delphi at any time up to the late eighth century BC (and it is
difficult, if not impossible, in these early periods, to distinguish between
what is a "secular" and what is a "cult" object). As we saw at the end of
the last chapter, some scholars argue for the possibility of a local oracle
existing at Delphi all the way back into the second millennium BC. Others argue that the arrival of tripod dedications from the end of the ninth
century and the beginning of the eighth signifies an oracular presence
(based on the tripod as a symbol of the oracle who, in later representations, sat on a tripod when giving her responses).[6] Others argue for the
oracle's inception, and certainly its growth (or rather the beginning of

its use not just by locals but by elites of different states) in the last quarter of the eighth century. Their reasoning is based largely on linking the sudden increase at Delphi in this period to the many elite/state level offerings given for consultation with the oracle, although again the link is considered by some not to be without its problems.[7] In short, we cannot, with the present archaeological evidence, prove the date of the origin of Delphi's oracle, or, in more positive terms, as the French archaeologist Jean-Marc Luce has put it, the "question remains open."[8]

But the observable quantum leap that Delphi underwent in the late eighth century and on into the seventh century does coincide with a growing need identified by several scholars among the developing political communities in Greece for new ways of solving emerging community problems (which the oracle may have provided), and with the many literary and historical sources that focus on the oracle's increasingly important role in three major aspects of the development of Greek society during the late eighth–sixth centuries BC: colonization, constitutional reform, and tyrannical power. Thus while we cannot prove when the oracle at Delphi started, we can investigate the extent to which, from the late eighth century, it seems to have acquired a new kind of purpose as well as audience.

There was a tremendous amount of change and growth in Greek society during the eighth century. By its end, the resultant increased opportunity and dynamism within the organization of different communities had created a significant amount of social instability. The seventh century would provide no letup. Fundamental to the process was the continued development of community self-definition, which led, in turn, to a variety of changes in the nature of warfare (the development of the hoplite phalanx based on cohesive group attack rather than on individual elite warriors); the nature and regulation of power exercised within political communities (the development of civic constitutions as an attempt to referee the power play between community elites and the emergence of an individual elite, tyrannical ruler); the expansion of communities into new landscapes (through trade, force, and active foundation); and a more clearly articulated set of relationships between the human and the divine (the development of identifiable myths, the investment in sanctuaries, the development of human figure sculpture and stone temples).[9]

Surviving within this increasingly dynamic and unstable melting pot often required a response from developing communities to problems not encountered before. Within a world that was, at the same time, firmly of the belief that the gods were in charge of everything, the attraction of a system of oracular consultation, which allowed for divine confirmation of community decisions, and therefore the ability to ensure the development of a consensus of opinion for particular courses of action, is eminently understandable.[10] That is, the oracle at Delphi—whether a longtime local practice or a recent institution—came into focus and importance at this time because it provided a new solution ideally suited to the particular and unfamiliar circumstances created by Greek social and political development. Not as an instrument simply for "revealing the future," but rather as an instrument for the adjudication of civic problems and the authorization of new solutions. As argued in the last chapter, we thus need to see the oracle at Delphi as more of a management consultant than a fortune-teller.

But before we look at the literary and historical evidence for consultation of the Delphic oracle during the late eighth and seventh centuries BC, we need once again to turn our attention to the warning label that comes with it. In most cases, the evidence for a particular consultation comes from sources dated several centuries after the consultation took place. At the same time, the events with which a consultation is associated are often themselves unclear and subject to metamorphosis in the different sources over time. As a result, a lake of scholarly ink has been spilled over the question of which consultations are "real" and which "fake," or which have been expanded and reworked over time. Some scholars go so far as to judge as false all accounts of oracular consultation from this period. Others are happy to accept some but not all. In what follows, this middle course has been adopted, with the understanding that all the evidence, just as with Delphi's earliest foundation myths, tells us as much about how Greeks of later centuries sought to understand Delphi's early history than it does about the early history itself.[11]

Strongly supporting the picture of the Delphic oracle coming to international attention when it did as a new way of resolving new community problems and tension is the fact that the first communities posited in the literary sources (and which we can be fairly sure are historical) to consult the oracle were all in regions that were in some way exceptional in the pace and nature of their development and the circumstances they had to confront: Sparta, Corinth, and Chalcis in Euboea.[12]

Sparta has often been highlighted for its close connection with the Delphic oracle. Herodotus (6.57.2) tell us that Sparta had special advisors to its kings, called *pythioi*, who were responsible for the relations between the city and the oracle. At some point between the late eighth and mid-seventh century BC (the date is the subject of much dispute), a new constitution came into force in Sparta; known as the Great Rhetra, this constitution was, by the fifth century BC, associated directly with Sparta's infamous lawgiver Lycurgus. This constitution is fundamental to understanding the unique nature of Spartan society: it regulated everything from the setting up of new temples, to the division of the Spartan population, the regulations of its council, and the power of its kings. Its adoption by Sparta, according to the later evidence for oracular consultation, was directly linked to approval from the Delphic oracle (who, in some versions, is even said to have dictated the constitution herself).[13] But while we cannot know exactly the extent to which Delphi was involved, we do know, thanks to a surviving fragment of the Spartan poet Tyrtaeus from the mid-seventh century BC, that, already by this time, the Spartan link with Delphi was strong:

> They heard the voice of Phoebus Apollo and brought home from Pytho the oracles of the god and words of sure fulfilment, for thus the lord of the silver bow, Far Shooting Apollo of the golden hairs, gave answers from out his rich sanctuary . . . for this has Phoebus declared unto their city in these matters.[14]

Indeed Sparta, it seems, from the evidence for further oracular consultations, was somewhat obsessed with the oracle, using it to confirm its social and political process, its pattern of oath swearing, and its system of land allotment. The oracle had even supposedly warned Spartans about their public morality and that their love of money would one day destroy them.[15] Yet the sources also indicate that Sparta had involved the oracle in its decision to expand its territory through conquest in what have become known as the first and second Messenian Wars (the second half of the eighth century through the first quarter of seventh century BC), resulting in the annexation of Messenia by Sparta and the subjugation of its native population as Spartans slaves, or *helots*. The surviving sources tell of oracular consultations at key points in the campaign: on the justification for its commencement, and on how best to improve their fortunes during (both the first and second) war.[16] Yet what is fascinating here is that Delphi also seems to have been consulted by the other side, Messenia, in both of these conflicts: on how best to maximize its chances of victory, on how to conduct itself during the war, and with desperate requests for tips on salvation as the end drew near (such help was not forthcoming).[17] The association between Sparta and the oracle about the former's expansion plans continued during Sparta's later attempt to take all of Arcadia, with the oracle consulted at the outset of the campaign and throughout, regarding revision of its goals and the best ways to proceed.[18]

For Corinth, whose economic and trading influence swept over Delphi and the surrounding region during the eighth century, the oracle provided a very different sort of management consultant role. Sometime in the first half of the seventh century BC, the Bacchiad ruling family of Corinth was confronted with a perhaps unsolicited warning from the oracle that they should take note of a "lion, strong and flesh-eating" who was to be born from an eagle. Sometime later, a man, Aetion, consulting the oracle on his inability to produce a child, was warned that his wife would conceive and that the baby would be a "rolling stone, which will fall upon the absolute rulers and will exact justice from Corinth." In the second half of the seventh century, when that child, Cypselus, was on the brink of seizing power as tyrant of Corinth, he was greeted by the oracle with another warning: "blessed is the man who enters my house, Cypselus, son of Aetion, king of famous Corinth, he himself and his sons, but his sons' sons [i.e., his grandchildren] no longer."[19]

Cypselus was not the first tyrant, or the last the oracle would seemingly foresee, encourage, and warn. In the late seventh century BC, the oracle was involved with a tyrannical coup in Athens by a man called Cylon. After consulting on the best way to achieve power, he was at first said to have misunderstood the oracle's response to attack during Zeus's great festival, which Cylon took to mean the Olympics. Eventually, however, Cylon secured power when he realized the oracle was referring to Zeus's great festival in Athens.[20]

Delphi's relationship with tyrants within Greece is often compared to its involvement with rulers in Asia Minor at this time. This involvement dates back to the legendary king Midas of Phrygia who was said, by Herodotus (1.14), to have dedicated at Delphi the royal chair upon which he sat to give judgment. But the oracular relationship really began with the slightly later king of Lydia, Gyges, in the late eighth century BC. The oracle was said to have arbitrated a dispute over the kingship of Lydia in Gyges' favor, again with a warning that his fifth descendant would be punished for the way in which Gyges had taken power.[21] In return (or perhaps in advance of this favorable oracle), Gyges was said to have showered Delphi with rich gold and silver offerings. In the late seventh century BC, this relationship with eastern kings continued in the form of King Alyattes, who consulted the oracle after he fell ill during a military campaign; the oracle refused to help until Alyattes rebuilt a temple he had destroyed on campaign. When Alyattes complied and the oracle brought him back to good health, Alyattes thanked the oracle by showering the temple with silver and iron dedications, one of which survived long enough to be seen by Pausanias in the second century AD.[22]

Delphi's relationship with tyrants, themselves a product of the fast-changing political system of the eighth and seventh centuries BC, has caused much controversy. Some scholars query the reliability of oracular responses that seem to contain unsolicited warnings and pronouncements, in place of a direct response to a question asked.[23] Others point to the way in which the literary traditions suggest a rebranding of Delphic responses over time. In later centuries, by which time tyrannical power had come to have the negative connotations it still does today, many of the ancient sources seemed keen to recategorize Delphi's interactions with these strong-men as foreseeing their coming, but paying them scant courtesy when they did.[24] However, such a changing picture of Delphic involvement does not mean we should discard the evidence for these consultations; rather, as the historian Irad Malkin has argued, we should imagine an oracle that embraced social and political change and moved (opportunistically) with the times, supporting new social and political ideas with the necessary redefining of its past involvement that this inevitably entailed as such ideas came and went out of fashion.[25] That is to say, as the world changed, so did the oracle. Thus, Malkin suggests, Delphi managed to become a force for change and innovation in social and political issues, and, because it always seemed to be on the "right" side, to eventually gain a reputation as a sort of elder statesman, thereby becoming a guarantor and arbiter of social order.[26]

In the late eighth century BC, Chalcis is said to have been involved in the Lelantine War with its nearby rival Eretria, on the island of Euboea (see map 2). The duration, nature, and even historicity of this war is open to debate, but, by the fifth century BC, Thucydides (1.15.3) marked it as the only conflict between the Trojan and Persian Wars in which Greeks came together to fight in multicommunity groups, that is to say, as larger unified elements. This seemingly epic struggle by eighth-century standards, over the boundaries of the Chalcidian and Eretrian communities and thus the ownership of the fertile Lelantine plains, may be seen as a result of processes of community self-definition, internal political instability, and population pressure omnipresent in the eighth century, and may help explain why Chalcis was said to have been drawn to consulting the oracle at Delphi over the question of founding new settlements elsewhere by the end of the eighth century (that of Rhegion and slightly later of Zankle in southern Italy; see map 1).[27]

The involvement of the oracle at Delphi with this process of "colonization," during the eighth–sixth centuries BC, has been the subject of more intense discussion than perhaps any other aspect of the oracle's business (see map 1). At stake has been everything from the form of oracular involvement to the existence of the process of colonization itself.

Scholars, particularly historian Robin Osborne, have been at pains to stress the problem of using the term "colonization," which suggests the nature of the Greek experience as akin to British colonial colonization. In place of such an organized territorial land grab, Osborne advocates seeing the number of new foundations around the Mediterranean in this period as "a manifestation of an exceptional degree of restlessness and ambition among individual Greeks. Some settlers will have been pushed by poverty, unpopularity, crime, or scandal; some will have jumped to get land, a foothold in foreign mineral resources, or just a new life free of irksome relatives."[28]

Such a variety of motivation is clearly crucial for understanding this complex process, as is, once again, the mutability of the literary record, which often offers not only a changing history of Delphic involvement, but also multiple, sometimes conflicting, versions of the responses, alongside a number of, famous, ambiguous riddlelike answers. The oracle is said to have suggested that a fish would point the way, and a boar lead the way, to those founding Ephesus. Aegae, the old capital of Macedon, was to be founded on the spot where its founder first saw goats. Over the foundation of Gela in Sicily, the record is split between an oracle that told a consultant who laughed to found a place called Gela (linked to the Greek for "to laugh"), and another source suggests the oracle told them to settle near a river called Gela. When Archias of Corinth consulted the oracle on the subject of founding a new settlement (Syracuse) c. 735 BC, it is said he was told to find Ortygia, which "lies in the sea on Trinakria, where Alpheius gushes forth mingling with the spring Arethusa." Such a reply, preserved in Pausanias (5.7.3), requires the belief that the river Alpheius in the Peloponnese somehow flows under the ocean all the way to Sicily to mix with the waters of the local spring. But yet another source (Strabo 6.2.4) suggests that the founders of Croton and Syracuse were allotted their locations on the basis of one prioritizing health and the other money.[29]

Herodotus gives two different versions of oracular involvement in the founding of Cyrene in North Africa at the end of the seventh century BC—one emphasizes the role of the inhabitants of the island of Thera (and is believed by the Therans), and the other attributes the founding to the individual Battus (seemingly preferred by the Cyreneans).[30] Further versions are found in other authors as well, and the story is complicated even more by the epigraphic evidence, as the Cyreneans in the fourth century BC erected steles relating to the granting of citizenship to Therans and to the institutionalization of their sacred laws, both of which were tied to the original founding and to the involvement of the oracle.[31]

The difficulty in assessing this complex and conflicting mass of evidence has led to some deep divisions over the nature of Delphi's involvement in colonization, and thus the nature, development, and importance of the Delphic oracle in the eighth and seventh centuries BC. What is indisputable, however, is that, by the last third of the eighth century, the pace of Greek cities and individuals establishing settlements around the Mediterranean had increased substantially. In southern Italy and Sicily during this period, a new settlement was founded about every other year. The cities already involved in different ways with Delphi, like Chalcis, Corinth, and Sparta, all appear to have consulted on such settlements (including a lengthy to-ing and fro-ing between the Spartans and the oracle on the foundation of Taras and its subsequent health and political organization).[32] But what also seems clear is that the history of the establishment of such settlements was an issue of recurring importance to both the new community, and its mother city, throughout their histories. It is, thus, no surprise that, as each developed, and the relationship between them changed, the foundation stories followed suit. In the sixth century BC, for example, intercolonial rivalry had developed to such an extent that colonies competed to have grander, older foundation stories and closer involvement with what was, by then, the prestigious institution of the oracle at Delphi. Croton, for example, even went so far as to put the oracular tripod on their first coinage.[33] And in the fifth century BC, many mother cities seem to have wanted closer, more colonial-style ties to *their* communities, which resulted in a rebranding of their heavier involvement in the settlement and thus their interaction with the oracle.[34]

So, how much can we see through this haze of changing priorities and changing stories to understand the place of the oracle in this process of expanded settlement during the eighth and seventh centuries? Opinions are still divided. On the one hand, scholars like the historian Jean Defradas have argued that we cannot be sure of any role for the oracle in colonization before the sixth century BC.[35] On the other hand, scholars like the historian George Forrest and the archaeologist Anthony Snodgrass have argued that the oracle acted from its inception as a clearing-house for the dissemination of geographical and political information to the widest possible audience, and was fundamental to the process of colonization.[36] In between them is a whole spectrum of viewpoints.[37] Yet I think we can sketch a timeline for the development of awareness across the ancient Greek world of the oracle's importance to the colonial process, as well as a timeline for the development of its actual involvement. For the latter, it seems probable that the oracle was involved in questions of new settlement foundation from the mid-late eighth century BC, particularly settlements founded in Sicily and southern Italy by Greek cities such as Corinth, Chalcis, and Sparta. During the seventh century, the range of Greek cities and individuals consulting the oracle on such issues widened to more of mainland Greece and spread east through the Cyclades to Paros, Thera, and Rhodes. Similarly the location of the resulting foundations also spread to North Africa and, very infrequently, the Hellespont. By the late seventh century, inquiries about foundations were even coming from Asia Minor, although it has long been noted that the number of such inquiries at Delphi (as well as resulting foundations in the Hellespont and Black Sea area) were always low, perhaps because there was a closer oracular sanctuary (in Miletus) for consultation.[38]

In terms of the progression of Delphi's reputation for involvement in this key process, scholars argue that a surviving fragment from the poet Callinus of Ephesus, of the first half of the seventh century BC, discussing the involvement of Pythian Apollo with the foundation of Colophon, suggests a recognition of Delphi's place in the process by this time. In 734 BC, a shrine to Apollo Archegetos (Apollo "the Founder") was established in the colony Naxos in Sicily. By the fifth century at the latest, this shrine was recognized (see Thucydides 6.3.1) as the place where all Sicilian cities were supposed to worship before setting out on their adventures. As a result, many have argued that the importance of Apollo as a god of "colonization," and the connection between Apollo's oracle at Delphi and colonization, at least for the Western Greek world, was assured by this time. In fact, we can be pretty sure such a connection was well known across the Greek world earlier in the sixth century BC. Herodotus (5.42) tells the story of Dorieus of Sparta who failed in his attempt to found a colony at Heracleia in Sicily. The failure was the result, everyone realized according to Herodotus's narrative, of Dorieus's having neglected to consult the Delphic oracle properly first.[39]

The picture painted here is of a Delphi gradually becoming involved in the ongoing process of new settlement foundation that gripped and expanded the Greek world in the eighth–sixth centuries BC. But it is, at the same time, also a picture of the reinforcement and expansion of that role for Delphi in the foundation process from the sixth century BC onward, as colonies and mother cities sought increasingly to reframe and often aggrandize their foundations and relationships by according often greater roles to a Delphi, which was, by that time, fully immersed in the center of the Greek world. Nothing breeds success like success. As the historian George Forrest put it, colonization thus did more for the spread of Delphi's influence and prestige than Delphi did for colonization.[40]

As a result of these developments, the oracle at Delphi, by the end of the seventh century BC, was, with very little doubt, an increasingly crucial institution for an increasingly wide circle of Greek cities and their new foundations spread out across the Mediterranean world. The oracle had been consulted by kings in the East and by tyrants in mainland Greece, and by communities and individuals on issues as diverse as constitutional reform, war, land allotment, oaths, purification, and the avoidance of famine (and many more issues if you are inclined to believe all the stories).[41] And yet, there is no evidence for any form of permanent temple of Apollo at Delphi for most of this time. The earliest possible date for such a structure at Delphi (the evidence for which is a few surviving roof tiles, and a couple of stone blocks) is 650–600 BC, with most scholars preferring the lower end of that register (approximately contemporary with the construction of the first temple of Hera at Olympia), although recent excavation has indicated we must revise that date even further, to the beginning of the sixth century BC (see the next chapter).[42] This is to say, throughout this crucial period of development for the oracle, and for Delphi, we have no real idea where, and in what circumstances, the oracle was consulted.

So just what was it like to visit Delphi during this period? We left the sanctuary in the late eighth century as a place of significant settlement, having recently suffered fire destruction, and yet with increasing numbers of expensive metal (particularly) tripod dedications associated with cult activity arriving from a widening circle of Greek communities as far away as Crete. During the seventh century, the site continued as a place of settlement, mixed in with increasing cult activity. Over the burned remains of the maison noire, the *maison jaune* (the "yellow house") was constructed. By the last quarter of the seventh century, this was replaced by the *maison rouge* (the "red house") which seems to have been one of several in the area. This house was comprised of three rooms, one of which was used for cooking. The nature of the finds suggests a wealthy owner (bronze vessels, golden rivets for some objects), but also cult activity (libation *phiale* [small vessels] have been found).[43] This house sat across what was later the boundary of the Apollo sanctuary, and its mixed sacred and secular use seems to sum up the indeterminate, unarticulated nature of what scholars presume was an early sacred area at the heart of the settlement that would later become the Apollo sanctuary.

As such, the settlement at Delphi, right through to the end of the seventh century BC (the house was not destroyed until the first quarter of the sixth century), seems to have been a melting pot of secular and sacred activity, with no properly defined or separated cult space (there is no evidence for a temenos wall marking out a sanctuary until the sixth century—see the next chapter). As Delphi's oracle continued to grow in importance through the century, even allowing for much of that early reputation only having been generated in later centuries, consultants and dedicators, on making their way up the Parnassian mountainside to Delphi, may well have been surprised to find such an unelaborated cult site for such an (increasingly) important institution, especially in comparison with the many sanctuaries in different cities and civic territories, which had been monumentalized from the late eighth century onward (e.g., at Corinth, Perachora, and Argos, and on Samos).

This lack of monumental elaboration, even articulation, of Delphi's sacred space through the seventh century is a crucial marker of three things. First, it underscores the importance of handling the literary sources with care to work out what Delphi was, as opposed to what it was later constructed to have been. Second, it reveals an important insight into the experience of early visitors to the site, especially in contrast to the sanctuaries at home. Third, it acts as crucial evidence for the generally late elaboration of sanctuaries, which would eventually become "Panhellenic"—sanctuaries common to all Greeks. These sacred spaces were less elaborate than sanctuaries within defined political territories because they were not the sole responsibility and territory of one community. But it was also precisely because of their indeterminacy of ownership, their "neutrality," that scholars argue they were *able* to grow as spaces for use by a much wider range of Greek cities and states.[44] This is to say, Delphi's late elaboration was a(nother) sign of its crucial impending significance.

Despite that Delphi could offer little in the way of articulated or monumental sacred architecture through the seventh century (and, as it has been argued, to some extent, *because* it could not), it *was* the recipient of increasing numbers of offerings from number of individuals and cities. We have already seen how Kings Midas, Gyges, and Alyattes from the East were said to have dedicated at Delphi a throne as well as a series of gold, bronze, and iron vessels and objects. Yet what is fascinating is what the dedication of these objects tells us about how different contributors interacted with the sanctuary. As far as we can tell, for example, all the monumental dedications coming from the East (from this period and on into the sixth century) were located on the eastern side of the (later temple of Apollo), in contrast to most other (monumental) dedications during the seventh and early sixth century, which gravitated toward the West (see plate 2). This has been explained as an eastern preference for the East, but also as a continuation of their traditional practice when making dedications at other sanctuaries (that is to say these eastern dedicators did what they were used to doing, without being influenced by what others were doing at Delphi).[45]

It was not only Eastern dedications that had their particular traits. During the seventh century BC, for example, Corinth does not seem to have continued with its dedication of bronze tripods, but only of pottery and, even then, only in the unelaborated sacred areas of the settlement. There is no Corinthian pottery in the maison rouge, for example, only locally made material.[46] Yet, around the middle of the seventh century, the new tyrant of Corinth, Cypselus (who had been so involved with the oracle), constructed Delphi's first (surviving) monumental dedication: a structure known as a treasury, because we think it was used as a treasure house to store other offerings (see plate 2).[47] This treasury, constructed in a highly visible location on a sort of natural crest in the landscape on the steep hillside, facing toward what scholars think was (or at least became) the earliest entryway into the sacred area, would have acted, at a time when Delphi had no official boundary markers, as an early marker of the sacred space. Cypselus, not only fundamental to the story of the oracle, is crucial in the story of the elaboration of Delphi as a sanctuary.[48]

In contrast to Corinth, Attica (and, at its heart, Athens) had a slow start at Delphi. Though some Attic bronze offerings can be identified as from the late eighth century, the numbers are low throughout the seventh century when Athenian pottery is nowhere to be seen. But at the very end of the century (and gathering speed from then on), the Athenians seem to have copied Cypselus and constructed a small treasury on the west side of the later sanctuary. Laconia, on the other hand, despite the number of consultations that associate Sparta with the Delphic oracle, was limited in its offerings at the sanctuary throughout the century. And despite the trade routes between Delphi and the North, the number of objects found at the sanctuary from northern and western Greece is also low, especially when compared with the numbers of Macedonian and Balkan objects found at Olympia, which is, after all, much farther south.[49]

Yet other areas of mainland Greece seem better represented. Several Boeotian cauldrons have been found, and a significant supply of armor from the Argolid seems to have been dedicated (though the Argolid does not seem to have offered any vases or terra-cottas). This trend for Argolid dedication was capped at the end of the seventh century BC by the dedication of a pair of over-life-size statues, which have often been identified with one of Argos's most famous myths, that of Cleobis and Biton (fig. 3.1).[50] Cyprus is also well represented—with shields, inscribed

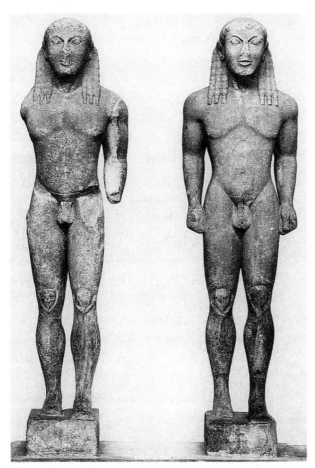

Figure 3.1. The Argive twins dedicated at Delphi, sometimes identified as Cleobis and Biton or simply as the Dioscuri (© EFA [Guide du Musée fig. 2a])

tripods, a number of cauldrons, and even a bronze bull.[51] So are Syria and Asia Minor, with lots of complex and beautiful cauldron decorations, ostrich eggs, glass human figurines, and even Phrygian belts (all found in recent excavations).Yet it is Crete that stands out, not only because of the number of tripods and shields, but also because of the way in which these offerings seem to be not isolated pieces but entire sets and series of dedications, and possibly even from the same area.[52]

Delphi, by 600 BC, may well have still been without a temple, or indeed any articulated, separated, sacred space, but it was, without doubt, already littered with offerings from the very small to the monumental, in a wide array of materials and styles, from a wide variety of dedicators. Once again, however, this material comes with a warning. While we label a piece "Cretan" because it is made in a style, procedure, or material we know to be associated with Crete, we cannot be sure that it was actually offered at the sanctuary by a Cretan, as opposed to its coming to the sanctuary via, say, a Corinthian trading network, or as the treasured possession of someone from outside Crete, or even as a prize dedicated by someone who was victorious over the Cretans in battle and took the piece as a victory trophy. Moreover, even some of the more monumental structures remain a mystery. A small, apsidal treasury-like structure was constructed around 600 BC in an area that would later be the temple terrace and even later be identified as the sanctuary of Gaia (see structure "B" in fig. 3.2). This, combined with its odd (and therefore supposedly religious) absidal-shaped end, as well as the literary myths about Delphi's early association with Gaia, the mother goddess, have led to this structure's often being called the Chapel of Gaia (as well as a possible early home for the omphalos). But in truth, there is not one shred of evidence that definitely connects this structure to Gaia. In reality, we simply have no idea who constructed it and why they did so.[53]

What we can do is begin to see increasing variation in the purpose and style with which different individuals, cities, and geographical areas interacted with Delphi in these crucial early phases of development. Not only in terms of their material offerings or trade connections, but by

Figure 3.2. The sanctuary of Apollo at Delphi c. 550 BC (© EFA [Courby FD II Terrasse du Temple 1920–29 fig. 156]).

putting these together with the literary evidence for oracular consultation and mythical involvement, we can begin to have a more three-dimensional view of how Delphi was perceived in the wider Greek world, and the different ways in which the different parts of that world chose to interact (and were represented as interacting) with it. What this brings into focus is the way certain communities interacted with particular parts of Delphic cult activity, but not others. The Laconians, for instance, had a close and ongoing relationship with the oracle, but dedicated very few offerings at the sanctuary before the sixth century BC. In complete contrast was Crete. Cretans dedicated many expensive smaller offerings (tripods, shields, etc.), but (probably) not a single monumental offering. They did not consult the oracle, unless you count one individual Cretan asking about the omphalos, which is probably a later creation. Yet Crete was fundamentally tied to Delphi from the late seventh century through the *Homeric Hymn to Apollo* as Cretans became the first priests of Apollo's temple.[54] Even more interestingly, no Cretan tripods have been found at Olympia, a sanctuary with which Delphi is often compared, but which, from its earliest history, seems to have attracted something of a different clientele from Delphi and seems to have been a center for different priorities and interests.[55]

Coming into focus also through this three-dimensional approach to early Delphi are the players, and tensions, that would, in the early sixth century BC, rip Delphi apart and catapult it forward. The dominant players at Delphi by the end of the seventh century seem to have been Sparta, Corinth, Lydia in the east, and increasingly Attica. Particularly these mainland Greek cities and city-states were users of the oracle, and to different extents, dedicators of cult offerings. In contrast, the longer-term influence of Thessaly on the site is not reflected in Thessalian interest in either of these activities during the seventh century.[56] Instead Delphi was changing, its focus turning from the trade corridor north toward the sea and land routes to the south, just as its livelihood seems to have become more dependent on the oracle and visitors to the sanctuary, who were themselves increasingly from polis city-states rather than older, *ethnos* political groupings (like Thessaly). Delphi itself was an increasingly rich settlement, full of treasures, its wealth now widely recognized and by now most probably the subject of one or more elaborate foundation stories. But, at the same time, Delphi had little architectural elaboration or protection, and was under the auspices of no major city. As the inhabitants of Delphi went about their business at the end of the seventh century, their treasures glistening in the sunlight in among their houses, few may have realized that there was a storm brewing. The great age of state activity in the Greek world was about to begin. Delphi, and its oracle, had, for a number of reasons, been turned into an increasingly crucial instrument in the dynamic and volatile processes of social and political change that Greece was undergoing, at the very moment when those processes were increasingly encouraging its constituents to butt heads. Delphi was a rich and unprotected place that many of these communities had a stake in. Who would try to claim it as their prize, and what would happen to Delphi as a result?

Gods! What may not come true, what dream divine,
If thus we are to drink the Delphic wine!

—Leigh Hunt, Epistle to Lord Byron on his departure for Italy
and Greece (published in the *Examiner* 28th April 1816

4

REBIRTH

In 590 BC, tension boiled over at Delphi. According to the ancient sources, inhabitants of one of the other settlements on the plain leading from the sea up toward Delphi, the town of Crisa, had not only been attacking those en route to the oracle, but had also been extracting heavy tolls from pilgrims arriving by sea, and even making raids on Delphi itself (see map 3).[1] The priests of the oracle at Delphi were said to be desperate to escape Crisa's malign and damaging influence. At the same time, a religious association of several cities and states, known as the Amphictyony, decided to come to Delphi's aid. Consulting the oracle over what they should do, they received this reply: "that they must fight against the Crisans day and night, and utterly ravage their country, enslave their inhabitants, and dedicate the land to Pythian Apollo, Artemis, Leto, and Athena Pronaia, and that for the future it must lie entirely uncultivated—they must not till this land themselves nor permit any other." Acting, according to some of the ancient sources, on the advice of Solon (the famous lawmaker of Athens), the Amphictyony, spearheaded by particular members (Thessaly, Athens, and Sicyon), launched a war against Crisa, which was said to have lasted as long as the Trojan War. The campaign was led, according to differing sources, either by Alcmaeon (head of the Alcmaeonidai family from Athens), by Cleisthenes (the tyrant ruler of Sicyon), or by Eurylochus (the Thessalian). Some sources report that the Pythia herself gave the lead on how to defeat Crisa, others that the Amphictyonic forces, after a long and protracted conflict, resorted to their own form of Trojan horse: they introduced hellebore into Crisa's aqueducts, subsequently rendering the city's inhabitants helpless thanks to the poison produced by the plant.[2]

Finally Crisa was destroyed, and the entire territory of the plain below Delphi was dedicated to the gods as sacred land (see map 3). The ancient sources trumpet how the oracle at Delphi was saved as an institution, freed from malign influence for all of Greece, and instead came under the influence of the Amphictyony, whose members not only safeguarded the sanctuary but instituted a series of athletic and musical games in honor of Pythian Apollo at Delphi, the prizes for the first of which were paid for with the booty seized from ravaged Crisa.[3] Delphi, in the first two decades of this new century, had been reborn, not only as a sanctuary free from the influence of any one city or state and instead under the protection of an multiregional association, but also as a sanctuary with games that would soon come to be considered on a par with the Olympics.

This war—known as the First Sacred War—has long been considered a watershed moment in Delphi's history. Yet in 1978, historian Noel Robertson challenged its existence, arguing that the war was an invention of the fourth century BC (at a time when Delphi was "once again" embroiled in a—now its third—Sacred War). His argument was strong: apart from possible allusions to the war in the *Homeric Hymn to Apollo* (in which, as we saw in earlier chapters, Apollo warns his priests against hubristic profiteering from the sanctuary) and the Hesiodic *Aspis*, the first reference to this great conflict is from fourth-century orator Isocrates (*Plataikos* c. 373 BC); followed by a cluster of material in the 340s BC (such as Speusippos's *Letter to Philip* 8–9; fragments from lost historians; as well as Aeschines in *On the Embassy* and *Against Ctesiphon*). Further references can be found in Diodorus Siculus (who quotes a lost fourth–century BC historian Ephorus) and Strabo, followed by nothing until the second century AD when the war resurfaces again in Pausanias.

Indeed, the most detailed narrative of the war comes from the Scholia to Pindar and Hypothesis to the *Pythian Odes* (II 1–5 ed. Drachmann).[4]

There is a dilemma here. Is the First Sacred War—the moment when Delphi was brutally reborn, at the expense of other settlements in the regions, as a sanctuary with international backing dominating a massive, and now off-limits territory—a necessary and important fiction used as justification for events in later Delphic history, or a later retelling (and potential enlargement) of an event that has its roots in historical truth? Most likely, it is the latter, and as such, we need to be careful in distinguishing between what we can known of what went on in Delphi in the early sixth century BC, from what later centuries portrayed as having happened for their own purposes. The circumstances surrounding the emergence of this First Sacred War in the fourth-century sources will be dealt with in detail in later chapters. For now, our focus is on what we can know to have happened in the early sixth century BC.

Key changes did take place at Delphi in the first half of the sixth century. The Amphictyony certainly came to have a heavy involvement there by, at the very latest, 548 BC.[5] The Pythian games were hosted for the first time in this period, although the date of their inception varies between 591/90 BC (according to the Parian Marble inscription) and 586 BC (according to Pausanias 10.7.4–5), with the first festival in which the laurel wreath was a prize occurring in 582 BC.[6] And the motivation for their inception is not, either, agreed upon in the ancient sources: some claim they were a celebration of the Amphictyony's victory in the First Sacred War, others that they celebrated Apollo's arrival at Delphi or Apollo's slaying of the serpent (their origins in the latter thus portrayed as funeral games).[7]

As well, the decision was made to leave the vast plain below Delphi uncultivated around this time, which, given its fertility and thus potential for profit, can only be explained by a significant turn of events like a Sacred War.[8] Coupled with this are stories in some literary sources from this period referring to bandits preying on Delphic pilgrims, which seem to echo elements of the Sacred War narrative. Moreover, some scholars have argued for a shift in the ideology underlying oracular responses from favoring Dorian powers to a more even-handed approach possibly tied with Delphi's rebirth as a "free" international sanctuary. And finally, there are a number of recognizable changes in the archaeological record at Delphi before and after this period that could be explained by the war: Cretan influence at Delphi, for example, which, as we have seen through the eighth and seventh centuries BC had been strong, tapered off by the beginning of the sixth century. Likewise, representations of scenes of Heracles stealing the Delphic tripod—a favorite used to epitomize conflict at (and over) Delphic—become extremely popular in vase painting 560–540 BC in the aftermath of the assumed occurrence of First Sacred War.[9]

Yet the most critical evidence for change at Delphi in the early decades of the sixth century BC has only recently come to light. As part of the excavations that revealed the series of houses (maison jaune, noire, and rouge) dating back to Delphi's earliest past, the excavators were able to date the first perimeter wall of the Apollo sanctuary (see fig. 3.2). As was stressed at the end of the last chapter, despite Delphi's increasingly important and international oracular and dedicatory record during the seventh century BC, there was still no separation between secular and sacred space, no bounded sanctuary or probably temple of Apollo during that time. The latest excavations show that all this changed in 575 BC, with the destruction of the maison rouge, and the building of the Apollo sanctuary's first perimeter wall over it, to which time should also probably be associated the building of a temple to Apollo (or at the very least the major elaboration of a structure that did not much predate it—see fig. 3.2).[10] By 575 BC, therefore, something had happened at Delphi to push the sanctuary headlong into a complete renovation and rearticulation of the settlement, which privileged the definition of a sanctuary space and prioritized the building of structures to worship Apollo.

The narrative of the First Sacred War fits neatly as an explanation for all these changes. Yet while recent scholarship has again become comfortable with the idea of conflict at Delphi in the early sixth century, it has sought to limit its scale and international nature. In particular, scholars have sought to emphasize the particular interests in Delphi of those

Amphictyonic members who took the lead in the war (Thessaly, Athens, Sicyon), and the corresponding absence of Amphictyonic members who were less directly related to the sanctuary.[11] Thessaly's long-term interest in Delphi has been noted in previous chapters, but, as a result of this conflict in the early sixth century, the Amphictyony (in which Thessaly held a prime role) became ensconced at Delphi, ensuring that Thessaly also maintained a say in affairs south of its own territory for the future.[12] Cleisthenes, the tyrant of Sicyon, is equally argued to have become involved in the war over Delphi because it offered a unique opportunity to challenge the supremacy of Corinth, itself long implicated in the sanctuary and surrounding area (not least as an ally of Crisa). This effort resulted not only in Sicyon fighting for the sanctuary, but in its dedicating substantial monuments there during the first half of the sixth century.[13] A number of groups in Athens (especially the Alcmaeonid family) have been argued to have been keen, given their rather difficult relationship with the oracle as a result of its involvement in Alcmaeonid as well as Athenian affairs, to reshape Delphi more on their own terms.[14]

Thus, while the conflict at Delphi in the early sixth century BC was most probably not on the scale of a Trojan War, which saw an international association fight for the freedom of Delphi (as those active in later centuries were keen to portray it), there does seem to have been conflict over Delphi at this time that arose because Delphi was an increasingly important and rich settlement that was not within a particular city's power but was on a vital trade corridor. The conflict was also the result of Delphi's being home to an oracle of increasing strategic power and value to an increasing number of city-states and communities with their own agendas. As a result, this conflict had the important effect of drawing Delphi into the auspices of the Amphictyony, potentially motivating the annexation of an extraordinarily fertile territory (the "untouchable" possession of the Delphic gods), most probably kick-starting the celebration of Pythian games, and, most importantly, prompting the final articulation of the Apollo sanctuary space through the building of a perimeter wall and the construction of a temple to Apollo— most likely by the Amphictyony themselves.[15]

Such an interest from developing city-states in the fortunes of a place like Delphi underscores an important shift in the nature of Greece during the sixth century BC. Internal civic development was still taking place at a scorching, sometimes brutal, rate: Athens suffered a coup, civic crisis, rebirth, and eventual tyranny, all in the last quarter of the seventh century through to the mid-sixth century BC. But that internal combustion was coupled with a perceived need to interact on a larger, comprehensive community scale within an ever-widening Mediterranean world. As a result, there was an increasing desire to have a stake in larger occasions and more international locations through which symbolic capital could be earned by city-state players. This is to say, the sixth century BC would become *the* century for the development of pan-Greek community occasions and locations. The use of long-known and increasing international, but still architecturally fledgling, sanctuaries like Delphi, Isthmia, and Nemea for a range of interactions (as worshipers, dedicators, and visitors) made increasing sense and was increasingly attractive to Greeks in the sixth century because they provided opportunities for interaction and an accretion of symbolic capital outside the city-state arena. It is no surprise, then, that it was during the first half of the sixth century BC that Delphi's fledgling Pythian games were joined by those of the sanctuaries at Isthmia and Nemea, and were all linked to the long-standing games at Olympia forming the Panhellenic *periodos* circuit (see map 2). And crucially, the prize for victory at each of these games was not money but a wreath made with branches of a plant sacred to the particular sanctuary and, with it, assured international renown and civic pride.[16]

The results of this increasing desire for action and interaction on the international stage were multiple. As we have seen, because communities now had, and sought a stake in, places like Delphi, such locations could expect to be the centers of more major investment and conflict. It is unlikely, for example, that there would have been the enthusiasm for a Sacred War over Delphi in the seventh or eighth centuries BC. As well, this new interest in international interaction provoked a tighter and more complex cultural and political network inside the Greek world. There was a noticeable increase in the development and uptake of a wider number of formal associations, agreements, and alliances between cities, and groups of cities, at this time. Such networks, however, also meant that individual city-states, and individual players within them, found themselves not only involved with the wider Greek world, but also occasionally at the mercy of it (as Crisa found to its cost). And at the same time, the increasing levels of interaction at places like Delphi and elsewhere ensured a growing cultural homogeneity within the Greek world. Regional pottery styles went into decline during the sixth century BC. In the early sixth century, artistic styles converged around the *kouros/kore* style of free-standing sculpture, and the construction of temples became de rigueur across the Greek world, with architectural sculpture starting to coalesce around a certain number of accepted themes. Coinage, too, first known at Ephesus c. 560 BC, began to diffuse across the Greek world during the course of the sixth century as an accepted style of financial interaction (if still with heavy local attachment, each city minting its own).[17]

Within this rapidly changing world, the Amphictyony came to have a good deal of control over Delphi. But just what was the Amphictyony and what was it for? These questions have exercised much scholarly debate, not only concerning the Amphictyony's composition and purpose, but also its nature, impact, and power in archaic and classical (and, indeed, Hellenistic and Roman) Greece. Translated literally, "Amphictyony" means those "who live around," and the name was given to a number of pluri-regional associations functioning in the archaic period (e.g., the Amphictyonic leagues of Calauria, Onchestus, Itonia, Delos, and Delphi), of which only the Amphictyonies of Delphi and Delos were to survive with any purpose into the classical world.[18] Each was centered in a particular sanctuary, and, as a result, the nature of these associations has been thought to have been primarily religiously motivated. The Amphictyony that came to be involved at Delphi, perhaps in the mid-seventh century BC and perhaps only in the run-up to conflict in the early sixth century, was not originally, or indeed, ever, centered entirely around the sanctuary at Delphi. Instead its heart was

the sanctuary of Demeter of Anthela near Thermopylae—still not archaeologically located (see map 2), and its own date of foundation as
an association varies in the ancient sources from the time of the Trojan War to the eighth century BC. Its traditional heartland was thus in
central/northern Greece, and its subsequent involvement in Delphi entailed an increase in its activities farther south. Its move to incorporate
Delphi also occasioned a change in its composition, with the result that
the Dorians of the Peloponnese, the Delphians, Athenians, and West
Locrians all gained membership, reflecting its new role in central Greek
affairs.[19] And noticeable from this list of new entrants, in addition to
the list of earlier members, the Amphictyony was a curious mix of more
recent polis city-states, older ethnos tribal groups, and even older loose
constructions of people from particular geographical areas. It was, thus,
always, an association of its time and and not of its time.

What was its purpose? The ancient sources outline it as anything from
ending conflicts that divided Greece, to ensuring its defense against the
barbarians, to the more modest protection of the goods of the sanctuary
(or sanctuaries) under its jurisdiction, and to stopping conflict between
its members. Many have, as a result, sought to portray the Amphictyony
as the Panhellenic body par excellence of the archaic period; some have
even seen it as a prototype European Union. On the other hand, some
scholars have argued that it was little more than an "old boys' club" and
a fairly ineffective talking shop. More recently, scholarly consensus has
characterized the Amphictyony as a multiregional but not Panhellenic,
old-fashioned, and yet supple institution that lacked permanence and
continuity and drifted in and out of usefulness and power as and when
it suited the needs of various of its members. As we shall see in later
chapters, we hear nothing about the Amphictyony in the fifth century
BC, for example, and its role at Delphi in the sixth century only comes
to the fore in fourth-century BC sources, when the Amphictyony strove
to be seen as a major force (once again) in Greek affairs.[20]

Why was the Amphictyony interested in Delphi? We have seen why
particular members (Thessaly, Athens, Sicyon) had their own interests
in Delphi, and some scholars argue that it was the attraction of the

sanctuary and settlement as a successful node on an important trade network that may have convinced the rest to decide on official Amphictyonic involvement. But it is clear that the involvement of this large pluri-regional association at Delphi catapulted the sanctuary into a new level of renown, as well as a new (or rather first-ever) bout of serious sanctuary construction, made possible not least in part thanks to new access to a much wider range of raw materials from the Amphictyony's constituent members.[21]

How did the management of Delphi change as a result of its incorporation into the Amphictyony during the first quarter of the sixth century BC? Who now "ran" the sanctuary, and what did that mean for Delphi? This is not an easy question to answer, because it is dependent not only on how the city and Amphictyony chose to represent it in later centuries (particularly the fourth century BC), but also on the fact that the available evidence suggests there were regular fluctuations in the management structure. In part it is also difficult because of the—most probably not inconsiderable—difference between the de jure and de facto positions, that is, what was supposed to be the case and what actually was the case. In reality, it is accepted that the Amphictyony was not a permanent body, but a council that met twice a year (and split its meetings between the sanctuaries of Demeter at Anthela and at Delphi). It had no permanent secretariat or bureaucracy (except for a time in the fourth century BC). As a result, while many scholars accept that "financially, politically, and administratively, the Amphictyony were entitled to have the first and final say in what went on," practically, their reaction times would have been "elephantine," their capacity to manage "intermittent," and their leverage power "minimal."[22]

In contrast, the authorities of the developing city of Delphi, which surrounded the newly elaborated sanctuary, are argued to have been in day-to-day control.[23] Some scholars have also sought to define the way in which the city of Delphi and the Amphictyony chose to carve up responsibility for different parts of the sanctuary's activities. Its reconstruction in 575 BC (and again after 548 BC) as well as the running of the Pythian games are considered to have been the responsibility of the

Amphictyony, whereas the oracle was the responsibility of the city of Delphi. Other scholars have argued that it is impossible to impose such neat divisions, because they never existed, and that the history of Delphi remains continually ambiguous, with, at best, assumptions that there existed periods of tension and forced relations between the Amphictyony and the city.[24]

Our picture of Delphi in the first quarter of the sixth century is thus uncertain in many ways. We know it was an increasingly important oracular center as well as a site for dedication, and we know that by 575 BC, the first dramatic articulation of the sanctuary of Apollo had been made, possibly combined with the construction of a temple to Apollo, and that by this time the Pythian games were also in existence (see fig. 3.2).[25] Yet what exactly sparked this rebirth, and the nature of the players involved, is unclear. We know, however, that Delphi was strengthened by the events of the first quarter of the sixth century BC: its safety and position in the immediate geographical region was secured, its access to a wider number of resources and its existence as a place of importance to a wider number of cities, ethnos states, and geographical areas across Greece were assured. But those same events had also demonstrated the conflicting interests of those who had a stake at Delphi. They had dictated, particularly with the demand for noncultivation of the fertile land below Delphi, that the fate and survival of Delphi's inhabitants was entirely tied to that of the oracle and the sanctuary. And they had formulated a management system for the sanctuary that in part thanks to its flexibility was open to manipulation and likely to cause tension in centuries to come.[26]

During, and in the aftermath of this war, who was consulting the oracle at Delphi? We saw briefly in the last chapter how Cylon's attempted coup at Athens in the late seventh century BC involved the oracle (and a misinterpretation by Cylon of the oracle's advice). Athens was seemingly racked by political struggle in this period, with political sympathies strongly linked to family ties: the surviving fragments of Draco's laws from the late seventh century suggest that the social and political instability in Athens at this time required a new and "draconian" legal code.

In c. 596 BC, the Athenians were back at Delphi to ask about a plague that had struck the city and how best to alleviate themselves from its grip. This was followed quickly by a number of consultations by the Athenian lawgiver Solon. Solon's initiatives in Athens—again the subject of bitter scholarly dispute because of the (mostly) later evidence for them—came at a time when political dispute seems to have come to a head in Athens, leading to major social as well as political unrest.[27] Yet his changes to the Athenian civic and political system were profound, not only because they offered a renegotiation of the social contract for the different classes of Athenian citizen, but also because they tied Athens, as Sparta had been in the previous century, to Delphi as an important element in Athens's own civic reform. We don't have surviving evidence for what Solon's inquiries consisted of, only that the oracle's replies advised a straight course from a single herald. At the same time, however, it's clear that Solon felt the oracle was an important part of his (and Athens's) decision-making system. In Solon's constitution for Athens, the chief magistrates of the city were required, upon entering office, to take a public oath in the Agora that, if they transgressed the laws, they would dedicate a life-size golden statue at Delphi. Solon also appointed three *exegetai pythochrestoi*, officials who were selected by the oracle from a short list of Athenians. Their function was to act as interpreters of the sacred law and ritual (not unlike the Delphic representatives in the Spartan constitutional system), and in practice, their appointment by the Delphic oracle cut across the traditional system of ancestral patronage for such positions, which had dominated in Athens in previous centuries.[28] Solon even returned to Delphi again in c. 570 BC to inquire of the oracle about the Athenian attempt to conquer Salamis, and was told to worship particular Salaminian heroes.[29] Given that Athens also constructed, or very soon would construct, a small treasury structure at Delphi in this period (on the site of its later marble treasury, whose reconstruction stands at the sanctuary today), it seems clear that Athens felt it had a close relationship with the sanctuary during, and directly following, the First Sacred War.[30]

Not all those, however, who were involved in leading the conflict over Delphi in the early sixth century BC seem to have been so favored as a result. While the Amphictyony's longer-term association with Delphi brought Thessaly, which presided over the Amphictyonic council, a say in events in mainland and southern Greece, Delphi failed to portray any real signs of favoritism toward Thessaly in return.[31] As well, the sanctuary did not repay another of its main supporters: Cleisthenes, the tyrant of Sicyon (who ruled c. 600–570 BC). Cleisthenes is argued to have been spurred into action over Delphi because of his Corinthian enemies' close interaction with the sanctuary.[32] In response Cleisthenes of Sicyon not only took a lead in the war over Delphi, but also seems to have been responsible for two of the most individualized and ornate monumental architectural dedications of the first half of the sixth century within the newly elaborated Apollo sanctuary: a *tholos* (a round colonnaded structure) and a *monopteros* (square colonnaded structure).[33] While we are not sure where exactly these structures were placed in this new building because they both fell prey to the redevelopment of the sanctuary in the second half of the sixth century (see the next chapter), it's likely that they were close to the newly built and improved (and perhaps still being built) temple of Apollo. More importantly, though in date the tholos and monopteros seem to have been dedicated some fifteen years apart, stylistically, it's likely they were planned as a unit. The tholos symbolized a monumentalized version of a traditional form of smaller stone religious dedication (the *perirrhanterion*), whereas the monopteros replicated the newly emerging temple, complete with carved metopes, each of which keyed in to the newly emerging Panhellenic Greek vocabulary of architectural sculpture themes, whose style and life (the sense of the scenes jumped across metope panels forcing the viewer's eyes to keep moving around the structure), however, are testament to its sculptural sophistication and individualization.[34]

Cleisthenes of Sicyon had thus ensured not only a position at the forefront of the fight to "free" Delphi, but had graced the sanctuary with its finest monumental dedications to date. He had even participated in the sanctuary's new athletic games, winning the chariot race.[35] What did it gain him? On the one hand, the first half of the sixth century saw the gradual transference of the allegiance of Corinthian tyrants away from

Delphi to Olympia.[36] Periander, Cypselus's successor, dedicated "Cypselus's" cedar-wood chest, covered in ivory and gold, at Olympia, where it was seen by Pausanias in the temple of Hera in the second century AD.[37] On the other hand, Cleisthenes received little for his investment in the sanctuary from the Delphic oracle. The one recorded consultation by Cleisthenes, on how to strengthen his rule at Sicyon by removing the bones of the Argive hero Adrastus that were acting as a focal point for his opposition, met with a stern rebuke from the oracle, who told Cleisthenes he was a mere skirmisher whereas Adrastus had been a king. It is perhaps no surprise that many have interpreted Cleisthenes' subsequent creation of athletic games in honor of Apollo Pythios at Sicyon—which were supposedly paid for our of his share of spoils from the First Sacred War—in the spirit of direct competition to those newly created at Delphi (rather than in praise of the Delphian games).[38]

It is testament to the increasing strength of Delphi in the Greek world, and indeed the wider world, at this time, as well as an example of the trend in the ancient literature to mark Delphi's credentials as increasingly antityrannical, that Delphi failed to treat well several powerful leaders who lavished its sanctuary with dedications when they came for oracular consultation.[39] The most famous examples are of Alyattes and his son Croesus, kings of Lydia. We have met this family before. Alyattes, king between 619 and 560 BC, had attacked Miletus and burned down a temple of Athena. He had subsequently fallen ill and sent to Delphi for advice. The oracle had apparently refused to reply until the temple of Athena was restored, and when it was, Alyattes recovered, and subsequently sent a huge, silver mixing bowl on a welded iron base to Delphi (one of those Eastern dedications that collected in front of the new temple's eastern front). Croesus, on the other hand, was not so fortunate. It is his story of oracular consultation at Delphi that is perhaps Delphi's most famous, and that we touched on in an chapter about the workings of the Delphic oracle as the classic case of how *not* to ask your question at Delphi and the perils of misinterpreting the oracle's answers. It was Croesus's generation that the oracle had foreseen (or was later said to have foreseen) would bear the revenge for Gyges' slippery usurpation of power (see previous chapters). Croesus, intent on gaining oracular approval for his upcoming military campaign is said to have first tested all the famous oracles around the Mediterranean to find out which one was the most accurate by sending messengers asking what he was doing one hundred days from the day they left Lydia (as Herodotus is keen to highlight, this was a very unusual form of question to an oracle). The oracle at Delphi was said to have answered correctly: Croesus was chopping up a tortoise and a lamb in a bronze cauldron with a bronze lid.[40] As a result, Croesus showered Delphi with dedications to sit resplendent in its newly articulated sanctuary. Different ancient sources claim he demanded contributions from individual Lydians, burned three thousand sacrificial victims along with encrusted gold and silver beads, casting the molten residue into 117 half-bricks (4 pure gold and the others white gold) to be surmounted by a lion statue of pure gold weighing ten talents. Nor did it stop there. Croesus also sent two extra-large mixing bowls, one of gold and one of silver, which would in Herodotus's day play a key role in Delphic temple ceremonies. He also sent four silver jars, two vessels (one of gold, one of silver), bowls of silver, a golden statue of a woman, and many other smaller dedications including the necklace and girdles of his queen.[41]

All this, scholars have argued, demonstrated not merely a routine diplomatic gesture to a foreign god, but an offer of generosity the likes of which had never been seen in the Greek world.[42] It was all also a payment in advance for the answer to the key question Croesus had had in mind all along, the oracle's answer to which became famous in antiquity. Croesus asked "whether he should make an expedition against the Persians and whether he should make any further host of men his friends?"[43] Many ancient writers record the response "Croesus, having crossed the Halys, will destroy a great empire." It is a reply that has become infamous for its ambiguity and misinterpretation, and subsequently for the danger inherent in consulting the Delphic oracle. Croesus of course did cross the river Halys, and he did destroy an empire: his own. Yet Croesus, interpreting it as meaning his enemy's empire, was so pleased by the response that he sent further gifts to Delphi (two gold staters for every

Delphic citizen), in return for which the Delphians gave him the right of promanteia (the right to skip the queue to consult the oracle), *ateleia* (the right to not pay the tax to consult the oracle), and *prohedria* (the right to front-row seats at the Pythian festival). Later, however, so upset was Croesus by what he saw as the oracle's failure to warn him that he asked permission of his now master—the Persian king, Cyrus—to take the chains of his captivity to Delphi and challenge the oracle to justify its conduct. The oracle is portrayed (in the later sources) as responding that Croesus was bound by destiny to pay for Gyges' actions, that he himself had misinterpreted the oracular response, and that, all in all, it was thanks to Apollo that he was even alive.[44]

Yet the oracle at Delphi was not only standing up to some of the most powerful men at the borders of the Mediterranean world at this time, it was also playing hardball with those closer to home. One Spartan, Glaucus, who had denied that his friend had previously entrusted him with his money, was asked to swear an oath to that effect. Glaucus, according to Herodotus, consulted Delphi about whether it was defensible in the eyes of the gods to perjure oneself under oath if material gain resulted. The oracle replied resolutely in the negative and mishap dogged Glaucus's family for generations. The oracle could also play hardball with the Delphians themselves. One consultation story, reported in Herodotus and dating to c. 563–32 BC, tells how Aesop (of Aesop's Fables fame), having insulted the Delphians for living off nothing except what Apollo gave them, was tricked by the Delphians into taking a sacred treasure away from the sanctuary.[45] Having set him up, the Delphians "discovered" his theft, convicted him, and had him thrown off the Hyampeia cliff high above Delphi. As a result, Delphi was smitten with plague and famine (we might think back again to the *Homeric Hymn to Apollo* and Apollo's warning to his priests not to abuse their position). Consulting the oracle, the Delphians were told that finding a relative of Aesop's was key to their atonement, and they conducted such a search at every major Greek festival till they finally found a candidate.

Among these oracles responding to queries of plagues, famines, world domination, civic rebirth, perjury, and tortoise and lamb boiling in bronze pots, Delphi also continued to answer queries about ritual practice, including the establishment of new rituals to different Greek divinities in various Greek cities.[46] Chief among these gods was Dionysus: in fact, there are more oracular responses recorded in the Delphic corpus relating to the worship of this god than any other. Dionysian cult practices may well already have been part of Delphic worship in this period—indeed it may always have been. But it is only epigraphically and archaeologically attested, for certain, beginning in the fourth century BC, whence it would grow into an essential part of Delphic mythology, indeed one that would remain when many other aspects of Delphic business had been forgotten.[47]

The oracle also continued, as in the previous century, to answer questions concerning the founding of new settlements. It was, after all, in the sixth century BC, that it became necessary to consult the oracle before a colonial adventure became a proverbial tale.[48] In the first half of the sixth century, Delphi continued to be consulted, for example, on the foundation of Heracleia Pontice by the Megarians and the Boeotians in the 560s BC and, in the same period, on the Athenian expedition to the Chersonesus (see maps 1, 2).[49] More importantly, foundations with which it had been involved (or, as discussed in the last chapter, with which it later became preferable to different parties to cast the oracle as being involved in) in the previous century, in turn, went back to the sanctuary. Syracuse, for example, is argued to have constructed a treasury at Delphi in this period (its presence known thanks to surviving roofing fragments in bright red Sicilian clay).[50]

In addition, the dedicatory record shows a swath of Western dedicators offering monumental structures at Delphi in this period, many of which do not seem to have had a direct connection to Delphi through a foundation oracle, but instead seem to represent the eagerness of these dedicators to ensure their presence at this increasingly important center of the ancient world. There are three treasury structures, for example, lined up opposite the western end of the new temple of Apollo, all leaning against the new perimeter wall of the sanctuary (structures C, D, and E in fig. 3.2). One of these (built c. 580 BC) has been associated with the Corcyrians because of its roofing style.[51] And two other treasury-like structures were dedicated in the southern part of the Apollo sanctuary behind the early Athenian treasury (see plate 2), which, again because of their roofing styles, have been associated with southern Italian (and probably Sybarite) dedicators.[52] All these structures seem to have taken advantage not only of the new perimeter wall, but also of new terracing walls within the sanctuary to claim positions of high visibility and dominate this new sanctuary space.

Also filling this new sanctuary space in the first half of the sixth century BC were a series of other treasury-like structures, whose function and dedicator we cannot claim with any certainty to know. One, perhaps two more structures, traditionally associated with the worship of Gaia but in reality uncertain, were constructed in this period. As well, a building, long labeled the Delphic city's bouleuterion but now the subject of disputed identification, was constructed near the Athenian treasury. We can also identify another series of monumental, and less monumental but incredibly ornate, dedications that graced the sanctuary at this time. The most ornate treasury yet, constructed c. 550 BC, was dedicated by the Cnidians in Asia Minor (see plate 2). It was the first at Delphi to be built in marble and in the ionic style. No treasury-like structure has ever been found in their home city of Cnidos, but here at Delphi the Cnidians seem not only to have followed the trend for treasury dedication, but to have embellished it considerably. In contrast, the inhabitants of the island of Naxos in the Aegean chose to dedicate c. 570 BC one of the sanctuary's most famous monuments, the Sphinx (see plate 2, fig. 4.1). This mythological creature with the body of a lion, the wings of a bird, and the face of a woman was something of a Naxian calling card in terms of artistic choice, as the Naxians had already dedicated a similar sculpture at the sanctuary of Apollo on Delos.[53] But it was also perfectly tuned to its location at Delphi: the sphinx's placement upon a tall column assured it was visible from all parts of the steep hillside.

In fact, we are only just scraping the surface of the ornate and expensive dedications that came from the eastern Mediterranean to Delphi in the first half of the sixth century BC. Herodotus tells us of the

Figure 4.1. The Naxian Sphinx, dedicated in the Apollo sanctuary at Delphi (Museum at Delphi).

Egyptian courtesan Rhodopis who chose to dedicate a percentage of the wealth gained from her profession to Apollo at Delphi in the form of iron spits.[54] And in the 1930s a whole host of dedications was discovered that date from the eighth to the fifth centuries BC, and had at some point been intentionally buried, it seems, underneath the central pathway through the sanctuary. Among them was the fabulous life-size silver bull (fig. 4.2) now on display in the Delphi museum, which had originally been the gift of an Ionian dedicator. In addition, there were two chryselephantine (ivory and gold) statues (see plate 5), as well as another ivory statue from an earlier date, all also of Ionian provenance.[55]

Delphi, by the middle of the sixth century BC, had thus changed dramatically. In just fifty years, it had been the subject of major international conflict (the First Sacred War); had come under the auspices of the Amphictyony; had had its sacred space of Apollo officially articulated with perimeter walls, a temple of Apollo built, an increasing stream of monumental treasuries constructed within its new sanctuary, alongside a plethora of jaw-dropping gold and silver gifts from eastern rulers and a wealth of ornate dedications from around the eastern Mediterranean. Its oracle had been consulted by eastern kings and by the tyrants and reformers of mainland Greece; had laid down the law with oath-breakers and Delphian misbehavers; had helped guide the institution of rituals of divine worship; had continued to play a role in the ongoing processes of settlement foundation around the Mediterranean, and had enjoyed the fruits of the success of the developing communities it had been involved with founding in the previous century.

Delphi was, without a doubt, a major player in the ancient world by the mid-sixth century BC. But that should not be confused with its

Figure 4.2. The Silver Bull, dedicated in the Apollo sanctuary at Delphi and subsequently found buried in the sanctuary (© EFA [Guide de Musée fig. 11])

having been a sanctuary for everyone. It was available only to those with vested interests in the Amphictyony during the conflict over Delphi, and to those who dedicated richly afterward. Much of mainland Greece did not choose to have a permanent presence within the sanctuary, and of northern Greece, there is almost no trace either in relation to the oracle or in terms of dedication. In contrast, this absence is countered by the overwhelming presence of many individuals and cities from the eastern and western boundaries of the Greek world. Delphi was international for sure, but, again, not open to everyone. Moreover, with its newfound success and importance came the difficult task of trying to negotiate a fast-changing and often cutthroat Greek world. The silver bull and chryselephantine statues discovered buried in the sanctuary of Apollo at Delphi all showed signs of heavy fire damage. Delphi was soon to be reborn—yet again—through fiery destruction.

PART II

Some achieve greatness

The sun blows down from Parnassus
and unhinges the centre of the world.

—Salvatore Quasimodo, *Delphi* (translated by Richard Stoneman)

5

FIRE

In 548 BC—less than thirty years after the Amphictyony had taken control of Delphi; separated out sacred from secular space; built the sanctuary's first boundary walls; and elaborated, if not built from scratch, its Apollo temple—fire broke out, once again, at Delphi. The new sanctuary, gleaming with its new ivory, limestone, gold and silver dedications, reveling in its busier-than-ever-oracle and brand new Pythian athletic and musical games that had become part of a recognized Panhellenic circuit, was consumed by the flames.[1] The fire was so intense that it was said to have melted the solid gold lion dedicated by King Croesus of Lydia along with the half-gold brick base on which it stood: four and a half of the twelve talents of gold the monument contained melted away never to be seen again.[2]

When the flames finally died away and the smoke cleared, the sanctuary was in a poor state. The temple must have been near ruin. Many of the sanctuary's most extravagant metal dedications, which had been placed around the temple, especially from rich eastern dedicators, were destroyed: only two of Croesus's offerings, the silver and gold amphora mixing bowls that had stood in front of the temple's entrance, had been removed in time to save them. A sanctuary, which

had increasingly been basking in the full focus of the ancient Mediterranean world, lay in tatters.

We don't know for sure how the fire started. Herodotus is insistent
that it was pure accident. The Greek word he used almost gives the sense
that the temple caught fire of its own free will.[3] Given the presence of the
continually burning sacred fire inside, and the regular use of the larger
altar outside for burning sacrificial offerings, it's easy to see how such
a fire may have been an accident. And we do know how Delphi, and
its new ruling Amphictyony, responded: by building bigger and better
than ever before. Out of the ashes of destruction, they created a sanctuary worthy of its reputation as the center of the world.

The Amphictyony seems to have taken charge of the rebuilding process (we can only imagine the chagrin this must have caused the inhabitants of the city of Delphi as *their* sanctuary was now rebuilt by an international committee). The upside, however, was a rebuilding program
beyond their wildest dreams. What the Amphictyony envisaged was a
construction scheme on a par with, if not surpassing, any that had been
seen in Greece. Building a new temple was just the beginning. It was to be
a bigger temple, which, because of the steep and treacherous mountainside on which Delphi was perched, required also the creation of a new,
monumental, supporting terrace that could provide a sufficiently large,
stable, flat surface on which to build. At the same time, the opportunity
was taken to expand the size of the sanctuary yet again, to push out its
(only recently created) boundary walls on all sides, perhaps to the chagrin of the inhabitants of Delphi, as it meant encroaching on what had
been residential areas (see plate 2). What is more, even though we have
no evidence to suggest the sanctuary of Athena, sitting below the Apollo
sanctuary on the same cleft of the Parnassian mountains, had been damaged in the fire, the Amphictyony seems to have decided to expand that
sanctuary too and build a new temple there as well (see plate 3).[4]

This was no mere patch-up of fire damage: out of Delphi's fiery destruction would come a rebirth of the Apollo and Athena sanctuaries on
a scale of size and grandeur never seen before. We should not underestimate the enormity of the project that the Amphictyony conceived of

at Delphi in the mid-sixth century BC. Temple building was the largest and most complex economic and management project the Greek world undertook at this time. This project not only sought to build a bigger temple, but to do it on incredibly unstable and difficult ground, requiring every ounce of engineering knowledge the Greeks had at their disposal. And at the same time, they sought to build a second temple in the Athena sanctuary, as well as enlarge both sanctuaries with new, monumental, boundary walls. Every block of stone, every piece of timber, every rope and pulley, every chisel had to be dragged and carried up to the sanctuaries. The stone had to come either from the local quarries in the Parnassian mountains or from farther afield, arriving by land through the mountains, or by sea to the Itean plain and then carted six hundred meters above sea level to Delphi (see fig. 0.1).[5] Working areas for the final cutting and shaping of the stone had to be created within and around the sanctuary, and the sanctuary itself became a building site for years. People with the necessary skills had to be found throughout Greece and the Mediterranean world, hired, and brought to Delphi, where they had to be accommodated. And, of course, all this had to be paid for.

For certain, Delphi had seen nothing like it in its history, and the Amphictyony had, almost certainly, never, as a council, undertaken a project on such a scale. It is arguable that the Greek world itself had never been party to such an undertaking, and that the Delphic rebuilding was fundamental to forcing the development not only of new skills in the Delphic and Amphictyonic communities (project management skills and alphabetic literacy, for example), but also the development of legal arrangements for building contracts and account keeping in Greece as a whole.[6] It also forced the Amphictyony to become good at raising money. The ancient sources tell us that the estimated total cost for this rebuilding was three hundred talents, which is the approximate equivalent of 3,600,000 days'-worth of wages for an Athenian juryman, or 1,800,000 days'-worth of wages for a skilled hoplite soldier. The Amphictyony took responsibility for raising among its members 225 talents, leaving 75 talents (still 450,000 days'-worth of hoplite wages) to be raised by the city of Delphi itself. This was a tall order for a small city whose main income came from the business of the oracle, and it would have to be done by appealing to the wider Greek world for support; as such, it would be a huge test of Delphi's popularity in and importance to the ancient Mediterranean community. The response to Delphi's call for funding is thus fascinating. We don't have the full picture of where the money came from, but we do know that Amasis, the pharaoh of Egypt, felt it important enough to contribute one thousand talents'-worth of alum—an Egyptian product highly valued in Greece—which could then be sold and the proceeds put into the restoration fund. To get a sense of the magnitude of this gift, the total contribution from Greeks living in Egypt came to twenty minas, one third of a single talent, which was itself thought to be very respectable.[7]

Raising such a huge amount of money, even with gifts like those of Amasis, must have taken a considerable amount of time. It is no surprise that, given also how complicated a building project this was, the construction of the new temples and sanctuary boundary walls was not completed until 506 BC, over forty years after the fire.[8] On the one hand, this left Delphi as a building site for the second half of the sixth century BC. It has been argued that, as a result, dedicators keen to continue their relationship with Apollo during this period went elsewhere, particularly to the sanctuary of Apollo Ptoios not that far from Delphi. Apollo Ptoios saw a leap in dedications of kouroi statues in exactly this period, which faded away in the early years of the fifth century BC as Delphi came back online.[9] Yet, on the other hand, this process of fundraising and rebuilding ensured that, for the first time, all the Amphictyonic members, as well as the inhabitants of Delphi and the wide range of people they tapped for money from all over the Mediterranean world, now had a financial stake in the fabric of Delphi.

Even more interestingly, despite the initial impression that Delphi was out of action at this time, the truth seems to have been quite the opposite. In the second half of the sixth century BC, Delphi, for better or worse, was becoming more and more deeply involved with the politics of ancient Greece. The oracle, despite the fact that the temple from which the Pythia made her responses was in ruins and under reconstruction,

continued to prophesize (we have no idea where or how). In part, the
questions put to her were business as usual. Questions about the founding of new settlements continued to come to Delphi (e.g., Abdera in 544
BC, Cyrnos in 545 BC); tyrants continued to consult and were (later)
recorded as being given the brush off: Polycrates of Samos consulted
about whether his new festival on the sacred island of Delos should be
called Delia or Pythia, and was told it didn't matter (he died soon after).
Equally important for Delphi's continued success was that settlements
with which Delphi had been involved at the time of their foundation
continued to return to the oracle for advice. When Cyrene in Libya
suffered political unrest in the second half of the sixth century, it consulted Delphi on how best to manage it, and was instructed to appoint
a mediator, Demonax of Mantinea. A little later, King Archesilaus III
of Cyrene, keen to reclaim complete control of Cyrene following the
process of mediation, consulted Delphi on how best to do so and was
told not to attempt to gain too much power. Ignoring the advice of the
oracle, he was eventually assassinated.[10]

Indeed, scholars have noted an increasing boldness of oracular responses in this period (even allowing for their recalibration in later
sources), borne out in the oracle's response to the residents of the city
of Cyme in Asia Minor, when they, just after the middle of the century,
consulted as to whether or not they should hand over Pactyes, a man
who had taken refuge in the city after having betrayed his Persian masters. The oracle is said to have replied that they should hand him over
(because that's what they wanted in reality to do), but that the city itself
would be punished for having even considered asking the oracle about
breaking such a fundamental rule of the rights of a refugee suppliant.
Underlying this chastisement, however, is a sense of Delphi's understanding of the changing balance of power in Asia Minor, and particularly the growing dominance of Persia after its defeat of Croesus of
Lydia. Delphi, after all, told Cyme to give in to Persian demands even
though it meant breaking a fundamental tenet of Greek society. Similarly, the oracle is recorded as responding to the Cnidians in Asia Minor,
who consulted on how best to fight against the Persians (they planned

to dig a canal through the landscape to make their city an island), that it would be best if they not resist.[11]

Delphi was thus, despite being a building site, still fundamentally active in the affairs of North Africa and Asia Minor in the second half of the sixth century BC. As well, it was consulted several times by settlements in the West during this period, particularly about public and private matters concerning the inhabitants of Croton in southern Italy.[12] But it was Delphi's involvement with the politics of mainland Greece that would be of crucial importance for its immediate future. More specifically, it would be Delphi's involvement (and noninvolvement) with two rival aristocratic families in Athens that would define the political landscape not only in Athens, but also at Delphi and set the stage for future events.

The first of those families were the Alcmaeonids. Back in the late seventh century BC the would-be tyrant Cylon, having consulted (and misunderstood) the Delphic oracle on how to take control of Athens, had been killed by the Alcmaeonid family. However, after performing such a service for their city, the Alcmaeonids dragged him out from the sacred refuge of a temple to Athena, their family thereby cursed forever because they had not respected Cylon's protected status while in the religious sanctuary. Despite this curse, however, the family continued to gain in wealth and importance. In the first half of the sixth century BC, Alcmaeon, had, it is claimed by Herodotus, helped the ambassadors of King Croesus of Lydia during their frequent trips to Delphi for consultation and dedication, and had gained great wealth as a result.[13] His son, Megacles, married the daughter of Cleisthenes, the tyrant of Sicyon (who, too, was very active at Delphi). Their son, also called Cleisthenes, was the famous Cleisthenes of Athens, who would eventually be fundamental in founding democracy in that city at the end of the sixth century.

Yet for most of the second half of the sixth century, the position of the Alcmaeonid family at Athens was far some stable, thanks to the emergence of another powerful family in Athens, the Peisistratids. Peisistratus, the head of this family, emerged in Athens as a powerful commander in the 570s and 560s. In time, he challenged the traditional power blocs in Athens (the "men of the coast" led by Megacles the Alcmaeonid and the "men of the plain" led by Lycurgus) by creating and harnessing the loyalty of a third group, the "men over the hills." His attempt at taking tyrannical power over Athens in the late 560s eventually ended in his exile. But in 556 BC he returned and married the daughter of Megacles the Alcmaeonid. This time, through trickery (according to Herodotus) or popular support (according to Aristotle), Peisistratus achieved tyrannical power over Athens.[14] The result of his ascension to power seems to have been the exile of the Alcmaeonid family (on the grounds of the curse that still hung over them from the seventh century BC), thus conveniently ridding himself of powerful political opponents.

In later times, the Alcmaeonids often claimed they were exiled from Athens for most of the rest of the sixth century BC (a claim important to their eventual antityrannical and pro-democratic credentials). But the inscriptional evidence demonstrates without doubt that their exile was much patchier than that: in 525/4 BC we know that Cleisthenes held the important civic position of eponymous archon in Athens (only possible with Peisistratus's favor).[15] Yet, despite their on-off appearances in Athens, the Alcmaeonids were also increasingly present at Delphi and the surrounding area in the middle and second half of the sixth century BC. In the early days of Peisistratus's tyranny, Herodotus reports that the Delphic oracle responded to the Dolonchi of the Chersonesus (near the Hellespont in the northeastern Aegean), who had asked a question about being hard-pressed in war, that they should persuade the first man who gave them hospitality to found a colony among them. That man turned out to be Miltiades the Elder, a member of the Alcmaeonids, who had been "disgruntled" with Peisistratus's tyranny. And in the 540s, BC, the early days of the Alcmaeonid exile, the brother of Megacles dedicated a victory monument for their win in a chariot victory (in Athens) at the sanctuary of Apollo Ptoios.[16]

Most crucially, however, it has long been argued that, during the second half of the sixth century BC, the Alcmaeonids increasingly built up their influence at Delphi. This picture of their influence is partly based on an argument from silence: Delphi never has anything to do with Peisistratus. Given Delphi's involvement with tyrants across Greece, the complete absence of any oracle to do with Peisistratus (for or against him) is surprising. More noteworthy is that even though Peisistratus was a great builder and founder of important events in Athens, he did not dedicate a single offering at Delphi. Indeed, he even founded (what many think was a rival) cult of Apollo Pythios in Athens, which would be continued and enlarged by his descendants who also ruled as tyrants. Moreover, according to some late sources, Peisistratus may have hated Delphi so much that he himself engineered the fire that burned the temple of Apollo to the ground in 548 BC.[17]

Yet the most positive proof of Alcmaeonid influence at Delphi comes in the last quarter of the sixth century. In 514 BC the new temple still lay uncompleted. The long process of securing the money, and then undertaking such a complex working project, had seemingly come to a halt, with the initial contractors responsible for the temple unable to finish the job. In 514 BC the Alcmaeonids stepped in and were awarded the contract to finish the temple.[18] This they did, according to Herodotus, not only completing it as required by 506 BC, but indeed going beyond their contract and paying themselves to adorn the east end of the temple (that facing toward the altar) in Parian marble rather than the prescribed poros limestone (fig. 5.1).[19] This was a grand gesture—the procuring, shipping, and sculpting of Parian marble was not a cheap undertaking.

Alcmaeonid largess toward Delphi came at the same time as the Athenians were becoming more and more resentful of the Peisistratid tyranny over their city and particularly their current tyrant, a descendent of Peisistratus, called Hippias. And it was also at this time that Herodotus records how the Spartans, every time they came to consult the oracle at Delphi on any matter, were told by the Pythian priestess that, before they did anything else, they must free Athens.[20] Alcmaeonid generosity had coincided with the Pythia's active support for regime change in Athens, a change that could not but benefit the Alcmaeonids. Is this a case of coincidence or the first attested case of bribery of the oracle at Delphi?

It is irresistible to think that Alcmaeonid beneficence did indeed incline the Pythia toward ensuring Spartan help to "free" Athens from the tyranny of the Peisistratids, even if the Pythia's intervention was only

Figure 5.1. A reconstruction of the east front of the sixth century temple of Apollo in the Apollo sanctuary at Delphi, with Apollo's arrival via chariot at Delphi represented in the pedimental sculpture (© EFA [Plate xxii Lacoste/Courby FD II Terrasse du Temple 1920–29])

the cherry atop a much longer-lasting series of negotiations between the Spartans and the Alcmaeonids, and something that, thanks to the increasing importance and potential of Sparta's own political network in the Peloponnese by the last quarter of the sixth century BC, was actually rather attractive to the Spartans themselves. But "freeing" Athens was no easy task: it took four separate campaigns by the Spartans to achieve Hippias's removal.[21] As a result, however, Delphi, more than ever, became an integral player in Athenian and Spartan politics and relations.

But while Delphi had become an integral part of the cut and thrust of Athenian politics, and Athenian/Spartan relations, how had Delphi itself been transformed? A visitor to Delphi in 506 BC, at the time of the completion of the temple, would have been hard-pressed to recognize the sacred complex in relation to what it looked like before the fire. In the Apollo sanctuary a gigantic terracing wall had been created to ensure a solid flat foundation for the new temple (see plate 2), and this wall towered over the sanctuary; it is known as the polygonal wall because this was the shape of the blocks of stone that composed it. Such a shape was preferred because the Greeks understood that such blocks would give the wall greater strength than square ones (polygonal-shaped blocks lock together in more complex ways). This new terrace also destroyed and swallowed up many of the old, unidentified structures (often associated with the cult of Gaia) that had surrounded the earlier temple, many of which had been built in the period 580–548 BC (see fig. 3.2).[22]

On top of this massive new terrace, a new temple was laid out, resplendent in Parian marble at its eastern end with entirely new pedimental sculpture at both east and west. Carved on the western end was a scene of Gigantomachy—the gods fighting the giants; and on the eastern side, the arrival of Apollo in a horse-drawn chariot (fig. 5.1). It has long been debated whether this should be seen as Apollo's arrival from the Hyperboreans as he returned to Delphi each year, or, more specifically, Apollo's arrival from Athens, surrounded by Athenians and welcomed by citizens of Delphi. If the latter, then the Athenians, or more specifically the Alcmaeonids, had successfully placed Athens at the very heart of Delphi's story and cemented their own special relationship with Apollo, in a temple they had completed and that would remain standing for over one hundred years.[23]

Those responsible for the rebuilding chose carefully: archaeologists have noted that blocks of stone from the pre-548 BC temple (built just after the First Sacred War) were often reused, but only in the "official" new temple complex: the temple, its polygonal wall and associated water conduits. And material from the old sanctuary boundary walls was also utilized to create the Apollo sanctuary's new perimeter walls, expanded to the south, east, and west by an exact 13.25 meters to create a perimeter some 3 kilometers long (making the Apollo sanctuary alone equivalent in size to a small polis, see plate 1). A new, major entrance to the sanctuary was created in the southeast, at the bottom of what would become the Apollo sanctuary's sacred way, and followed today by visitors to the site (see plate 2, fig. 0.1). But we should not be led into thinking that the sacred way itself was laid out at this time. In fact, the path taken today is a creation of the last phase of Delphi's ancient existence in the fifth–sixth centuries AD (see later chapters).[24] In the late sixth century BC, in contrast, while the sanctuary's major entrance was where it is today in the southeast area, there were several other entryways in the new boundary walls at each of the terracing levels of the sanctuary, with short staircases and pathways leading between these terraces inside the sanctuary (see plate 2). Rather than only one path of movement, we thus need to imagine a more complex sequence of movement in and around the Apollo sanctuary for much of its history, allowing visitors more flexibility to engage with and admire the increasing number of monuments that filled it.[25]

Attention was also paid in this period to the Athena sanctuary, which, despite being undamaged by the fire, perhaps represented the Amphictyony's first attempt to exercise control over this sanctuary as well as Apollo's. The Athena sanctuary's boundary walls were expanded and rebuilt to treble the size of the sanctuary, incorporating what were probably unofficial cult locations to several other deities, including Artemis (see plate 3). A monumental entrance to this newly expanded sanctuary was added in its northeast corner and may have doubled as the official entrance to the Delphic polis (see plate 1). A new temple to Athena was built, and a carbon copy of the pedimental sculpture from the new Apollo temple was probably given to it.[26] As a result, Delphi grew in international appeal during this period, and seems also to have expanded not only the number of gods within it, but also the respect with which they were worshiped.

It is almost impossible to map this landscape of divine worship at Delphi with any precise detail, even less to give it a solid chronology. But it is crucial to realize that, by the end of the sixth century BC, and increasingly rapidly from then on throughout Delphi's long history, Delphi was home to the worship of a large number of gods, goddesses, demigods, and heroes. Alongside Apollo Pythios, Athena Pronaia, Artemis, Dionysus, and Poseidon, inscriptions attest to the worship in and around the Apollo and Athena sanctuaries (as well as at the port of Cirrha, which served Delphi, and in the Corycian cave) of Hermes, Gaia and the Muses, Zeus Machaneus (the artisan), Moiragetus (the master of fate), Polieus (the protector of the city), Soter (the savior), Athena Ergone (the workman), Zosteria (the warrior), Artemis Eucleia (of marriage), Leto, Aphrodite Epiteleia (of birthing), Harmonia (of harmony), Epitymbia (goddess of tombs), Demeter Hermouchus (the carrier of Hermes), Amphictionis (of the Amphictyony), Core, Asclepius, Hygaia, Eileithyia, the Dioscuri, Pan, the Nymphs, the Thries (the nymphs of Parnassus), and, later, Roma.[27] In addition to this is the attested worship of a host of demigods, personifications and heroes developed over Delphi's history: Heracles, Delphus, Castalius, Parnassus, Amphiction, Phylacus, Neoptolemus, Aigle (the cult of the winds), and a later Imperial cult dedicated to Antinous Propylaius (Guardian of the Gates).[28] Delphi, as it grew in international appeal, was a place of worship for a relative pantheon of divinities and heroes, reflecting not only its own history and focus, but also that of those who went there. Over the following chapters, we will examine some of the known occasions when these different divinities and heroes came to the fore of Delphic history. In addition, the many festivals associated with them, and that created a packed sacrificial calendar for the city of Delphi (it was a well-known joke in ancient Greece that Delphians always had a sacrificial knife in their hands), will be examined in the context of the time period in which the evidence for their existence derives (most of which comes from the writings of Plutarch in the first century AD).[29]

What happened to those wanting to dedicate monuments in these sanctuaries during this period of rebirth and expansion? Some, as we have seen, may have rerouted to other nearby sanctuaries, like that of Apollo Ptoios. But many seem to have recognized the opportunity this rebuilding presented. In the Athena sanctuary, the Massalians, from the Greek colony at modern-day Marseilles, used the remnants of the old boundary wall in the Athena sanctuary, along with bits of the old

Athena temple, as "ready-made" foundation material for a new treasury building (see plate 3). It was a fascinatingly cosmopolitan structure: Delphi's most western dedicator building an Ionic, eastern-style, treasury at the center of the ancient world, perhaps reflecting the eastern origins of its settlement founders (the Phocaeans), as well as perhaps commemorating a recent Massalian battle victory over the Carthaginians.[30]

In the Apollo sanctuary as well, many dedicators seem to have taken the opportunity of the concentration of workmen, materials, and the remnants of the now-discarded old boundary wall to offer treasury structures that would gain height (and thus visibility) by using the outgrown boundary wall as their foundation. And in the last quarter of the century, as the building of the new perimeter walls and the new temple really got under way, two dedicators seem to have bitten the bullet and moved into the newly acquired, expanded space of the Apollo sanctuary. The first were longtime users of Delphi: the Sicyonians. The tyrant of Sicyon, fully involved in the First Sacred War, and responsible for the unique tholos and monopteros dedications in the sanctuary in the first half of the sixth century BC, was gone. As the new temple terrace expanded, his old dedications faced destruction, and so an extraordinary decision seems to have been made. Once dedicated in a sanctuary, each offering belonged to the god; it could not, thus, simply be removed. But it could be used for a different purpose. The Sicyonian people, surely in conjunction with those masterminding the rebuilding at Delphi, thus decided to take down both of its former tyrant's buildings piece by piece and pack every bit of both structures into the foundations of a new treasury structure, which was placed up against the sanctuary's new perimeter walls (see plate 2) and faced the new sanctuary entrance in the southeast corner[31]

Just to the west, in line with the new Sicyonian treasury up against the sanctuary's new perimeter walls, was the offering of a dedicator new to Delphi. The tiny island of Siphnos in the Aegean, with a population of perhaps two to three thousand people, had, according to Herodotus, recently discovered silver- and gold mines on their island. To begin with, they divided the revenues among themselves. But

Figure 5.2. A reconstruction of the front of the Siphnian treasury, dedicated in the Apollo sanctuary at Delphi (© EFA/E. Hansen [G. Daux & E. Hansen FD II Le tresor de Siphnos 1987 fig. 133])

by 525 BC, they had created a community fund. With a percentage of the profits, this get-rich-quick, nouveau riche island community that had never had any impact on the Greek world stage, launched a program to build the most lavish treasury structure Delphi had ever seen (see plate 2, fig. 5.2). It shipped marble from Siphnos to construct the treasury walls. The Siphnians used the Greek world's finest Parian and Naxian marble for the treasury's frieze and pedimental sculpture (because Siphnian marble was too brittle to carve in small detail). They used caryatid (female-figured) columns for their entrance. In the frieze, at the north of the building alongside which visitors would most often pass, they copied the new temple's pedimental sculpture and carved a Gigantomachy scene in exquisite relief (fig. 5.3). We know they had an eye for showing off to the visitor because the frieze on the other side of the building, which could only be seen from farther away, was not finished in anything like such detail as was the Gigantomachy. The sculpture was also painted, and particular details worked in bronze and other precious metals. This monumental and lavish offering was the most extraordinary confirmation of Delphi's newfound fame and importance in the Greek world. But it was also an important example of the lengths a dedicator would go in order to shape their "message" for Delphic space. The Siphnians were likely in lengthy discussions with

Figure 5.3. A close-up of the north frieze of the Siphnian treasury with detail of the Gigantomachy (Gods versus Giants) scene (Museum at Delphi)

those responsible for masterminding the sanctuary's rebuilding and expansion over the position of their treasury; they seem to have carefully ensured their sculpture reflected the new themes of the Delphic sanctuary (in their pedimental sculpture they also had a scene of Heracles stealing the tripod, which was, at this time, a popular Delphic motif); and they had even made sure that the offering presented its best side to visitors seeing it up close.[32]

The Siphinian treasury marked the beginning of an upsurge in elaborate Delphic dedications, ushering in an era of building über-rich treasury structures as cities attempted to outdo one another. In the last quarter of the sixth century BC, Croton (a regular consulter of the oracle in this period) likely offered a treasury, as did the Megarians, the Clazomenians, the Etruscans, and possibly the Potidanians. Having a permanent presence at Delphi now mattered, and keeping that presence up to date, it seems, mattered just as much. The Corinthians, who had, by the second half of the sixth century ejected their tyrant rulers (the line of Cypselus and Periander whom we met in the last chapters), were desperate to update the prominent dedications of those tyrants at Delphi and Olympia to reflect their newfound political freedom. We know from inscriptional and literary evidence that they officially petitioned the authorities at Delphi and Olympia to change the name of Cypselus's treasury to the "Corinthian" treasury, and, while Delphi allowed the name change, Olympia did not.[33]

The Siphnians, not long after completing their splendid treasury, asked the oracle if their good fortune would continue for long. The oracle's response is uncertain but both Herodotus and Pausanias offer us a story of what happened next. In Herodotus, the newly acquired riches of Siphnos inspired envy, and some islanders were held hostage for an enormous ransom by the Samians (for one hundred talents—a third of the total cost of rebuilding Delphi). In the writings of Pausanias, the story is darker. Apollo demanded a percentage of Siphnian wealth, but the Siphnians became lax in their payments thanks to their own greed, and so Apollo saw to it that their mines were flooded and their revenue stream lost forever.[34]

But the oracle was not occupied at this time with only nouveau-riche upstarts. The struggle for power in Athens continued, with the result that the oracle was sucked deeper into Athenian and Spartan politics. Sparta, after four attempts, had successfully removed the tyrant Hippias from power in Athens, on the prompting of the Delphic oracle (in turn probably thanks to the persuasion of the Alcmaeonids). In the political vacuum that followed, Cleisthenes the Alcmaeonid (grandson of Cleisthenes the tyrant of Sicyon), returned to Athens and, among other elite members of Athenian society (such as Isagoras) began to canvas for political support. In the race for political leverage in the last decade of the sixth century, Cleisthenes added "the mass of the people" to his "faction," promising sweeping constitutional reform.[35] But Isagoras seems to have still had the upper hand, leading to Cleisthenes' exile once again from Athens (on account of the age-old Alcmaeonid curse). In the meantime, however, the Spartan king Cleomenes (who, along with his co-king Demaratus, had been responsible for the ousting of Hippias on Delphic prompting) sought to intervene in Athenian politics still further by invading Athens to bolster support for Isagoras. By 508 BC, following a defeat of Cleomenes' force by Cleisthenes' supporters (even though Cleisthenes was in exile), something akin to a riot unfolded in Athens as all sides grappled for power. Because the Athenians felt so threatened by Sparta, Cleisthenes was allowed to return from exile (and the city even asked for Persian support). Cleisthenes' support was further strengthened by subsequent attempts of Cleomenes of Sparta to intervene in Athenian affairs, first to support Isagoras again, and eventually to reinstate Hippias, whom he had removed in the first place. This melee gave birth to democracy, as Cleisthenes eventually took control and set about a thorough re-formation of Athens, its political constitution and civic system.[36]

What role did Delphi play in this complex and fast-paced civic change? One of Cleisthenes' reforms was to organize the Athenians into ten tribes, each named after an Athenian hero. In 508/7 BC, Cleisthenes submitted the names of one hundred Athenian heroes to the oracle at Delphi, and the Pythia picked ten. The oracle of Apollo thus lent its authority to Cleisthenes' civic reforms. But scholars have also argued for the importance of these reforms in relation to military events. Athens was under threat from Sparta but, in 506/7 BC, was also called onto the battlefield to defend itself against the Boeotians and Chalcidians. The new Athenian tribes were not just civic units, but also served as military units. In turning to Delphi, Cleisthenes thus ensured the Pythia had personally chosen the heroic figureheads for Athens's new fighting force.[37]

Thus, when the new temple was completed in 506 BC by the Alcmaeonid family of Athens, the Pythia had already been heavily implicated not only in securing Spartan support for an Alcmaeonid return, but also for implementing the new constitutional system spearheaded by Cleisthenes the Alcmaeonid. In addition, the Pythia was said to have discouraged Athens from pushing its might too far, and discouraging other cities from attacking Athens: in this period, Athens was told to wait thirty years before attacking the nearby island of Aegina (its on-again, off-again enemy), and Thebes is reported to have consulted the Pythia, having suffered defeat in battle with Athens, on how to seek revenge, to which the oracle, in a particularly ambiguous reply, seems to have suggested it not bother.[38]

At the very end of the sixth century BC, Delphi was thus in an extraordinary position. Its new Apollo and Athena temples and expanded sanctuaries were complete (see plates 1, 2, 3). In place of many of its older dedications, some destroyed in the fire of 548 BC and some purposefully destroyed as part of the renovations, these sanctuaries were now quickly being filled with new treasury structures. Some of them pushed the boundaries of sculptural and architectural excess. All of them testified not only to the increasing plethora of gods worshiped at the sanctuary, but also to the vast stretch of Mediterranean from which Delphi commanded offerings, and the care to which these dedicators manipulated their offerings to ensure maximum visibility and appropriateness to Delphic themes. Now, on and around the new temple terrace, marble sculptures from craftsmen who had worked on the rebuilding jostled with kouroi statues from Aegean islands, individual dedications from the king of Cyprus, a new statue of Apollo from the Massalians, precious metal dedications from Apollonia in Illyria, over two thousand shields and several statues dedicated by the Phocians following victory in battle over the Thessalians, the new great altar of Apollo dedicated and paid for by the island of Chios (for which they were given promanteia), and the texts of treaties between states like Boeotia and Locria.[39] Hundreds of meters above Delphi, in the Corycian cave (see map 3, figs. 0.2, 1.2), which had begun to gather momentum as place of cult worship in the early sixth century, the number of offerings increased greatly, marking the beginning of an era of high popularity that would continue for three centuries.[40] Delphi was increasingly a place not only in which to worship a variety of gods, and particularly Apollo, but also to advertise and proclaim wealth, military victory, deference to the gods, diplomatic relations, family and civic pride, and membership in the Greek world. And all the while, the Delphic oracle not only continued its role in issues of settlement foundation, but became increasingly attractive to particular cities in the West (like Croton) and in North Africa (like Cyrene), as well as deeply involved in the politics of mainland Greece's two major cities, Athens and Sparta, a politics that would come to define Greece in the following century.

In the first decade of the fifth century BC, Cleomenes from Sparta was back at Delphi. He had a long history of interaction with the oracle: it was this man who was persuaded by the oracle to oust Hippias, and who, earlier, was famously tried in Spartan courts for not attacking Argos as he'd been ordered to do (and exonerated on the basis of his defense that he had interpreted a Delphic oracular response to mean an attack would prove fruitless). In his subsequent involvement with Athens, first removing Hippias, then trying to oust Cleisthenes, Cleomenes had become increasingly exasperated with his co-king Demaratus, since Demaratus had been reluctant to support Cleomenes' attempts to influence Athenian politics.[41] But in the first years of the fifth century BC, Cleomenes was once again given a chance to become involved with Athens. It seems that Athens had become increasingly worried about the loyalty to Greece of the nearby island of Aegina, given the increasing power of the Persian Empire across the Aegean and its recent attacks on Greek colonies on the shores of Asia Minor.[42] Athens requested Cleomenes' help in "securing" Aegina. But Demaratus was a friend of the Aeginetans and so resisted Cleomenes' attempts to answer Athens's call.[43]

It seems that Cleomenes' patience finally ran out with Demaratus, and a scheme was hatched to remove him from the throne, a scheme that required the participation of the oracle at Delphi. Cleomenes utilized a local Delphian contact, Cobon, who in turn persuaded/bribed the Pythian priestess Periallus to confirm (in response to a question put forward by a Spartan on Cleomenes' request) that Demaratus was not the legitimate son of his father (the Spartan king Ariston), hence rendering him unfit to continue in office. The Spartans initially bought the lie, and Demaratus was exiled, fleeing to Persia where he was welcomed by the Persian king. Cleomenes was free to attack Aegina, but his bribery of the Pythia was eventually discovered. His contact in Delphi, Cobon, was exiled from the city; the Pythia Periallus was removed; and Cleomenes himself was forced out of Sparta, only later to return and disembowel himself in what was considered a shameful suicide.[44]

In 490 BC, one year after the Pythia's corrupted response, the Persians landed at Marathon, accompanied by none other than Hippias, the exiled tyrant of Athens who cherished hopes of being reinstated as master of the city. The Athenians, it seems, did not consult Delphi ahead of this battle—there was likely not enough time to do so. Instead, against the odds, the Athenians repelled the Persian invasion on the plains of Marathon. Soon, stories arose that a mysterious figure had appeared on the battle scene to help the Athenians, and that he was slaughtering Persians with his plowshare. The Athenians, in the aftermath of the battle, consulted the oracle at Delphi about whom they should worship in thanks for this divine aid.

The Athenians also chose to commemorate their victory at several sites inside and outside Athens, including Olympia and Delphi. At Olympia, as was the tradition, they offered armor taken from the battlefield, then inscribed with the names of the victors. At Delphi however, they competed in Delphic style with a new and expensive treasury. Knocking down the small treasury that had been at Delphi since the early sixth century BC, the new Athenian treasury was the first treasury outside of Attica made of Attic Pentelic marble; the first to have its columns built in drum form; the first Doric structure to fill all its metopes with carefully carved reliefs, the themes of which (Theseus and Heracles) were brought together for the first time in sculptural history on this building (see plate 2, fig. 5.4). Its position perched on the steep hillside made it an imposing monument (you still get this impression when you visit the rebuilt Athenian treasury at Delphi today), and its architectural style, combined with the forecourt laid out around it, made it almost a miniature copy of the new Apollo temple, which was, after all, Athenian built, too. Linked to this gleaming new treasury, along its southern flank, was a statue group with the ten eponymous tribal heroes of Athens (those picked by the Delphic oracle) and an inscription making clear to all that this monument commemorated the Athenian victory at Marathon. If this was not enough, the Athenians also appear to have hung shields captured on the battlefield from the metopes of the new Apollo temple, making their ownership—of what was supposed to be a temple of Apollo paid for by the Amphictyony, Delphi, and the wider Greek world—even clearer, and even perhaps to have etched an inscription to their victory onto the temple itself.[45]

While they were building themselves into the sanctuary of Apollo at Delphi, the decade 490–480 BC saw no letup in the activity of Athenian politics, interpolis Greek relations, or the changing role and position of Delphi in the wider Greek world. The Alcmaeonids in Athens were accused of scheming to act as traitors at the battle of Marathon.[46] Megacles, the new prominent Alcmaeonid in Athenian politics, and nephew of Cleisthenes, was exiled in 487 BC, but maintained Alcmaeonid influence at Delphi by winning the chariot race in the Pythian games the following year. His victory was enshrined in an ode by the poet Pindar, the language of which suggests that Megacles, or at least Pindar, realized the need for a more conciliatory approach to the Athenian people, making Alcmaeonid achievements pan-Athenian ones, including the building of the new Apollo temple.[47]

At the same time, the principal foreign policy issue was preparation for an expected return invasion by the Persians. In Athens, the debates in the assembly focused around whether or not to channel funds from Athenians silver mines into building a substantial fleet. Other cities struggled with the question of whether to submit to such a powerful empire, or attempt (what seemed like) futile resistance. Several put the question to the oracle at Delphi. Argos asked if it should join the anti-Persian alliance, but the response suggested a more defensive, neutral policy. Crete asked if it would be better for them to defend Hellas, and the response suggested that they should keep out of the war entirely. Sparta consulted and was met with the (later-recorded) response that either Sparta or a Spartan king must fall. The Delphians themselves, when the Persians were already marching through Macedonia, consulted on their own behalf and that of Greece, and were told to pray to the winds as allies.[48]

None of these responses are particularly inspiring: Delphi, the center of the ancient world, seems unenthusiastic about Greece's chances in the coming titanic struggle. Much has been made of Delphic ambiguity in this period, suggesting that the sanctuary was pro-Persian. Scholars have also pointed to the fact that Gelon, the tyrant of Gela (and later Syracuse), who had been begged for help against the Persians by the Athenians and Spartans but had evaded giving help by attaching impossible conditions to his offer, sent gifts for the Persian king to Delphi.[49] Even more questionable in some eyes is Delphi's amazing ability to survive intact the subsequent Persian invasion. Such a rich jewel, deep in Persian territory for much of the war, survived without a scratch. Later stories insisted the sanctuary had been saved by supernatural aid: the Delphians had consulted on what to do with the sanctuary's treasures,

Figure 5.4. The imposing Athenian treasury in the Apollo sanctuary at Delphi (P. de la Coste-Messelière & G. Miré *Delphes* 1957 Librarie Hachette p. 98)

but were told to evacuate (many seem to have taken refuge in the Corycian cave and the surrounding area) and leave everything to Apollo (a small garrison of sixty stayed in the sanctuary). The invading Persian force was said to have been knocked back by giant rock falls, the subsequent Persian retreat assured by two long-dead local heroes who took to the battlefield once again.[50]

Does this amount to a tangible charge of betrayal by Delphi in Greece's critical hour? Not really—it is more useful to think of the oracle in the context of its surroundings. Much of northern Greece, to which Delphi was historically linked, took the view that it was powerless to resist the Persian invaders. Equally it can be argued that Gelon sent his gifts to Delphi not because it was pro-Persian, but because it was a conveniently accessible point in the middle of Greece (and he sent them on condition that they should be returned if Xerxes did not win).[51] It is worth noting that Xerxes himself did not send gifts to Delphi, but instead to the nearby sanctuary of Apollo Ptoios. Moreover, the Persians may never have attempted to attack Delphi, if Herodotus is to be believed, since he reports that Mardonius, the Persian commander, believed in an oracular response given by a different oracle that if the Persians attacked Delphi, the sacrilege would ensure that the gods made their campaign fail.[52] The divine defense of Delphi thus spoken of in the literary sources (and for certain promulgated by the Delphians themselves in later years) may, thus, be a made-up story, not to hide Delphic Medism, but to give the city and sanctuary at least some honor and crucial role in what was to become a famous war in Greek history.

Critically, whatever the whispers in the air about Delphi in the run-up to the Persian invasion of Greece in the late 480s, the Athenians, determined to oppose the Persians, prepared a full embassy to be sent, with all the proper rites and rituals, to consult the oracle at Delphi just before the battle of Thermopylae in 480 BC. Having entered the temple, but before they could even ask their question, the Pythian priestess, Aristonice (the replacement for the disgraced Periallus), was said to have addressed them advising them to give up and escape. The ambassadors were appalled and reluctant to return home with such a response. Instead they took the advice of a Delphian, Timon, who suggested they return as religious suppliants of Apollo to ask for a second oracular response. Praying to Apollo, they asked for a "better oracle about our land" and begged the god "to respect these emblems of suppliants which we have come bringing into your presence, or else we will not leave the shrine, but remain here thus even unto death." The Pythia's response this time is infamous: that they should trust in their wooden walls.[53] Much scholarly ink has been spilled regarding the veracity of this response, but it has all the hallmarks of a traditionally ambiguous Delphic reply, in that it required the ambassadors to return to Athens and submit it for further discussion and debate among the Athenians. Some took it to mean building a wooden palisade around the Acropolis. Themistocles, the Athenian general who had convinced the Athenians some years before to build up their fleet, argued it meant to take to the sea and fight the Persians from their wooden triremes. His proposed interpretation was accepted, and, according to an inscription surviving from the third century BC from Troizen, which purports to be a copy of the decree passed at that fraught assembly in which Themistocles won the day, the assembly agreed, "beginning tomorrow," to evacuate the city and take to their ships.[54]

In responding to the Athenians, the oracle is shown to have initially kept to its line of non-opposition but, when pressed, to have offered a traditional response that motivated deliberation and decision. Moreover, it is clear that Delphi continued to matter to the Greeks.[55] Herodotus records that those fighting against Persia took a roll call of all those who had submitted to Persian authority, and made an oath promising to destroy the Persians and bring a percentage of the booty extracted from those who had submitted to be dedicated to Apollo at Delphi.[56] The Athenians also returned to consult again just before the final showdown against the Persians at the battle of Plataea asking which gods they should pray to in order to secure victory.[57] And in the aftermath of those battles, which led to the legendary stories of the Spartan stand at Thermopylae, the Athenian sea victory at Salamis and again at Plataea, as Robin Osborne puts it: "<~?~hrspace>'what did this city do in the Persian wars?' [became] the first historical question whose answer mattered that could be asked of all Greek communities."[58] It is no surprise, then, that stories later circulated about a divinely led defense of the Delphic sanctuary, no surprise that every city, whatever its stance and role in the war, was keen to immortalize (and often realign) the part they had played, and even less a surprise that Delphi, whatever suspicions some may have harbored about the sanctuary, was to be the place where that commemoration would be felt more keenly than anywhere else.

Lord of Lycia, O Phoebus, you who rule over Delos
and who loves Parnassus' Castalian spring,
willingly take those things to heart and make this a land of brave men.

—Pind. *Pyth.* 1.38–40

6

DOMINATION

As the Persians retreated from Greece during 479 BC, the victorious cities turned to Delphi to consult the oracle on the right way to celebrate their triumph. The response integrated Delphi more than ever into the fabric of the Greek world. The Pythia instructed the cities to erect an altar to Zeus Eleutherios (the liberator), but not to sacrifice anything on it until they had extinguished every fire in the land (as the altars had all been polluted by the barbarian invaders) and taken fresh fire from the sacred hearth at Delphi to relight the hearths and pyres of Greece. Euchidas of Plataea is said to have offered to run to Delphi and bring back the sacred flame to his city, completing the return journey in a single day, after which tremendous achievement he promptly dropped dead and was buried in the Plataean sanctuary of Artemis "of Good Repute" with an epitaph to commemorate his journey to Delphi.[1]

As a result, Delphi became—literally—the common hearth of Greece, the origin of its fire, the center of its world. Any notions that Delphi had strayed to the Persian side before and during the conflict were forgotten, and the victors set about commemorating their victories at different sanctuaries across Greece, but most especially at Delphi (they had, after all, sworn an oath to dedicate at Delphi a percentage of spoils taken from those who had betrayed Greece for Persia). First to commemorate the Persian Wars were the Amphictyony, the governing council at Delphi, who not only set up a monument at Thermopylae to commemorate the famous Spartan stand, but also established at Delphi a statue group of two mythical heroes who were supposed to have helped the Greek fleet at the near-simultaneous sea battle, which had taken place at Artemisium. The council also put a price on the head of Ephialtes, the man who betrayed the Spartans at Thermopylae.[2]

In quick succession a second monument was established at Delphi to commemorate the Greek victory at Salamis. This, we know from the ancient sources, was a giant statue of Apollo six meters high, a trireme in his hand, placed on the temple terrace directly facing the great Chian altar and temple front (see plate 2, fig. 1.3). And while no trace of the statue now remains, French archaeologists have argued that the base survives, complete with its dedicating inscription, which, however, is damaged, leaving a tantalizing puzzle for modern scholars, for the one word missing from the dedicating inscription is the name of the dedicator. But thanks to the sentence structure and grammar, along with the neat alignment of letters on different lines, we know we are looking for a name that is eight letters and in the plural. The most tempting possibility is "Hellanes"—"the Greeks." If correct, this would mark an exceptional moment in Greek history. The Greeks, torn as they were by city rivalry, rarely referred to themselves as Greeks. This monument, here at Delphi in the early fifth century BC, would represent perhaps the first time the Greeks had publicly described themselves as such. This dedication thus encapsulates the recognition and display of a community forged in the heat of battle, set up at the sanctuary that was the mythical center of the ancient world and now literally the common hearth of the Greeks.[3]

Those contributing to the dedication of the Salamis Apollo asked the Pythia if Apollo was satisfied with the monument established in his honor. The reply was ambiguous: he was, but he required more from the Aeginetans. Aegina, as we saw in the previous chapter, had most certainly wavered at the approach of the Persians and had been frequently accused of Medism ("having Persian sympathies") by other Greek cities. Yet, in reality, this request for a second monument from the oracle provided the Aeginetans with a useful opportunity. Delphi was quickly becoming the place in which to commemorate one's role in the Persian defeat and, as a result, an excellent place in which to stake a claim not to what actually happened, but rather to what the dedicator would prefer to remember as having happened. The Aeginetans certainly took the opportunity not only to make their presence felt, but also to make a strong statement of their (now) pro-Greek credentials. They offered a bronze palm tree with golden stars to be placed on the temple terrace.[4] And while this offering was specifically requested by Apollo, other cities also actively chose to emphasize their role at Salamis by putting up their own monuments to commemorate their own role in that same victory, and all of these were placed on the terrace area in front of the Apollo temple, turning it into an unmistakable "Persian Wars zone."[5]

Yet it was in the commemoration of the battle of Plataea, the final land victory against the Persians in 479 BC, that Delphi's key role in commemorating the Persian Wars became clearest. Whereas at the sanctuaries of Zeus at Olympia and Poseidon at Isthmia, the alliance of Greeks offered yet another Zeus and Poseidon statue (they had done the same to celebrate Salamis at these sanctuaries), at Delphi a unique monument was born, one that would come to epitomize Delphi itself: three bronze serpents coiled together into a column standing nine meters high with the serpent heads (partly made in gold) supporting the legs of a golden tripod (see fig. 1.3). The symbolism of the serpents (referring to Apollo and his fight with the serpent Pytho) and the tripod (the Pythia's tripod) is clear. This was a monument designed for Delphi that sought to evoke Delphi: the ultimate expression of victory and of the Greeks' close relationship with their gods, especially Apollo. It stood on the temple terrace, towering over the Salamis Apollo and other monuments around it. Thucydides would later report that the Spartan commander, Pausanias, tried to hijack the monument and have it inscribed as if it were a dedication from him alone. But he was punished, and instead, the names of all the Greek cities—not just those that fought at Plataea, but those that had any involvement in the fight against Persia at any stage—were inscribed on the serpent coils of the column.[6] As a result, an evocation of a more comprehensive Greek community evoked by the Salamis Apollo (potentially the "Hellanes"), paid homage to Apollo and to Delphi as the common hearth of Greece. Yet swiftly, the serpent-column monument was surrounded by other offerings from individual cities that sought to commemorate their own particular role in the battle at Plataea, or, more often, to recast that role. The Carystians offered a statue of a bull for victory at Plataea, even though they had fought on the Persian side, and Alexander I of Macedon, who was keen to establish his credentials as having been on the Greek side the whole time, offered an enormous golden statue of himself.[7]

Yet, despite this overwhelming deluge of monuments and oracular consultations, which not only embedded Delphi more strongly at the center of the ancient Greek world, but also highlighted its role as a space in which to tell, and perhaps more importantly retell, history, some notes of the trouble to come were also being sounded. Themistocles, the Athenian general, after bringing his dedications to Delphi, was told by the Pythia to remove them from the sanctuary: the only instance in Delphic history of the oracle refusing a dedication. At the same time, Sparta proposed that the Amphictyony should become an anti-Persian league, excluding every city that had not fought actively against the Persians. Themistocles, whose dedications had been refused, argued against this proposition claiming it would shift the balance of power within the Amphictyony toward two or three main cities rather than its current wider representation.[8] The proposal was dropped, but it sounded a note of disquiet that was all too familiar to the citizens of Delphi and was, in part, to define their future over the next two centuries. As Delphi and its council became more important and valuable, more people came to have designs on dominating them.

For the time being, however, the hum of tension over Delphian ownership was most probably drowned out by the increasing popularity the city and sanctuary enjoyed in the first half of the fifth century BC. And none more so than among the Greeks of the western Mediterranean world of Magna Graecia. Gelon (the tyrant of Gela and now Syracuse

in Sicily, who had refused to help the Greeks during the Persian invasion) now sought not only to establish a permanent marker of his power
at Delphi, but to put his own military victories against the enemies of
the Greek world to the west (especially the Carthaginians) on a par with
the great victories against the Persians to the east. Where better to do
this than at the sanctuary where the Persian Wars had been so insistently
commemorated? On the temple terrace, near the Salamis and Plataean
monuments, Gelon erected a tall column and tripod monument (see
fig. 1.3). The likeness of its style to that of the Plataean serpent column
was supposed to underscore the similar magnitude and importance of
Gelon's victory (and no doubt cover his own refusal to contribute to the
fight against the Persians).[9]

Nor was he the only western Greek dedicator anxious to find a place
in Delphi's growing collection of monuments. The city of Croton, a long-
term user of the oracle, set up a similar enormous tripod dedication on the
temple terrace, and even represented Delphi on its coinage in this period.
Rhegion, too, put up offerings in the sanctuary, as did the Etruscans. Most
famous, however, were those of Gelon's successor, Hieron, and the latter's
successor, Polyzalus. Hieron not only dedicated monuments to military
victory (similar to those of Gelon and the Plataean serpent column), but
also to his own victories in the Pythian games. The Delphi charioteer, discovered buried in the ground in the first years of excavation at Delphi and
now holding pride of place in Delphi's museum, is part of Hieron's athletic victory monument (plate 6). Placed just beside the temple of Apollo,
originally composed not only of the charioteer, resplendent as he is in
bronze, silver, and precious metals, but also of a life-size representation of
the entire chariot and horses, this would have been an awesome offering
(see fig. 1.3). So much so that Polyzalus decided not to try and top it for
his athletic victories, but instead simply rededicated the statue in his own
name. Theirs was not the only chariot dedication at this time: Archesilaus
IV, king of Cyrene, also dedicated his winning chariot and placed it on the
temple terrace in honor of his victory in the late 460s BC.[10]

This investment in the commemoration of victory in the Pythian
games emphasizes the continued, if not growing, importance of these

games in the wider fifth-century Greek world. The games, lasting for five days, were held during the Greek month of Boucation (sometime between our mid-August and mid-September), beginning on the seventh day of the month (events were often scheduled on the seventh day of a month at Delphi because, as has been said, this was thought to be the day of Apollo's birthday). The Amphictyony and the city of Delphi devoted huge resources into their organization. They sent out Delphic citizens as *theoroi* (ambassadors) six months before the games on pre-agreed routes to announce the games and call for competitors to come to the events. They prepared the facilities at Delphi for the competitions (it is around the middle of the fifth century BC that the area of the later stadium may have first been used for contests—see plate 1). They ran the games themselves, which involved undertaking large-scale religious rituals (over a hundred animals were sacrificed and their meat roasted for consumption at just one of the rituals on the first day of the games), and coped with the sheer practical needs of so many spectators in one place for a week.[11] In 484 BC, the Amphictyony expanded the competitions to include a running race in full armor (the *hoplitodromoi*), and in the mid-fifth century BC, a contest for painting appears to have been introduced, which complemented the important and ancient musical competitions that had always been part of Apollo's games (a dance competition was added in the fourth century BC and, later, competitions in acting, mime, and pantomime).[12]

The first day of the Pythian festival was dedicated to religious sacrifices and a re-enactment of the mythical clash between Apollo and the serpent, the second day to communal banquets, the third day to musical and artistic competition, the fourth to athletics, and the final day to chariot racing. This last was the day perhaps more than any other on which all eyes were focused, especially as it was the richer and more powerful individuals of the Greek world who were competing against one another through the horses they owned and entered into the competition, each chariot in turn driven by a professional charioteer. It is no accident that most of the surviving odes to athletic victory at Delphi written by the praise-poet Pindar during the fifth century BC are for chariot victories (he can't have been cheap to hire): Hieron of Syracuse, Archesilaus IV of Cyrene, Xenocrates of Agrigentum, Megacles of Athens all paid for praise odes from Pindar for their chariot victories at Delphi between 490 and 462 BC.[13]

Pindar's victory odes and hymns are also important because they give us the first evidence for the existence of a particular cult at Delphi: that of Neoptolemus, son of Achilles. Pindar's *Paean 6* (117–20), produced c. 475 BC, tells of the death of Neoptolemus at Delphi (see fig. 6.1). How he died, however, is heavily disputed among the literary sources (including by Pindar, himself, who offers a different version of the story in *Nemean* 7.59–69). Whatever the manner of his death, the Delphians likely offered an annual sacrifice to him as a hero. In addition, according to Pausanias, the Aenianes sent a sacred embassy to Delphi during the Pythian festival to honor Neoptolemus, since he had been their king. In the following centuries, the area of the cult tomb of Neoptolemus in the sanctuary would be a popular one for dedication (just northeast of the temple of Apollo), and the dead spirit of the hero himself was later said to have

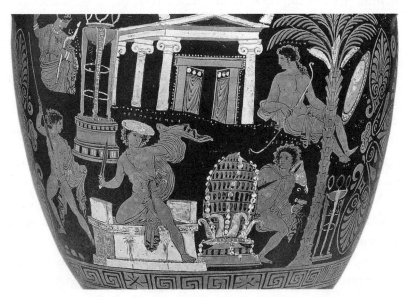

Figure 6.1. The murder of Neoptolemus at Delphi (identified by the tripod and omphalos) represented on a volute krater by the Iliupersis painter c. 370 BC (© Intesa Sanpaolo Collection inv. F.G-00111A-E/IS)

fought alongside other heroes and demigods to protect Delphi against invasions in the third century BC.[14]

As the sanctuary was expanding in terms of cult locations, myths, and monumental dedications, the oracle was by no means silent: forty-five different oracular consultations are known to have occurred between 479 and 431 BC.[15] The Spartans in particular continued their long tradition of consulting the oracle on a range of issues concerning military endeavors, diplomacy, and, sometimes, their own misdeeds. Pausanias, the Spartan general who had tried to hijack the Plataean serpent column as his own monument, was found guilty of treason by the Spartan elders. Pausanias fled for sacred refuge into the temple of Athena on Sparta's acropolis. There, under the protection of the gods, the Spartans could not touch him but instead chose to starve him into submission. He died in the temple's forecourt. Before long, Sparta was subject to a series of signs of divine disfavor and promptly consulted Delphi on what to do: they were told to bury Pausanias where he had fallen; they did, alongside putting up two statues of him in the sanctuary.[16]

We also know that in 476–75 BC, the Athenians—busy building an anti-Persian alliance (the Delian league) that would before long become the Athenian empire—consulted the Pythia regarding cult practice on one of the Aegean islands, Scyros, in which they happened to have strategic interests. The result was that, in order to "follow" the "advice" of the oracle, the Athenians moved in to annex the island, discovered (as instructed) the bones of their hero Theseus, and built a temple over them.[17] As well as being a useful tool in explaining Athenian expansion, the oracle at this time played an increasingly important role in the cultural mindset of Athens thanks to the development of Greek tragic theater. It is in the fifth century BC—and specifically with the plays of Aeschylus, Sophocles, and Euripides, which have survived into our time, starting with Aeschylus's *Persians* in 472 BC—that we begin to gain an insight into how the Athenians conceptualized the Delphic oracle, its origins and its role in Greek society. As we saw in earlier chapters, the tragic plays from Athens are some of our most significant sounding boards for learning how the Greeks (or more specifically the Athenians) understood (the various and changing) stories regarding Delphi's origins. But they also show us the extent to which Delphi was conceived of in this period as an enforcer of civic values, a place that was on the path toward conflict resolution and active justice: although the actual resolution and justice are themselves (perhaps unsurprisingly) eventually always to be found in Athens (e.g., Aeschylus's *Oresteia*). As can be seen, Delphi is portrayed on the Athenian tragic stage as an institution for the maintenance of order in the Greek world and, at the same time, as emphasizing the special role of Athens in Greek society.[18]

Thus the Delphi's oracle was undoubtedly held in high regard in the first part of the fifth century BC. Compare this, however, with the use of the sanctuary for other purposes, particularly monumental dedication, and a picture emerges of a Delphi in which its oracle is, in reality, no longer the only prime motive for going to, and investing in, the sanctuary. We have already seen that the Pythian games attracted important and powerful individuals to invest and display their triumphs at Delphi. But in the first half of the fifth century BC, there was also a growing tendency by different dedicators to attempt a monopolization of the Apollo sanctuary through offering a series of monumental structures, often to advertise military victories, on the many terraces that comprised the Apollo sanctuary. In short, the value of having a permanent and obvious presence that advertised one's military and cultural prowess in this sanctuary complex—firmly embedded at the very core of the Greek world, and to which more and more people were coming—was as attractive and useful as the oracle's ability to provide guidance at moments of difficult decision.[19]

Western dedicators were at the forefront of this trend. The Liparians, just off the coast of Sicily, erected vast numbers of Apollo statues on both the temple terrace and in the lower half of the Apollo sanctuary, perhaps deliberately opposite dedications by their frequent enemy, the Etruscans.[20] The Tarentines, in southern Italy, who had been among the first to use Delphi to announce military victory through a monumental sculptural dedication at the very beginning of the fifth century (and in doing so had bagged the first spot visitors saw as they entered the Apollo sanctuary at its new southeastern entrance) now returned in the 460s BC to erect another sculptural group on the temple terrace to commemorate military victory, placing it just in front of the already well-known Plataean serpent column (see fig. 1.3).[21]

But this new trend of "spatial monopolization" was not only practised by Western dedicators. Cnidus, on the coast of Asia Minor, having dedicated a marble treasury in the sixth century BC, returned in the fifth century to offer not only a group of statues squeezed in next to the Siphnian treasury in the new lowest terrace of the sanctuary, but also to take advantage of the newly laid-out northern part of the sanctuary above the temple terrace to offer a cultural tour-de-force in the form of a *lesche* (see plate 2). A lesche was a place for meeting, conversation, and contemplation, and the Cnidian lesche at Delphi, constructed in the 460s BC, provided ample material for discussion since its walls were covered in paintings by the famous artist Polygnotus, none of which have survived, but all of which were described in exacting detail by Pausanias in his second century AD tour of the site. The paintings described numerous Greek myths and stories, offering a space for visitors to contemplate the mytho-history of the Greek world, having just walked up through a sanctuary that was itself increasingly stuffed with monuments to moments in Greek history, and over which the lesche (and its attached terrace) provided one of the most unobstructed views.[22]

Yet no one monopolized the Apollo and Athena sanctuaries in the period 479–460 BC more than the Athenians. Already well represented in the sanctuary with a new treasury, shields and inscription on the temple, as well as in the Persian War dedications, the Athenians scattered-bombed Delphi with dedications to their military and cultural prowess in this period. They likely erected a treasury in the Athena sanctuary in the 470s BC; built Delphi's first-ever stoa along the bottom of the polygonal wall as a shelter for the display of booty from naval and land victories; and constructed a bronze palm-tree dedication with a golden statue of Athena in its branches on the temple terrace in the 460s BC to commemorate Athens's military victory at the battle of Eurymedon (see plate 2, fig. 1.3). Finally, the Athenians supplanted the Tarentines as the first to be seen by visitors entering from the southeast with a new monument that restated the importance of their victory at Marathon in 490 BC. This new monument mixed the eponymous heroes of Athens, whose names had been chosen by the Pythia in 508 BC, with figures more closely connected to the battle of Marathon itself (plate 2, fig. 6.2).[23]

Delphi was not the only place in which Athens commemorated its prowess in this period, but, in comparison with the other major sanctuaries of Greece, it received far more insistent and visible attention than any other (except of course for the acropolis in Athens itself). Such

Figure 6.2. A reconstruction of dedications by Athens and Sparta at the entrance to the Apollo sanctuary at Delphi. 1 Fourth century BC Argive semi-circle dedication. 2 End fifth century BC Spartan stoa. 3 Fourth century BC Arkadian dedication. 4 Fifth century BC Athenian statue group dedication. 5 End fifth century BC Spartan dedication to victory at Aegospotamoi. 6 Later Roman agora. 7 Entrance to Apollo sanctuary.

domination at and of Delphi is not unexpected as this was the period in which Athens moved to dominate the Greek world with its great empire. But Athenian monumental presence at Delphi also underscores a crucial point for understanding the changing perception of Delphi within the Greek world, and the motivation for what would happen next in Delphi's life story. Take away the popular participation of western and eastern dedicators in the first half of the fifth century BC, and, in the period 479–60, we are left with almost no one except Athens. While Sparta and a host of other cities and individuals continued to consult the oracle, the physical space of the Apollo and Athena sanctuary was unmistakably dominated by Athens at this time because Athens had created for itself an empire within the Greek world, and had, almost mirrorlike, created a similar hold over the microcosm of the Greek world that was Delphi. It was unlikely that other powers in Greece would put up with either for long.

By 457 BC, Athens's influence had extended from dominating the Delphic complex through dedications to political dominance and control over all its nearest neighbors.[24] As a result, when Athens decided to support Phocis in its claim to incorporate Delphi within its political territory (since the time of the arrival of the Amphictyony in the early sixth century BC, Delphi had had a position of independence from any regional political unit), there was little the citizens of Delphi could do about it. Athenian domination of the sacred space of the Delphic complex through monumental dedications to the gods in honor of its own military victories had been transposed into, by proxy, control over Delphi itself. It is no surprise that many scholars date two preserved oracular responses, which encouraged and justified growing Athenian power, to exactly this time when Athens was effectively the master of Delphi.[25]

In 449 BC, however, the balance of power began to change in Greece and at Delphi. The first hint of this change was perhaps Sparta's decision to make monumental dedications in the Apollo sanctuary. Despite being a long-term and constant user of the oracle, and despite a presence in terms of small dedications for much of Delphi's history, Sparta had never invested much in monumental artistic and architectural offerings (except of course for the Spartan general Pausanias's attempt to hijack the Plataean serpent column). This is perhaps not unexpected: Sparta was, after all, famously Spartan in its approach to such projects. Which makes it all the more interesting that, at the midpoint of the century, Spartan monumental dedications begin to arrive at Delphi. This statement of dedicatory presence within the sanctuary was accompanied by a military presence: Sparta sent troops to Delphi to champion the cause of the city, remove its Phocian overlords, and return Delphi to its (historic) independent state.[26] In honor of which, the Delphians granted Sparta promanteia and had the decree inscribed on the brow of a bronze wolf statue that the Delphians themselves had dedicated in the sanctuary (in honor of the story of a wolf who had helped defend the site). The symbolism of placing this inscription of thanks for Spartan defense of the sanctuary on this monument originally made to commemorate the defense of the sanctuary must have been palpable to sanctuary visitors. The Delphians may have gone even further to please their Spartan saviors: Herodotus reports that one of Croesus's precious metal offerings that survived the great fire of 548 BC, was now reinscribed to make it look as if the Spartans had dedicated it.[27]

Yet, before long, Athens, under the leadership of Pericles (another Alcmaeonid—their involvement with Delphi never ceased), went back to Delphi with its own military force so as to return Delphi to the Phocians once more. In response, the Athenian accepted a grant of promanteia from the Delphians (as if the Delphians had any choice but to offer it) and inscribed their acceptance of this honor on the same bronze wolf dedication that had recently been inscribed with the same honor for the Spartans.[28]

By 445 BC, Delphi had once again been freed from Phocian control and returned to independence. This almost slapstick era of repeated Athenian and Spartan attempts to control and free Delphi, and their blatant one-upmanship in representing each stage of that struggle in the sanctuary (on different sides of the same wolf statue), is often referred to as Delphi's Second Sacred War. Scholarship is split about how it ended. The debate focuses around reports in the later historian Diodorus Siculus that the Delphians laid a compensation claim against the Phocians for their take-over of the city before the Amphictyonic council, who resolved to fine the Phocians, the proceeds of which went into making a colossal bronze Apollo statue for the sanctuary.[29] Yet whether or not the Amphictyony was strong enough in the fifth century BC to impose such demands, it is clear that the atmosphere at Delphi changed drastically in the first decades of the second half of the century. For it was during the 440s and 430s BC that not only did Sparta begin to dedicate in the sanctuary, but many other mainland Greek cities and states also returned to dedicate to Apollo. In particular Thessaly (closely associated with the sanctuary's long-term development, and heavily involved in the Amphictyonic council as its permanent president), and Thessalian cities like Pherai, returned to the sanctuary to offer monuments to their military victories over none other than Athens.[30] The age of Athenian dominance—at Delphi at least—was over. Indeed, Athens, in contrast to the monopolization of the sanctuary space it exacted in the first half of the century, would not offer a monumental dedication there again during the fifth century BC.

At the same time, Delphi seems to have begun to receive offerings from parts of the Greek world that had never been connected with Delphi, like the Greek colonies of the Black Sea (in whose original settlements Delphi had not played a role) and from Sardinia. Aegean islands, like Andros, arrived to offer monuments to their original founders, and even professional associations put up monuments to Apollo, which simultaneously advertised their skills. And it is at this time that we find the first hard evidence for a cult of the old mother goddess Gaia at Delphi: the Delphians erected statues to Gaia and Themis by the Castalian spring (see plate 1, fig. 0.2), a symbol of a gathering sense of the ancient lineage of this sanctuary, and, no less important, the need to demonstrate that lineage publicly in an age of increasing competition among the many important oracular sanctuaries of Greece.[31]

Amid this renewed enthusiasm for Delphic dedication from around the Greek world, the oracle continued its traditional role in the founding of new settlements, even for Athens, who was advised by the Pythia on how and where to settle what would become the colony of Thurii on the southern Italian coast. The oracle was also likely involved in Athenian settlement in Amphipolis in northern Greece.[32] In addition, the oracle was said to have been involved in the appointment of religious officials in Athens in the 430s, and, most famously, gave support to Athens's Imperial First Fruits Decree (argued to be c.435 BC). Repeated twice in the inscribed text of this decree is a report of an oracle from Delphi encouraging that "first fruits" (a percentage of revenue) be dedicated to Demeter at the Athenian sanctuary of Eleusis by the Athenians, by their allies, and indeed by everyone.[33] At the same time, the oracle remained of use to settlements as they continued to develop: in the 430s BC, Epidamnus was torn apart by *stasis* (civil unrest) and appealed to its original founder, Corcyra, for help. None was forthcoming, so the Epidamnians approached the oracle at Delphi for guidance on whether they should appeal instead to Corinth (the city that had founded Corcyra).[34] The oracle, it seems, despite the intensifying political and military disagreements over the sanctuary itself, was still a useful port of call in times of tricky international Greek diplomacy.

Yet, at the same time, the new ascendency, and physical presence through its dedications, of Sparta at Delphi meant that the sanctuary was now an attractive place in which to hammer home military victories over that city too. Argos constructed no less than four different offerings at Delphi in this period, all of which celebrated victory over Sparta. It is most fascinating that experimentation with different sculptural and architectural styles of monument at Delphi seems to have helped crystallize the city's identity at home. The Argives erected a semicircular statue base in the lower half of the Apollo sanctuary at Delphi, complete with statues of the seven Argive heroes who had fought against Thebes, an almost identical copy of which was later erected in Argos itself (see plate 2).[35] Delphi had become not just a place in which to tell (and retell) a (monumental) version of history, but an incubator for emerging identities within a constantly shifting world, of which Argos, developing its own democracy in the period after 460 BC, seems to have taken full advantage.[36]

The second half of the fifth century BC was thus critical for Delphi. On the one hand, it bore witness to the development of the many stories that surrounded Delphi's origins, which pushed its ancient lineage further and further back into mythical time (as we saw in earlier chapters). On the other hand, it bore witness to the development and widening of its role within the contemporary Greek world, both as a sanctuary that was decidedly international, and as a space that offered a range of opportunities for individuals, cities, and states to consult on difficult issues, tell and retell the past, as well as crystallize their own identities. As tensions in the Greek world continued to grow—as its city-states hardened in their attitudes to one another; as what was once, albeit only briefly, a united Greece fractured into two competing superpower blocs that would, in the following thirty years, tear the Greek world apart—Delphi stood as a mirror of the history that had brought Greece to this point. It was a religious space and institution to which access for all was jealously guarded, but also a small, unprotected city whose inhabitants, the Delphians, would once again have to strain every muscle and sinew to navigate the treacherous waters of Greek politics in the tumultuous years ahead.

The sources report that the Pythian oracle made a strong opening play in the first act of this unfolding tragedy. When, in 432 BC, the Spartans consulted the Pythia on whether or not it would be better for them to go to war against Athens in response to what they saw as Athens breaking the terms of the agreement left over from the Second Sacred War, the oracle's response was said to be, uncharacteristically, *un*ambiguous: "if you go to war with all your might, you will have victory, and I Apollo will help you, both when you call for aid and when you do not."[37] During the following decade, Delphi was a crucially important strategic location for Spartan forces and its allies: it was probably almost constantly in the hands of the Peloponnesian league, to the extent that it was even suggested Delphi could contribute financially to Sparta's campaign against Athens, and is reported as sanctioning a further strategic Spartan settlement from which "Ionians, Achaeans, and certain other tribes" were banned.[38] And even though the Delphic oracle was said to have been involved in yet another case of Spartan bribery in 427–26 BC, this time helping to reinstate in Sparta a long-exiled king who was keener on peace with Athens than war, it seems that Athens's disillusionment with Delphi, perhaps

understandably, grew considerably during this period.[39] Scholars have
pointed to the rather bitter representation of Delphi in the Athenian
tragedies of the time (particularly to Euripides' *Andromache*, performed
between 428–25 BC), and the searing sarcasm reserved for oracles in
general in Aristophanes' comedies (particularly *Knights*, performed 424
BC).[40] And yet, perhaps because a thing lost is a thing missed most, it is
telling that representations of Delphi in Athenian vase painting increased
a lot in the same period: locked out of the sanctuary they had so recently
dominated and claimed as their own, Athenians sought to visualize it in
their every-day lives.[41]

When peace was agreed upon between Sparta and Athens in 423 and
again in 421 BC, Thucydides makes clear the extent to which Delphi was
center in the minds of both parties. In the agreement of 423 BC, the first
clause ran as follows:

> concerning the temple and oracle of the Pythian Apollo, we agree
> that whosoever wants shall consult it without fraud and without
> fear, according to the usages of our forefathers. . . . concerning the
> treasure of the god we agree to take care to find out all wrong-
> doers, rightly and justly following the usages of our forefathers.

And in the renewed agreement two years later, the first clauses again
concerned Delphi:

> with regard to the common sanctuaries [Delphi and Olympia],
> whosoever wishes may offer sacrifices and consult the oracles and
> attend as a deputy according to the customs of the fathers, both by
> land and sea, without fear. And the precinct and temple of Apollo
> at Delphi, and the people of Delphi shall be independent, having
> their own system of taxation and their own courts of justice, both
> as regards themselves and their own territory, according to the cus-
> toms of the fathers.[42]

As a result of the privileged position at the heart of these treaties, it is
possible to see Delphi as once again reaching out to a more varied crowd
in the last twenty years of the fifth century BC. Its oracle was involved in

encouraging the development of an Arcadian confederacy under Mantinea; in continuing its evolving role as arbitrator in a dispute between Thasos and Neapolis; in dealing boldly with Athens to insist Athens returned the Delian exiles to Delos after Athens had sought to purify the island by expelling its citizens; and in advising Athens about how to recover from plague (for which Apollo Alexikakos (the averter of evil) was henceforth worshiped in Athens).[43]

Yet, in reality, and especially for Athens, relations with Delphi were still strained. Thucydides' rendition of the peace treaties evoked the need to convince all the separate parties to agree to the terms, which, in relation particularly to Boeotia, was difficult. Relations between Athens and Boeotia remained tense, with a treaty between them repeatedly agreed upon every ten days. The result, given that Boeotian land stood between Athens and Delphi, was that the sacred processional route from Athens to Delphi was only accessible with Boeotian permission. As Aristophanes lamented later in 414 BC: "if we wish to go to Pytho, we have to ask the Boeotians for passage through their territory." That sense of ongoing frustration with Delphi continues to be palpable in Athenian tragedy, too, for example in Euripides' *Ion*, where, despite the fact that the play is staged at Delphi, and Delphi continues to be represented as an interpretive space through which solutions for future actions could be found, Pythian Apollo is presented as something of an ambiguous villain.[44]

Perhaps because of the ongoing difficulties of access to Delphi, and the perceived reception waiting for them when they did get there, the Athenians do not seem to have consulted to the same degree as they did during the Persian Wars in the run up to launching their infamous Sicilian expedition in 415 BC. Indeed, if anything, the sources indicate that the oracle was supporting the Spartans once again as conflict resumed in the aftermath of that campaign.[45] Visitors to the sanctuary over the last decade of the fifth century would be left in no doubt either about how the war was going. Neither Athens nor its allies dedicated monumental offerings at Delphi during this period, but their enemies most certainly did. Over the course of the Peloponnesian War, almost all of Athens's proud monuments from the first half of the fifth century were opposed—spatially, artistically, and architecturally—by monuments constructed by its enemies: the Acanthians, the Syracusans, the Megarians, and, of course, in the aftermath of 404 BC and Sparta's final victory over Athens at Aegospotamoi, the Spartans. The latter made their new ascendancy particularly clear: at the southeastern entrance to the Apollo sanctuary, where Athens had constructed its second group monument to Marathon and positioned it so as to be the first seen on entering the sanctuary, the Spartans now trumped that position with a group comprising thirty-eight statues in two rows: in total, three times the size of the Athenian offering on a base eighteen meters long (fig. 6.2). On the opposite side of the entrance path, they built a stoa that towered over the entrance, and whose construction required heavy engineering to ensure its stability on the mountainside; in it, valuable offerings were placed by the Spartans and their victorious general Lysander.[46]

The changing tide of Greek history had once again been written into the Delphic complex in marble, stone, and bronze. But if Plutarch, writing in the first century AD, is to be believed, this was also the moment when monuments at Delphi began not only to represent the victories of their dedicators, but their fates as well. Not simply in the sense that they were eventually upstaged, opposed, and overshadowed, but, more powerfully, in the sense that the monuments themselves crumbled as their dedicators crumbled. As the Athenians set off on their fateful Sicilian expedition in 415 BC, Plutarch records, the brilliant bronze palm tree topped by a golden statue of Athena dedicated by the Athenians on the temple terrace in 460 BC (see fig. 1.3) was pecked at insistently by crows, till it was disfigured.[47]

According to some later (and doubtful) sources, at the end of the Peloponnesian War, victorious Sparta and her allies asked the Pythian priestess whether Athens should be destroyed; she replied that the victors should spare "the common hearth of Greece."[48] But as the Greek world slowly shook itself free of the dust that had settled in the aftermath of the Peloponnesian War, how would the Delphians have taken stock of their position in the Greek world? It is telling that at this point in Delphi's story, one of its most enduring legacies comes into focus. By the end of the fifth century BC, somewhere on the architecture of the *pronaos* (the front section) of the temple of Apollo at Delphi, the now-famous maxims of Delphi had been inscribed and were viewable by all who came to the sanctuary. *Gnothi sauton*—"know thyself"; *meden agan*—"nothing in excess"; and the less well-known *eggua para d'ate*—"an oath leads to perdition."[49] The statements of wisdom inscribed on the temple at Delphi were—from the fifth century BC—ascribed to the Seven Sages, a group whose existence was much noted in the ancient sources from the early sixth century BC onward. Some argued that the Delphic maxims were actually responses from the oracle to the Seven Sages, while other later authors attempted to assign each of the Delphic maxims to a particular Sage (and adopted four more sayings so that each of the Sages could have their own).[50] But whoever came up with them, it is almost certainly without accident that it was during this time of crisis and uncertainty in the Greek world that they came to have such public renown.

At the end of the century, if the Delphians had contemplated what drew people to the oracle, they would have recognized its role as a central resource of advice for issues affecting individuals and city-states across the Greek world, and yet, that it was also a place inaccessible to some thanks to political and/or military conflict. If they contemplated their sanctuary, they would have seen something that had survived intact the Persian and Peloponnesian Wars, and was now groaning under the weight of dedications, many of which testified to the tensions, ambitions, and animosities that had shaken Greece to its core. And at the same time, they would have felt a sense of irony about the Delphic ideals of "know thyself" and "nothing in excess," which were now emblazoned across their temple. Here was a religious complex that screamed excess, and one that, while often tripping up others who had failed to know themselves and understand the words of the oracle properly, was itself part of a wider world whose identity was anything but known, certain, or stable.

When I stood up, everything rose with me, and the whole
of great Delphi accompanied my movement.

—Amendée Ozenfant (1939: 394–96)

7
RENEWAL

In the years immediately following Sparta's great victory over Athens at
Aegospotamoi in 405 BC, as Athens was forced to submit to the humili-
ation of being stripped of its fleet and even the very walls that had for so
long protected its city, a young Athenian by the name of Xenophon came
to consult the oracle at Delphi. His mind was fixed not on the conflict at
home, but on an opportunity presented by a conflict abroad, in Persia.
The throne of the Persian empire was up for grabs, and he had been invited
to join the army of the man intending to usurp it: Cyrus. Journeying to
Delphi on the advice of his friend Socrates (the man whom no one was
wiser than, according to the Delphic oracle), Xenophon asked the oracle
which gods he should sacrifice and pray to so that he might best and most
successfully perform the journey he had in mind and, after meeting with
good fortune, return home safely. The Pythia responded, and Xenophon
returned home to perform the appropriate sacrifices. Socrates, however,
pointed out that he had not asked the key question: Should he go? Xenophon had consulted the oracle with his mind already made up.[1]

Within five years, Xenophon would have returned from his campaign, having heroically led his men out of Persia following Cyrus's defeat and death, and Socrates would have been put to death by the city of

139

Athens as it sought to come to terms with political revolution and instability. In thanks for his lucky escape, Xenophon promised a half tithe (percentage) of the spoils of his campaign to Delphi, which he placed in the treasury of the Athenians. Yet within another thirty years, Xenophon would have transferred his allegiance to Sparta and moved to live near that city, even enrolling his own children in the Spartan education system, and Sparta, preeminent in the years after Aegospotamoi, would have fallen from power, crushed in battle by the combined forces of several Greek city-states.[2]

The Greek world was turned on its head more than once in the first decades of the fourth century BC, and Delphi could not hope to be immune to this tectonic movement. Several scholars have argued that the effect of such world change was to decrease interest in the Delphic oracle. With very few exceptions, questions about colonization cease at Delphi in the early fourth century BC, no appeals for arbitration are known after 380 BC (when Delphi was called in to arbitrate a dispute between Clazomenae and Cyme over the island of Leuke), and even questions about fighting wars came to a halt after the middle of the century. Parke and Wormell go further and claim that the Spartan consultation about whether to go to war against Athens back in 432 BC was the last time the Pythia was consulted on a major question of policy not connected with cult or ritual in Greek history.[3] Yet such checklist approaches only highlight one aspect of Delphic business and gloss over the various critical ways in which Delphi was still immersed in the fabric of Greek society at this tumultuous time, acting both as a reflector, but also as a cultivator, and even occasionally as an instigator, of the changes that so fundamentally shook the Greek world.

Partly because Sparta had been banned by the city of Elis from Olympia for the last decades of the fifth century BC (as a result of a disagreement between them), Delphi had received the brunt of Sparta's monumental dedications following its victory over Athens. These dedications, thanks to the plethora of Athenian monuments at Delphi, were able to artistically, architecturally, and spatially oppose and outdo those of the Athenians. In the following years, as Spartan power was projected across the Greek mainland, Delphi continued to benefit. King Agis of Sparta set up a dedication paid for with money from his plundering in central Greece: it was placed high on top of a tall column to ensure its visibility and prominence inside this increasingly crowded sanctuary. Yet Sparta was soon troubled by the zealous empire-building of one of its most successful generals, the architect of victory over the Athenians, Lysander. It was later said that Lysander had designs on the kingship of Sparta and sought constitutional change to alter the kingship to election rather than family right (with the ultimate aim of taking the title himself). To do so, he was said to have turned to the one authority with the power to convince Spartans of the need for such dramatic change—the Pythia— seeking to bribe her with vast sums of money. But, for once, his advances were rejected, and a second plan, to employ Delphi as the legitimator of a scam involving a supposed son of Apollo, was thwarted by Lysander's death in battle in 395 BC.[4]

Sparta, despite its powerful position in Greece, was by no means the only consulter of the oracle at this time: it was claimed in the fourth century AD by the pagan emperor Julian that Athens had been instructed by Delphi at the end of the fifth century BC to build a temple to the Mother of the Gods (the foreign deity Cybele) to ease her anger at the city; this structure became the Athenians' archive house in the city's agora.[5] Also, it is from this period, the end of the fifth century and the first half of the fourth century BC, that two of the crucial inscriptions for evidence regarding the costs of consulting the oracle (that we met in the first chapter) seem to have been set up as part of public statements of the close relationship between the oracle and different city-states across the wider Greek world. The inscription of Phaselis (in Asia Minor) set out the tariffs for public and private consultations, and that of Sciathus (in the Aegean) set prices for both public and private consultation of the oracle, and perhaps, as well, for the lot oracle available at Delphi.[6] In the same period, inscriptions were also set up at Delphi to record the privileges granted to particular associations. The most well-known is that for the Aesclepiads (a religious association tied to the god of healing Asclepius), who set up their own inscriptions to publicize their Delphic honors in the sanctuary. Nor was Sparta the only dedicator in the sanctuary: Pythian victors (including those from Athens) represented their victories with statues in the Apollo sanctuary, and individuals increasingly celebrated their close relationship with Delphi (e.g., their status as proxenos) with statues, or were honored for their abilities with statues put up by others (e.g., the orator Gorgias of Sicily was honored in this way with a statue on the temple terrace).[7]

Despite this plethora of individuals and associations, it was impossible to ignore the presence of Sparta at Delphi in the first three decades of the fourth century BC, and increasingly impossible to ignore Sparta's rather heavy-handed projection of power across Greece. King Agesilaus of Sparta dedicated a percentage of the hundred talents'-worth of war booty extracted from his campaigns in Asia Minor at the occasion of the Pythian games in 394 BC. He also manipulated the oracular network to assure divine approval for his attack on Argos during a religious festival. Agesilaus first went to the oracle of Zeus at Olympia (which was now much more firmly under the Spartan thumb than it had been in the last decades of the fifth century BC) to ask for approval for the attack, then traveled to Delphi, an oracular shrine with more international weight than that of Olympia (but less under the thumb of Sparta), where he asked simply if the son agreed with his father. Apollo, son of Zeus, could hardly not agree with his father, king of the gods, and by implication, the response Agesilaus had extracted from the oracle of Zeus at Olympia. Agesilaus had manipulated the system to perfection.[8]

Such stories underscore the irony of Delphi's position in the Greek world. It was a well-respected oracle, with centuries of authority behind it, in the midst of a lavish sanctuary filled with hundreds of monumental dedications from across the Mediterranean world; it was a host of international athletic and musical games that were respected throughout Greece; and it was managed by a pluri-regional association of cities and states. Yet it was also a small community living by its wits, clinging to a mountainside in central Greece. It is estimated that Delphi had one thousand citizens (with a total population, including foreigners and slaves, of perhaps five thousand) in the early fourth century BC. The population was not divided into demes spread out over the landscape as at Athens and the territory of Attica: the very nature of the Delphic landscape (the sanctuary and city surrounded by the 150–200 square kilometers of sacred land that had to remain uncultivated) meant that citizens of Delphi had to live in, or in the immediate vicinity of, Delphi itself (see map 3, plate 1). Moreover, the overwhelming success of the sanctuary in the preceding centuries had warped the population to such an extent that most other settlements in the surrounding area had withered away; Delphi was extraordinarily isolated for such a small and yet powerful community.[9] The surviving inscriptions do indicate that it had some control over areas of land beyond the sacred "no-man's" land, from which it could draw income. As well, surveys of the land immediately around the city show that it was cultivating its own cereal crops, as well as maintaining sheep on the mountain plateau around the Corycian cave (see map 3, fig. 0.2).[10] But, to all intents and purposes, Delphians were dependent for their livelihood on the sanctuary, as the *Homeric Hymn to Apollo*, composed approximately two centuries before, had forecast they would be. This was reflected in the fact that the city's key civic structures—the meeting place of the civic assembly, the council chamber (bouleuterion), and the prytaneum (smaller executive council chamber)—were all located within, or very close to, the sanctuary of Apollo itself.[11] The very success of Delphi had provided its small community a living, but it had also left its citizens isolated within the wider landscape, and tied their fortunes tightly to that of the sanctuary. As a result, Delphi's identity was always not only that of independent authority, but also of vulnerable prize as well as of tool susceptible to manipulation.

All three aspects of this identity were on display during first decades of the fourth century BC. In Plato's detailed analysis of an ideal state, Delphi was to occupy a prominent role. All legislative affairs relating to the establishment of shrines, sacrifices, and other form of cult for gods, daimones and heroes, as well as the graves of the dead and the services to be performed for the spirits of the dead, were to be overseen by the oracle at Delphi. Such a prominent role for Delphi would also be echoed in Plato's later work: Delphi was to be master of all laws about divine matters, final arbiter in the appointment of interpreters of the sacred laws, and consultant about all public festivals and sacrifices.[12]

Yet at the same time as Delphi's importance was being firmly established, both civic and Amphictyonic bodies at Delphi seem to have felt the need to bolster and restate their own importance. It is most probably during this period that one of the *phratries* (civic units) of Delphi, the Labyadai, chose to reinscribe and publicize in the sanctuary of Apollo their traditional rules, regulations, and oaths (an older version of which could be seen on a different side of the same stone that carried the new updated fourth-century inscription). A similar desire to update and redisplay seems to have motivated the Amphictyony in 380 BC to bring together their regular responsibilities with those regarding special events like the Pythian games and have them inscribed on steles not just at Delphi but also in other cities. Our surviving copy comes from Athens, and in it, the Amphictyony claim responsibility for inspecting the sacred land, for carrying out the necessary repairs before the Pythian games (including to bridges along the roads to Delphi in each of the Amphictyonic members' respective territories), and for taking the opportunity to set out a potpourri of their own legislation about behavior in the sanctuary. This is not the only set of Amphictyony laws that was updated and displayed at this time. In the first half of the fourth century BC, a number of Amphictyonic laws and decrees seem to have been similarly treated at Delphi and elsewhere.[13]

This is perhaps part of a bigger picture: some scholars, as we saw in a previous chapter, have argued that it was in this era—particularly the 380s and the 370s—that we should locate the creation of the stories surrounding the First Sacred War over Delphi, the very event that brought the Amphictyony into relation with the sanctuary. And this need to restate, publicize, and even invent particular roles, rules, and perhaps even historical events, among key Delphi players was furthermore motivated by the fact that this was a period during which Delphi began to feel increasingly vulnerable about its position in the wider world. In 385 BC it was whispered that the warlord tyrant Dionysius of Syracuse had designs on the sanctuary and that his treaty with the (not very distant) Illyrians was merely a precursor to launching an attack on Delphi itself. In 373 BC the Athenian general Iphicrates intercepted and captured a ship bringing gold and ivory statues to Delphi and Olympia, thus denying the sanctuaries their latest dedications. In the same year, Delphi fell victim to a serious earthquake and rockslide, which seems to have devastated the Apollo and Athena sanctuaries and their temples. In 371 BC, Sparta, master of Greece for the previous thirty years, finally fell from power, crushed in pulverizing defeat at the battle of Leuctra. In its place was the city of Thebes, not far from Delphi. And most worryingly, by 371 BC, a man called Jason from the city of Pherai in Thessaly had risen to such extraordinary heights of power that he was able to claim mastership of northern Greece, and to act as a strong supporter of Thebes in its challenge to Sparta. In 370 BC, as the sanctuary of Delphi lay in tatters following the earthquake, Jason of Pherai planned to preside over the Pythian games, bringing with him an immense army of sacrificial animals—one thousand oxen and ten thousand other animals—collected from all his dominions. What the Delphians feared most was the rumor that he came not simply to celebrate the games, but to lay claim to the sanctuary itself.[14]

The Delphians were able to dodge the bullet in 370 BC, because Jason of Pherai—however correct the rumors had been about his intentions—was assassinated earlier in the year before he could preside over the Pythian games at Delphi. Yet the repercussions of events in the last years of the 370s would be felt at Delphi for the rest of the century. First and foremost, the sanctuary was in need of drastic renovation. The temple, it seems, was so badly affected by the earthquake that the oracle was unable to function: no oracles are known certainly to have emanated from Delphi between 372 and 262 BC, although later tradition supplies several examples, especially after the 340s, not least the "discovery" of a number of century-old oracles that seemed to prophesize the Spartan downfall at Leuctra. We know also, from later inscriptions detailing repairs, that parts of the north and south boundary walls, or else (depending on how you read the inscription) the entire east wall of the Apollo sanctuary had collapsed (see plate 2).[15] The question was, who would lead the charge in fixing it? Scholarship has long been divided about where the germ of the massive reconstruction project that dominated Delphi through until 310 BC began. For some, it was the brainchild of the organization that had led the previous redevelopment of Delphi: the Amphictyony, who, despite their low profile in the fifth century BC, had recently demonstrated publicly their role and power at Delphi. For others, however, the initial plan may have been formulated among the individual city-states at the several peace conferences that, eventually, failed to prevent the seismic military clash on the plain at Leuctra in 371 BC, with the Amphictyony taking over the project only in the years immediately afterward.[16]

Yet at the same time as the temple and sanctuary reconstruction project gathered momentum, the sanctuary was also playing host to commemorating the victory over Sparta at Leuctra. Just as Athens had proved a tempting target because of the number of monumental dedications at Delphi for Sparta, so too now Sparta found itself spatially, artistically, and architecturally confronted (see fig. 6.2). The Argives erected a semicircular statue group (directly opposite the similar semicircular monument they had offered in the fifth century) that stood next to the Spartan stoa, which had been built to commemorate victory over Athens, at the very entrance to the Apollo sanctuary. But the Argives did not simply build their monument next to the Spartan monument: theirs physically cut into, and cut off access to, the stoa. This was Delphic monument war in a whole new phase: dedications to victory inflicting wounds on dedications of their enemies. No wonder stories of dedications "dying" at the same time as their real-life dedicators cluster around the monuments of this period: Sparta's dedicated golden stars were said to have crashed to the ground at the time of the battle of Leuctra, the statue of Lysander to have fallen apart, and another to have crumbled.[17]

The visibility of the Spartan stoa was further reduced in 369 BC when the Arcadians, celebrating the development of their new confederacy, placed an imposing statue group directly in front of it (see fig. 6.2). The dedicating inscription on the monument read "for victory over the Spartans."[18] Nor were they the only city-states to commemorate the Spartan downfall. Thebes constructed a new treasury in the sanctuary (the first for many decades), and Thessaly offered statues of the victorious generals.[19]

Sparta seems to have retaliated as best it could, by returning to update its statue group to victory at Aegospotamoi from 404 BC with a new victory inscription written by Ion of Samos.[20]

As the power vacuum left by the collapse of Sparta was filled with city-states like Thebes and Athens fighting for ascendancy in the years after 371 BC, Delphi, still in a state of partial collapse following the earthquake, continued both to play host to that competition and to provide opportunities for a wide number of city-states to realign and recharacterize their histories to fit with the swiftly changing power balance.[21] Several dedicators returned to the sanctuary in the following decades to update their previous monuments to military victory by reinscribing their dedicatory epigrams, sometimes to emphasize their religious rather than political nature, and sometimes to make those victories more visible and emphatic.[22] Several cities also returned to make their close relationship with Delphi clearer: the Siphnians returned to their treasury built in the sixth century BC to inscribe the fact that they had promanteia across the lintel of its doorway, and the Naxians returned to their sphinx (also a dedication of the sixth century BC), standing high on its column, to inscribe a record of their own promanteia (lower down on the column where it was highly visible to visitors).[23]

Rewriting history was not the only role for Delphi in this period. In 368 BC, a(nother) peace conference was held at Delphi to try and settle the ongoing political and military disputes in Greece that would eventually culminate in another major clash in 362 at the battle of Mantinea. It was organized by Philiscus of Abydus, an undersatrap of Arioborzanes from Asia Minor, and its main participants were Athens, Thebes, and Sparta. That a Persian should be interested in cultivating peace with Greece is understandable only because the former had need of the (by now) battle-hardened Greek mercenaries for its own wars—men it could obtain only if there was peace in mainland Greece. The conference was a failure, according to some ancient historians, because, though it was held at Delphi, it did not consult the oracle (if indeed the oracle was functioning enough to be consulted).[24]

The failure of the peace conference, and the failure to settle the ongoing political and military disputes in mainland Greece through the 360s, began to take its toll on Delphi. For sure, the commission for the rebuilding of the Apollo and Athena sanctuaries continued to meet every spring from 370 until 356, but progress was slow—unsurprising when it was a project likely involving a large number of Greek city-states at a time when they were at loggerheads with one another.[25] At the same time, however, a surviving inscription from this period related to the lowering of interest rates at Delphi is perhaps testament to an economic slowdown, which would eventually cripple even the major cities like Athens in the 350s. It was more worrying still that the command structure at Delphi was becoming increasingly thwarted by the political and military struggle that was dividing Greece. On the one hand, most of the citizens of Delphi, led by a man called Astycrates, were keen to support the people of Phocis (and by extension Athens) against the increasing Theban supremacy. The Amphictyony, on the other hand, seem to have increasingly leaned toward supporting Thebes. In spring 363 BC, this internal rift came to a head: Astycrates and ten other Delphians were condemned, by a decree of the Amphictyony (proposed by the Thessalians), to permanent exile, and their property was confiscated. This band of eleven refugees fled the sanctuary and was given refuge in Athens. Later that year, the city of Delphi, no doubt under duress from the Amphictyony, granted the Thebans the right of promanteia at a level unlike any they had granted before: the Thebans had the right to consult the oracle not simply before everyone in their particular group, but before *everyone in the entire world* except the Delphians. The (enforced) political bias of Delphi (or rather the Amphictyony) could not have been clearer, although the Thebans still thought it worthwhile to inscribe their new rights at Delphi on the treasury they had built a decade earlier.[26]

More internal Delphic strife erupted soon after. A wedding was planned at Delphi between Orsilaus, son of one of the Delphic archons (magistrates), and the daughter of a man called Crates. In preparation for the wedding, during a ritual libation pouring, the vessel cracked. Seeing it as a bad omen, Orsilaus refused to go through with the ceremony. In revenge for the spurning of his daughter, Crates orchestrated for Orsilaus and his brother to be accused of stealing sacred objects from the sanctuary (the same trick the Delphians had used on Aesop a couple of centuries before). Found guilty, the brothers were thrown off the Hyampia cliff to their deaths. Crates, it appears, was still not satisfied and, going insane, murdered a number of Orsilaus's family members and friends in the sanctuary of Athena at Delphi. This story of revenge for a spurned marriage may well have had a political undertone: Orsilaus's family was said to have been pro-Theban, and that of Crates pro-Phocis. As a result of the conflict, Crates' family was heavily fined and the proceeds supposedly dedicated to the goddess whose sanctuary had been defiled by the murder: Athena. Scholars have argued that the money in fact went toward paying for a new structure in the Athena sanctuary: a beautifully constructed and sculpturally adorned tholos, whose exact function is still hotly debated, although the surviving remnants ironically, given how little we know about the use of the building, make up one of the most well-known images of Delphi in today's tourist literature (see plate 3).[27]

The changing power balance and resulting tension, both at Delphi, and in the wider Greek world, soon erupted into renewed conflict, but this time over Delphi itself. The Phocians, no longer supported by a now weak Sparta, were targeted by the Thebans at a meeting of the (pro-Theban) Amphictyonic council. They accused the Phocians of sacrilege and ensured that the Amphictyony imposed on the Phocians a heavy fine. The Phocians were between Scylla and Charybidis: paying meant financial penury and submission to Theban supremacy; not paying put them at risk of becoming the target of an Amphictyonic sacred war. In 356 BC, the Phocians decided to gamble everything: they moved in with their troops, under the leadership of their general Philomelus, to occupy the sanctuary, and they asserted their ancient claim to Delphi. About a century after the Athenians had pushed the Phocians to take over the sanctuary in the middle of the fifth century BC, precipitating the Second Sacred War, the Phocians tried the same tactic again. Their actions would begin the Third Sacred War in Delphi's history.[28]

In summer 356, under Phocian occupation, the exiled Delphian Astycrates was welcomed back to the city, and the pro-Thebans elements were driven out. This was, for now, a conflict between Phocis and Thebes: the

Phocians even began to pay the fine originally imposed on them by the Amphictyony. Indeed they did everything they could to demonstrate their ritual respect for the sanctuary: their general Philomelus promised he would respect the sanctuary's treasures and even managed to turn the chance remark of the Pythia (along the lines of "do as you please") into an oracular response to support his occupation.[29] But a year later, in 355 BC, the Amphictyony were forced into action to protect the sanctuary they were supposed to be running: sacred war was declared on Phocis for their occupation of the sanctuary. It was not, however, a united front. Several Amphictyonic members chose to remain neutral. Athens, though often represented on the Amphictyonic council, in reality supported her old ally Phocis, and, in a complete volte-face from the time Phocis had occupied the sanctuary a century before, Sparta now also supported Phocis (because Sparta was now anti-Thebes, having suffered defeat at their hands at Leuctra in 371).

It must have been an odd experience to visit Delphi in the 350s BC. On the one hand, the sanctuary was still a building site, its oracle functioning in some kind of temporary setup. On the other hand, the sanctuary was militarily occupied by the Phocians. They had destroyed the stele in the sanctuary on which the original Amphictyonic charge of impiety against them had been inscribed. And they had even begun to build fortresslike protective walls across the crags of the Parnassian mountains around Delphi to defend their position from attack (the remnants of which can still be seen today).[30]

But the Phocian bravado disguised despair. The Phocian general Philomelus threw himself off a cliff in 354 BC, and his brother Onomarchus took over and was later replaced after being killed in battle (the Phocians proceeded to dedicate statues of Philomelus and Onomarchus in the Apollo sanctuary in their honor). The Phocian force faced opposition from within Delphi as well: Onomarchus was forced to expel seven families from the city and confiscate their property to keep control. As the conflict continued, the Phocians were even forced to go back on their promise not to mistreat the sanctuary's many sacred dedications. Money was needed to pay for the occupation, and the only source available was the money at Delphi gathered for the temple rebuilding and from oracular consultation, and, when this ran out, they started melting down Delphi's precious metal offerings. The list of fabulous dedications destroyed during the years 356–46 BC is heart-rendering: the gold tripod cauldron from the serpent column of Plataea; the crater of Alyattes, the sixth century Lydian king; what had survived from the 548 BC fire of Croesus's golden lion; his gold and silver mixing bowls along with most of the rest of his dedications; the statue of Nike from the Sicilian tyrant Gelon along with other offerings from Sicilian rulers and probably the golden statue of Alexander I of Macedon offered after the Persians Wars. In total, Diodorus Siculus tells us that ten thousand talents'–worth of silver were melted down.[31]

And yet, between 353 and 351 BC, the committee for the reconstruction of the temple met each year at Delphi to discuss the rebuilding, which was supposedly still under way.[32] Similarly, at least the pro-Phocian states seem to have continued to relate issues to the oracle. Dating from the middle of the fourth century BC, there is a series of inscriptions relating to changes in ritual practice in Athens, all of which seems to indicate backing from a Delphic consultation. At the same time, however, these consultations may have been cloaked in a degree of suspicion about Delphic bias. It is not without irony that the fullest contemporary report we have of the process of decision making involved in consulting the Delphi oracle comes from Athens at exactly the time when Delphi is experiencing one of the oddest periods in its history. In 352 BC, according to inscribed reports in Athens, the Athenians were debating what to do with sacred lands belong to the sanctuary of Demeter and Core at Eleusis, which were subject to long-running disputes over ownership between the Athenians and Megarians. They could not decide whether or not to allow cultivation of the sacred land, and referred the issue to Delphi. But instead of simply sending their ambassadors to Delphi with this question, they recorded in the inscription that they had written out the two options (to cultivate or not to cultivate) on sheets of tin. These sheets were subsequently wrapped in wool, then placed in a bronze jug, shaken around, and one was placed inside a gold jug, the other inside a silver jug. Both jugs were then sealed, so that no one knew which jug contained which option. The question the Athenians decided to put to the oracle was simply which jug they should pick. This is an extraordinary procedure and without parallel: that the Athenians chose to inscribe and publicly display the complex lengths they went to in order to ensure that no one—in Athens or at Delphi—could influence the response from the god. Only the god would know what was in each jug and indeed what the real question was in the first place. The answer came back that they should leave the land uncultivated, and the Athenians subsequently obeyed.[33]

We know too that during this period of occupation, a number of Delphic festivals continued. In the period 356–46 BC, the Thyades, female worshipers of Dionysus from Delphi, joined the Thyades from Athens who had processed from their city to the sanctuary, in order to take part in their regularly held (every two years) joint festival in honor of Dionysus. This ritual celebration took place not in the sanctuary of Delphi, but high in the wilds of the Parnassian mountains. The Delphian and Athenian celebrants processed together from the sanctuary by torchlight up into the mountains to take part in a series of Dionysiac revels. In this particular period, at the end of one such celebration, the Thyades lost their way returning down from the mountains to Delphi and strayed into Amphissan (enemy) territory. The women of Amphissa, keen to ensure the lost female worshipers were not maltreated, looked after the group and made sure that they found the path that would take them home.[34]

This was not the only festival in honor of Dionysus celebrated at Delphi. Plutarch in the first century AD tells us of several others (which will be examined in a later chapter). The difficulty, as always, is with knowing whether Plutarch's testimony should be extrapolated back in time. Despite the fact that Dionysus may always have been worshiped at Delphi, it is only now in the fourth century BC that his cult can be archaeologically attested to. From the middle of the century, dedications appear to Dionysus in an area just to the east of the Apollo sanctuary that would become (or indeed may have been already) the established cult location of the god (see plate 1). In 339–38 BC, a paean was written by Philodamus honoring Dionysus at Delphi, and complemented by the introduction of a statue of the god offered by the Cnidians set up in the area of the theater (see plate 2).[35] And Dionysus even made it on to the temple of Apollo itself. The temple construction, interrupted by the different wars of the fourth century, would finally be completed in the 320s BC. The new pedimental sculptures adorning it were the work of Athenian sculptor Praxias and finished (probably by c. 327 BC) by another Athenian, Androsthenes. Made in Pentelic (Athenian) marble, the east pediment displayed Apollo, hunched on his tripod, while the west pediment portrayed an Apollo-like Dionysus, playing the lyre (fig. 7.1). Much scholarly ink has been spilled over the meaning of the sculptural choice for these pediments, and particularly the elevation of Dionysus to equal billing with Apollo. Some have

Figure 7.1. Statues of the gods Apollo (*left*) and Dionysus (*right*) from the east and west pediments, respectively, of the fourth century BC temple of Apollo in the Apollo sanctuary at Delphi (Museum at Delphi).

seen it as a result of Macedonian influence, others of Athenian. Yet what it reflected above the politics of influence was the increasingly wide and public scope of worship at Delphi, with major cult areas dedicated not only to Dionysus but also to Asclepius and Hermes in the fourth century, alongside the continued worship of a variety of other gods.[36]

By 351 BC, the Phocian cause looked almost lost, although they managed to hang on to control of Delphi until 346 BC. They were supposedly so desperate for money by this time that one of their last commanders, Phalaecus, even resorted to following lines from Homer's *Iliad* that intimated there might be wealth beneath the temple of Apollo. He set his soldiers to work digging up the area around the sacred hearth and tripod, but to no avail.[37] What finally brought their occupation of Delphi to an end, however, was not so much the absence of money, as the arrival of one man: Philip, king of Macedon.

Philip had in fact already been involved with Delphi in the first year of the Phocian occupation. In his dealings with the Chalcidians in 356 BC, he had negotiated a treaty, which he called on the oracle at Delphi to put its stamp of approval to; a copy of this was later set up at the sanctuary.[38] Now, however, at the request of the Amphictyony, he came with his forces to expel the Phocians from the sanctuary. This he did in 346 BC, having first successfully neutralized Athens's support for Phocis through another peace treaty of his own with Athens.[39] The Phocians were expelled from the temple and the Amphictyony. Those who had fled abroad were put under a curse, as was anyone who had touched the money that came from the melting down of the sanctuary's treasures. Those who remained were forced to break up their cities within Phocian territory into villages of not more than fifty houses. Phocis was handed an enormous fine—an annual tribute of sixty talents—until such a time as they had repaid everything they had destroyed at the sanctuary (valued by Diodorus Siculus at ten thousand talents). The sanctuary was given back to the Delphians. The pro-Phocian families (including that of Astycrates) were once again expelled, and those exiled by the Phocians were allowed to return. In a statement of the seriousness of Phocian actions, the statues of their generals dedicated in the sanctuary during their occupation were targeted for removal and destruction: the only instance of such a decision in Delphic history.[40]

In contrast, Philip of Macedon was feted as the savior of Delphi. Even though Thebes had borne the brunt of the conflict, Philip took the glory. He presided over the Pythian games in 346 BC and was given the seats on the Amphictyony formerly occupied by the Phocians. Indeed in the lists of attendees at their meetings, his representatives came second, while the Thessalians, who presided over the council, came in first (the latter were pro-Macedonian in any case). Philip was voted promanteia by the Delphians, and a statue of him was erected in the Apollo sanctuary, possibly by the Amphictyony themselves. In turn, the Amphictyony was later said to have proclaimed itself at the center and beginning of a new era, an era of *koine eirene*—"common peace."[41]

Athens—increasingly wary of Philip's actions—especially after their peace treaty with him had not delivered the rebalancing of power in central Greece they had hoped for, boycotted the Pythian games celebrated by Philip in 346 BC, lost their right of promanteia with the oracle (just as Philip got his), and even considered going to war against Philip and the Amphictyonic league. Demosthenes, the famous Athenian orator whose anti-Philip stance would eventually convince Athens to face Philip in battle at Chaeroneia in 338 BC, characterized life at Delphi during the 340s under Philip's auspices by saying that the new government at Delphi was so tyrannical that if anyone mentioned the sacred treasures, they were thrown off a cliff. And Philip, Demosthenes argued, was so intent on holding on to to authority at Delphi that, if he could not be there to celebrate its games, rather than allowing another city to do it, he would send his slaves.[42]

The impression one gets of Delphi through the speeches of Athenian orators like Demosthenes is of a place of critical importance not only due to the authority of its oracle, but also to its own long existence and long-standing interaction with Athens over that time. Delphi was a source of authority and tradition, an important element of Greek society, which the orators, especially Demosthenes, increasingly portrayed as besmirched by Philip.[43] And at the same time as Delphi was characterized in this way by the Athenian orators, Athens's physical involvement with

Delphi was very selective: the Athenians were boycotting its games, offering no civic dedications in the sanctuary, and refusing to contribute financially to the reconstruction of its temple. Yet the Athenians were active as part of the commission tasked with overseeing the rebuilding (as *naopoioi*), and as craftsmen and suppliers for it. Nor is this patchwork approach to Delphic interaction only true for Athens, the plentiful inscriptional evidence from this period allows us to form a picture in which many different cities and states made particular decisions about what kinds of activities at Delphi they wanted to be involved in.[44] And at the same time, the inscriptional evidence reveals the degree to which individuals throughout the Greek world sought to be part of the construction: many individuals gave small amounts, most half a drachma (about a day's wage for an Athenian juror), but some gave only enough to cover the cost of their donation being inscribed (and sometimes even less than that). Donating was, however, clearly a huge source of pride: Clearistus of Carystus brought his children to Delphi in order to donate to the reconstruction fund and, while there, showed them the statue of his grandfather Aristocles of Carystus, who was represented on the monument to Spartan victory at Aegospotamoi.[45]

In the years after 346 BC, the rebuilding of the temple and sanctuary moved forward apace, reinfused as it was with energy and money thanks in no small measure to the Phocian fine flowing annually into Delphi's coffers. The renovations were extensive: the terracing wall to the temple terrace was raised in height, the entire floor plan of the temple was moved farther north, necessitating excavation and rebuilding of the terracing wall to the north to create extra space. Sets of stairs were inlaid into this new terracing wall to lead to the area later occupied by the theater. There was significant investment in systems to channel water as it flowed down the mountainside around and underneath the temple platform. A new temple was planned with new pedimental sculpture, so the surviving pedimental sculpture from the previous Apollo temple, like the famous charioteer statue, was buried just to the north of the temple terrace, along with dedications damaged in the 373 BC earthquake. New access routes were laid out above these burials between the north of the sanctuary and

the temple terrace, with previous dedications moved around and repositioned to line these routes, and at the same time areas of cult worship to
a variety of deities and heroes were likely more fully developed, for instance, the cult area around the "tomb" of Neoptolemus just to the north
of the temple (see plates 1, 2; figs. 1.4, 7.2).[46]

But the Phocian fine, it seems, had encouraged the Amphictyony
to develop their plans even further. Some of the dedications that were
melted down by the Phocians (particularly Croesus's gold and silver craters) were remade. Money was also put to use to create new structures at
Delphi: a gymnasium and stadium, for instance, to provide better facilities for its increasingly popular Pythian games (fig. 7.3). The stadium,
dramatically positioned now up above the Apollo sanctuary, had copies
of its older rules and regulations laid into its stone walls (see plate 1). One
inscription, still in place today, forbids the taking of sacrificial wine out
of the stadium on pain of a large fine. It seems that those tasked with the

Figure 7.2. The fourth century BC temple of Apollo in the Apollo sanctuary at
Delphi as seen today from the theater above it (© Michael Scott)

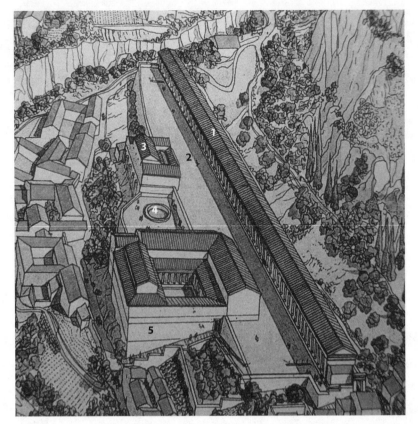

Figure 7.3. A reconstruction of the gymnasium at Delphi (aquarelle de Jean-Claude Golvin. Musée départemental Arles antique © éditions Errance).
1 Covered running track. 2 Outdoor running track. 3 Roman baths. 4 Washing pool. 5 Palestra.

reinscribing of this old rule were uncertain how to render it in fourth-century style. The result is an inscription in which the letter forms are a curious mix of centuries: an archaic theta but a fourth-century alpha, for example, and even a misspelling of the word "wine" because, by then, an entire letter that used to be in the word (the digamma) had slipped out of usage and was unrecognizable to the fourth-century letter cutters.[47]

The gymnasium, on the other hand, was built nearer the Castalian fountain, next to the Athena sanctuary, on land mythically considered the location where Odysseus had been wounded in the thigh by a boar (see plate 1, fig. 7.3). It was one of the first architecturally complex gymnasiums built in Greece, putting Delphi at the forefront of Greek architectural and athletic development, and it consisted of both a covered and outdoor running track, a wrestling area, and bathing facilities. The Pythian games benefited from the building of these new facilities: additional events were added to the games in the fourth century, and it is now, in the late 340s and 330s, that the first attempts are made—by Aristotle and his nephew Callisthenes no less—to record a list of all the Pythian victors stretching back to the beginnings of the games in the sixth century, a list eventually put on display in the sanctuary, and for which laborious effort Aristotle and Callisthenes received honors from the Delphians.[48]

If all this was not enough, the Phocian fine was also channeled by the Amphictyony toward their other sanctuary, that of Demeter at Anthela, and used to produce the Amphictyony's first, and only, currency (fig. 7.4). The one place conspicuously not to benefit from the fine seems to have been the sanctuary of Athena at Delphi (although its damaged tholos and temple were repaired). At the same time, its two treasuries seem to have been converted for use in some kind of civic/private function and were surrounded by inscribed steles documenting civic affairs, perhaps an indication that this sanctuary had come more recognizably under the control of the Delphic polis at a time when relations between the Amphictyony and Delphi must have been strained (see plate 3).[49]

Figure 7.4. Coinage issued by the Amphictyony at Delphi between 336 and 335–35 BC. This stater coin has Demeter on one side (due to the Amphictyony's responsibility for the sanctuary of Demeter at Anthela), and Apollo sitting on the omphalos on the other. "Amphictyony" is spelled out on the coin around the rim (© EFA/Ph. Collet [Guide du site fig. 2.f])

Despite tense relations at Delphi, this burst of building activity and reflowering of the Amphictyony, coupled with the ongoing articulation in the literary sources at this time of the events surrounding the First Sacred War in the early sixth century, seems to have once again encouraged dedicators to invest in the sanctuary. The Cnidians returned to spruce up their lesche and the surrounding area. The Thebans and Boeotians celebrated the outcome of the war with new dedications. The Cyreneans, fundamentally tied to Delphi throughout their history, and now contributors to the fund to rebuild the temple, returned to dedicate a marble treasury in the Apollo sanctuary (see plate 2), for which they were awarded promanteia, to complement their other fourth-century dedication: a chariot sculpture with a figure of the god Ammon. Likewise, the Rhodians, chose to build a sculpture of the god Helios with his sun chariot, which was placed atop a high column on the eastern edge of the temple terrace, directly on the axis of the new temple (see fig. 1.3).[50]

But it was this temple that was soon again to spark controversy. By 340 BC, it was complete enough for the Athenians, still spoiling for a fight having felt cheated by Philip of Macedon in the peace agreed in 346 BC, to rehang the Persian shields the Athenians had placed on the metopes of the previous temple after their great victory against the Persians at Marathon in 490 BC. In a sanctuary already teeming with examples of the rewriting of history to suit present circumstances, this was one in which history was deliberately not rewritten to make a point. The rehanging of the same old shields pointed to the continued glory of Athenian history, but also, more specifically, to the past misdemeanors of Thebes, a city now enjoying considerable influence, but which, according to the inscriptions on the shields, had fought with Persia against Greece back in the fifth century BC.[51]

Such an undiplomatic slap in the face could not go unnoticed. At a meeting of the Amphictyonic council in 340 BC, the representative of the Ozolian Locrians accused the Athenians (without doubt, pushed by Thebes and Philip) of impiety for not performing the proper rituals before erecting the shields. Athens's man at the council was Aeschines, an orator who, in Athens, was a natural supporter of Philip (and thus archenemy of Demosthenes), but who now was called on to defend Athens on a larger stage against Philip's machinations. His speech to the assembly, as he himself later recalled, brilliantly turned the tables on Athens's accusers. The Locrians were guilty, he argued, of a greater impiety in cultivating sacred land. His rhetoric was enough to spark a military attack then and there against the Locrians, an attack the Locrians easily repelled because neither the Amphictyony nor the city of Delphi had a proper standing army. As 340 gave way to 339 BC, the Amphictyony called a special meeting to organize a proper military force. But by this time, Athens had realized that pushing this war was not in their best interests long-term: the city was conspicuously absent from the emergency meeting, as were the representatives of their main enemy Thebes. The result was that the paltry forces of the Amphictyony were able to evict the Locrians—and particularly the citizens of Amphissa—from the sacred land, but unable to enforce any kind of permanent solution. In exasperation, the Thessalian commander of the Amphictyonic forces turned (once again) to Philip of Macedon.[52]

It was exactly the invitation Philip had been waiting for. Fed up with Athens snapping at his heels, Philip used the invitation to sweep south with his forces. Instead of marching on Amphissa, he set up camp at Elatea, just a couple of days march from Athens. Athens's diplomatic posturing had led to the prospect of its invasion. In desperation, Athens was forced into an alliance with the same city it had hoped to antagonize in the first place: Thebes. In late September 339 BC, Athens consulted the Delphic oracle on ill omens witnessed at their festival of the Mysteries at Eleusis. Demosthenes, Philip's most vocal opponent, architect of the new alliance between Thebes and Athens, denounced Delphi's response with the bitter words "the Pythia is Philipizing." In the winter of 339–38, Athens and Thebes marched to occupy Phocis and Delphi as a brave forward move against Philip. In return, in the summer of 338 BC, Philip turned to meet them. He occupied Locris, punished Amphissa as per his original agreement with the Amphictyony, and faced Athens and Thebes on the battlefield at Chaeronea, just on the other side of the Parnassian mountains from Delphi. It was a cataclysmic event in Greek history: the forces of Athens and Thebes were decimated, leaving Philip triumphant and in charge of mainland Greece.[53]

So ended what became known as the Fourth Sacred War. Amphissa, terrorized into submission by Philip, promptly put up a statue of him in the Apollo sanctuary at Delphi, calling him "*basileos*" ("king") (it was their first and only civic dedication in the sanctuary).[54] It was a moment, finally, for the Greeks, and particularly the Delphians, to catch their breath. In a single century, their sanctuary had been used as a space in which to trumpet Athenian defeat and Spartan ascendancy, followed by Spartan defeat and Theban ascendency. It had been in ruins since 373 BC, during which time the Delphians had faced prospective takeovers from Thessaly; actual occupations by the Phocians; two Sacred Wars; the dramatic loss of many of their most precious offerings; the adrenaline shot of the Phocian fine, which had not only replenished their coffers, but had seen their sanctuary rebuilt and expanded; the articulation not only of a newly empowered Amphictyony but of a mythic history of their involvement with the sanctuary dating back to the First Sacred War; and the arrival and imposition of Philip and the power of Macedon over mainland Greece. It had been a roller coaster ride. Perhaps now, they thought, things would settle for a while? They could not have been more wrong.

One tries to imagine all these as they were when they breathed
intact. They must have looked, from a distance, like cypresses,
shiny, multicoloured, around the temple of Pythia. One just tries . . .
one is still trying.

—George Seferis, *Dokimes* vol. 2 (1981), trans. C. Capri-Karka

8

TRANSITION

In the immediate aftermath of Philip's victory over Athens, his conquest
of mainland Greece, and his conclusion of the Fourth Sacred War over
Delphi, Philip's allies continued to dedicate at the sanctuary: Daochus, a
Thessalian, erected a statue group of his entire family in the Apollo sanctuary near the cult area of Neoptolemus. The temple construction also
continued, indeed its organization became more professional with the instigation of a new level of financial oversight in 337 BC in the form of the
tamiai (treasurers). At the same time, Philip reinforced the importance of
Delphi in Greek affairs by making it one of the sanctuaries in which his
Hellenic league would be based, and through which it would act. This
league, which only Sparta refused to join, sought to unify Greece under
Philip and to work in tandem with the one thing that had always worked
best to unify the Greek city-states: an attack on Persia. Philip even returned to the Delphic oracle to ask if he would conquer the Persian king.[1]

Yet in July 336 BC, just before setting out on his campaign and while
celebrating the marriage of his daughter, Philip was murdered. Later
sources commented that the Pythia had foreseen the event: her reply to
Philip's inquiry about conquering Persia had been "the bull has been gar-
landed, the end is come, the sacrificer is at hand." Just who the "sacrificer"

was, and why, was as much a matter of debate in the ancient sources as it is in modern scholarship. Some point to the involvement of Philip's (recently) ex-wife, Olympias, the mother of Alexander the Great. Centuries later, Olympias, using the name she had used as a little girl, Myrtale, was even said to have dedicated the sword used to kill Philip in the sanctuary of Apollo at Delphi. Yet whoever was responsible for Philip's death, it marked yet another sea change in the tide of Greek history, one the sanctuary authorities at Delphi were quick to respond to. The Amphictyonic accounts for autumn 336 BC contain a space meant to read "*para Philippou*" ("from Philip") but at the last minute the stone cutters managed to squeeze "*para Alexandrou*" into the space instead.[2]

As a result of Philip's murder, however, Greece was once again plunged into a period of high tension and instability. Alexander assumed the Macedonian throne and leadership of Greece, with only a short window of time in which to make his authority clear. Delphi's position in this period was complex. No Delphic oracles addressed to Alexander can, according to the still preeminent volume on the Pythia by Herbert Parke and Donald Wormell, be classed as genuine, but rather seem to be later creations to suit Alexander's future achievements.[3] So, the famous story—that Alexander went to the oracle, like Philip, to ask about his campaign against Persia, but arrived on a nonconsultation day, forced the Pythia to prophesize for him, to which she replied "boy, you are invincible," a response Alexander was happy to take and promptly left for Asia—is unlikely to be historical. Indeed it bears (a little too much) remarkable resemblance to the consultation by the Phocian general Philomelus during his occupation of Delphi in the Third Sacred War.[4]

At the same time, however, it does seem that Alexander was both suspicious and respectful of Delphi. He did not dedicate there (although his generals did), and this personal avoidance of Delphi stands in stark contrast to his expensive dedications at Olympia and his use of the Olympic games for the announcement of his achievements and commands. He may have held his first session of the Amphictyonic council at their other sanctuary near Thermopylae rather than at Delphi, and is said to have always dealt with embassies to him from sanctuaries in the order Olympia,

Ammon (in Egypt), Delphi, Corinth, Epidaurus (see maps 1, 2). Nevertheless, Delphi seems also to have been one of the sanctuaries in which Alexander planned to construct a temple (costing fifteen hundred talents). As well, Delphi is portrayed as having been supportive of Alexander when Thebes rebelled against him, a rebellion that ended in the total destruction of Thebes by Alexander and his forces. At the time of the rebellion, the roof of the Theban treasury at Delphi was said to have become stained red with blood.[5]

Yet, just as Alexander seems to have shown a mix of respect and disregard for Delphi, the city of Delphi itself may not have been wholly pro-Alexander either. Indeed, it may well have been attempting to keep the good will of all sides, particularly through the awarding of civic honors (proxenia). In 335/4 BC, the year after Philip was murdered and Alexander was struggling to assert his authority, the city of Delphi offered collective promanteia to the people of Aetolia in northern Greece (see map 2). Aetolia was, despite being an ally of Philip at Chaeronia in 338 BC, now little less than a confirmed enemy of Alexander and Macedon (it sided with Thebes against Alexander). As such, the city of Delphi seems to have engaged in a serious, and potentially dangerous, game of, at best, hedging its bets over the future of Macedonian ascendancy, and, at worst, taking an openly rebellious stance against Macedon.[6]

Such an independent strategy continued through the rest of the 330s and 320s, with the city of Delphi awarding proxenia to Thessalians, Aetolians, and Macedonians.[7] In 324–23 BC, however, as resistance to Alexander grew in Greece following the proclamation of his exiles decree (at Olympia), the stance of the Amphictyony seems to have hardened against Macedon. At the meetings of the Amphictyony in 324–23, the representatives of Alexander were "not seated." At the same time, money that had been voted by the Amphictyony in 327/6 BC to purchase gold crowns to honor Alexander's mother, Olympias, was, by 324–23, diverted to other uses and the crowns never purchased.[8] In contrast, in the aftermath of Alexander's death, Delphi once again sought to position itself as a friend to all in an uncertain world, even extending its first (surviving) proxeny decree to a citizen of Phocis, Delphi's territorial neighbor and (recent) military overlord who were still paying the heavy fine for their occupation of the sanctuary during the Third Sacred War.[9]

At the same time as Delphi was playing the odds creating (and denying) relationships with Macedon and Aetolia in the 330s BC, Athens was demonstrating its independence once again at Delphi. The city had suffered under Philip and, as a result, boycotted the Pythian games at Delphi because of Macedonian involvement with the sanctuary. Yet Athens now celebrated its return to competition at the Pythian games with statues and precious dedications in honor of its victors, and as active dedicators in the Athena sanctuary. Crucially, it was perhaps the Athenians who dared to cut off access to the not-long-dedicated statue group of Philip's ally, the Thessalian Daochus, with their own dedication of a high acanthus column topped by dancers and a copy of the sanctuary's holiest of holies: the omphalos, marker of the center of the world (see fig. 1.3).[10] This bold statement did not, however, mean that Athens exerted the kind of influence at Delphi it had done in the early fifth century: in 332 BC, its failure to pay a fine on behalf of its athletes who had cheated at Olympia was taken up by the oracle at Delphi, with the result that the Athenians were instructed by the Pythia to set up six golden statues of Zeus at Olympia as recompense.[11]

The Greek world was re-formed fundamentally by Alexander's conquests, but it was subsequently torn apart by Alexander's death in 323 BC. He left no adult male heir, but a host of competing generals and a pregnant (foreign) wife. The resulting power struggle lasted for the remainder of the century and saw Alexander's empire carved up into numerous new kingdoms, his mother Olympias and his young son eventually killed, and his generals beginning their own dynasties in his place. Delphi was not immune to these seismic events and the uncertainty they created. It is to this period at the end of the fourth and beginning of the third centuries BC that a number of watchtowers have been dated; constructed across the landscape around Delphi, they ensured their users the ability to survey (not to mention control) the valley east and west of Delphi. Who built and used these towers, and why, is uncertain, but it is not without importance that such a surveillance/defensive network came into operation at this unstable time in Greek history.[12]

Despite the apparent dangers in traversing the wider landscape around Delphi at this time, the ritual use of the Corycian cave seems to have continued unabated. Indeed, it is during the end of the fourth century BC, and particularly during the third, that a number of inscriptions (some on elaborate marble bases and some cut directly into the rock of the cave) were set up in honor of Pan and the Nymphs, including one in the third century BC by a patrolman from the Phocian city of Ambryssus who seems to have been tasked with keeping watch in this area of the Parnassian mountains.[13]

Moreover, despite the fact that Herbert Parke and Donald Wormell have argued that in the fifty years after Alexander's death, there is no evidence for the oracle's being consulted on anything but local matters, it is clear that the sanctuary was not abandoned in this period.[14] The building of the new stadium, for example, continued through to its completion c. 275 BC (see plate 1, figs. 0.1, 0.2). Equally the Phocians, so long damned by their actions during the Third Sacred War, seem to have returned to the sanctuary to dedicate for victory in the Pythian games and in thanks for victory on the battlefield. The sanctuary, it seems, was also becoming something of a subject for study. Just as Aristotle had written a study of the constitution of the Delphic polis earlier in the century, now, at the end of the fourth century BC, the first books specifically about the vast numbers of Delphic dedications seem also to have appeared. In fact, as knowledge and interest in Delphic dedications spread, dedicators were becoming more and more sophisticated in their manipulation of the dedicatory landscape within the sanctuary. The Orneates of the Argolid, at the end of the fourth century BC, dedicated a statue group to a military victory they had won back in the sixth century BC, which had now become an important part of their civic identity. To make it look like this dedication had been at Delphi all the time, and thus a marker which the Orneates could point to as symbolic of their long-term importance and affinity with Delphi, the monument was sculptured in an archaic style, reminiscent of that from the sixth century, and placed in an area of the Apollo sanctuary that had been popular in the early fifth century for military dedications.[15] Delphi had become a place studied for its history, but was also, at the same time, a place that offered the perfect story board through which to retell history.

We have great difficulty reconstructing a history of oracular consultation in the centuries after Alexander's death, with some of the stories of consultations memorably labeled by Herbert Parke and Donald Wormell as "sanctimonius humbug." In many cases oracles said to have been given to the Hellenistic kings who came to Delphi seem to be simple rehashings of oracles given to the tyrants and kings before them. In any event, many scholars have argued that Hellenistic monarchs were not interested in a decision-making mechanism like the oracle. After all, they alone, and not a complex civic system of government, now called the shots. In fact we hear that rulers like Demetrius Poliorcetes (Demetrius "the Beseiger") in Athens, were themselves treated as oracles.[16] Yet the oracle continued to be useful to many Hellenistic city-states, particularly in providing them with a rich and varied historical record (as it did for Messenia), or in securing a grant of sacred protection (*asylia*) for their sanctuaries, or indeed in the process of founding new sanctuaries.[17] In one case, it also continued to be the bearer of bad tidings. The Locrians, who abandoned, after a thousand years, the tradition of sending to Troy human tribute (in the form of Locrian maidens) as a recompense for the rape of Cassandra by the lesser Ajax, were beset by disasters in the first part of the third century BC. They returned to the Pythia, who informed them that there was nothing to do but resume sending human tribute, and to continue this indefinitely.[18]

More importantly, across the Mediterranean to the west, there was another society whose leaders continued to engage with the oracle throughout the third century BC: that of Rome (see map 1). It is reported in the ancient sources that Rome's first consultation at Delphi dated back as far as its last king, Tarquinius Superbus; and we know that two centuries later, Rome consulted Delphi during the fourth century BC in regard to its military expansion into northern Italy; and that its victorious generals, like Camillus, even vowed dedications to Delphi during that time. In the late fourth and early third centuries BC Rome was back to consult Delphi during the course of the Samnite Wars, when it was told by the Pythia to put up statues of the bravest and wisest of the Greeks in the Roman forum. Delphi seems to have been involved also in the Roman efforts to bring the cult of Magna Mater to Rome, and Ovid reports that the Pythia was involved as well in the transfer of the cult of Asclepius to the city.[19]

In time, Rome would come not only to consult the oracle, but to "free" Delphi—and Greece—from its "oppressors," and eventually (not to mention ironically), to turn Greece into the Roman province of Achaea. But such a fate was far from the minds of Delphians at the beginning of the third century BC because a much closer power was in the process of taking over the sanctuary, the Aetolians, the same group to which Delphi had offered a collective grant of promanteia as part of their rebellious stance against Macedon in the 330s BC. The Aetolians were a *koinon*, a grouping of tribes in northern Greece. They were, like their Macedonian neighbors, something of an enigma to the southern Greeks, who would have had a hard time understanding their dialect and cultural priorities, and who would have considered them something of a backward federation. But, despite this reputation, and despite the fact that the Aetolians had had little to do with Delphi during the last thirty years of the fourth century BC (despite them being awarded promanteia by the Delphians), by 290 BC, they controlled the sanctuary to the extent that they could ban the ruler of Athens, Demetrius Poliorcetes, from attending the Pythian games (he set up his own in Athens instead).[20]

In the years immediately after 290 BC, that control only strengthened. An Aetolian governor was installed at Delphi along with a garrison of soldiers, and though Aetolia was never a member of the Amphictyony per se, it came to control enough of the members to ensure it could control the council. By 280 BC, Aetolian control over Delphi was strong enough to precipitate a war to free Delphi in the spirit of the four Sacred Wars already fought over the sanctuary during its history. The king of Sparta rallied a group of city-states to repel the Aetolians, claiming that the sacred land around Delphi, which should not be cultivated, had been occupied. The force perished miserably and, with it, the cultivation of sacred land as a cause for war. The Aetolians erected a victory offering in the Apollo sanctuary at Delphi in honor (ironically) of their victory. It was the Aetolians' first civic offering at Delphi.[21]

But the following year, in 279 BC, Greece faced a much bigger threat: an invasion of Gauls from the North. At first it seemed their advance was unstoppable. The Macedonian king was killed in battle, and the Gauls reached Thermopylae. Fighting their way past this narrow gateway into central Greece, they headed to Delphi. The Greek army was in tatters, and the only people who stood against them as they approached Delphi were a small contingent of combined Phocian, Amphissan, and Aetolian forces: at most a few thousand men.[22]

The ancient sources are quick to make this standoff over Delphi echo that of the Persian invasion and attack on Delphi two hundred years before. The Delphians, just as they did then, were said to have consulted the oracle on what to do, and, just as then, were told to leave everything as it was. As the Gauls began their attack, they were met, just as the Persians had been, with earthquakes, thunderbolts, and rockslides. Some of the same mythical heroes, like Phylacus, who defended the sanctuary against the Persians appeared again alongside the Aetolian forces, and were joined by a range of other heroic figures associated with the sanctuary including Neoptolemus. The priests of Apollo from the Delphic temple proclaimed joyfully that even Apollo, Athena, and Artemis had joined in the fray.[23]

Some of the ancient sources indicate that the Gaulish leader, Brennus, despite this divine onslaught, was still able to penetrate the Delphic defenses and enter the temple of Apollo itself. There, the ancient historian Diodorus Siculus claims, Brennus was unimpressed by all the wooden and stone images, contenting himself with carrying off gold—gold that was, as a result, it was later said, cursed and that brought misfortune and death to anyone who handled it.[24] Whether or not Brennus made it into the temple, by the end of the day of their attack, the Gauls had been beaten back, and that night, Delphi was covered in snow. Now in unfamiliar territory and difficult conditions, the Gauls made easy prey for local Phocian raids. Brennus was eventually wounded and the Gauls withdrew. Soon after, the Greek forces, including the main Aetolian army, were able to regroup and comprehensively defeat the Gauls in battle and repel the invasion for good.

Most of the ancient sources for this invasion are late, and none are from before the second century BC. But we can be more confident in the nature and importance of this victory thanks to the inscriptional evidence dating from soon after 279 BC. In spring 278, the island of Cos expressed votive thanks to the gods for saving Delphi, and in the following years, a number of decrees showered honors and rewards on individuals who had given information leading to the recovery of the sacred money belonging to Apollo, presumably that taken by the Gauls. Soon after, Gaulish shields were hung on the metopes of the temple of Apollo on the sides opposite where the Persian shields had been hung (and re-hung) by the Athenians.[25] The desired symmetry of the two victories against the Persians and the Gauls, separated as they were by almost exactly two hundred years, was complete.

The Phocians, in thanks for their role in saving Delphi, were given back their seats on the Amphictyonic council (which they had lost to Philip of Macedon after the Third Sacred War), and their ongoing fine to Delphi (which they had in all probability stopped paying many years before) was officially canceled. In response they seem to have dedicated a statue in the sanctuary. But the real winners were the Aetolians themselves. Their occupation of Delphi had never been sanctioned, indeed they had been attacked by the Greeks for it. However, now they were no longer Delphi's occupiers, but its saviors. This victory, this defense of Delphi, confirmed their right to occupy the sanctuary, and more importantly, confirmed them once and for all as defenders of Greece, and thus Greek. The Aetolians seem to have received their own seat on the Amphictyonic council and been recorded in the subsequent attendance records of the Amphictyonic meetings as second only to the presiding Thessalians.[26] But they also ensured their victory was represented among the growing monumental history book of Delphic dedications. Stretching out from the west side of the Apollo sanctuary is Delphi's biggest single structure bar the temple of Apollo, the West Stoa, occupying a 2,000 square meter terrace (see plate 2). Its origins are uncertain, and scholars have been unable to precisely date its construction. Yet, it is certain that in the years immediately after 279 BC, this structure became a focus for the commemoration of the Aetolian victory over the Gauls. On the back wall of the stoa was inscribed in large letters a dedication from the Aetolians offering to Apollo armor taken from the Gauls, which seems to have been displayed on long planks of wood attached to the stone back wall.[27]

The stoa, coupled with the hanging of Gaulish shields on the west and south faces of the temple Apollo, was not the end of Aetolian commemoration. A statue of the personification of Aetolia was erected at the west end of the Apollo temple. The female Aetolia sat triumphantly atop a carved set of Gaulish weapons and was accompanied by not only a further statue elsewhere on the temple terrace, but also, according to Pausanias, a monument with statues of all the Aetolian chiefs as well as a special monument dedicated to the general Eurydamus.[28]

How did the Delphians feel about this renewed (and now largely accepted, especially by the Amphictyony) imposition of Aetolian control over their sanctuary? On the one hand, of course, they and the sanctuary would benefit hugely from such a backer (and controller), especially in terms of investment in the sanctuary and its games. But the Delphians' record of offering proxenia during the course of the third century BC gives a hint of a different story. Four hundred people were awarded proxenia by the city of Delphi during that time, and only thirteen of those were Aetolian (six of which were awarded before the Aetolian victory against the Gauls in 279 BC). It could be argued that Aetolians didn't need grants of proxenia, such was their involvement with the sanctuary. But, on the other hand, it seems that the city of Delphi worked awfully hard to maintain its own relationships with a number of other parts of the Greek world at the same time.[29]

The 270s BC, as a result of the saving of Delphi from the Gauls, was a decade filled with renewed focus on Delphi as, once again, the symbol of Greece's freedom from invasion. It is not surprising that several previous dedicators to the sanctuary saw this as a fitting time in which to return and update their monuments. The Athenian statue base, originally dedicated after Marathon, and that ran along the southern flank of the Athenian treasury, was extended in the aftermath of this new victory to include new figures paying homage to Delphi's new rulers. The Chians returned to their great altar in front of the Apollo temple not only to repair it after almost two hundred and fifty years of use, but also to re-inscribe their rights to promanetia (see fig. 1.3). And at the end of the century, inscribed steles relating to their ambassadors to Delphi were also erected as close as possible to the altar. Alongside these individual revamps, the sanctuary seems to have undergone a series of rearticula-tions. To the south of the central open space just below the temple terrace (known as the *aire* and thought to be used for religious festivals), a series of previously dedicated monuments were repositioned along a newly cre-ated pathway, which in turn led to a new flight of steps leading directly to the aire performance space (see plate 2).[30] The greatest change, however, at Delphi, during these years was in its festival calendar. The saving of Delphi required a new festival celebration, and the Soteria (quite literally "the saving") was created in response. Performed annually in the autumn, this new festival mirrored the athletic and musical contests held during the Pythian games, in addition to competitions for tragedies and come-dies. Its creation also heralded the probable final completion of the new stadium at Delphi high above the temple, and ushered in a new era of popularity for Delphic games and festivals (see plate 1, figs. 0.1, 0.2).[31]

And yet, despite this outpouring of celebration, renovation, and in-novation at Delphi, it would have been impossible not to notice Delphi's more lackluster place in a changing wider Greek world during this pe-riod and over the next thirty years. Many scholars have noted that while the Aetolian dedications, both public and private individual offerings, continued to flow at Delphi, most of the Hellenistic kingdoms and their ruling monarchies were dedicating not at Delphi, but at Apollo's other well-known sanctuary on the island of Delos, the place of his birth, as well as at sanctuaries like those on Samos (see map 2). The Ptolemies of Egypt were absent from Delphi, so were the Seleucids, so too the kings of the Black Sea, as well as Pyrrhus, king of Epirus, despite his constant campaigns against the Romans. The Greek cities of the Western Medi-terranean—so long the dependable stalwart of Delphic dedications and oracular consultation—were also largely absent at this time.³² Walking around the sanctuary in the middle of the third century BC, it must have felt like Delphi had in some way slipped from being an international sanctuary to a regional one, and this was, to some extent, the reality. It was no longer a sanctuary whose independence was jealously guarded in peace treaties and fought over in sacred wars. It was now a sanctuary under the increasingly strong control of the Aetolians, which meant that dedicating great monuments at Delphi no longer served predominantly to glorify the dedicator as much as it glorified the owners of the sanctuary.³³ Coupled with the fact that this was now a world in which monarchical rule already had much less use for a conflict-resolving mechanism like the Delphic oracle and thus less reason to come to Delphi—as well as a world in which many of the traditional dedicators no longer had the money or reason to put up expensive votive offerings—a contraction in Delphi's appeal was, in reality, unavoidable.

But the story is not one of total decline. Several city-states continued to dedicate, particularly in order to celebrate their victories in the Pythian games or to honor particular Aetolians (e.g., Abydos, Clazomenai, Cnidus, Cyzicus, Elatea, Boeotia, Eretria, Megara, and Erythrai near Thermopylae), as well as particular associations like the Pylaioi (thought to be linked with the Amphictyony's other sanctuary of Demeter at Anthela). In the second quarter of the century, one king, Dropion of Paeonia, a region above Macedon in Thrace, was attracted to dedicate at Delphi first a statue of his grandfather and subsequently a statue portrait of the head of a bison.³⁴ In 260 BC the Aetolians celebrated their latest victory over the Archarnians with a new victory monument, representing victorious Aetolian generals alongside Apollo and Artemis.³⁵ Athens too had recovered from the banning of its ruler from competing in the Pythian games in 290 BC and was now in a much closer relationship with the sanctuary: not only had it updated its statue group monument to victory against Persia, which lay alongside its treasury (which also began in this period to be used as a notice board for recording Athenian victories in the Pythian games), but the Delphic Amphictyony had publicly granted ateleia (exemption from oracular consultation taxes) and asylia (religious

Plate 1. A watercolor reconstruction of the ancient city and sanctuaries of Delphi with main areas labeled (aquarelle de Jean-Claude Golvin. Musée départemental Arles antique © éditions Errance) 1 Parnassian mountains. 2 Stadium. 3 Apollo sanctuary. 4 City of Delphi. 5 Castalian fountain. 6 Gymnasium. 7 Athena sanctuary.

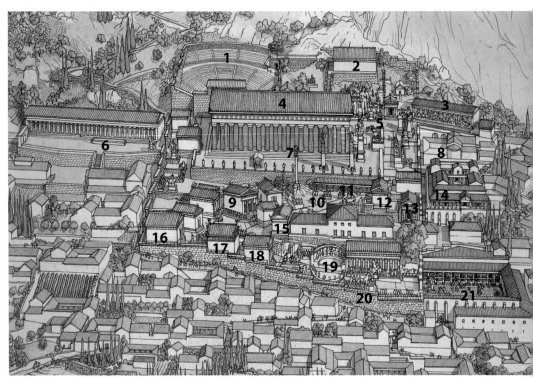

Plate 2. A watercolor reconstruction of the Apollo sanctuary at Delphi with main structures labeled (aquarelle de Jean-Claude Golvin. Musée départemental Arles antique © éditions Errance) 1 Theatre. 2 Cnidian lesche. 3 Stoa of Attalus. 4. Temple of Apollo. 5 Temple terrace. 6 West Stoa. 7 Naxian Sphinx. 8 Roman baths. 9 Athenian treasury. 10 Aire. 11 Athenian stoa. 12 Corinthian treasury. 13 Cyrenean treasury.14 Roman house. 15 Cnidian treasury. 16 Theban treasury. 17 Siphnian treasury. 18 Sicyonian treasury. 19 Argive statues. 20 Post-548 BC sanctuary boundary wall. 21 Roman agora.

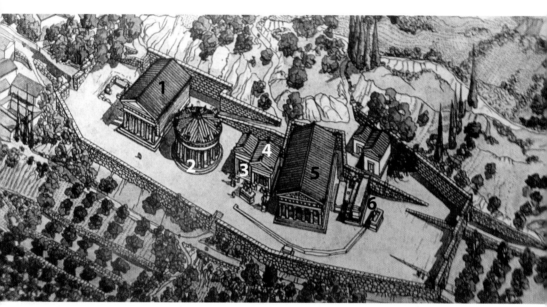

Plate 3. A watercolor reconstruction of the Athena sanctuary at Delphi with main structures labeled (aquarelle de Jean-Claude Golvin. Musée départemental Arles antique © éditions Errance) 1 Fourth century BC temple of Athena. 2 Tholos. 3 Treasury of Massalians. 4 Doric treasury. 5 Sixth century BC temple of Athena. 6 Altars.

Plate 4. The *Priestess at Delphi*
as painted by John Collier
1891 (© John Collier, Britain
1850–1934, Priestess of Delphi
1891, London oil on canvas,
160.0 x 80.0 cm, Gift of the
Rt. Honourable, the Earl of
Kintore 1893, Art Gallery of
Southern Australia, Adelaide).

Plate 5. The remains
of a Chryselephantine
(gold and ivory) statue
dedicated in the Apollo
sanctuary at Delphi, and
subsequently buried in
the sanctuary (Museum
at Delphi).

Plate 6. The Delphi Charioteer
(Museum at Delphi).

Plate 7. A view of Castri/Delphi painted by W. Walker in 1803 (© Benaki Museum).

Plate 8. The still very visible remains of a rockfall at Delphi in 1905
at the temple of Athena in the Athena sanctuary (© Michael Scott).

sanctuary) to the Dionysiac artists of Athens. In addition, the close connection between Athens and Delphi was symbolized by the synchronization of the worship of Apollo Patroos and Apollo Pythios in Athens during the course of the century, rendering Apollo Pythios the paternal god of the Athenians.[36] Rome also returned to dedicate during the First Punic War (when it was itself fighting the Gauls in northern Italy), with one of its generals, Claudius Marcellus, copying the act of his predecessor Camillus in the previous century and sending a golden mixing bowl to Delphi as a symbol of the plunder taken in the battle.[37]

Despite growing Aetolian control over the sanctuary (the Aetolians took over from the Thessalians as president of the Amphictyony in this period), and despite their developing military power, particularly in contrast to that of Macedon, the Aetolians seem to have been keen to avoid confrontation on the international stage. They avoided any conflict with Macedon, refused to take sides when Pyrrhus of Epirus turned his attentions from Rome to invade Macedon in 274 BC, and despite a possible alliance with Athens in the 260s, seem to have kept clear of a resurgent Macedon's attempts, following the defeat of Pyrrhus's invasion, to take control of Athens and much of central Greece during the 260s.[38] Yet from 262 BC, there was also a significant shift in Aetolian attitudes at Delphi toward a much more public degree of control over the sanctuary, a move not perhaps unwelcomed by the local Delphians who must have been excited by the prospect of some stability after so much change. In 243 BC, the Aetolians felt confident enough in their position to relaunch the Soteria festival not simply as an annual Delphian festival, but as their own festival dedicated to Zeus Soter. Scholars often refer to "Aetolian audacity" in this period, both at Delphi as they took over more and more of what had traditionally been Amphictyonic and Delphic business, and also on the international stage as Aetolia started to exercise greater dominance at sea and become more aggressive on land.[39]

In autumn 242 BC the first Aetolian Soteria festival was celebrated at Delphi in honor of Zeus Soter and Apollo. The Aetolians had proclaimed the festival *isoPythian*—equal to the Pythian games—and changed the timing of its celebration so that it coincided with the Pythian games to produce, in effect, one large and long festival. In the years preceding this new celebration, the sanctuary at Delphi seems to have been spruced up considerably. More work was done to the stadium, and inscriptions record that twenty-three contractors undertook to complete about forty different projects around the Delphic complex, from clearing plant growth around the gymnasium and stadium to plowing and leveling the competition surfaces and fixing wooden seating apparatus.[40] The Aetolians also seem to have asked other cities in the Greek world to recognize their new festival. We have surviving inscribed records of affirmative replies from five cities including (perhaps predictably) Athens and Chios, but also Tenos, another Cycladic city, and Smyrna. Chios was so keen on the idea that their inscription also records that they immediately picked three individuals to be sent to represent them at the celebrations (and no doubt to admire their still new-looking altar).[41]

In response to this new phase of Aetolian domination at Delphi, individual Aetolians seem to have been encouraged to dedicate increasingly ornate and immense dedications in the sanctuary. In fact, they began an entirely new artistic and architectural style for individual dedications at Delphi. The Aetolian Aristaineta was the first to erect a statue resting on a piece of architrave that was supported by two columns, a style that would prove to be *the* Aetolian monument style of choice. It was soon followed by a statue of the Aetolian general Charixenus in a similar fashion atop two columns.[42] The power of the Aetolians over the sanctuary in this period is indicated by the fact that a number of these dedications from individuals (in particular those of Aristaineta and Charixenus) began to encroach on what had hitherto, throughout Delphi's history, been the open, almost reserved, space around the Chian altar in front of the temple. But individual Aetolians also chose to honor other rulers of the Hellenistic world (even though they had ignored Delphi). Lamius the Aetolian, for example, erected a long line of statues to the Egyptian royal family (the Ptolemies).[43]

The sanctuary was not, however, playing host only to Aetolians in the second half of the third century BC. Cities in Western Locris also dedicated (even if one of their dedications was a statue in honor of an

Aetolian), as well as cities in Boeotia and Epirus. Yet by far the most striking dedication in this period—not only in its form, size, and extravagance, but also in the identity of its dedicator—was the stoa of Attalus (see plate 2, fig. 1.3). King Attalus I of Pergamon in Asia Minor was the first of the Attalid dynasty, which was in turn the only Hellenistic dynasty to pay close attention to Delphi at this time. Erected between 241–26 BC, this stoa summed up the way in which Delphi was now more at the mercy of the rulers of the Greek world than it had ever been. It broke through the eastern boundary wall of the Apollo sanctuary on the level of the temple terrace, something not done by any dedication (apart from the monumental west stoa) since the walls had been constructed in the second half of the sixth century BC; and, in fact, this was something that would never be done again. The stoa was accompanied by its own terracing wall to ensure a large courtyard space outside it, and completed with a monumental offering just in front of the stoa, as well as a statue base in the courtyard terrace.[44]

The Amphictyony were clearly keen to keep the Attalids on their side. In 223–22 BC they issued a law, inscribed in the sanctuary, that no other dedications were to be put within the Attalid stoa complex except those from the Attalids themselves.[45] Why was Attalus, and the Attalids, so keen to dedicate at Delphi when the other Hellenistic ruling families had snubbed it? Partly it was to do with cultural identity. The Attalids modeled themselves on Athenian artistic and architectural supremacy. They built in Athens and copied Athens in Pergamon, so it was only natural that they should dedicate where once Athens had been so dominant. Yet it was also to do with current politics. Attalus was an ally of the Aetolians, and would be fighting his own war against the Gauls in the period 238–27 BC, a war that eventually brought him mastership of much of Asia Minor. As a result it was natural for Attalus to turn to Delphi, place of his allies' victory against the Gauls (and its celebration), and in particular to create a monument that demonstrated his newfound power (by breaking through the boundary wall), and mirrored the west stoa that was (or had been turned into) the Aetolians' own monument to victory over the Gauls after 279 BC.[46]

In 239 BC, Antigonus II, king of Macedon, died at the age of eighty. He had been a fearsome warrior, and the Aetolians had shied away from open conflict with Macedon despite their growing power and authority during his lifetime. But with his death, there was a rush to capitalize on a vulnerable Macedonian kingdom, particularly by the Aetolians. In the period 239–229, the so-called war of Demetrius eventually ended with a marked increase in Aetolian power, including the usurpation of Thessaly (traditionally an ally of Macedon) to Aetolian control. As a consequence, the year 226 BC marked the apogee of Aetolian dominance at Delphi and in mainland Greece. Aetolia had fifteen representatives on the Amphictyonic council that year, and even the Delphians set up a statue in their sanctuary to one of the Aetolian generals. The Aetolians, it seems, through the Amphictyony, also saw fit to extend the protection enjoyed by Delphi to other sanctuaries. Surviving Amphictyonic decrees attest to the granting of asylia to the sanctuary of Dionysus at Thebes, to the festivals and sanctuary of Apollo Ptoios (the same sanctuary that had, in the mid-sixth century BC, operated as a replacement for Delphi while its temple renovation was under way), and to another sanctuary in Boeotia.[47]

The other outcome of the war was that the city of Athens regained its independence, which had been lost to Antigonus II in 268 BC. As a result, the 220s saw a renewed closeness between Athens and Delphi. There was a steady stream of proxeny decrees between Delphians and Athenians, indicating regular Athenian consultations with the oracle and interactions with the sanctuary. More interestingly, the Athenians seem to have returned to the sanctuary once again to update a previous dedication. This time their focus was on the statues of Eponymous and Marathon heroes that had been erected at the southeastern entrance to the sanctuary in 460 BC, where they had been spatially opposed, at the end of the Peloponnesian War, by Spartan monuments (see plate 2, fig. 6.2). The Athenians extended this now centuries-old dedication to include statues of the new tribes it had established in Athens in honor of its own recent rulers and those of the Hellenistic monarchies whom it was impossible to ignore.[48] Once again, a Delphic dedication had been rearticulated to keep pace with current events.

Yet Aetolian dominance was to be short-lived. In 221 BC a more effective king, Philip V, came to the throne in Macedon, and just a year later, the Aetolians found themselves at the receiving end of a new campaign to "free" Delphi, the likes of which had not been seen since 280 BC. The campaign—the War of the Allies—did not change Delphi's status, which remained resolutely under Aetolian control, but now much nearer the Aetolian front line than it had been. A warning bell had been sound, and Delphi was once again much more open to outside influence and interest, symbolized by the fact that Sicyon, a member of the Achaean league (an alliance resembling the Aetolian league but mainly centered in the Peloponnese), which had fought against Aetolia during the war, was able to consult the Delphic oracle in 213 BC on how to bury the recently deceased Achaean general Aratus, and to which Delphi not only replied but proclaimed him a hero. Likewise, it is a sign of how much Delphi had been reopened to the wider world that in 211 BC, the city agreed to act as a proxenos for visitors from Sardis in Asia Minor wishing to consult the oracle (rather than the normal practice in which it was the responsibility of an individual Delphian who was known to those wishing to consult the oracle to act as proxenos) because, as the inscription records "the men of Sardis have not been able to come to the oracle for a long time."[49]

Yet just as this War of the Allies came to an end, a player critical in the future history of Delphi and Greece appeared back on the scene: Rome. Rome was once again engaged in conflict with Carthage in the Second Punic War (218–201 BC), during which it sent numerous questions to the Pythian oracle. Quintus Fabius Pictor, for example, was sent to consult Delphi on the proper ritual by which to secure victory in 216 BC. Delphi duly responded with a traditionally mysterious set of instructions, added to which was a request that they return and thank Apollo (in the form of a costly dedication) when the situation improved. In 207 BC, after a resounding victory over the Carthaginians, the Romans returned to Delphi with gifts and were greeted by another oracle who indicated they could soon expect an even greater victory.[50]

Yet Roman interest was not only in the West. Increasingly, Rome was also being drawn into affairs in the eastern Mediterranean. In fact, its consultations at Delphi during the Second Punic War marked the last official civic consultation of the Delphic oracle by the Romans, presumably because it made no sense to consult an oracle belonging to what was increasingly becoming an enemy to be conquered.[51] The process by which Rome came to see Greece as its enemy, however, was a complicated one. Philip V of Macedon, buoyed by his recent successes against the Aetolians, formulated a plan for much greater Mediterranean domination which led him to make an alliance with Carthage, which was still in bitter conflict with Rome. As a result, the kingdom of Macedon was now an enemy of Rome, and Aetolia, in its weakened state, saw an opportunity to bolster its position. In September 212 BC, Aetolia concluded an alliance with Rome against Philip V of Macedon (unsurprisingly, Attalus of Pergamon also joined), in what became known as the First Macedonian War. Yet, more surprisingly, the combined forces of Aetolia and Rome did not swiftly bring an end to Philip's plans. In fact, the Aetolians were so worried about their ability to hold on to their "capital"—Delphi—that troops from as far away as Messenia in the Peloponnese (another Aetolian ally) had to be sent twice in 207–206 BC to Delphi for its protection.[52]

In the final analysis, it was actually fear of losing Delphi that pushed the Aetolians to desert their Roman allies and sue for peace directly with Philip in 206 BC, for which they were forced to give up large areas of territory. At Delphi, it was once again time for a delicate and diplomatic game of ensuring good relations with all the major players as an uncertain future lay ahead. The surviving inscriptions reveal the city of Delphi returning to its game of giving honors to both Aetolia and her enemies, but also indicate that the city increasingly had to take over what had been Amphictyonic and therefore Aetolian responsibilities as Aetolian control and interest in the sanctuary slackened in the face of an increasingly stiff fight for its own survival.[53] By this time, Delphi had been under the Aetolian thumb for almost a century, the longest period in its history without independence. But freedom was, once again, just around the corner.

PART III

*Some have greatness
thrust upon them*

"Lector, si monumentum requiris, circumspice."

"Reader, if you are looking for something monumental, look around you."

—Epitaph for the Delphic scholar Pierre de la Coste Messelière (1894–1975), which is on display at the French dig house at Delphi. The same wording was famously first used by Sir Christopher Wren in (his) St. Paul's Cathedral, London (1723).

9
A NEW WORLD

At the dawn of the second century BC, the Delphians found themselves in a curious limbo. On the one hand, their sanctuary was overwhelmingly still under the thumb of the Aetolians, who interfered in Delphic civic life, dominated many aspects of the sanctuary and its business, and even appointed informal "overseers" (*epimeletai*) to keep an eye on things in the city. The Delphians were at pains to honor the overseers (who seem to have been given rights even to keep herds of cattle on Delphic public land) on a regular basis.[1] At the same time, visitors to parts of the Delphic complex—particularly the Corycian cave in the Parnassian mountains above—were beginning to decline. And even the oracle, according to Parke and Wormell, can be shown to have had only one genuine consultation in the entire second century BC, despite the fact that the Delphians during that time, in a single inscription, granted proxenia to the citizens of 135 different cities in the ancient world.[2]

And yet, on the other hand, the territory this small city controlled was larger than that of a number of central Greek cities. The surviving lists of those whose gave hospitality around the Greek world to the *theoroi*—the messengers sent out from Delphi to announce its athletic and musical games—grow longer than ever in the second century BC, testifying to the importance and popularity of Delphi's contests. In 200 BC, one of the winners, Satyrus of Samos—victor as an *auletes* (flute player)—was apparently so delighted with his win that he immediately played two impromptu concerts in the stadium at Delphi as a gesture to the gods and spectators. At the same time, far away at the Greek settlement of Ai Khanoum in modern-day Afghanistan, a man named Clearchus was in the process of erecting a monument telling of his journey all the way to Delphi and back. The monument spelled out the purpose of his journey: to copy with his own hand the words of the Seven Sages inscribed on the temple of Apollo, so that his fellow citizens could benefit from their public display at home. As well, the Amphictyony had recently given the go-ahead to a near four-meter-high bronze statue of the people of Antiocheia, as well as to a statue of similar height for Antiochus III (to complement another statue of this king atop a horse already dedicated in the sanctuary), both of which were placed in a prime position to the west of the temple of Apollo.[3] As the century began, then, Delphi was not independent but increasingly cosmopolitan, in decline and yet never more popular.

But all this was about to change. In 200 BC, as Delphi became less and less subtle in its call to be freed from its Aetolian "oppressors," Rome was once again drawn into Greek affairs. King Philip V of Macedon, this time seeking to expand his territory by annexing parts of the Greek world belonging to the Ptolemaic (Egyptian) ruling family, had set his sights on the island of Rhodes, as well as on the city of Pergamon (see map 1). Pergamon was the seat of Attalus I, friend of Rome, Aetolia, and Delphi. Initially reluctant to fight Philip again, having just emerged from the Second Punic War against Carthage, Rome at first counseled peace to Philip. But soon enough, particularly after Philip had also set his sights on taking Athens, in October 200 BC, Rome went to war again against Philip V of Macedon.

The resulting victories of Rome were based on the slogan "liberty for the Greeks." Macedon was forced to withdraw back into its own kingdom. In May 196 BC, at the Isthmian games, the herald proclaimed that the Roman Senate and consul Titus Quinctius Flamininus, had defeated

Philip V, leaving "free without garrisons, without tribute, governed by their ancestral laws, the Corinthians, Phocians, Locrians, Euboeans, Achaeans, Magnesians, Thessalians, and Perrhebians." Flamininus celebrated the victory, or rather liberation, at Delphi. He sent his own shield along with shields of silver and a crown of gold, decorated with a series of poetic inscriptions, as dedications to Apollo. The Delphians in return later put up a statue of the general in the Apollo sanctuary.[4] Yet, almost as soon as the Romans had liberated Greece, they were gone. Despite staying in contact with the city of Delphi (as witnessed by a series of proxeny decrees for Romans inscribed in the sanctuary), by 194 BC, there was not a single Roman solider left in Greece.[5]

What brought them back was their one-time ally, the fading Aetolian league who were still—barely—masters of Delphi. In 193 BC, just a year after the Romans had left Greece, the Aetolians rallied their allies, including king Antiochus of the Seleucid empire in the East (the same king who had recently been honored by the Amphictyony with an enormous statue of himself in the sanctuary). In October 192, Antiochus landed in mainland Greece with ten thousand men, five hundred cavalry, and six elephants. The king came to Delphi to offer sacrifice, and, in the spirit of the place which had, twice before, been the scene for defeats of forces invading Greece (the Persians and the Gauls), Antiochus proclaimed himself champion of Greek freedom against Roman domination (despite the fact that the Romans had proclaimed the freedom of Greece just four years earlier and subsequently left).[6]

This declaration of war against Rome was a threat the Romans could no longer tolerate. Landing in Greece almost immediately after Antiochus's sacrifice at Delphi, the Roman forces, under the control of Manius Acilius Glabrio, dislodged those of Antiochus and the Aetolian league from the their stronghold at the infamous pass at Thermopylae, the "bottle-neck" of Greece. It is testament to the fast-changing nature of alliances in this period that Philip V of Macedon, defeated by the Romans in 197 BC, now fought, just six years later in 191, with the Romans against Antiochus. Equally so is the fact that Philip also fought alongside Eumenes II of Pergamon, who had become king on the death of his father Attalus I in 197 (Philip had tried to conquer Pergamon less than a decade before, nearly capturing Eumenes' father several times in the process). Within months of the onslaught from this Roman, Macedonian, and Pergamene force, the Aetolians sued for peace. Antiochus remained to be dealt with.[7]

To the Delphians, having seen Antiochus's proud arrival followed in such a short space of time by news of Glabrio's victory, the world must have seemed a very uncertain place. But they did know for sure now where their allegiances needed to be.[8] Between September 191 BC and March 190, Glabrio not only seems to have turned over a series of confiscated Aetolian properties in the vicinity of Delphi to the "city and the god," and made a series of changes to the boundaries of Delphi's sacred land, but also wrote a letter to the Delphians, saying he would support in Rome the sanctuary's return to its ancestral ways of governance and the autonomy of the city and sanctuary.[9] In response, the city of Delphi not only welcomed their "liberation" by the Romans, but engraved Glabrio's letter on the base of the statue they set up in his honor, along with a list of all the people—mostly Aetolians—they promptly chucked out of the city.[10]

Glabrio's initiatives probably engendered some regional hostility—particularly his changing of land boundaries, which brought Delphi into conflict with its long-term local rival, the city of Amphissa (see map 3). His offer to the Delphians may well also have begun (or indeed been responding to) a tussle for power at Delphi between the city (which some sources intimate attempted to push Glabrio to give them sole control of the sanctuary and shut out the Amphictyony entirely) and the Amphictyony, who wanted Glabrio and the Roman Senate to restore the traditional Amphictyony/city divided system of control over the sanctuary.[11] But, for the moment, Glabrio had a more important enemy to deal with: Antiochus III. In 189 BC, Antiochus was finally defeated by a combined Macedonian, Pergamene, and Roman force at the battle of Magnesia, with Eumenes II of Pergamon personally leading the cavalry charge that was crucial in bringing victory.[12]

In 189 BC, just as Antiochus was defeated, Delphi sent three ambassadors to Rome to confirm Glabrio's offer of the city and sanctuary's independence. Spurius Postumius Albinus wrote in response to Delphi to confirm the Roman Senate's official decision to uphold Glabrio's offer. As a result, Delphi's Amphictyonic council was reformed so that, for the first time in its history, the Delphian representatives now chaired its meetings.[13] But on their way home, the Delphian ambassadors were murdered by Aetolians. Later that same year, Delphi sent two more ambassadors to Rome, this time to announce the creation of a new Delphic festival, the Romaia, in honor of Rome, and also to bring to Roman attention the murder of the previous ambassadors and point the finger at those responsible. The Senate commanded M. Fulvius Nobilior to search for the culprits, and G. Livius Salinator wrote to Delphi to confirm the Senate's acceptance of the new festival in Rome's honor, the text of which was inscribed publicly at Delphi on the base of Glabrio's statue, which was fast becoming the central notice board in the sanctuary for the developing relationship between Rome and Delphi.[14]

In 189 BC, therefore, Delphi was once again in a very different sort of limbo from that in which it had found itself at the beginning of the century. On the one hand, it had a degree of liberty—guaranteed by the Roman Senate—it hadn't had since the Aetolians had taken control of the sanctuary in the early third century BC, and indeed perhaps a degree of liberty it hadn't had in its entire history. On the other hand, it was still a small city without an army; it was in only partial control, with the Amphictyony, of the sanctuary. Its civic ambassadors had been murdered by Aetolians, it was surrounded by Aetolian communities or those in sympathy with Aetolia; and its livelihood—the sanctuary— was still to some degree dependent on Aetolian business. That position became even more precarious when the Romans, having again asserted their interests in Greece, decided again to leave. In 188 BC, they withdrew, leaving behind no troops, veterans, garrisons, governors, political overseers, or indeed even any diplomats. Delphi—whatever the Roman Senate had promised and Delphi had inscribed on its walls—was once again on its own.[15]

Delphi did have one clear ally, Eumenes II of Pergamon. Like his father before him, and unlike other Hellenistic rulers, Eumenes II happily pumped money into the sanctuary. In the 180s BC he sent slaves to help with the construction of Delphi's theater, another testament to the continuing popularity of the sanctuary's musical competitions at this time in that Delphi now had need of a dedicated stone-built structure in which to house the competitions and spectators.[16] In response, the Amphictyony were happy to recognize the status of asylia for the sanctuary of Athena Nikephoros in Pergamon and the Nikephoria games set up by Eumenes. In addition, Eumenes II was honored with statues in the sanctuary, one by the Amphictyony and one by the Aetolians, testament to their lingering presence at Delphi, especially since the statues were placed center stage on the temple terrace of the Apollo sanctuary.[17]

We hear little about Delphi in the remaining years of the 180s and early 170s BC. On receipt of a gift of 3,520 drachmas from the Calydonian Alcesippus the sanctuary was happy to establish a festival celebration called the Alcesippeia.[18] The Rhodians were called in to arbitrate on a question of land border dispute between Delphi and Amphissa in 180–79 BC.[19] Aetolian use of the sanctuary seems to have petered out after 179 BC, and, in 178 BC, the Amphictyony unusually called itself, in the inscribed list of delegates for that year's meeting, "a union of the Amphictyons from the autonomous tribes and the democratic cities"; this was thought to be not only a celebration of Delphi's newfound independence, but also a dig at the Amphictyons' former enemies, particularly the Aetolians and Macedonians.[20] A question to the oracle about an issue of colonization by the island of Paros in 175 BC represents a distant echo of Delphi's almost continuous role in these processes back in the seventh and sixth centuries BC. Also in 175 BC the father of the Delphian Eudocus erected a statue of Eudocus in the sanctuary, in honor of the latter's athletic victories.[21]

Yet, at the same time, pressure was again building in the wider Greek world that would change Greece's, and Delphi's, future for good. In 179 BC, Philip V of Macedon, having waged war against and then alongside the Romans, died. He had been slowly and successfully rebuilding Macedonian power within the constraints of burgeoning Roman influence. Yet in his last moments, he seems to have attempted to stop his son from succeeding him. Perhaps it was for fear of what his son, Perseus, would attempt once on the throne.[22]

Taking control despite Philip's final efforts, King Perseus of Macedon initially walked a careful diplomatic line, pacifying Rome and flattering Greece. Delphi too was flattered, as one of the sanctuaries chosen as the place of publication for Perseus's call for the return of all exiles to Macedonia, and for his treaty of friendship with the Boeotians.[23] Yet in 174 BC, Perseus crushed a tribal rebellion against him in Macedonia and subsequently set off on a leisurely tour with his army through central Greece, which brought him to Delphi. His arrival was timed to coincide with the celebration of the Pythian games, Perseus grandly sweeping in to sacrifice at the sanctuary as part of the festival.[24] Perseus continued to use Delphi as a place for acts of public propaganda. He consulted the oracle in what was to become (although he could not know it at the time) the last ever consultation by an independent monarch of the oracle at Delphi.[25] Yet Perseus also used Delphi as the location for his more cutthroat activities, including the attempted murder of his enemy, and longtime Delphic supporter, King Eumenes II of Pergamon, who had, in 172 BC, traveled to the Roman Senate to warn them of the threat Perseus posed to Roman interests. With the help of Praxo, the wife of an eminent Delphian who later became a priest of Apollo, Perseus set up an ambush on the road leading from the port of Cirrha up to Delphi. Eumenes' party was slain and Eumenes himself left for dead.[26]

By 171 BC, Rome had awakened to the threat Perseus posed to Roman interests in Greece. Delphi, in part because it had been a focus for Perseus's propaganda, in turn acted as a primary focus for the Roman articulation of Perseus's wrongdoings. In particular, the Romans focused on Perseus's armed participation at the Pythian festival in 174 BC at a sanctuary whose independence was, at the end of the day, guaranteed by the Roman Senate. In addition, they focused on his attempted murder at Delphi of Eumenes II, a friend of Rome, as well as his wider alliances with the same barbarians who had invaded Greece and sacked the temple of Apollo at Delphi just over a century before. These grievances were inscribed and publicly displayed in the sanctuary at Delphi.[27]

In the years that followed, Roman troops flooded back, this time under the command of Lucius Aemilius Paullus, to fight in what has become known as the Third Macedonian War.[28] On 22 June 168 BC, Paullus crushed Perseus at the battle of Pydna, a victory that was commemorated most pointedly at Delphi. Perseus had been in the process of building himself another ten-meter-high statue at Delphi, intended as a victory monument in which a golden statue of him on horseback would stand atop a marble column, and be located on the temple terrace. It was unfinished when his hopes were crushed at Pydna. In a brilliant piece of propaganda, Aemilius Paullus chose to complete the monument, putting a statue of himself on horseback in place of that of Perseus, and adding a sculptured frieze around the base depicting his victory at Pydna (figs. 9.1, 1.3). In addition he erased the Greek inscription already carved in anticipation of Perseus's victory and replaced it with his name, titles, and a short but pointed explanation in Latin: "de rege Perse Macedonibusque cepet" ("[that which] he took from King Perseus and from the Macedonians").[29] Apollo is absent from Paullus's declaration: this monument is not about thanking the gods for victory, it is about making a political statement of that victory in the most public and forceful way possible. This new monument stood on the temple terrace of the Apollo sanctuary at Delphi in the area where the major monuments to Greek victory over foreign invading enemies had stood for centuries (see fig. 1.3). Yet this time it was a Roman general commemorating his victory over a Greek force, and in so doing preserving what Rome had guaranteed: Delphian independence and Greek "freedom."

Yet the victory at Pydna also marks a critical moment in the nature of the freedom that Rome offered Greece. Rome abolished the Macedonian monarchy, replacing it with a series of republics. More widely, 168 BC represents the tipping point for Greece (and the rest of the Mediterranean) in what political scientists call "unipolarity": the arrival of Rome as the only political and military force in the Mediterranean. Rome had emerged victorious from the wars at the end of the third and beginning of the second centuries BC against Carthage, Macedon, and the Seleucid Empire. In previous Greek conflicts, it had subsequently completely withdrawn. But after 168 BC, there was to be no withdrawal. Greece's "multipolar anarchy" of the Hellenistic world was replaced by Roman unipolarity, which would be imposed on the country in an ever increasingly forceful manner.[30] Delphi had not only, once again, been an important factor in the events that had brought Greece ever more closely under Roman control, it had also been the place in which to make that transition clear through the dedication of the remarkable victory monument of Aemilius Paullus. But to what extent would and could Delphi's freedom continue in this new phase of Roman unipolar dominance?

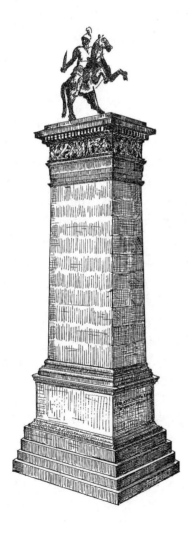

Figure 9.1. A reconstruction of the column, frieze, and statue erected by Aemilius Paullus following his victory over King Perseus of Macedon at the battle of Pydna (© Dietrich Reimer-Verlag [Front Cover image, H. Kähler *Der Fries vom Reiterdenkmal des Aemilius Paullus in Delphi*]

The great survivors of this sea change in Greece's history were old friends of Delphi: the Attalid ruling family of Pergamon and particularly its current ruler Eumenes II. He had fought with Rome against Antiochus of Syria, informed against Perseus of Macedon to the Roman Senate (in part following Roman suspicions of him being a Perseus supporter), been left for dead after being ambushed on the road to Delphi by Perseus's operatives, and now lived to see the downfall of Macedon and the rise of Roman power.[31] In 159 BC, Eumenes II finally passed away and was succeeded by his brother Attalus II. At Delphi in that year, celebrations were held in honor of Eumenes II and Attalus II on the back of a huge financial donation to the sanctuary by the Attalid rulers themselves. New festival celebrations and sacrifices, the Eumeneia and the Attaleia, were initiated at Delphi on a huge scale. Fifteen hundred liters of wine were prepared for the festival banquet, and financial sanctions imposed on those who failed to carry out their appointed roles in the celebration.[32] The Delphians went further and erected a statue of the new Attalid ruler in the sanctuary right by the sacred processional area in front of the Athenian stoa in the Apollo sanctuary (see plate 2). Attalus II was clearly in awe of the variety and standard of artistic accomplishment at Delphi. He sent painters to Delphi to make copies of its many monuments, and especially the paintings by Polygnotus from the fifth century BC Cnidian lesche building. Delphi, in return, not only accommodated Attalus's artistic mission, but honored his artists in inscriptions engraved onto the monument of Eumenes II erected in his honor earlier in the century.[33]

The Amphictyony did not, however, fare quite so well following Roman victory at Pydna. The French epigraphist Georges Daux argues that there are only two certain instances of Amphictyonic action in the entire period 166–46 BC, that of their participation in the arbitration of a dispute over the city of Lamia between Sparta and the Dorians of the Metropolis (an Amphictyonic tribal grouping); and that of their honoring of an Athenian. This lull is perhaps to be associated with a further rearrangement of the Amphictyonic council conducted around 165 BC to reflect the altered political map of Greece following Roman victory.[34]

Yet the Amphictyony and the city of Delphi survived much more successfully than other parts of Greece. In the early 140s, Roman forces were back in action at Pydna, this time to dispatch a pretender to the Macedonian throne. Two years later, in 146 BC, in the same year in which the Romans won their historic victory over Carthage and destroyed that city, a league of Peloponnesian cities, known as the Achaean league, which had been on good terms with Rome, turned against Rome. The Roman general Lucius Mummius, with approximately 23,000 men including forces from Crete and Pergamon, marched on the league in what has become known as the Achaean War. At the end of 146 BC, Mummius defeated the league in the battle of Corinth and in punishment plundered and burned the city of Corinth to the ground. Every Greek city that had been part of the league was put under direct Roman control.[35]

The destruction of Corinth in 146 BC marked another turning point in Rome's relationship to Greece and, along with the destruction of Carthage in the same year, a new phase in Roman domination of the Mediterranean. Mummius celebrated his victory in part by sending dedications to Delphi: ironically the sanctuary was increasingly becoming the location for the commemoration of Roman victories over Greece. But as a result, perversely, Delphian interaction with the wider Greek and Mediterranean worlds seems to have shrunk. The surviving accounts of proxeny decrees—honors offered by the city of Delphi to individuals from elsewhere—show that in the first half of the second century BC, Delphi was welcoming and forming relationships with people from all over the Greek world. But from 146 BC onward, that circle shrinks considerably, to almost only its immediate neighbors and mainland Greece (although Delphi continues to honor Romans—almost a prerequisite given the increasing Roman control of Greece), with an almost total absence of the Aegean islands, Asia Minor, and Africa.[36]

The one benefit of this closer-to-home focus after 146 BC seems to have been the renewed presence of Athens at Delphi. An inscription on the wall of the Athenian treasury at Delphi records Athenian involvement in 140 BC as arbitrators in a local dispute over the extent of

Delphian territory. In 138 BC Athens revived the Athenian Pythaïs festival, which had not occurred since the late fourth century BC and was intended to celebrate Apollo's arrival at Delphi thought to be via the Athenian territory of Attica. The heart of the festival was a procession along the sacred road from Athens and Delphi and a return to Athens bringing fire from the sacred hearth of the Apollo temple. The festival was intended to stress the close historical, religious, and geographical links between Athens and Delphi; and its renewal, at a time in which both, given recent Roman actions toward other Greek cities, felt the need for mutual support and comfort, is particularly understandable. The Pythaïs, which had been an irregular event undertaken only in relation to particular divine signs (like lightning) was now turned into a regular festival, celebrated every eight years, with the event recorded each time in inscriptions on the walls of the Athenian treasury, which tell us not only that there had been many oracles in the past prescribing the festival, but also that some three hundred to five hundred people were involved in the sacred procession. It was also on the occasion either of the first Pythaïs in 138 BC, or a decade later in 128 BC, that the Athenians composed and then inscribed on the highly visible southern wall of their treasury at Delphi not only the words but also the musical notations for two hymns to Apollo (see plate 2, fig. 5.4). These hymns, which have been fundamental to the study of ancient music, and were discovered early on in the initial excavation of the sanctuary at the end of the nineteenth century, record the celebration of Apollo through sacrifice, song, and prayer.[37]

Yet this (re)blossoming of the relationship between Athens and Delphi did not stop here. In 134 BC, the Amphictyony, having received five ambassadors from Athens, appear to have confirmed the privileges accorded to the Dionysiac guild members of Athens back in the third century BC. On the treasury of Athens in Delphi, as well as in the theater of Dionysus in Athens, the record of both the original honors and their restatement over a century later were inscribed and published. Crucially, though, the Amphictyony highlights in the inscription that their confirmation of such privileges is contingent on Roman approval (a smart and perhaps necessary move in the wake of increasing Roman control after the destruction of Corinth in 146 BC).[38] These privileges were later augmented, after the actors' star performance at the Pythaïs of 128 BC, with a series of further rights in 125 BC, and would be restated again after the Roman Senate had also commented on Athenian prowess in 112 BC.[39] Indeed, the language used in these inscriptions is not only testament to the strength of relationship between Delphi and Athens, but also, more widely, to Athens's increasing reputation as a cultural powerhouse. In its public inscription of 125 BC, the Amphictyony honored the "people of Athens, who are at the origin of everything that is good in humanity, and who brought mankind up from a bestial existence to a state of civilisation."[40]

At the very same time, however, as the city of Delphi and the Amphictyony were honoring Athens in such fulsome terms, Delphi itself was embroiled in scandal. Traditionally dated to 125 BC, but perhaps occurring as late as 117 BC, the Amphictyony were called to an emergency session, the only one in their history for which the inscribed list of attendees named both the official representatives, the *hieromnemons*, and their advisors, the *pylagores*. In the aftermath of the event, the entire dossier of documents relating to the affair was inscribed on the side of the temple of Apollo, and it tells a story not only of conflict at Delphi, but of continuing Roman interest in the sanctuary.[41] It appears that a group of Delphians linked to the son of Diodorus had usurped a series of objects belonging to Apollo for their own purposes, breaking one of the fundamental tenets of the sanctuary and of Greek religious belief (and for which in the past the punishment had been death). Thirteen Delphians in return, led by Nicatas, son of Alcinus, reported on their actions in the first instance to the Amphictyony, but, fearing for their lives while the slow wheels of Amphictyonic bureaucracy turned, fled from Delphi to Rome. There, they appeared before the Roman Senate pleading for its support. The Senate decided to take up the case and, through the Roman proconsul of Macedonia, put pressure on the Amphictyony to deal speedily and properly with the situation, thus precipitating the Amphictyony's emergency session. Following their investigation, serious mistakes were found in the sacred accounts thanks to objects wrongly appropriated and the need to redefine the boundaries of Apollo's sacred land.[42] Elite Delphians were charged with taking sacred treasures, and were forced to make good the god's financial loss.[43] The total fines imposed came to fifty-three talents and fifty-three mines. Yet at the same time as this scandal appears to show equally Delphian misbehavior, Amphictyonic action, and Roman willingness to engage in the minutiae of Delphic management, it perhaps also indicates a certain reluctance on the part of the Amphictyony to acquiesce beyond the necessary to the will of Rome. The engraving of an inscription recording praise from the Amphictyony for the thirteen brave Delphian whistle blowers was actually left unfinished, and, despite the large fine supposedly imposed, those responsible for the sacred theft seem to have suffered little more than a rap on the knuckles: some of them appear as priests of Apollo in the sanctuary a few years later.[44]

One of the downsides of the Roman defeat and subsequent carving up of Macedon during the course of the second century BC was that mainland Greece was left without a well armed and coordinated buffer zone between it and the "barbarian" tribes to the north. As a result, raids by northern tribes became more frequent during the second half of the century and into the first twenty years of the first century BC.[45] Delphi—as it had been in the past—was an obvious target, given its large collections of precious dedications and minimal armed protection. In 107 BC, the Delphians honored M. Minucius Rufus for protecting Greece against barbarian raids. The threat, and resultant gratitude, was obviously very real. The Delphians offered one statue with a Greek inscription and another with a Latin inscription, the only known occurrence of such bilingual honors in Delphic history.[46] Surviving texts from Delphi also attest to Roman concern for safe passage around the wider Mediterranean at this time. An inscription from 100 BC, carved into the base of the victorious monument of Aemilius Paullus, relates a Roman law (translated into Greek) asserting the rights of Romans to safe passage across the seas and urging all Greeks not to give aid to pirates. In the same year, the threat to local Delphians was also made clear. Kidnappers were reported operating in the vicinity of the sanctuary.[47]

Yet it is also apparent that despite these threats, the sanctuary continued to enjoy a good deal of patronage, especially at the time of the Pythian games. At the turn of the first century BC, the stadium seems to have
undergone a refitting; in 97 BC the city of Delphi honored an Athenian
comic poet Alexandrus with a statue in the sanctuary, and the eastern
Locrians honored their Pythian victor Aristocrates with a statue. In 90
BC we hear that Antipatrus of Eleuthernai was invited by the Delphic
polis to play the water organ for two days during the Pythian games, as
paid entertainment for visitors, in addition to the musical and athletic
competitions.[48] It is also during the first century BC that we first hear of a
cult at Delphi in honor of Dionysus Sphaleotas and the establishment of
an official cult shrine in his honor near the terrace of Attalus at Delphi.
The surviving inscription claims that this cult dated back to the Trojan
War, and that the cult would go on to be respected into late Antiquity.[49]

Yet the beginning of the first century BC, not withstanding the threat
of foreign invasion, also represented the start of a broader downturn in
Delphic fortunes. In 87 BC, the Roman general Sulla, having marched
on Rome only the year before, was on campaign in Greece against the
forces of Mithridates, the latest threat to Roman control of the eastern Mediterranean. In part thanks to his precarious relationship with
Rome, Sulla found himself in need of money. He turned to Greece's
best bank vaults: its sanctuaries. Taking the treasures from Olympia
and Epidaurus, he wrote to the Amphictyony at Delphi to warn them
of his intention to raid the sanctuary. He sent his agent in Phocis, a man
named Caphis, to Delphi to organize the plunder. Once there, Caphis
was said to have heard the sound of Apollo's lyre and took it as a sign of
the god's displeasure at what was being done. He reported this to Sulla,
yet Sulla replied that the sound of the lyre meant the god's pleasure not
displeasure and instructed Caphis to continue. Sulla was not ignorant of
Delphi's importance; he had most probably consulted the oracle himself
several years before and was said to carry with him everywhere a small
golden statue of Apollo from Delphi, which, when in particularly tight
situations, he was said to have always kissed. But he was also a canny
political and military operator in a tight spot: he found himself at odds

with Rome to the west and at war with Mithridates to the east; neglecting the treasures he had at his disposal was simply not an option.[50]

Delphi was thus—once again—raided and the larger objects that could not be transported whole, like a giant silver mixing bowl said to have been one of King Croesus of Lydia's dedications back in the sixth century BC, were broken up on-site for ease of transportation. In return, Sulla, after his subsequent victories, took land belonging to Thebes and reapportioned its revenues to those sanctuaries from which he had taken money. It was little more than a gesture, however, never likely to reach the financial value of what had been taken and most certainly unable to repair the damage to the sanctuary's reputation and relationship with the Roman world.[51] Up to this point, Delphi had been the recipient of Roman dedications to Roman victories, even those over fellow Greek cities. Now Delphi had become the bankroller for the destruction of Greece (ostensibly of course in the name of saving Greece from Mithridates).[52] When Sulla laid siege to the city of Athens between the summer of 87 BC and 1 March 86 BC, some Athenian citizens fled to Delphi and asked the oracle whether Athens had finally met its fate. All the oracle could do was repeat the words it had supposedly said to the Athenians hero Theseus centuries before: "be not too distressed within your heart, and lay your plans. For as a leathern bottle you will ride the waves even in a swelling surge."[53]

Delphi should have celebrated the Pythian festival in 86 BC, the year Athens fell to Sulla. Certain competitors certainly presumed the celebrations would go ahead. Polygnota, a woman from Thebes, arrived at Delphi accompanied by her cousin, ready to take part in the musical competitions as a harp singer, only to find that the festival had been canceled. Given that she had already made the effort to come, she offered a free performance to those present. She was apparently so good (or the need for anything cheering so intense) that the city of Delphi commissioned her to perform for three days for the price of five hundred drachmas, and threw in civic honors for her as well. The uncertainty surrounding the Pythian celebration of 86 BC was understandable. Athens had fallen to Sulla. Mithridates was still a prominent threat both to Sulla and to mainland Greece, and another set of Roman legions, under the command of Lucius Valerius Flaccus, was also crossing northern Greece on route to Asia.[54]

Things got worse the following year. Tribes from the north, including the Illyrians, Thracians, Scordisci, Maedi, and Dardani, having defeated the Roman army stationed in northern Greece, invaded central Greece and sacked a number of cities, including, by 84 BC, Delphi. Accounts differ as to the extent of damage, but it appears the invaders were able to get to the heart of the sanctuary, cause significant damage to the temple of Apollo, extinguish the sacred hearth, and carry off a number of dedications.[55] Funds at the sanctuary seem to have been so low that no immediate repairs were carried out. The only upside was found in stories that later circulated about how anyone who came in contact with the booty taken in the barbarian raid was met with a curse. The Illyrians suffered a plague of frogs; earthquakes drove the Celtic tribes from their homes; and even the Roman governor, Lucius Cornelius Scipio Asiaticus (who would be consul at Rome in 83 BC), having acquired a share of the booty from the Illyrians, was said to have taken home with him the curse of civil war that would plague his consulship and Rome for the remainder of the decade, and indeed for a good part of the rest of the century.[56]

We know relatively little about how Delphi fared in the rest of the first century BC. The traditional picture is that it entered a period of steady decline: its temple not repaired, its sanctuary deprived of its sacred treasures first by Sulla and then by barbarian invaders. Yet there are signs that this picture may be overly pessimistic. Some have recently argued that the Amphictyony was active in and around this period, even trying to establish Athenian tetradrachms as the coinage of preference throughout the Greek world. Others have argued that the damage to the temple, traditionally thought not to be repaired until the time of Emperor Domitian 150 years later, was repaired much sooner. Three Spartans received awards of proxenia in 86–85 BC, and later, in 29 BC, the Spartans even honored a Delphian, in recognition of his help to Spartans visiting Delphi: they set up a monument in his honor in the sanctuary. We know that Cicero, an ambitious young man, came to consult the oracle in 79 BC to ask about how he might win fame and was given the response that he make his own character his guide in life (Cicero comments in one of his writings that the oracle had by now stopped giving its answers in verse form).[57]

Moreover, Delphi continued to play host during this period to a relatively new form of business begun (or at least more publicly and permanently displayed) in about 200 BC: manumissions. Since 200 BC, and continuing through until the end of the first century AD, Delphi seems to have become a key space in which to publicize the contract for the freeing of a slave. There are over thirteen hundred known manumission inscriptions at Delphi, covering the massive polygonal wall that supported the terrace of the temple of Apollo, as well as a series of other monuments around the sanctuary (see plate 2, fig. 9.2). These inscriptions reveal the sanctuary's development of a new public function for a changing clientele list, which, over time, encapsulated not only Delphi's controllers and the Delphian community, but also a wider local market.[58] In the fifty-seven manumissions known through to 190 BC, for example, forty-three were undertaken by Aetolians and only twelve by Delphians. As well, in the year 179–78 BC, just as the Aetolians were cut out of Delphi, no Aetolians undertook a manumission in the sanctuary. After 167–66 BC, the two biggest groups undertaking manumissions were the western Locrians and Phocians, suggesting, that at least for this particular element of Delphic business, the sanctuary was particularly (and understandably) attractive to those living within striking distance of it.[59]

Yet undoubtedly, Delphi was at best a bystander in the titanic struggles that were about to grip the Mediterranean world in the second half of the first century BC. In the midst of the war between Caesar and Pompey, Julius Caesar, in the lead up to the battle of Pharselis in August 48 BC, records Delphi simply as another Greek town occupied by one of his lieutenants, Q. Fufius Calenus, several months before the battle. Yet one of Pompey's lieutenants, Appius Claudius Censorinus, whom Pompey had put in charge of Greece in 49 BC, seems to have taken Delphi more seriously, and consulted the oracle in the run up to the conflict about whether to support Pompey or Caesar. It was, it seems, only due

Figure 9.2. Manumission inscriptions carved into the retaining wall of the temple terrace in the Apollo sanctuary at Delphi (P. de la Coste-Messelière & G. Miré *Delphes* 1957 Librarie Hachette p. 53)

to his influence as a Roman official that he could persuade the priests of Apollo to conduct a full consultation ceremony. The Pythia replied, in typically enigmatic fashion, that the war did not concern him (he fell ill and died before he had to take a side). In turn Anthony would pay more attention to the political value of Delphi. Having won in 42 BC, with the help of Octavian, the battle of Philippi in northern Greece against Caesar's murderers, Brutus and Cassius, Anthony is said to have flattered the Greeks in part through his respect for the temple of Pythian Apollo.

Later he is also said to have attempted to win the good will of the Roman Senate by promising to repair the temple of Apollo following a visit to the sanctuary. Later, while resident in Athens, Anthony seems to have been involved in the dispatch of a sacred embassy to Delphi c. 40 BC, only Athens's second since the time of Sulla, which was followed up in 36/5 BC by a renewal of friendship and exchange between Gephyraei (a *genos* [family group] of Athens) and Delphi.[60] Anthony's offers and embassies, however, would come to naught, not least because of his own death in Alexandria, bringing to an end the civil war that had split the Roman world in two. Its winner, Octavian, became Rome's first emperor in 27 BC. As Augustus, he faced significant challenges in healing and controlling his Roman Empire. The question was, what role would there be for Delphi in this—a yet another—new world?

The guest of Phoebus claps his hands and shouts,
"There is but one such spot: from Heaven Apollo
Beheld; —and chose it for his earthly shrine!"

—Aubrey de Vere lines written under Delphi 1850

IO

RENAISSANCE

Rome's first emperor, Augustus, is not known to have visited Delphi.
But the sanctuary did feel the force of the new emperor in three particular ways. First, because Augustus reorganized the Amphictyony.
Following his victory over Anthony at the battle of Actium in September 31 BC, Augustus set up a new city, called Nicopolis (the "city of
victory"), in the vicinity of the battlefield (see map 2). This new town,
according to the geographer Strabo who wrote a tour guide for the entire Mediterranean world in the first thirty years of the first century AD,
was bolstered by Augustus with all the necessary accoutrements for its
survival. And at the same time, Augustus reengineered the composition of the Amphictyonic council at Delphi to give his new city a seat
in this ancestral grouping; he also formally instituted a bureaucratic
position in the Amphictyonic hierarchy—the epimeletai, "overseers"—
effectively the emperor's agent attached to the Amphictyonic council.[1]

On top of this rather domineering insertion, Augustus and his wife,
Livia, are said to have sent dedications to the sanctuary at Delphi. Livia's
was especially atuned to the particularities of Delphic practice and
belief. Alongside the wise maxims said to have been inscribed on the
pronaos of the temple of Apollo at Delphi ("Know thyself," "Nothing

in excess," "Give an oath and face perdition") was the mysterious letter "E." Plutarch, who, in the early second century AD, was a priest of Apollo at the temple, recorded an entire discussion about the meaning of this letter, about which none of his friends could agree. But he relates the fact that the original letter "E" had been made in wood and attached to the temple, that the Athenians had replaced this wooden letter with one in bronze, and that Livia, in turn, replaced it with one in gold, although he does not relate what drew her to be particularly interested in—of all things at Delphi—the mysterious letter.[2]

Augustus's final link with Delphi revolved around the increasingly close relationship between the sanctuary and Athens that had blossomed in the final quarter of the second century BC, at which time not only had Athens reinstituted its ceremonial procession festival, the Pythaïs, but the Amphictyony had also heaped praise on Athens as the savior of civilization. Now, just over a century later, under Augustus, the Athenians chose to rename the Pythaïs the Dodekais. In so doing, they linked the sacred procession to the date of the new emperor's birthday, the twelfth day of the Athenian month Boedromion. By extension, because the month of Boedromion was also Apollo's birthday, the Athenians were able to underscore the Apollonine nature of the emperor (who liked to think of himself as under the protection of Apollo) and to link the emperor to both Athens and Delphi.[3] Once again, Delphi had proved extremely useful to the Athenians in helping them navigate and articulate their position in this new world and power hierarchy.

Yet, despite these actions and interactions, and despite that some scholars have claimed Augustan monuments in the east seem to have deliberately copied the style of dedication epitomized by the famous serpent column at Delphi from the fifth century BC, Augustus never showed particular interest in the oracle or temple of Apollo at Delphi, especially in contrast to the "lively interest" he took in the Olympics and Olympian sanctuary. Some scholars have seen this as a sign of things to come. Emperors, because of their all-powerful positions, did not have need of oracles to help them in times of difficult or contested decisions (and if they did, there were forms of oracular divination much closer to

home than Delphi). Others have argued that Delphi, despite its fantastic collection of art and architecture, lacked the one thing that always
fascinated a Roman world obsessed with Greek cultural achievement:
a chryselephantine (ivory and gold) statue made by a famous sculptor,
like the statue of Zeus made by Pheidias at Olympia, which captured
the imaginations of a host of Roman writers.[4] Others still have argued
that longer-term Imperial interest in Olympia rather than Delphi was
the result of Olympia's claim to be the original home of Greek athletics,
which continued to play a part in the culture and power-broking of the
Roman world.

But perhaps Augustus's actions need also to be seen in the wider
context of his attitude toward Greece and indeed to the whole of his
empire. After 27 BC, he reorganized the provinces of his world. Greece,
which had hitherto been part of the province of Macedon, was established as its own province (Achaea, covering mainland Greece and the
Aegean islands) and put under the governorship of the Senate. As a result, Achaea, unlike other provinces under direct political and military
control, was given the privilege of having no Roman army stationed
within its boundaries. At the same time, Augustus's move to place
Nicopolis within the Amphictyonic council underlines the importance
he attached to the council and its famous sanctuary and its ability to act
as a source of legitimization for his new creation. More crucially, it also
highlights what would be a continuing misunderstanding within the
Roman world of what the Amphictyony was supposed to represent. The
Amphictyony had never, in its history, represented all of Greece, but instead had always been a partial representation composed of a mixed assembly of some of Greece's oldest tribes, more recent poleis, occasional
Macedonian rulers and the Aetolians, and nearly always been dominated by cities and states from northern Greece. Nevertheless Augustus, and the Romans more generally, seem to have understood the Amphictyony, in the Roman writer Pliny's words, "as the general council of
Greece."[5] Such a view not only helps us understand why Augustus was
so keen to ensure his new city had a voice in this "general council," but
also to understand why the Romans—over the next centuries—would

pay it so much attention when interacting with the province. Delphi, and its governing Amphictyony, had—in Roman eyes—a role it had never had at any point during its already long existence. Indeed, rather than Delphi occupying a meager role in Imperial history, thanks in part to the Roman confusion over Delphic and Amphictyonic history, the sanctuary was set to play a much bigger role than even the Delphian authorities could have hoped for or anticipated. Delphi, thanks to a Roman misunderstanding, was to have greatness thrust upon it.

Despite the continuing and increasing importance in what was now a much bigger world, however, there is no getting away from the fact that, especially in comparison to its active centrality in centuries past, Delphi was no longer quite the place it had been. It is telling that in the first century AD Delphi stopped paying performers who had been hired to entertain the crowds at its festivals in between the sacred athletic and musical competitions in cash, and rewarded them only with civic honors and titles. This was now a Delphi relying on its cultural worth rather than its financial muscle (much like the rest of Greece in this period). So keen perhaps were the Delphians to ensure that those receiving these new honors did not realize the change or feel cheated by it, they seem to have erased the mention of fees paid to performers in inscriptions already set up in the sanctuary. Polygnota, who had been paid to perform during the difficult Pythian festival of 86 BC in the midst of Sullan robbery and barbarian invasion, for example, had her fee erased in the inscription testifying to her performance, as did Antipatrus of Eleuthernai, who had been similarly paid for his playing of the water organ during the Pythian festival in 90 BC.[6]

At the same time, the list of dedications at Delphi from the first century AD makes rather sad reading. The overwhelming majority are from Delphians or the Amphictyony, the two communities with a direct connection to (and interest in) the sanctuary. Yet neither of them seems to have put up a statue to Augustus. It is perhaps more than a little surprising that this latter was done instead by one of the exceptional "outsider" dedicators of this period, who had made an active effort to incorporate their honoring of Augustus into their relationship with

Delphi: the city of Athens, who erected a herm in honor of the emperor in the Apollo sanctuary.[7]

We know relatively little about life at Delphi under the first Emperors. In AD 15 the Emperor Tiberius, who maintained Augustan interest in the Olympics by participating in the equestrian races, took the province of Achaea away from the Senate and made it an Imperial province under the control of the *legatus* of the northern province of Moesia, only for it to be restored again to the Senate by Claudius (AD 51–54) as part of his show of respect for the Senate and Augustan ancestral ways.[8] At the same time, the city of Delphi and the Amphictyony seem to have fallen into a pattern of honoring the emperor, which mirrors most towns around the empire. Both the city and the Amphictyony, for example, put up statues of Tiberius in the Apollo sanctuary, and the Amphictyony also put up a statue to the grand matriarch related to Augustus, Tiberius, Caligula, Claudius, and Nero: Agrippina Major.[9] At the same time, the city of Delphi seems to have embraced both Augustus's new epimeletai (his overseers attached to the Amphictyony), and Tiberius's choice of governor relatively quickly. The city put up a statue in honor of Poppaeus Sabinus, the governor, with an accompanying inscription in which they honored him for "saving the Greeks." And they put up a statue of Theocles—the first of the epimeletai whose name survives to us (from the reign of Tiberius AD 14–37)—in the sanctuary while he was in the post, and then another after he retired. It is not without irony (or indeed design) that Theocles was son of Eudamus of Nicopolis, Augustus's new city, only recently itself a member of the Amphictyony, and that the link between Nicopolis and the epimeletai would continue all the way through to the end of the second century AD. The very last of the epimeletai we can identify in the surviving records is M. Aurelius Niciadas, from none other than Augustus's city of Nicopolis.[10]

The Emperor Caligula (AD 37–41) was even more honored with statues, this time not only by the Amphictyony (who also put up a statue of his sister Drusilla), but also by a koinon (a "community alliance") of Achaeans, Boeotians, Locrians, Phocians, and Euboeans, who must have felt Delphi was the appropriate place for such a gesture.[11] Yet it was under Claudius, who had returned Greece to the control of the Senate, that we first see sustained interest by the emperor in Delphi itself. A series of measures seems to have been undertaken by the senior Roman administrator, L. Iunius Gallio, at the emperor's instigation, to help repopulate the town surrounding the sanctuary and restore its former territory. Claudius himself, in the spirit of the Roman generals and the senators who had written to Delphi during the second and first centuries BC, wrote about these measures in an open letter to Delphi, marking the beginning of an almost unbroken chain of correspondence between Delphi and the emperor from the time of Claudius right through to the rule of Gallienus in the second half of the third century AD. This correspondence with Claudius—after the splendid isolation of Delphi during the reigns of Tiberius and Caligula—clearly meant a lot to the Delphians. It was inscribed publicly in the sanctuary, not just anywhere, but rather as part of the first set of correspondence inscribed on the western end of the south wall of the temple of Apollo (see plate 2).[12] Previously reserved for the records of the most serious moments in Delphic civic history, it now became the place for demonstrating the connection between Delphi and the emperor, not least because it was one of the most visible corners of the temple to visitors. Delphi was once again making sure that any greatness thrust upon it was as conspicuous as it could be.

Claudius seems to have been seen, particularly by the Delphians, as something of a heroic refounder of the sanctuary and city, not least because he had planned the city's repopulation and helped bolster its reputation as a place of importance even for the emperor. That gratitude is most evident in terms of dedications within the sanctuary. While no evidence for a statue of Claudius erected by the Amphictyony has survived, he was most certainly honored by the city of Delphi with a plethora of statues (including one set up 150 years after his reign). This makes sense: it was, after all, the city that benefited most from Claudius's patronage. Claudius, in response perhaps to the city's worship, even seems to have taken on the position of eponymous archon (chief magistrate) in the city, and by so doing he became the first Roman emperor to hold an honorific magistracy in Greece.[13] The city of Delphi had managed to secure its own greatness and renown by attracting, involving, and holding onto Imperial attention and interest.

It is perhaps to this period, too, that we should date something of a reshuffle and revival in Delphic organization and fortune. New officials, like the "secretary of the archives," were appointed. The inscribed records of honors given out by the city of Delphi in this period also show Delphi once again playing to a much wider, more international and cosmopolitan field, especially courting those who were stars of the stadium or the theater. It was in this period, too, that the theater at Delphi seems to have been embellished with a new frieze representing a series of mythical events (see plate 2). And perhaps most innovative of all, it is in this period that the first records appear of women competing, not in their own separate games, but on a par with the men in the same competitions. In the 40s AD, a surviving inscription attests that a woman called Tryphosa had victories in the running races at Delphi and Isthmia, the "first of maidens to do so."[14]

The arrival of the Emperor Nero to the throne, and subsequently in Greece, and indeed, at Delphi after AD 54, must have been something of a shock for the sanctuary and its citizens, not least because he was most probably the first emperor actually to visit Delphi. Nero's desire, many have argued, was to achieve the status of a *periodonikes* (a victor in at least four of the six "Panhellenic" festivals). To that end, he began a tour of Greece, during which, he entered competitions at several of the Greek periodos games, inevitably winning, even in contests that were specially inserted into the competitions just for him. At the end of his tour of Greece, in a speech at Corinth on 28 November AD 67, Nero is reported to have declared the freedom of Achaea from financial tribute to Rome. It was an action, which was said later by Plutarch to have won Nero a reprieve when being judged for his other harsh actions in the underworld, but was, in the world of the living, quickly revoked by his successor Vespasian in AD 69.[15]

At Delphi, Nero had been honored with a statue of himself by the Amphictyony in the sanctuary in the first year of his reign, and his mother, Agrippina Minor (who had been the fourth wife of Claudius) was similarly honored with a statue by the city of Delphi. The Amphictyony's move to honor Nero seems to have paid off, as he reorganized the Amphictyony, returning it to its "ancestral order," in particular giving the presidency and a majority of seats back to the Thessalians. On his visit to the sanctuary, Nero entered the athletic and musical competitions at the Pythian festival, and, not surprisingly, won. He was also said to have consulted the oracle. The Pythia's response, according to later sources, was said to have warned Nero to beware the seventy-third year. In return for this oracular advice, Nero gave ten thousand sesterces to the sanctuary, probably the largest sum given for an oracular consultation since King Croesus of Lydia had showered the sanctuary with gifts in return for his oracle responses in the sixth century BC. And just as that response had not turned out to be so straightforward (or indeed positive) for Croesus, so it was to be with Nero and, in part, for Delphi. It was not Nero's seventy-third year that turned out to be the difficulty. Rather it was his rival's, Galba's, who, in *his* seventy-third year, revolted against Nero and became his successor. Once again, it seems, the oracle's ambiguous response to Nero had been "proved" right. But any increase in the oracle's reputation must have been marred by the fact that Galba also reclaimed for Rome the ten thousand sesterces originally given by Nero to Delphi.[16]

Yet whatever Nero had given (or tried to give) with one hand, he had taken away with the other. He sent veteran soldiers to live on the Cirrha plain, on what had been for centuries land sacred to the god Apollo. He also took, according to Pliny, some five hundred statues from the sanctuary at Delphi to adorn his Golden House in Rome. In some cases this action simply led to the removal of dedications from the sanctuary altogether—as if they had never been there. In others, it left a forlorn reminder of the removal and a confused, if not meaningless, role for the remainder. Nero, for example, was said to have taken a shine to one of the statues from the group of Scylla and Hydna, dedicated by the Amphictyony after the sea victory against the Persians at Artemisium in 480 BC. Now, over five hundred years later, Nero chose to remove the statue of one of these mythological heroines, leaving the other behind.[17] The *damnatio memoriae* that took place after Nero's death only placed emphasis more strongly on the negative aspects of Nero's interaction with Delphi. Later sources speak of a further series of oracular responses to Nero: that the oracle had told Nero it would prefer some poor man's meager offerings to the emperor's lavish gifts, and that it had alluded to Nero's murdering of his own mother (whose statue stood in the sanctuary) by saying "Nero, Orestes, Alcmaeon, all murderers of their mothers." In response, according to these later sources, Nero's uncontrolled fury led him to attempt to block the mouth of the cave (from which vapors emerged to inspire the Pythia) with the bodies of slaughtered men.[18]

Delphi fell into a lapse again after Nero's self-serving (or victimizing) attentions, symbolized more broadly by the reyoking of Greece to the Roman cart following Vespasian's reversal of Nero's declaration of freedom. In fact, scholars have pointed out that Nero's desire to compete in Greek games was unusual not least because he was one of very few ethnic Romans (as opposed to Greeks under Rome or who were given Roman citizenship) who chose to compete at Delphi. Most ethnic Romans who chose to compete in Greek games (and there were never many) chose Olympia rather than Delphi. Delphi's games—though continuing in their popularity—were popular, it seems, only with the inhabitants of the wider Greek world, not its Roman masters.[19]

Yet Delphi's isolation did not continue for long. The Emperor Titus, who came to power in AD 79, followed in Claudius's footsteps and became the eponymous archon of the city of Delphi, for which he too seems to have received a statue from the city of Delphi in the sanctuary. This "seems" qualification is necessary because many scholars disagree over whether this statue is of Titus, or of his successor, Domitian, who also held the archonship at Delphi. The latter's investment in the sanctuary has long been recognized. Indeed it is unavoidable. A gigantic inscription, measuring 4.75 meters by 0.65 meters, etched into stone plaques, has been found at Delphi. It can be dated to between 6 January and 13 September AD 84, and testifies to Domitian's undertaking of the refurbishment of the temple of Apollo at his own expense (the restored inscription can be seen in the Delphi museum today). Scholars are undecided whether this inscription was placed upon the eastern architrave of the temple, or set up on the ground by the temple. There has also been recent significant debate about exactly what refurbishments Domitian undertook. Traditionally, they have been thought to be those needed for well over one hundred years, since the temple of Apollo was damaged during the barbarian raids on Delphi in 84 BC. Yet, more recently, the argument has been made that the damage Domitian undertook to repair was caused more recently, perhaps during the earthquake that struck Greece in AD 77 and which, we know, caused significant damage at Corinth. It is, however, telling that at least one of the plaques onto which the inscription was placed had a series of older inscriptions on the reverse side. The plaques had, it seems, been appropriated from a former dedication thought by some to be the Cnidian treasury originally built in the sixth century BC (see plate 2), which, by this period, may well have fallen into disrepair and thus been seen as a convenient source of material. Domitian may well have restored the temple, but he made his motivations clear, it seems, by taking material from monuments he chose not to restore.[20]

Both Titus's and Domitian's reengagement with Delphi may have been part of a bigger picture of a return to more earnest ancestral religious observance as a result of a string of the disasters that befell Rome and Italy: there had been fire and an outbreak of plague in Rome in AD 80, and Pompeii and Herculaneum had been destroyed by Vesuvius in AD 79. Furthermore, Domitian's interest in the sanctuary did not end with the restoration of the temple. He was involved in the sacred procession festival between Athens and Delphi, renamed the Dodekais, as indicated earlier, to honor Augustus in the last years of the first century BC. He engaged in correspondence with the city of Delphi when they asked him about the organization of the Pythian festival, and his response belies something of the importance he attached to traditional religious observance: "it is naturally right and pious to keep to the appointed time of the Pythian contest in accordance with the

Amphictyonic laws and not to tamper with any part of the ancestral customs." This letter, like all Imperial letters, was inscribed publicly at Delphi, and in AD 86, it seems Domitian introduced the Capitoline games to Rome, which were themselves based on the model of the Pythian games at Delphi.[21]

Yet, at the same time as he likely imported the Delphic model to Rome, his influence at Delphi seems to have started a process of returning the Delphic games to Greek control. Since the time of Augustus, alongside the introduction of an emperor's overseer (the epimeletai) attached to the Amphictyony, it is indicated that the position of an *agonothetes* (president of the games) was created. Yet it was during and after the time of Domitian that this role began more regularly to be filled by Greeks, and particularly citizens of Hypata, chief city of the Ainianians (part of Thessaly). This coincided also, from the time of the Flavian dynasty onward (Vespasian, Titus, and Domitian), with the appointment of more and more Delphians as epimeletai.[22] Delphi, under the Flavians, is reputed to not only have been physically restored, engaged with, and encouraged to uphold its ancestral customs, but also to have had its games actively copied in Rome, and their organization and management restored to more local groups.

Domitian was also likely honored with a statue erected alongside the temple he restored (and that mirrored in style and placement the monument of Aemilius Paullus from 168 BC) as well as perhaps with a second statue set into a niche created in the northern wall of the Apollo terrace (see fig. 1.3).[23] Perhaps this gratitude was more well deserved than we have already recognized. Delphi itself also seems to have been the beneficiary of much other new construction during Domitian's reign and in the period immediately afterward. The gymnasium, for example, was given a new bathhouse in the later first century AD/early second century AD; a library and a dining room were added to the gymnasium complex under the auspices of the epimelete Tiberius Flavius Soclarus, and the covered running track (the *xystos*) was also given a new colonnade (see fig. 7.3). Too, just outside the sanctuary of Apollo, along its eastern boundary wall, a large house was erected at the end of the first century AD, 100 square meters, with an ionic colonnaded courtyard at its center. Known as the "peristyle house," it has been interpreted as either the new home of the Pythian priestess (we know from inscriptions that the epimelete of the period, Tiberius Flavius Soclarus, built a new home for the Pythia), or as the new prytaneion council house for the city of Delphi (see the "Roman house" in plate 2).[24]

The end of the first century and beginning of the second century AD were an important time for Delphi. The writer and orator Dio Chrysostom (Dio "the golden-mouthed"), while in an exile forced on him by Domitian for his overzealous support of the emperor's rivals, visited the sanctuary and undertook a consultation of the oracle in the period AD 82–96. The Emperor Nerva, who would eventually end Dio's exile, received a statue from the city of Delphi, as did Trajan from the Amphictyony, and several other dedications by the Amphictyony and the city of Delphi suggest the sanctuary was both well plugged in to the wider political world, and the beneficiary of a number of visitors, especially its games. The Amphictyony honored the proconsul of Asia, T. Avidius Quietus, with a statue in AD 91–92, and the city of Delphi honored his successor Caristanius Julianus in the same way in AD 99.[25] The Amphictyony honored an agonothete from the city of Nicopolis (who just happened to be a member of the Amphictyonic council as well), and the city of Delphi also honored the wife of one of the epimeletes in this period, as well as two of the Greek-born (Hypatian) agonothetes and a grammarian. But Delphi also attracted new dedicators in this period. The city of Gortyn made their only dedication at Delphi in the sanctuary's history around AD 100: to commemorate a victor in the Pythian aulos competition from their city. In addition, Hypata, whose citizens were increasingly involved with the games as agonothetes, offered a statue of Trajan in the sanctuary, and a group of sophists dedicated a set of statues to different individuals at Delphi at the same time. And in the early second century AD, a certain Memmia Lupa, seems to have made a large enough contribution to the sanctuary to receive no less than ten reserved seats in Delphi's theater, each inscribed with her name, as well as a statue in her honor (see plate 2).[26]

The Emperor Trajan responded to a number of Delphic letters during his reign, including accepting their request for him to reconfirm Delphi's status as an independent city and sanctuary during his reign. Yet he also seems to have been responsible for sending in a series of financial administrators to ensure the books were balanced.[27] At Delphi, this *corrector*, as he was known, was C. Avidius Nigrinus, and in AD 116–17 , he, according to inscriptions engraved onto the temple of Apollo, arbitrated yet another series of disputes over land boundaries between Delphi and Ambryssus, Amphissa, and Anticyra, with the resulting decisions inscribed in both Latin and Greek.[28] Nigrinus however seemed to have fallen foul of the new emperor, Hadrian, soon after he came to power in AD 117: he was executed on a charge of conspiracy.[29]

Yet Nigrinus is not the only individual we know of at Delphi from this period. Much better known, in fact, is Plutarch, son of Autobulus, from the city of Chaeronea, not far from Delphi, and famous for being the site of a series of decisive battles in Greek history. It was where Philip of Macedon won hegemony over the Greeks by beating the Athenians and Thebans in 338 BC; and the place in which the Roman general Sulla defeated Mithridates in 86 BC. The inhabitants of both Delphi and Chaeronea were often close friends. Plutarch's grandfather Lamprias had been good friends with a doctor called Philotas, who had settled and practiced in Delphi, and an inscription was even set up at Delphi during the first century AD to commemorate the *homonoia* (the "equality") between the two cities. Plutarch himself was born in AD 47 and later became a Roman citizen, thanks to being recommended for the honor to Trajan by his close friend the Roman L. Mestrius Florus, from which Plutarch took his Roman name: Mestrius Plutarchus. Plutarch was well educated and traveled extensively across Greece, Asia Minor, Egypt, and Italy, and his philosophy and learning was widely respected. He was well connected to powerful men in both the Greek and Roman worlds: he was friends with Sosius Senecio, a friend of the Emperor Trajan and consul in AD 99, 102, and 107; and he was also friends with the son of Plutarch's brother, who became a stoic philosopher and was a tutor to the future Emperor Marcus Aurelius.[30]

Yet Plutarch is especially important for our story because he spent a great deal of time at Delphi. Though there is no evidence that he possessed a house or land in the city, we can first place him there at the time of Nero's visit to Greece, when he visited the sanctuary in the company of his brother. From that time on, Plutarch seems to have taken a keen interest in Delphi, and throughout the rest of his career worked in a series of important civic and religious roles in the city and its sanctuary: he was an agonothetes, a *proedros* of the Amphictyonic council, as well as an epimeletes of the Amphictyony, and even, in very old age, he was procurator of Greece. He became a citizen at Delphi, and was a priest of Apollo at the sanctuary at the time of the arrival of Trajan's corrector, Nigrinus, with whom Plutarch became friends (indeed he dedicated one of his philosophical writings, on the subject of brotherly love, to Nigrinus). And following his death in AD 120, just after Hadrian became emperor, he was honored by both Chaeronea and Delphi with a portrait bust in the sanctuary (fig. 10.1).[31]

Yet Plutarch is even more important for our story because, in addition to being a well-connected and active member of the Delphic community, he was also a great writer, publishing two weighty tomes known collectively as the *Moralia* and the *Parallel Lives*. The *Lives* is a series of individual biographies that paired particularly important Greeks and Romans because of their similar characteristics or achievements. It was a masterwork of historical and psychological analysis drawing on a wide range of previous sources, and has often provided critical insight for modern scholarship, not least for our understanding of Delphi as a place many of his personages passed through or impacted.[32]

His *Moralia*, however, is, for our understanding of Delphi at least, perhaps an even more precious survival. It is composed of sixty or so individual treatises on a wide range of subjects from religion to philosophy, ethical matters, politics, science, and literary criticism, some of which are responses to official requests and others notes of his philosophical dinner conversations at his home in Chaeronea and those of his friends. Within this sprawling feast of intellectual abundance lie three treatises explicitly located at, and concerned with, Delphi. All

Figure 10.1. Bust of a man of Delphi, often identified as Plutarch but now labeled simply as a philosopher type, dating to the second century AD (© EFA/ Ph.Collet [Guide du musée chapter 2, fig. 101])

seem to have been written before Plutarch became priest of Apollo (circa AD 95) and were sent by Plutarch as a first installment of his musing over Delphi to Sarapion, a poet living in Athens who wrote verse on scientific subjects.[33] The first is a discussion of the meaning of the mysterious letter "E," one of the philosophical maxims attached to the pronaos of the temple (which, as indicated above, Augustus's wife, Livia, as Plutarch tells us, replaced with a version in gold).[34] The text takes the form of a discussion, at first initiated by Plutarch's son in conversation with strangers at Delphi and later with Plutarch, who, in turn relates a previous discussion he had on the matter when he was a young man with his friends and a priest of Apollo, and which concludes, after offering several explanations motivated by logic, metaphysics, and mathematics, that there is no certain interpretation of the symbol.

The second treatise concerns the issue of why the Pythian priestess no longer gives oracles in verse.[35] Plutarch is not present in the discussion, which takes place just outside the temple of Apollo at Delphi. Instead, his friends meet, one of them having been on a tour of the sanctuary that included in the group a rather overzealous questioner from the city of Pergamon in Asia Minor. The tour discussion is repeated ranging over a series of issues including the particular color of bronze at Delphi (said to be affected by the unique quality of the air); reasons for the bad verse responses of the Pythia and particular statues and dedications within the sanctuary. The final treatise has been entitled "On the obsolescence of oracles" and also does not include Plutarch, but is a discussion once again among his friends in the sanctuary.[36] The occasion for the discussion is the meeting at Delphi of Demetrius, who is at Delphi en route from Britain to Tarsus in Asia Minor; and Cleombrotus, who is en route to Sparta having come from the Red Sea. The discussion is once again far ranging—covering issues of spiritual inspiration, depopulation in Greece, Demetrius's experiences in Britain—and ending with a discussion about how the Pythian priestess at Delphi is inspired.

These texts have been fundamental (as we have seen in earlier chapters) for our reconstruction of how the oracle at Delphi functioned, and particularly how it continued to function in Plutarch's time at the end of the first century AD.[37] Yet what I want to concentrate on here is how these texts are also fundamental in opening up for us a sense of how the sanctuary as a whole was engaged with, understood, and enjoyed by visitors and locals at the end of the first century AD. Most important, Plutarch's dialogues show us that there were a steady stream of visitors to Delphi, and that Delphi still acted in some ways as the center of the world (the meeting point of a man coming from Britain and another from the Red Sea). There were enough people coming to

Delphi to ensure the need for guides to lead tours, even if those guides are characterized by Plutarch as being fairly ignorant and unwilling to engage in serious philosophical discussion. The dialogues also show us that there was a huge range of interpretation over the practices of the sanctuary, and the many dedications that were on display there. Some visitors reacted with horror and disgust to dedications such as the iron spits offered by the prostitute Rhodopis, which had lain at Delphi since the sixth century BC; and others were mystified by the artistic and architectural choices made by dedicators, such as the island of Tenedos choosing axes as their symbol.[38]

What this opens up for us is a Delphi that has become a popular tourist location, a place in which to engage with history and memory as much as, if not more than, a place that was the focus of religious pilgrimage. This comes on the back of a, by now, long-standing tradition of texts written about the many magnificent dedications seen (or rather, not seen) at Delphi, starting with analyses by Theopompus in the fourth century BC and Anaxandridas at the beginning of the second century BC of those objects pillaged from Delphi, followed by more general discussions of Delphic treasures by Polemon of Ilion, Alcetas, Apollonius, Melisseus, and Apollas from the second century BC through the first century AD. The guides present at the sanctuary by the end of the first century AD seem to have had a set tour that always started with the Spartan monument to victory at Aegospotamoi (404 BC; see plate 2; fig. 6.2). Similarly, the presence of a number of small terra-cotta lamps from this period at the Corycian cave up above Delphi suggests that it too (see map 3, fig. 0.2), having fallen into decline as a place of religious observance by the end of second century BC, was reborn as a tourism venue, perhaps with lamps (which were discarded, or dedicated, there afterward) provided so that visitors could see into the depths of the cave.[39] In short, Delphi, had begun to feel a little like the commercial theater it does today, where tours also often start with the Spartan monument for Aegospotamoi.

It is also through Plutarch, indeed sometimes only through Plutarch (although at other times combined with various epigraphic and literary sources), that we hear about many of the different festivals that made up the religious calendar at Delphi, and indeed the division of the Delphic year into the periods when Apollo and Dionysus were respective masters there. Some of the festivals had been celebrated for centuries, like the Pythian games, and some of them continued right through Delphi's lifetime.[40] Others were begun in response to special events and may have petered out in turn, like the Soteria, started in 279 BC, taken over by the Aetolians in the later third century BC, and, after their fall, by the time of Sulla in the first century BC, likely forgotten.[41] Others were begun as the result of particular donations to the sanctuary, like the Eumeneia and Attaleia following donations from the Pergamon rulers, or the Alcesippeia on the back of a donation of Alcesippus of Calydon. Others reflected the current political climate: the Romaia was introduced following Rome's victories in Greece after 189 BC, and the Sebasta seems to have been introduced at Delphi in honor of the Roman emperors, possibly linked to the conversion of the tholos in the Athena sanctuary into a temple of Roma and Augustus and the shrine for Imperial cult.[42]

These were, however, but a handful in the midst of a heavy festival calendar. Most months in the Delphic calendar had at least one annual festival celebration, many named after the month itself, like the Theoxenia in the month of Theoxenius (our February), which celebrated the return of Apollo to Delphi from the Hyperboreans and his resumption of mastership of the sanctuary. Others were conducted by only certain members of the Delphic priesthood, like the secret rites for Dionysus mentioned by Plutarch and conducted by the hosioi. When Apollo left Delphi each year in the winter, Plutarch tells us there was another ceremony in which the Thyades—young female worshipers of Dionysus, under the leadership of the Thyia, the priestess of Dionysus—"woke Licnites" (what this entailed we don't known) and the hosioi made secret sacrifices to Dionysus.[43]

These were in addition to the festivals, which were celebrated every two, four, and eight years. We have already discussed the festival held every two years in honor of Dionysus, in which the Thyades of Delphi and Athens came together to revel in honor of the god in the Parnassian mountains. The Pythian games were famously held every four, and there were also at least three festival celebrations performed every eight years: the Septerion, the Herois, and the Charila. Little is known about the Herois, which seems to have involved once again a set of secret ceremonies known only by the priestess of Dionysus and involved worship of Semele, the god's mother. In the Charila, for which Plutarch is our only source, the priest of Apollo distributed barley and pulses in front of the temple, received a doll from the priestess of Dionysus, struck it, and gave it back to the priestess who buried it in the mountains. In thus doing, this festival supposedly replayed a myth in which the local king dispersed grain during a time of famine but refused to give any to a small boy (Charila) who later hung himself, for which the city suffered plague and pestilence.[44]

The Septerion, however, celebrated Apollo's victory over the Python serpent and was an elaborate affair. In the open space below the temple terrace (see plate 2), a wooden hut was constructed. A boy, chosen to represent Apollo, went to the wooden hut at night, with an escort, and they proceeded to burn down the hut and overturn nearby tables. The participants then turned and ran out of the sanctuary with the boy having to re-create Apollo's supposed journey to the valley of Tempe in order to secure forgiveness for the murder of the serpent (see map 2). The boy eventually returned with gifts of laurel from Tempe, which was used later in the year, at the Pythian games, for crowns. Yet it is interesting to note that even regarding these established Delphic festivals, there was much dispute. Plutarch himself discusses doubts over the association of the ritual with the serpent, and that some thought the hut represented the palace of a king.[45]

All this points to a Delphi in the first decades of the second century AD poised on the brink of, if not a return to its former glory, then certainly a golden age of a different kind. While its oracle may not, as Plutarch's dialogues make clear, have been functioning as it had in the past (and he famously comments that now only one priestess is needed rather than two or three), the sanctuary (and city) of Delphi was doing a good business as a place of cultural memory and history as well as of religious celebration, which placed it in good stead of having an unusually high degree of contact with, and attention from, the emperor.[46] It had highly respected and well known individuals like Plutarch undertaking its important civic and religious positions. The city itself was relatively stable, with at least three well-respected and Romanized Delphic families exerting strong influence for much of the period, many of them, according to one surviving inscribed "dramatis personae" list, taking most of the important roles in the Septerion festival celebrations if not others.[47] Moreover, in the fading years of Plutarch's life, it fell to him to honor and welcome to Delphi an emperor whose love of Greek culture would lead to an even greater Delphic renaissance: Hadrian.

Such in my day are the objects remaining in Delphi worth recording.

—Pausanias 10.32.2 (second century AD)

II
FINAL GLORY?

In AD 117, Hadrian became emperor of the Roman Empire. Almost immediately, a correspondence began between him and Delphi that would continue for his entire reign, all of which was inscribed publicly on the outer wall of the temple of Apollo. Within a year of Hadrian's accession to power, he wrote to Delphi twice. The second of these was in response to a letter from Delphi, congratulating him on becoming emperor and asking him to confirm that he would accord Delphi the status of liberty and autonomy accorded by his predecessors. Hadrian replied verifying exactly that. In response, one of Plutarch's last official acts as priest of Apollo at the temple before his own death circa AD 120 was to oversee the setting up of a statue to Hadrian in the Amphictyony sanctuary The city of Delphi also set up their own statue to the new emperor.[1]

There was no letup in the exchange of letters after this first volley. Delphi consulted Hadrian at the end of AD 118 on how to honor an individual called Memmius, and between AD 118 and 120, Hadrian ordered that a series of works be erected in the area, the special power for seeing them through delegated to C. Julius Prudens. In AD 125, the relationship between Hadrian and Delphi became even closer as Hadrian embarked on his own visit to central Greece and visited Delphi. That year, he became, like several emperors before him, the archon of the city. During his visit, he is (later) said to have consulted the Pythian oracle, asking a series of questions on Greek culture, in particular where Homer came from and the identity of Homer's parents. Hadrian's visit to the sanctuary prompted the erection of another statue of him in his honor, this time the combined effort of the Amphictyony and the city of Delphi.[2] Nor was this the only one. T. Flavius Aristotimus, priest of Apollo at the sanctuary and who had already been sent as ambassador from Delphi to Hadrian in Rome, erected a private statue of Hadrian in the sanctuary of Athena (see plate 3). This was one of the last statues to be dedicated in this sanctuary, which had for many years acted as something of an easily accessible mine when ready stonework was needed elsewhere in the Delphic complex.[3]

There also seems to have been a series of new issues of Delphic coinage during Hadrian's reign, bearing the head of the emperor on one side, and images related to the sanctuary on the reverse (e.g., Apollo, the omphalos, the façade of the Apollo temple with the celebrated and mysterious "E," the serpent surrounding the omphalos). Some coins even featured the mouth of the Corycian cave, suggesting its return to prominence and its full inclusion in the standard tour guide of the sanctuary and its religious landscape.[4] Perhaps the most interesting coins from this period feature a new figure in Delphic cult at this time: Antinous Propylaius ("Guardian of the Gates"). Antinous, famous for his relationship with the emperor, died in mysterious circumstances on the Nile in AD 130. In response, Hadrian set up a cult in his honor at several places around the Mediterranean (and particularly in the east), including one at Delphi (on the instigation of the priest of Apollo, Aristotimus, who had been responsible for a statue of Hadrian in the Athena sanctuary). This cult, whose location in the Apollo sanctuary is uncertain, was the recipient of a stunning 1.8 meter–high statue of Antinous in Parian marble, which is one of the masterpieces on display in the Delphi museum today (fig. 11.1).[5] Nor did improvements under Hadrian cease with the introductions of new cults. The columns of the covered running track (the xystos) in the gymnasium were redone in a bluish marble in ionic

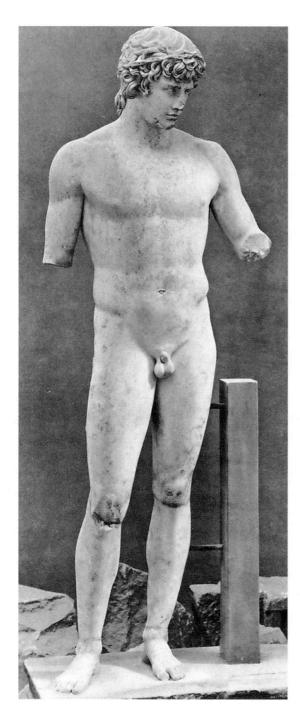

Figure 11.1. Statue of Antinous
dedicated in the Apollo sanctuary
at Delphi (P. de la Coste-Messelière
& G. Miré *Delphes* 1957 Librarie
Hachette p. 202)

style (see fig. 7.3). The first articulation of what would become a built Roman agora—by the Apollo sanctuary's southeast entrance—also seems to have been made at this time, comprising small workshops perhaps making items to sell to visitors (see plate 2), and the Amphictyony seem to have undertaken work on the small Asclepieion shrine within the Apollo sanctuary at the foot of the temple terrace wall in the final years of Hadrian's reign.[6]

In the run-up to, and aftermath of the visit in AD 125, Hadrian's proximity to Delphi seems to have prompted the city to consult him on a number of issues associated with the religious and athletic traditions of the sanctuary. The Imperial correspondence from AD 125 that was inscribed onto the Apollo temple wall concerned the organization of the Pythian festival and expressed Hadrian's concerns (in response to Delphic queries about changing some of the procedures related to these games) that no traditions should be lost or changed. In the following years, as part of his wider Greek agrarian policy, Hadrian also seems to have been consulted and, as a result, have made significant changes to the management of the sanctuary's sacred land (which was now known simply as "territory"—see map 3), and to the reorganizing of its citizen classes to create a new category of citizen, the *damiourgoi*, who were to be given full civic rights and larger land allotments. The purpose of this reorganization seems to have been to manufacture a particular class of wealthy citizen at Delphi who could fulfill the role of a local governing class. Though not all the letters between Hadrian and Delphi have survived in full, we know that regular correspondence continued through to Hadrian's death in AD 138, with Delphic praise for the emperor becoming more and more overt. They praised him for assuring the "peace of the universe," marked the days of his first (and second) visit to Delphi as sacred days in the Delphic calendar, and wrote a number of letters on no particular issue except to express their adoration of him.[7]

But Delphi also had something of interest to Hadrian: its Amphictyony. Part of one of his letters to Delphi, dated to around the time of his visit in AD 125, concerned a reorganization of the Amphictyony council. Several emperors, as we have seen, undertook reorganizations, yet Hadrian's letter is instructive because of the articulated purpose behind the reshuffle. The letter outlines a reduction in the large Thessalian representation (which had in fact been reinstituted by Nero only in the previous century), and the redistribution of those votes on the council between the Athenians, Spartans, and other cities so that, in the words of the letter, "the council may be a council common to all Greeks."[8]

Such a purpose focuses our attention on two critical facets of the Roman relationship to Greece and particularly to Delphi. First, as we saw in chapter 10 regarding reorganizations before him (and particularly that of Augustus), the purpose of Hadrian's was to develop a particular kind of council that could undertake a role that, in reality, the Amphictyony had never had during its archaic, classical, and Hellenistic lifetimes. Its council membership had never been a fair representation of all the Greek people; and it was not, despite many modern attempts at analogies, an ancient United Nations or European Union though this is how Romans (and many in the modern world) choose to see it, use it, and characterize it.[9]

The second, connected, point concerns Hadrian's wider plan for Greece. In AD 131–32, Hadrian famously formed the Panhellenion—a union of Greek cities in the Roman province of Achaia that was specifically designed to allow Greece's cultural and historical eminence to sit on equal terms with the more current economic and political muscle of other parts of the Roman Empire, particularly Asia Minor. Constituent members had to prove Hellenic descent, and its members were the famous *metropoleis* of central Greece and their overseas colonies. Many scholars have argued that Hadrian's first instinct was to use the Delphic Amphictyony as the core of such an organization, and that this is why we see this critical restructuring of its membership in AD 125 in preparation for the formation of the Panhellenion in AD 131. Yet, what careful study of the documentation has recently pointed out is that Hadrian's letter to the Delphi inscribed on the temple terrace wall in AD 125 is actually the report of a Roman senatorial commission about potential reform of the Amphictyony (reflecting the Roman misconception of what the Amphictyony was supposed to be), which was in fact later rejected by Hadrian. Hadrian's Panhellenion was, it seems, always, in Hadrian's mind at least, a separate entity that would in fact be centered around Athens, and that led, in Athens, to the creation of a sanctuary of Hadrian Panhellenius, Panhellenia athletic games, and the embellishment of the nearby sanctuary at Eleusis.[10]

Yet, even though Delphi and its Amphictyony may not have been the inspiration or original focus of Hadrian's plans for a united Greece, the Greeks certainly responded to Hadrian's keenness for the concept of a united Greece articulated specifically through the sanctuary at Delphi. In the early years of Hadrian's reign, and before the creation of the Panhellenion, a statue of the emperor was erected at Delphi by the "Greeks who fought at Plataea."[11] This is the only dedication made in the sanctuary's history by this particular grouping, although of course it made an instant connection to Delphi's perhaps most famous monumental dedication, the three twisted serpents supporting a golden tripod set up for the victory at Plataea in 479 BC by the Greeks. The united Greek front achieved during the Persian Wars had been, ever since, a key part of any call for Greek unity, and it is not unsurprising that a collection of Greeks chose to reactivate this banner to demonstrate unity to Hadrian through honoring him with a statue in the very sanctuary in which such unity had originally (centuries earlier) been most monumentally displayed.

The level of contact and care lavished on this sanctuary by Hadrian during his reign represents without doubt a high point in Delphi's history. It was a blessing Delphi was to enjoy, after Hadrian's death in AD 138, for much of the rest of the second century AD, and it came in several forms—first, through continued interaction with the emperor and other important Roman officials. Hadrian's successor, Antoninus Pius, became archon of the city, and his image appears on a series of Delphic coins, the last major series of coins minted at Delphi in its history, most probably struck for the occasion of its ongoing and successful Pythian games. And Valeria Catulla, the wife of Tiberius Claudius Marcellus, a Roman official in Greece during the second half of the second century AD, set up a statue in the sanctuary in Antoninus's honor with the agreement of the Amphictyony.[12] Second was through a growing interest in and use of the sanctuary as a base for philosophical thinking. Since the end of the first century AD, Delphi had been acquiring a reputation as a locus for philosophical discussion, thanks to its unique combination of history, oracle, philosophical heritage, and athletic and musical competitions, which even other Panhellenic periodos sanctuaries could not match. It was a reputation much enhanced by Plutarch's time as priest of Apollo and the dissemination of many of his philosophical discussions about Delphi and other matters (see fig. 10.1).[13] As a result, Delphi was visited by a significant number of philosophers and sophists during the second century AD, such as Aulus Gellius who attended with his students to watch the Pythian games in AD 163. At the same time, a number of statues of Sophists were erected in the sanctuary both by the city of Delphi and by other cities like Ephesus and Hypata, and by groups of Sophists in honor of respected members of their circle.[14]

Combined with (and partly as a result of) this Imperial favor and reputation as a philosophical hotspot, Delphi's games also continued strongly in popularity during the second century AD. The sanctuary's increasingly packed confines were populated with a plethora of statues to athletic winners and to those tasked with organizing the games (in particular the agonothetes) from the Amphictyony, as well as from cities around the Mediterranean who had previously dedicated in the sanctuary, and sometimes from cities that had never dedicated at Delphi.[15] Ancyra, in Asia Minor, for example, made its only dedication in the sanctuary's history at the end of the second century AD, erecting a statue of its victor in the Pythian musical competition. Likewise, Myra (in Lycia in Asia Minor) erected its only offering in the sanctuary's history during the second century AD: a statue for its own Pythian victor. So, too, Sardis (in Asia Minor) erected a series of monuments to one of their extremely successful athletes (who had been victorious in a number of the periodos Greek games) at the end of the second century AD and the beginning of the third century.[16]

This interest in Delphi's athletic and musical competitions reflects Delphi's importance all across the Mediterranean (but especially in the east) during the second century AD.[17] But at the same time, the sanctuary was the focus of one of Greece's own greatest benefactors from this period: Herodes Atticus. A millionaire aristocrat from Athens, but also of Roman citizenship (and who would be consul in Rome in AD 143), Herodes Atticus was born at the very beginning of the second century AD and died in AD 177. During his lifetime, he saw Greece flourish under the spotlight of successive Roman emperors (many of whom he encouraged to take an interest in Greece, and with whom he was on excellent terms). More importantly he was himself prolific in building projects designed to enhance both Athens and other cities in the Greek world. At Delphi, he turned his attention—perhaps unsurprisingly, given the amount of interest in the Pythian games at this time—to the stadium. What you see today when you visit the site is largely the work of Herodes Atticus (fig. 11.2). The stadium's length was reset to measure six hundred (Roman-measured) feet. For the first time in its history, the stadium was given stepped seating in local limestone: twelve levels on the northern side, six on the southern, with curved seating at the western end that allowed for approximately 6,500 spectators. At its eastern end, a monumental entrance was created with arched doorways and niches for statues. As a result of Herodes' enormous benefaction, a number of statues were put up in his honor. One, predictably, comes from the city of Delphi, which also erected one to his wife, Regilla, and to Herodes' disciple Polydeucion. In contrast, it is interesting that we have no record of the Amphictyony erecting a statue in Herodes' honor. But Herodes Atticus seems also to have been keen to erect statues in honor of his own family and circle in the sanctuary—of his wife, more than one of his daughter and son and Polydeucion; and in turn his wife set up a statue of him And all these were placed prominently near the temple of Apollo.[18]

Herodes Atticus died in AD 177, during the reign of Marcus Aurelius (AD 161–80), who had himself taken the cue from his predecessors (and indeed his co-emperor Lucius Verus AD 161–69) and continued a close relationship with Delphi. Both Lucius and Marcus confirmed the continued independence and autonomy of Delphi as a city, and Marcus Aurelius seems to have kept up a lengthy correspondence with the sanctuary.[19] We can get some sense of the wealth of Delphic citizens in

Figure 11.2. A view of the stadium at Delphi following a makeover thanks to the benefaction of Herodes Atticus in the second century AD (© EFA/P. Aupert [Aupert FD II Stade fig. 142])

this period from their tombs, collected in burial areas (necropoleis) surrounding the city and sanctuary (see plate 1). We know, for example, that an underground crypt was created during the Imperial period in one of the necropoleis to the west of the sanctuary. While it is difficult to date the crypt specifically, we can be more certain of the date for a large, ornate, and expensive sarcophagus from the second century AD, now on display outside the Delphi museum (fig. 11.3). It is known as the sarcophagus of Meleager because of the mythological scene carved around it, and it was an expensive choice for whomsoever was originally

Figure 11.3. The Meleager sarcophagus, at the moment of its discovery
in the nineteenth century (© EFA [La redécouverte de Delphes fig. 86])

buried in it. Indeed it was so much admired that it was reused as many
as fifteen times for additional burials between the second and fifth centuries AD.[20]

Moreover we catch brief glimpses of the continued use of the oracle in
this period, mostly for private inquiries, but also for more official ones.
A Spartan *theopropos* was sent to consult during Marcus Aurelius's reign
(about what, we do not know), and stories circulated that the oracle had
even been involved in ensuring that Galen, one of the most famous med-
ical practioners in the ancient world, give up his studies in a different
field to concentrate on medicine.[21] Yet with renewed attention paid to

the oracle, so too was it subjected to greater criticism in a world that was fast changing and would, in less than 250 years, officially reject paganism entirely in favor of Christianity. One writer, Lucian of Samosata, writing in the middle and second half of the second century AD, chastised the Delphians for being at the beck and call of dedicators because their fates were tied to that of the oracle, and railed against the famed obscurity and ambiguity of Delphic oracular responses, a trope that would continue to play well with Christian writers keen to undermine oracular sanctuaries and paganism in general in the years to come.[22]

Yet it was during the reigns of Antoninus Pius, Lucius Verrus, and Marcus Aurelius in the second half of the second century AD that Delphi was immortalized in another set of writings: those of Pausanias. Despite the survival of Pausanias's *Description of Greece*, we know almost nothing about the writer himself; indeed we are not even sure of his name. He seems to have come from Asia Minor, possibly Magnesia in Lydia. Born during the reign of Hadrian, circa AD 110–15, he was old enough to have seen Antinous, Hadrian's lover, alive before Antinous drowned in the Nile on 30 October AD 130. Compared with other famous men of his time, he was about the same age as Ptolemy of Alexandria, and a little older than Lucian of Samosata and Galen of Pergamon. His writings belong to the period AD 155–80 and fit into a broader genre of literature known as *periegetic*: tour guide mixed in with, among other things, geography, history, mythology, art history, and ethnography.[23] His *Description of Greece* appears to do just what it says on the tin. Starting in Athens in book 1, Pausanias claims to deal with "*panta ta hellenika*" ("all things Greek" 1.26.4) and proceeds to travel around Greece, describing Olympia in the middle (books 5–6) and Delphi in the final book (book 10).[24] As a result, his detailed descriptions of many Greek sites are instantly recognizable to those studying ancient Greece today and were a fundamental guide to the early excavations of those sites, Delphi included.[25]

And yet, there have always been a number of questions about how to understand his text. At the same time as it was an indispensable aid to excavators in the nineteenth century, literary and textual scholars like von

Wilamovitz Moellendorff intensely criticized his work. More recently, there has been a concerted effort to highlight the difficulties in taking Pausanias at face value, and even a question about his usefulness for archaeological research.[26] No longer do we see him as simply recording what he saw, but as a writer with particular interests and views writing to a very particular agenda, and shaping what he reported to fit that mold. As such, Pausanias's text is now considered not simply a straightforward tour guide, but rather a cognitive map created to express a particular ideology of Hellenism contiguous with the greater project of reshaping (and creating) a unified Greece as seen in other initiatives like Hadrian's Panhellenion. Pausanias's focus, scholars have stressed, was on stories, places, objects, and moments that spoke to Greek unity, and most definitely to Greece's past rather than its present: with only two exceptions, no monument discussed by Pausanias at Delphi was erected later than 260 BC (the exceptions being the stadium and a structure in the Athena sanctuary). Pausanias's present-day Delphi, indeed any part of Delphi's history subsequent to the assumption of full control by the Aetolian league, seems not to have fit with Pausanias's project, which sought to stress the antiquity, cultural history, memory, and importance of an (ancient) unified Greece.[27]

Pausanias's goals are understandable. His *Description of Greece* came at a time of heightened interest in, and prosperity for, the country; as well as at a time of recognition that Greece's trump card in a fast changing Mediterranean world was its claim to an unrivaled historical and cultural contribution. But, was he successful in his literary goals? In two ways, it could well be argued that he was not. His own work, the *Description of Greece*, seems not to have been much read in antiquity. The first surviving mention of him and his text is 350 years after his death, in the time of the Roman Emperor Justinian subsequent to Rome's conversion to Christianity. But perhaps more importantly, and indeed what might explain his lack of success, is that by the time of his death circa AD 180, the brand of philhellenism ignited by Hadrian had begun to splutter slightly.[28] It is telling that one of the two monuments Pausanias mentions in his description of Delphi, and which dates from after 260 BC, is the stadium, and that his description of it differs from what we find today (see fig. 11.2). Pausanias claims that Herodes Atticus paid for the spectator banks to be made out of marble. But the surviving ones are of local limestone. Scholars have discounted the possibility that the marble has been lost. Instead they believe it was likely never there. Pausanias may well have written about what he heard was intended, but, after the death of Herodes Atticus in AD 177, it seems the plans were scaled back. The opulence was no longer justified, and stone from the local quarry was used instead. At the same time, when Pausanias writes about the sacred lands belonging to Apollo, and which had remained uncultivated since the sixth century BC, it is telling that no one at Delphi seems to know exactly why this is the case. He hears some say it is because they are cursed, and others that it was not good earth for olive trees.[29] Respect for Delphi, it seems, was beginning to falter, and Delphi's trump card—its reputation as a place of cultural memory and unsurpassed history—was threatened by its own lack of knowledge about its own history.

But this was by no means a sudden downfall. At the end of the second century AD, with the arrival of Septimius Severus as emperor (AD 193–211), Delphi once again sent ambassadors to congratulate him on his military victories over rivals (that had brought him to power), and, no doubt, to ask him to reconfirm the liberty and autonomy of the city and sanctuary in accordance with his predecessors. This he did, and the Delphians duly wrote up his response on the walls of the temple of Apollo. In addition, during the reigns of Severus and his son Caracella, a further restoration of the temple of Apollo seems to have been undertaken and overseen by the proconsul of the Roman province of Achaea, Cn. Claudius Leonticus.[30] Indeed, at least for the city and citizens of Delphi, the end of the second century AD and the beginning of the third seems to have been a relatively prosperous and stable time. One Amphictyonic secretary from this period, M. Junius Mnaseas, could claim to be the grandson of a Pythian priestess and descended from a number of priests of Apollo; such, it appears, was the stability of the governing class within the city. Moreover Delphi's inhabitants were wealthy enough for numerous statues to be put up in the sanctuary for members of their own families, as well as for a number of important Romans and Roman officials.[31] The Imperial governor (and corrector of Delphi), Cn. Claudius Leonticus, who was probably responsible for a series of renovations of the temple, is thanked with no less than five statues set up by individual Delphians for taking care of all Delphi's affairs. Moreover, although the dating is notoriously difficult, the initial elaboration of the Roman agora space at the entrance to the sanctuary of Apollo continued, and seems to have been accompanied around this time by an expansion to the south with the construction of a complex originally thought to be a set of baths, but now thought likely to have been a complex of housing, shops, and service workshops (see plate 2).[32]

It seems, thus, that the celebrations by people like Clement of Alexandria at the end of the second century AD, that the time of oracles was over, were premature in a number of ways. Not only do we have evidence that the oracle at Delphi continued to give responses right through into the fourth century AD (and even the Christian writer Origen of Alexandria writes about the Pythia in the present tense in the mid-third century AD), but also it seems that the oracular sanctuary at Delphi continued to be respected enough by the Roman state and its citizens to ensure that the Delphians did well enough for themselves to continue embellishing their sanctuary and city during that time.[33] At the same time, as we saw in the introduction to this book, it was in the third, or even, fourth century AD that Delphi starred as the setting for Heliodorus's fictional novel, *Aethiopica*, which portrayed Delphi not only as the center of (and well connected with) a wide Mediterranean world, but also as a busy and prosperous sanctuary.

In one aspect of Delphic business, however, there were signs of change, and this was the Pythian games, which had long been a stalwart of Delphic business, and a major reason for the sanctuary's continuing success. But the sanctuary was to become something of a victim of that success. On the one hand, certain communities, like that of the Hypatians, seem to have been stalwart supporters of the games, and even to have taken the opportunity of the festival to conduct a ritual in honor of Neoptolemus at his small cult area in the Apollo sanctuary from the second century AD onward. But on the other hand, from AD 180 AD through to AD 268, there seems to have been a massive exportation of the Pythian games, at the command of successive emperors, to twenty-seven cities in the Balkans, Asia Minor, and Syria. At first sight, this might seem good news only for Delphi, and without doubt, the spread of the Pythian games must in some part have been inspired by the high regard in which the Delphi Pythian games were held. But in reality these were not carbon copies of the Delphic games. They were loosely based on them, but incorporated a wide range events and practices. Moreover, in no way does the spread of the Pythian games seem to have been officially linked to their original location: not a single epigraphic attestation of this expansion survives at Delphi.[34] Instead these new sets of games are known predominantly through the publicity generated in their new-found homes. So, while the "original" Pythian games would with little doubt have continued to hold a particular attraction, these new ones throughout the Roman world must have drawn attention away from Delphi. This was especially the case because these new games seem to have been motivated in the third century AD by a shift in the worship of the emperor away from temple building and sacrifice toward the performance of agonistic festivals and ceremonies in his presence. Given that the way to honor the emperor was increasingly through games, no one city or sanctuary could expect to hold the monopoly on these activities, and indeed we should expect increasing rivalry between the different events, which meant increased competition for the Pythian games at Delphi, especially as new Pythian games were hosted in cities closer and closer to Delphi. A Pythian festival, almost identical to that at Delphi, was founded at Thessalonike under the Emperor Gordian III (AD 238–44). As a result, despite the liveliness of the Pythian games at Delphi depicted in the sources for mid-late second century AD, the inscribed catalogs of victors shows a marked decline in numbers during the first half of the third century AD.[35]

One of the reasons the Pythian games, as opposed to the Olympic games, became the model for export was their association with the god Apollo. During the course of the third century AD, Apollo, and particularly Apollo Helios (Apollo "of the Sun"), who was deemed the Greek equivalent of the Roman Sol Invictus ("Invincible Sun"), became a more and more popular patron deity for emperors. Yet the third century AD was also a period of prolonged crisis for the Roman empire: confronted by ongoing invasion from multiple directions; dealing with a continued, bitter, and violent struggle for Imperial control within Roman society; suffering from brief fractures in the empire itself and accompanied by economic difficulties and even plague.[36] On the one hand, Delphi did its best to keep up with this continually changing, fractured, and fraught political landscape. Emperor Gordian III (despite his approval for the setting up of identikit Pythian games at Thessalonike) was honored by the Amphictyony and the city of Delphi with a statue in the sanctuary. So, too, the city of Delphi honored Valerian (AD 253–56) and his son Gallienus who was co-ruler with him for a time (AD 253–60), and then sole ruler (AD 260–68). Likewise, the city of Delphi set up a statue of his successor, Claudius Gothicus (AD 268–70), and later for Carus, who ruled for only a year in AD 282–83.[37] At the same time, the sanctuary itself was not unattended to or unpopulated. The first phase of the eastern baths, completed on a terrace between that of the stoa of Attalus and the Roman agora, can be dated to the second half of the third century AD (see plate 2). Likewise, dedicators still came to the sanctuary from far afield. Sinope, on the Black Sea, erected a statue to its own athletic superstar in AD 250–75, and, in keeping with the military and political instability of the period, a group of mercenary soldiers erected a statue of their leader in the sanctuary at some point during the third century AD.[38]

Yet, there were also signs that the institutions running Delphi were beginning to struggle in a number of ways. The statue set up to Gordian III is the last known statue in Delphi's history set up by the dual authority of the Amphictyony and the city of Delphi. While the city would continue to set up statues of later emperors, the Amphictyonic record is much more hazy. Its final known dedication in the sanctuary is that of a statue of Philiscus, a governor of the Roman province of Thessaly (created by Emperor Diocletian at the turn of the third–fourth centuries AD). But that came 150 years after the last surviving record of an Amphictyonic meeting—a time about which we know little. The Amphictyony itself seems to have continued, but, though scholars debate the degree to which it maintained itself as a functioning force at Delphi and in the wider Greek world, there is general agreement that it had passed its prime.[39]

At the same time, those statues that were erected by the city of Delphi during the third century show signs of increasing thrift. The statue of Claudius Gothicus was erected (and inscribed) on a base that had been originally placed in the sanctuary in the fifth century BC, when it had carried a statue of a horse, which had been dedicated (and inscribed) by the Pharsalians of Thessaly for one of their own military victories. This process of reuse is by no means uncommon in the ancient world (and indeed at Delphi), and it would become more prevalent in the sanctuary over the course of the century. Carus's statue base, for example, was reused for another emperor almost immediately. But its reuse now—even for statues of, and honoring, the emperor—is a very real testament to the uncertain political landscape. Claudius's reign was only three years long and came almost immediately after the Delphians had set up statues to two recent predecessors, and Carus's reign was only one year. Given such short periods of rule an investment in an entirely new stone might have been deemed unnecessary and not worthwhile, especially in view of the generally worsening condition of Delphic finances. Nor is reuse of the statue base the only change in attitudes toward the monuments of the Apollo sanctuary at this time. It is during the third century AD that we first see hints that the treasury of the Athenians—for centuries one of the most prestigious structures at Delphi—was being used as a home to pawnbrokers, a practice that continued well into the fourth century AD (see plate 2, fig. 5.4).[40]

Given this picture, and that the following century saw the emergence of Christianity as the Imperial religion of choice, and eventually the official religion of the Roman world, it is logical that Delphi continued its slow slide into decline from this point on. But, if anything, the opposite seems true. Delphi's governing class—the damiourgoi created under

Hadrian—was still exerting a good deal of influence (if not more than ever) at Delphi in the fourth century AD, even though its meetings were now held in Hypata. Statues of philosophers dedicated during the first half of the fourth century AD have been discovered in the sanctuary.[41] Carus's statue base was reused as the base for a statue of Constantius Chlorus (the father of Constantine the Great) at the turn of the century. All of this, in fact, seems to have been part of a wider reenergizing of the sanctuary—at the very moment in which the fate and direction of the wider Roman world was turning toward Christianity on the battlefield of Milvian Bridge near Rome.[42] As Constantine the Great swept through the Roman Empire, defeating his co-emperors and reuniting the territory under his command (and under his Christian standard), at Delphi, the city and sanctuary seem to have been playing host to almost the last major building project we know about in the site's pagan history. A surviving inscription from AD 319 attests to the generosity of L. Gellius Menogenes, president for life of the college of the damiourgoi (and also a man with important roles in the religious life of the city of Athens), who handed over 500,000 coins (of an unknown denomination) for the cleaning of the Delphic baths, a donation matched by a woman: Aurelia Julia Sotia. This money seems to, at least in part, have gone to not only cleaning the baths, but also to renovating them substantially, including an upgrade of the heating system (see plate 2).[43]

It is instructive that Constantine the Great, the emperor—who conquered under the Christian standard, reunited the Roman Empire; set about establishing a new capital for the empire at Constantinople (Istanbul); and in the process removed some of the greatest works of art from across the Mediterranean to grace his new capital, including the Plataean serpent column that had stood at Delphi since the fifth century BC—received no statue at Delphi from the city of Delphi during his lifetime.[44] In contrast to the statues erected for emperors who survived only a year (like Carus), this lethargic behavior toward Constantine, who ruled for much longer, might indicate the uncertainty of the times—Delphi felt it politically inappropriate to honor an emperor who was making war on his co-rulers. Or indeed it might suggest the sadness

Figure 11.4. The Serpent column dedicated in 479 BC at Delphi following the battle of Plataea, now in the hippodrome built by Constantine in Constantinople (© Michael Scott)

they felt at Constantine's removal of their most famous dedication to his capital at Constantinople (fig. 11.4). In the aftermath of Constantine's death, however, in AD 337, and as a result of the more settled (if new) Roman order, the city of Delphi erected not one but two statues to Constantine.[45] It was at this time as well that the Roman agora, which, since the time of Hadrian had been through several renovations, was rebuilt again in its grandest form, using material taken from various parts of the Delphic complex (including the marble columns that, during Hadrian's reign, had been installed in the covered running track of the gymnasium). Stoas on three sides of the agora square were constructed, with the agora's axis corresponding to the entryway into the Apollo sanctuary, and with its own vestibule entrance to the east (see plate 2). More importantly, this new space was, it seems, identified as the choice location for Imperial statues (which had until this time been placed mostly on the level of the temple terrace). After AD 330, all Imperial statues were likely placed in the Roman agora.[46]

The steady flow of Imperial statues also resumed in this period of religious flux. Dalmatius, junior emperor from AD 335 to 337 with control of—among other provinces—Achaea, received a statue from the city of Delphi, employing a base that had previously been used for one of the statues of the Emperor Hadrian.[47] Flavius Constantius, son of Constantine the Great, was honored with a statue by the city of Delphi in period AD 337–40, possibly since, though he co-ruled in his early reign with his brothers, his sphere of influence included Illyricum (nowadays part of the Balkans) and was thus more important for Delphi to impress. But this statue, too, employed a reused base, one that had originally been set and inscribed as the base for the statue of Polydeucion, the disciple of Herodes Atticus in the second century AD.[48]

Delphi was caught in the same catch-22 as all the pagan sanctuaries in this period. They were erecting statues to honor Christian emperors in pagan sanctuaries, as both people and emperors negotiated the difficult task of being Christian in a still overwhelmingly pagan world; some estimates put Christian numbers at perhaps 10 percent of the population in the 320s AD.[49] And though these emperors were diplomatic enough to allow pagan worship to continue (Delphi received in AD 342–44 an Imperial reply assuring the continuing liberty of its cult), the increasingly loud voices of Christian writers also focused in on the practices of these sanctuaries as evidence not only for their decline, but also, curiously, for historical support for the inevitability of Christian victory.[50] The Christian historian Eusebius, for example, records that in his time only the oracles of Apollo at Delphi, Clarus, and Didyma were still working, and when someone asked why this was so, the explanation offered had to do with earthquakes and the natural passing of time.[51] At the same time, Eusebius reports a consultation by the Nicaeans, who asked Apollo whether, in view of the lapsed oracle, they still needed to honor Pythian Apollo with the traditional sacrifices. According to Eusebius, the oracle said it was now impossible to renew the spoken oracle at Delphi since "it has put on itself the keys of prophetic silence," but that it was still important to continue the offerings.[52] Other writers portrayed the oracle's silence as a direct consequence of the coming of Christ, and, in this period, the story circulated that when, at the time of Jesus's birth, the Emperor Augustus himself had consulted about his successor, the oracle remained dumb and, when asked why, replied, "a Hebrew boy bids that I leave this house and go to Hades. Depart therefore from our halls and tell it not in the future."[53]

Yet even in this climate, Delphi had its supporters, and none of them was bigger than the man who attempted to turn the Christianization of the Roman world on its head: Julian the Apostate, the last pagan emperor. Ruling from just AD 361–63, Julian was a committed pagan whose attempts not only to deny Christianity but to sideline it within the Roman system may well have had a great deal of success if his reign had not been cut short by his death on the battlefield. As it was, this was paganism's last hurrah, and Delphi had a famous role to play. Julian not only wrote extensively against Christians, defending how it was the oracles had gone silent, but also paid significant tributes particularly to Delphi, and commented on its athletic events. But even more famously, he sent a doctor, Oribasius, from Constantinople to act as Imperial *quaestor* in Achaea and to consult the Pythian priestess at Delphi. The response (if indeed the sources have not been confused and Julian actually consulted the oracle at Daphne rather than Delphi) is the last recorded oracular response from Delphi and is (as one might expect) dramatically (and perhaps too suitably) final: "Tell the king the fair wrought hall is fallen to the ground. No longer has Phoebus a hut, nor a prophetic laurel, nor a spring that speaks. The water of speech even is quenched."[54]

In AD 365, just two years after Julian's death, Greece was rocked by a devastating earthquake. In the latest scholarly publication by French archaeologists concerning the temple of Apollo, it is argued that the damage done by this earthquake might have been similar to that of the 373 BC earthquake, and that it was certainly enough to distort the east-west axis of the foundations of the temple (a distortion still visible today—see fig. 7.2).[55] We don't know how much damage was done to other parts of the Delphic complex, but it's likely there were some who believed it was a sign that Delphi's end was finally approaching. It was, however, not to be, at least not quite yet. The Christian emperors, Valens and Valentinian (AD 364–75), were honored at Delphi with an imposing (and new rather than reused) base topped with statues in the Roman agora in the early 370s AD, which thanked them for their benefaction to the city.[56] Perhaps that benefaction came in the form of repairing any damage from the AD 365 earthquake. If so, it was an important example of the kind of religious peace Valens and Valentinian sought to create between paganism and Christianity during their rule: Christian emperors giving help to a famous pagan shrine and being honored in return, in a far more generous way than Delphi had honored Constantine and his family successors.[57] But, at the same time, the inscription relating to the honoring of these emperors also reveals a crucial public change in Delphic status. For centuries Delphi had described itself in its official inscriptions as "*hiera*," a "sacred place." Even in honoring the Constantinian emperors, Delphi had proudly continued to claim its (pagan) holy title.[58] But in the inscription honoring Valens and Valentinian, Delphi drops it. It is only a city, it claims, perhaps because, despite the era of religious peace (and indeed because of it), it is no longer advisable to draw attention to one's pagan credentials. The monument to Valens and Valentinian is the last known pagan monument at Delphi.[59] In the last thirty years of the fourth century AD, the Roman world witnessed increasingly damaging attacks by Christians on pagan shrines; the official outlawing of paganism by the Roman Emperor Theodosius in the early 390s; and, as a result, the official end to the pagan sanctuary of Apollo at Delphi.

What I found stranger still was that the most famous place in
the world should have suffered such a reversal of fortune that
we were obliged to look for Delphi in Delphi and enquire
about the whereabouts of Apollo's temple as we stood on its
foundations.

—J. Spon, *1678 Voyage d'Italie, de Dalmatie, de Grèce et du Levant*

12
THE JOURNEY CONTINUES

It is at first sight surprising that we find a Christian writer, Claudian,
during the time of the Christian Emperor Honorious in the early fifth
century AD, talking with enthusiasm about Delphi and its pagan mythology, a religious sanctuary officially shut down with the outlawing
of paganism. As Greece was once again menaced by northern invaders,
Claudian imagines that the god Apollo must have rejoiced after his victory in the third century BC over these barbarians, a victory that assured
"no barbarian [would drink] with defiled mouth the Castalian waters
and the streams which have fore-knowledge of fate." What Claudian's
dream highlights is not only the difficult times in which Greece found
itself during the early fifth century AD (no Apollo to come to the rescue
this time), but also that Delphi's pagan days, like those of many other
pagan sanctuaries, may not have been so abruptly cut short (as we may
have initially supposed) at the time of Theodosius's official outlawing
of paganism in AD 391. Instead we see a much slower, more muddled,
transition from paganism to Christianity.[1]

During this slow evolution over the course of the fifth and sixth centuries AD, what was Delphi like (see plate 1)? Houses, ceramic workshops,
ovens, and at least two cisterns seem to have been built into and over the

athletic compound. At the Athena sanctuary, for centuries having been treated as something of a readily available quarry, there was no letup in the reuse of the blocks from its temples and structures. The areas to the west and east of the Apollo sanctuary seem to incorporate expanding arenas of habitation (with the eastern side seemingly slight poorer than the western side). Immediately around the Apollo sanctuary perimeter wall, in the period up to the middle sixth century AD, a number of fairly wealthy houses and baths have been identified. Some of these had their origins in previous periods; some were new and employed reused material from monumental dedications in the Apollo sanctuary, and some were simply monumental dedications turned into houses (like the west stoa).[2]

Within the Apollo sanctuary itself, much of the northern half (including the Cnidian lesche) seems to have been slowly occupied by houses (see plate 2). The Chian altar in front of the temple was dismantled. Most of the still-standing treasuries around the sanctuary were turned into utilitarian buildings of one sort or another, and baths were established in the niche of Craterus to the northwest of the temple of Apollo. Over the course of the fifth and sixth centuries AD, the sanctuary of Apollo was absorbed into a seemingly prosperous urban settlement, with the Roman agora continuing to act as a busy commercial center (it was the only area not to be invaded by private buildings). And it is as part of this slow transition that Delphi offers us, once again, an important irony. Today, tourists visiting the sanctuary are guided through it by the zigzag stone pathway leading up to the temple terrace (see plate 2, fig. 0.1). Most maps of the sanctuary highlight this pathway, and it is often labeled the "sacred way." Yet it is entirely the creation of the final phase of Delphi's life: a pathway constructed out of reused pieces of stone from around the Apollo sanctuary to service the town that grew up in the abandoned confines of Apollo's precinct.[3] In the over one thousand years of Delphi's history as a sanctuary, there was no single pathway that led to the temple, but instead a myriad of entrances and paths at different terraced levels. The final phase of Delphi's ancient life has left an indelible impression on the way we see and move through the sanctuary today.

What place for the worship of Christ within this changing community, and what happened to the temple of Apollo itself? Scholarship in
the early twentieth century emphasized the sheer variety of Christian-
era architectural fragments found at Delphi, most of which came from
the fifth century AD and were thought to have been part of an adap-
tion of an already existing building. At the same time, these fragments
demonstrate the continued use of well-known pagan-era motifs like the
acanthus. As a result, an argument was made that the Delphians were
once again doing what they did best: actively trying to attract (now
Christian) pilgrims to the city as a place of now Christian worship by
quickly building (or rather altering current buildings in order to create)
an ornate Christian basilica.[4]

More recent investigation has emphasized, in conjunction with the
picture outlined above for Greece's slower movement toward a wholly
Christian outlook, a more gradual and less opportunistic development
of Christian worship at Delphi, beginning slowly in the town that had
always surrounded the temple complex, and growing organically over
time to engulf the sanctuary and temple of Apollo at its heart. We know
of at least three Christian basilicas that were eventually constructed at
Delphi, but none can be dated to before AD 450.[5] Indeed, it seems to
have been in the second half of the fifth century AD that Christian worship really took root at Delphi (see plate 1). The French archaeologist
Vincent Déroche, in his study of Christian-era structures, records three
basilicas at Delphi. First, a basilica "of the new village" west of the sanctuary (beyond the west necropolis of the ancient town), built mostly
from recycled material circa AD 475–500, and with a well-preserved mosaic floor. Second, a newly built basilica in the gymnasium to the east of
the Apollo sanctuary (later covered by the Church of the Virgin built
in 1743); and third, another newly built basilica constructed inside the
sanctuary itself.[6] But this basilica did not occupy the temple of Apollo.
Instead it was most probably constructed just to the north of the temple,
on the terrace between the northern terracing wall of the temple terrace
and the area of the theater (see plate 2). Built in a rich and cosmopolitan style, it appears to have been the bishop's official basilica, following

Delphi's establishment as an episcopate, and it remained the site of a Christian church right through until its excavation in the late nineteenth century. In addition to these three certain basilicas, there may have been a fourth, dating to perhaps the end of the sixth century AD. Pieces of mosaic have been found on the roadside approaching Delphi (above the gymnasium area—see plate 1). This mosaic was found beneath a later chapel dedicated to Saint George, which was itself only removed as part of the excavations in the late nineteenth century. As such, scholars have argued that the mosaic may have belonged to a pre–Saint George chapel basilica.[7]

Delphi, then, was a curious mix. On the one hand, it had, by the beginning of the sixth century AD, a significant Christian community centered around three (possibly four) basilicas, compared to ancient sanctuaries like Olympia that had only one. But this community did not actively destroy the pagan sanctuary or, importantly, the temple of Apollo.[8] Instead, we have to imagine a community in which the abandoned temple, still a massive and imposing structure, stood almost parallel to the new, itself rich and ornate, basilica immediately to its north, at the center of a developing urban (and increasingly Christian) community that slowly expanded to take over the rest of the Apollo sanctuary. And at the same time, while there is no sense that the inhabitants of Delphi tried to preserve any parts of the pagan sanctuary (and thus, it seems, had no interest in living off the rewards of Delphi's long-term reputation as a place of valued history and memory), there is no evidence for any kind of organized or willful destruction of it either.[9] Indeed, what is fascinating about these changes at Delphi is the way in which Christians seem to have synthesized and incorporated pagan traditions. A lamp, for example, found in the eastern baths at Delphi (those renovated at the beginning of the fourth century AD), bears an image of Christ with a serpent at his feet, merging Delphi's snakey mythology with the worship of Christ. Moreover, the fourth basilica dating to the end sixth century AD, discovered above the gymnasium, may have been dedicated at this stage (and definitely was later in its history) to Saint George, a saint whose fight with the dragon overlaps directly with pagan Apolline and Delphic mythology.[10]

Apart from the possible construction of a Saint George basilica toward the end of the century, the second half of the sixth century AD likely bore witness to a downturn in the degree of opulence apparent in the structures and architecture of the fifth and early sixth century. Houses were abandoned, doors shut up, and cisterns no longer used. At the same time, the area inhabited by the citizens of Delphi significantly contracted. The countryside was abandoned and people huddled together in among poorly built houses and workshops in the central area of the old sanctuary and city. This downturn and contraction may have been the result of the plague of Justinian, but it may also have been the result of a fresh wave of uncertainty in relation to increasing territorial invasion.[11] And in the early seventh century AD, Delphi's luck finally ran out. A new series of invasions from the north by the Slavs caused huge devastation across Greece. At Delphi a hastily constructed defensive wall from this era cuts across the gymnasium, abandoning the remains of the Athena sanctuary and city around it—a final attempt to protect the core of the city (see plate 1). But it was not to be. The final layer of the city of Delphi shows signs of destruction and wholesale abandonment.[12] We hear little from Delphi for over eight hundred years, apart from the occasional inference that small pocket communities were living in among the ruins during the medieval period.

The appearance of the Italian merchant Cyriac of Ancona in the Parnassian mountains of Greece for six days from 21 March AD 1436 must have caused quite a stir among the sparse local population.[13] Cyriac is the first foreigner visitor we know of who went searching for Delphi after the site was abandoned in the early seventh century AD. In that time, Delphi had simply faded away. The remnants of its once proud buildings gradually crumbling; its glistening marble and local limestone either buried under, or incorporated into, a new, impoverished and ramshackle settlement known not as Delphi but as Castri; its inhabitants seemingly unaware of the remains over which they built and that, in some cases, still stood visible above the earth.[14] It is one of the most humbling facts in Delphi's long history that even with its important and glorious past it could be forgotten and lost—even by those who lived on top of it.[15]

What brought Cyriac here in AD 1436? His interest in the physical remains of the ancient world reflected the growth of the Humanist movement and the First Renaissance in Italy from the early fourteenth century and led by scholars such as Petrarch. Up to this point, western European interest in Greece, let alone Delphi, had been confined to the study of its surviving literary texts. The idea of actually visiting—of seeking the physical remains of classical antiquity—was distinctly unattractive. Since the church schism of AD 1054, Greece, as part of the Eastern Orthodox Church, had been viewed with suspicion: a place difficult to travel to, unsafe to travel in, and with little assured reward.[16]

Yet by Cyriac's time, there was increased agreement among the Humanists that the rediscovery of classical antiquity was an important step in the process of applying its lessons to the contemporary world. In the early fifteenth century, the Florentine monk Cristoforo Buondelmonti's *Description of Crete* (1414) and *Books of the Islands of the Archipelago* (1422) were best sellers. Cyriac took the search one step further with the idea that "monuments and inscriptions are more faithful witnesses of classical antiquity than are the texts of ancient writers." His task, as one companion put it, was "to restore antiquity, or redeem it from extinction."[17]

Cyriac traveled throughout the Mediterranean between 1435 and 1453. He recorded in great detail what he saw, but his notebooks were all but lost in a library fire in Pesaro in 1514. The scant remains tell of his journey to Delphi in March 1436, when he saw the stadium and its theater (which would later disappear from view entirely as generations of rock fall, earth, and habitation covered it); a round building he thought was the temple of Apollo (in fact the Argive semicircle in the southeastern corner of the Apollo sanctuary—see plate 2, fig. 6.2); several tombs and statues still intact, as well as a large selection of inscriptions.[18]

What would also have been clear to Cyriac as he traveled around Greece and elsewhere during those years—as was becoming increasingly clear also to the rest of Europe—was the advancing power of the Ottomans. In 1453, just seventeen years after Cyriac's visit to Delphi, the sultan launched his final assault on Constantinople, closing the book on the Byzantine world and rendering Greece part of his dominions. It is a bizarre note in the story of the first person seeking to save the remains of the ancient world from extinction that our last glimpse of Cyriac, in May 1453, finds him standing at the sultan's side (and reading to the sultan relevant sections from the great ancient writers) as the sultan prepares to take Constantinople.[19]

Cyriac's visit to Delphi was an exception. We have no record of anyone else making this journey for over two hundred years after this, until the English mathematician Francis Vernon made his way there on the 26 September 1675, by which time the village of Castri had grown, and the sanctuary of Delphi had sunk further into the ground. In the meantime, despite the difficulty of obtaining access to, and traveling in, the region, the great interest in classical antiquity had continued to grow, particularly in the French and English courts. By the late seventeenth century, the idea that there was much to see, that it was important to see it and if possible own it as well was established. The acquiring of such artifacts was particularly valuable as an instrument of international power politics between royal families and aristocrats. It was in this atmosphere that two famous travelers reached Castri a year after Vernon, on 30 January 1676: the French doctor Jacob Spon and the English naturalist George Wheler, both crucial to the history of the development of archaeology. Spon was the first to use the word "archaeology," in the preface to his publication about the diverse monuments in Greece. At Delphi, they identified the gymnasium that lay beneath the monastery of the Panagyia (which would later keep a register of all visitors to the area), but otherwise "had to stop there and be satisfied with what we could learn from books of the former wealth and grandeur of the place: for nothing remains now but wretched poverty and all its glory has passed like a dream."[20] Jacob Spon's thoughts continued in the epigraph to this chapter. He was overwhelmed and sobered that a place as famous and as wonderful as Delphi could disappear. For Spon, Delphi was the ultimate warning about what could occur as the result of human hubris.

Soon after their visit, in 1687, the Venetian assault against the Turks in Athens led to the igniting of the gunpowder store in the Parthenon, whereupon large sections of the building were destroyed. Yet this did nothing to slow the passion for antiquities, both as possessions for the powerful, and as important windows into the past for those interested in history. In 1734 the Society of Dilettanti was formed in London for aristocrats who had visited Italy and who had, at least according to Horace Walpole, been drunk (preferably in Italy). The discovery of Herculaneum in 1738 and Pompeii in 1748 fanned the flames of interest. In France, there was a craze for Greek inscriptions, not only because they were considered the most useful type of evidence for illustrating history, but also (and perhaps more importantly) because they could be used as meaningful mottoes for medals struck to commemorate the exploits of Louis XIV (for which the Academie des Inscriptions et Belles Lettres had been established in 1701).[21]

By 1748, just as Pompeii was being uncovered, the English architects James Stuart and Nicholas Revett found willing ears to their call that "unless exact drawings can be speedily made, all [Athens's] beauteous fabricks, temples, theatres, palaces will drop into oblivion, and Posterity will have to reproach us." Volume I of their detailed drawings of monuments in Greece was published in 1762, and it was as part of their work that they came to Delphi in 1751. During their stay en route from Thermopylae, they were bewitched by the romantic feel of the natural landscape, but also took time to investigate in among the buildings of the haphazard village of Castri. They found part of the enormous polygonal wall covered in inscriptions that supported the temple terrace (see plate 2). The stones of the wall were so large, they lamented, that they were unable to take them away.[22]

Some laughed at this newfound love of all things Greek, but many would have agreed with Gavin Hamilton, a dealer in Rome, who (with great advertising aplomb) said in 1779, "Never forget that the most valuable acquisition a man of refined taste can make is a piece of Greek sculpture." The "gusto Greco" was now in full maturity, fueled also by the crucial writings of the German scholar Johann Joachim Winckelmann in the second half of the eighteenth century on the beauty and importance of Greek sculpture. Although Winckelmann never actually set foot in Greece, more and more travelers did make the arduous journey to Athens, and a handful made the even more difficult journey to Castri nestled in the Parnassian mountains. Some even went so far as to drink from the water of the Castalian Spring, famed in the surviving literature as the bathing place of the oracular priestess (see fig. 0.2). Richard Chandler, on an expedition sanctioned by the Society of the Dilettanti, bathed in the waters in July 1766 and, despite the summer weather, was overwhelmed by the coldness of the water to the extent that he shook so badly he was unable to walk without aid. Returning home, he wrapped himself up, drank large quantities of wine, and began to sweat profusely. Perhaps, he mused, this was what the ancients had taken for the oracular priestess's possession by the god.[23]

But despite this kind of ancient amusement-park activity, what could Delphi really offer its visitors? Inscriptions were all the rage, and Delphi had many of them to offer. Late eighteenth-century visitors write with glee of finding more inscriptions than they had time to record. But the disappointment felt by Spon and Wheler at the meager remains of what had been, according to the ancient literary sources, one of the most extraordinary sites in the ancient world, continued to pervade visitors' thoughts. As they arrived with their literary texts in hand—particularly Pausanias, who, as indicated above, had written the first tour guide of the sanctuary back in the second century AD—Delphi's first modern tourists were continually disappointed in their inability to see the site itself. William Gell's drawing of Castri from 1805 outlines the little that was on view (fig. 12.1). As the Swedish priest A. F. Sturtzenbecker put it following his visit in 1784: "Delphi has kept nothing of its former splendour. Everything is lost bar its name."[24]

The beginning of the nineteenth century witnessed a quickening in the pulse of interest in, and travel to, Greece. For the English, this was in part because the Napoleonic Wars had made travel to Italy, the traditional destination for those interested in the ancient world, difficult. Greece was the next best alternative as part of the Grand Tour. "Epidauria" claimed the English naturalist Edward Clarke in 1801, "is a region as easily to be visited as Derbyshire." At the same time, painting at the

Figure 12.1. A drawing of Castri/Delphi in the nineteenth century AD by William Gell (1805) (© The Trustees of the British Museum)

beginning of the nineteenth century began explicitly to take its inspiration from the classical landscape as *the* example of the picturesque, and Greece became a kind of idyllic Arcadia mixed with pure fantasy and occasionally accurate depictions of surviving ruins. This longing for the idealized, however, also clashed with an increasing interest in securely identifying ancient sites in the Greek landscape, spurred on by the wider availability of key texts like Pausanias (translated into English for the first time at the end of the eighteenth century). In two campaigns, 1805–1807 and 1809–10, British army officer William Martin Leake, for example, mapped the Greek landscape in meticulous detail, which led to the discovery of sites like the Temple of Bassae in 1812.[25] In response, in 1813, the Society of Friends of the Muses was set up in Greece to help uncover and collect antiquities, assist students, and publish books.

Yet such an interest in the landscape, among western Europeans, also chimed with, and indeed helped provoke, an increasing interest in owning, and exporting, its contents. From 1810, the topographers started to lose ground to the collectors, spurred on as the latter were by Elgin's work in bringing the Parthenon marbles to England 1801–1803 and displaying them in a public exhibition in 1807 before they were bought by the British Museum in 1816. It was an act matched by the French, who, in 1833 brought the Luxor Obelisk to the Place de la Concorde in Paris, and by the Bavarian King, who bought the sculptures of the Temple of Aphaia at Aegina in 1811. The overarching feeling was that modern Europe was now worthy of ancient Greece, and thus had the right to take what remained of it.[26]

The village of Castri, and ancient Delphi, were not indifferent to this three-pronged European interest to idealize, record, and physically capture/walk off with ancient Greece in the first decades of the nineteenth century. William Gell's paintings, despite his rather desolate drawings, offer Arcadian images of the Castalian fountain, and those of William Walker offer encouraging visions of the site as one in which ancient ruins complement modern structures (plate 7). George Hamilton, Earl of Aberdeen and later prime minister, engraved his name on a marble by the Monastery of the Panaghia in 1803 (in the area of the ancient gymnasium). Henry Raikes mapped the topography of the Parnassian landscape and located for the first time the Corycian cave eight hundred meters above Delphi, in 1806 (see map 3). Yet the burial of most of the site underneath the village frustrated any real attempt at excavation or removal, despite the fact that Sir William Hamilton, better known for his discovery of Greek vases in Etruria, had persuaded Lord Nelson at the end of the eighteenth century to ship to England a small altar found at Delphi (it now sits in Castle Howard in Yorkshire), persuasion successful perhaps because Hamilton's young wife was also Nelson's mistress.[27]

It is difficult to underestimate the myriad ways in which Greece impacted western Europe during the first quarter of the nineteenth century: King Ludwig of Bavaria even claimed he would rather be a citizen of ancient Greece than king of Bavaria. Crucial to understanding this impact is the fact that there was often little agreement (and not less than a pinch of hypocrisy) between its strongest advocates. The Society of

Figure 12.2. A copy of graffiti found on a column in the gymnasium at Delphi, including the signature of Lord Byron ([La redécouverte de Delphes fig. 28])

Dilettanti actively tried to undermine the authenticity of Elgin and the Parthenon marbles because they were examples of the naturalistic style of sculpture, which the Society detested in comparison to its preferred "Ideal" style. The poet Lord Byron in turn sought to disgrace Elgin for his denuding of Greece (see *Childe Harold's Pilgrimage*; *The Curse of Minerva* 1812), caring little for Elgin's stated aim "to improve the arts in England," preferring instead to honor the glory that was Greece by recreating it in poetry and action. Yet Byron also happily engraved his name on ancient stones at a number of ancient sites, including on a column from the gymnasium at Delphi (fig. 12.2).[28]

Despite this cultural, intellectual, and political storm of which Greece was the center—because of the difficulties of seeing the ancient site—the overwhelming feeling was nevertheless of nostalgic sadness and disappointment at the gap between the literary accounts of Delphi's past glory and its meager present. Byron complained bitterly of having to sample a half a dozen stagnant brooks before finding the Castalian fountain, which he pronounced "ugly." The artist Louis Dupré complained in 1819 about finding not the "superb Delphi, but the miserable village of Castri."[29]

Yet a larger storm was brewing that would fundamentally affect the future of the site. In 1771, following his travels in Greece, Pierre Augustin Guys, a French merchant turned proto-anthropologist, had published his thoughts on the parallels between ancient and modern Greeks claiming not only to see much connection between them, but also that modern Greeks preserved a simplicity lamentably lost in Western Europe. Even more importantly, his work offered the idea that the modern Greeks were not without hope, that their spirits were dormant, waiting for the right moment to rise up to glory once again. His work won great acclaim with Catherine the Great in Russia, who meddled in Greek politics in the 1770s, persuading the Greeks that Russia would support them if they rose up against the Turks. The putative revolution was a disaster. But it sowed the seeds for European support for the Greek war of independence when it came in 1821. In that war, the heritage of ancient Greece was crucial both as an incitement to revolt, and as a marker for what a newly liberated Greece might achieve.[30]

The end of the war of independence, and the linking of Greece and Germany through the crowning of Otto, son of Ludwig of Bavaria, as king of the Hellenes in 1833, marked the beginning of a new phase both for Greek archaeology and for German scholarship in Greece. In 1829, Greek authorities had permitted a small excavation at Castri, which revealed the extraordinary sarcophagus of Meleager (now on display in front of the museum at Delphi—see fig. 11.3). In 1831 the German Friedrich Thiersch made the first complete description of the site of Castri and its visible Delphic remains. In 1834 Ludwig Ross (a German scholar who was professor at the University of Athens) brought King Otto and his wife, Queen Amelie, to Delphi. The king even made the ascent up to the Corycian cave (see figs. 0.2, 1.2). In return the local inhabitants petitioned the king for the construction of a small museum at Castri to safeguard finds that were turning up with increasing frequency. How to manage and protect the legacy of ancient Greece was an increasing concern. The first archaeological site, the acropolis in Athens, had been officially designated in 1834. The Greek Archaeological Society was formed in 1837, and the first law concerning the selling and transportation of antiquities was passed in 1836. In 1838 Delphi was included in a list of sites where it was illegal to give as a dowry any piece of land on which there were antiquities.[31]

Yet at Delphi, visitors' responses to the site were simultaneously turning in three different directions. First, the by now traditional lyric wonder and nostalgic disappointment. The Greek historian Andréas Moustoxydis, visiting the site in 1834, recommended that you travel by night to experience Delphi's mystery and then see at dawn its misery, as the site appears "in front of you, behind you, on top of you, all around you." In September 1836 Prince Hermann von Pückler Muskau commented that "full of reverence, I hesitated to enter this sanctuary, even though all that I saw on the site of the temple was a lamentable village of wretched ruined houses."[32] The second response was to attempt excavation where possible in among the village buildings. In 1840 Carl Müller undertook a small excavation of part of the Apollo temple substructure and polygonal wall (a part of which had first been exposed by Stuart and Revett less than a hundred years before). Müller's aim was to once again gaze on the temple sculptures, which scholars knew from the literary descriptions of Pausanias and Euripides. What the excavation produced, however, was not the hoped-for sculpture, but more and more inscriptions. Müller contented himself with recording as many of them as possible. But conditions at Delphi were harsh, particularly the summer heat. On 26 July 1840, Müller wrote to his wife:

> I gambled on my ability to endure the heat and began to copy the inscriptions on an upturned stone, hanging upside down with the sun beating on my face. I paid dearly for this, however. I felt a burning in my skull, together with pain and irritation. I have reached the point where I am able to do no more at Delphi since every new attempt on my part re-awakens the pain, and I cannot even escape this incessant heat.

Just four days later, Müller died of sunstroke at the site.[33]

Figure 12.3. An early photo of the town of Castri above Delphi before excavations began (© EFA [La redécouverte de Delphes fig. 48])

The third response, however, was to have the most important ramifications for the local villagers and, ultimately, for Delphi as well. From 1838 there was an attempt to begin the systematic release of ruins from under the village as part of a larger policy for rebuilding following the war of independence (fig. 12.3). The plan was for a gradual transfer of houses to a new site through a stick and carrot approach. The carrot was the offer to pay the locals to undertake the move. The stick was to forbid any more repairs to their current houses. The first stage in this process was to value all the properties and agree on a price with the local community. The locals responded, now all too well aware of the gold mine they seemed to be sitting on, by trebling the value of their homes. As a result, the plan ground to a halt, leaving the local villagers in the curious, and rather unhelpful position of not being able to repair their homes, yet with no agreement over what they might be paid to move, when they would move, or even where they would move. In 1841 three separate requests were made to the authorities to either get on with the plan and excavate or let them repair their homes (see fig. 12.4). Some

Figure 12.4. An early photo of conditions in the town of Castri above Delphi before the excavations began (© EFA [La redécouverte de Delphes fig. 52])

locals took the matter into their own hands. The flamboyant Captain Dimos Frangos, capitalizing on the fact that all excavations so far had not been left open but had been refilled, took over the land that Müller had excavated (and died studying) in 1840 and built atop it the ancillary rooms of his house.[34]

In part thanks to the lack of success of the grand plan to completely uncover the site, the predominant activity at Delphi during the 1840s and 1850s was ongoing wonder coupled with nostalgic disappointment, fueled by small excavations where possible conducted both by the Greek archaeological service and by predominantly French and German scholars. In 1843 the German scholar Ernst Curtius published his *Anecdota Delphica*, and in 1858 the local villagers were proud enough of the heritage of their village, not to mention increasingly savvy about its implications for their own future wealth, to change the name on the door lintel of their village school from Castri back to Delphi.[35] Twelve hundred years since its abandonment in the early seventh century AD, Delphi was officially back on the map.

Yet in reality, Delphi was left out of the huge leaps forward in Greek archaeology during these decades. From the 1850s to the 1870s, significant discussions about the material culture of the ancient world were taking place in universities across Europe and transforming interest in ancient Greece from romanticism to erudition; and the poster-site for this transition was not Delphi, but Olympia. As Curtius, who had focused on Olympia since his early work on Delphi in 1843, demanded in his Berlin lecture on 10 January 1852, "When will the womb be opened again, to bring the works of the ancients to the light of day? What lies there in the dark depths is life of our life."[36] Olympia, given its famous games, had the promise to deliver examples of the ideal of Greek physical beauty and architectural excellence the modern world clamored for, and scholars of ancient Greece thought key to understanding its culture. In 1874 the German Archaeological Institute was opened, and on 25 April 1875, the first legally explicit agreement between Greece and a foreign country for the excavation of an entire ancient site—Olympia—was signed.

What was going on at Delphi during these years? Throughout the 1850s, the Greek authorities sought to keep records of objects found and the state of the site, noting with increasing concern that what was left would further disintegrate and perish if not more carefully looked after. So exasperated was Kyriakos Pittakos, the head of the Greek

Archaeological Society, that he even proposed in committee that a rich Greek be found to buy the entire site for purposes of excavation; and so worried was the Society about the survival of what was left at Delphi that it took official note of his proposition. Meanwhile, small excavations continued in 1861 and 1862, particularly by French scholars who, following the establishment of the French School in Athens on 11 September 1846, had a permanent base in the country. At the same time, the Committee of Antiquaries, founded in 1862 in Greece, declared its aim to raise money for excavating Delphi, money it hoped to earn through running a regular Greek lottery game. In 1867 a commission for excavating Delphi was formed, with one member of the committee, P. Kalligas, lawyer for the National Bank of Greece, pronouncing a harrowing assessment of the pitiful conditions found in the village of Castri/Delphi, which had, according to him, the highest infant mortality rate in Greece (see figs. 12.3, 12.4). The fountain of Castri, it was pointed out, which had been cleaned out earlier in the nineteenth century, was, by the mid-1860s, once again filthy. But their efforts to prepare the ground for an excavation of Delphi to match that of Olympia also met with increasingly stiff resistance from local inhabitants who continued to demand a high price for their homes. The Committee of Antiquaries, with its grand aims, was dissolved in 1869.[37]

The lack of progress in the 1860s is not surprising. Greece's focus was elsewhere, following the exile of King Otto, and the arrival of his replacement, King George I, in 1862, and the Cretan revolution in 1869. But on 20 July 1870, a wake-up call was delivered in the form of an earthquake. The village of Castri/Delphi was bombarded with rocks falling from the high cliffs of the Parnassian mountains, and thirty locals were killed. Here, amid the disaster, was an opportunity: the locals were understandably keener to move, the need to protect the ancient site clearer than ever. A new commission, this time diplomatically called "the Commission for the establishment of the inhabitants of Delphi," was formed, with the aim of identifying a new site for the villagers to live in. The search was on to raise the money to effect the change. In 1871 the Greek Archaeological Society took the Russian ambassador to

Delphi to discuss the possibilities of excavation; and, though there was no money forthcoming from that quarter, in 1872, the Greek Archaeological Society was able to offer a loan to the Greek government in the amount of 90,000 drachmas for expropriation of the village. But negotiations were stifled by arguments first over the interest rate the Society could charge, and second by the locals' refusal to give up rights not only to their houses but also to their fields, and their demand that recompense be paid in a single sum and not in dribs and drabs.[38]

Once more, the plans to excavate Delphi were on the back burner, but it was not long before wider events forced further action. The decade of the 1870s was a momentous one for excavation in Greece. In 1873 Schliemann found "Priam's treasure" at Troy (he visited Delphi in 1870). In 1875, work started at Olympia. In 1876 the French began to dig at Delos, just as Schliemann did at Mycenae, where he soon uncovered the shaft graves. Given such a spectacular rostra of discovery, the pressure was on for a place as important as Delphi to be excavated. The Greek Archaeological Society, which had been raising funds via the only legal lottery in Greece since 1876, began in 1877 to negotiate with individual locals to buy their property, thinking if they convinced a few key individuals, everyone else would follow suit. Captain Dimos Frangos was their target, and in 1878, he eventually agreed to sell his less-than-luxury house and property for the staggering sum of nine thousand drachmas.[39] But even if they managed to convince all the locals to sell up (and had enough cash to pay them), who would undertake such a massive and difficult excavation?

On 28 December 1878, Paul Foucart became director of the French School in Athens. He was one of the first of what have become known simply as "Delphiens": scholars dedicated to Delphi. Foucart had uncovered parts of the polygonal wall in 1860 and was convinced the French should secure the right to excavate the site. He was not alone: since the Germans had signed an agreement to excavate Olympia in the mid-1870s, there had been tacit promises that the French could have the same deal elsewhere. In the corridors of the Congress of Berlin in June and July 1878, while the main business at hand was stabilizing the Balkans in the wake of diminishing Ottoman power, the French prime minister made the first official request to the Greek delegation to excavate Delphi, and in 1880 the Greek Archaeological Society made a small area of land they had bought at Delphi available to the French for excavation. The results were promising, with parts of the Athenian stoa coming to light (see plate 2). Even more promising was the state of international affairs, particularly Greece's desire for further territorial gains at the expense of the Ottoman Empire, which inclined Greece toward doing what it could to secure French goodwill in return for support in the international negotiations. In 1881 a flurry of diplomatic activity between the Greek prime minister Alexandros Koumoundouros; the French ambassador in Athens le Comte de Moüy; and Foucart, the director of the French School, resolved most of the issues in less than four months. On 13 May 1881, Koumoundouros announced his intention to the Greek Archaeological Society to give France the right to excavate Delphi, and the 13 June 1881 was set as the date for signing the agreement.[40]

It was not to be. In fact, the negotiations took another ten years, an amount of time, as French scholars are fond of pointing out, equal to the length of the Trojan War. The delay was not due to a lack of interest in archaeology—in fact, quite the opposite. Foreign interest continued to build: in 1882 the American School of Classical Studies was opened, and in 1885 the British School. At the same time, the Greek Archaeological Society had become better funded and more sure of itself, so much so that it objected to Koumoundouros's plan to give the French the right to excavate Delphi, instead requesting to undertake the job itself.[41] The real problem, however, was still the inability to agree on a price or a process for moving the village of Castri. In the days before the planned signing of the 1881 agreement, the Greek government realized the ridiculous sums it would have to pay (Captain Frangos, remember, had secured nine thousand drachmas for a property worth perhaps one hundred). The deal was delayed, pending the passing of a law that would force the villagers to accept a market value for their property.

In the meantime, on 2 February 1882, a convention was signed between the French and Greek governments on the terms of the excavation. On 12 March, however, Koumoundouros resigned in the wake of elections following the annexation of Thessalia and Arta as part of Greek territory. He died just under a year later. In his place, Charilos Tricoupis was asked by the king to form a new government. Tricoupis took a very different approach to the negotiations, one centered on Greek currants. Since the 1850s, the latter had been the principal export of Greece. England imported large quantities for all its rich puddings, and the French began importing larger quantities after a disease killed off many French vines in the 1870s. Production of Corinthian currants rose, as a result, from 104,000 kg in 1878 to 162,000 kg in 1888. France alone, by 1889, was importing 69,500 tons a year. Greek currants were big business, and France needed them in the 1880s. Tricoupis saw an opportunity to link business to archaeology, and inferred that it was impossible to give France the honor of Delphi until France gave Greece a cut in French import taxes on Greek currants. The standoff continued into 1883, Tricoupis, floating the notion that the French might also have to help pay the costs of moving the locals, until such a stalemate was reached that everyone stopped talking about currants and Delphi.[42]

We hear little more about negotiations for Delphi until June 1886, when the same positions resurfaced. However, by 6 November 1886, the French had agreed to a commercial deal on currants. On 31 December 1886, negotiations over Delphi sprang back to life, and on 4 February 1887, a new agreement about Delphi was signed, limiting Greek expense for moving the inhabitants to 60,000 drachmas. On the Greek side, the renewed enthusiasm to push for both bills made sound economic sense, and was helped by the fact that the minister for foreign affairs at the time, Stephanos Dragoumis, had visited and enjoyed Delphi a decade before. But what caused this French willingness to compromise? In part, new principal actors. Le Comte de Moüy had been replaced by le Comte de Montholon, a canny political operator. But more important, the French realized they were not the only ones interested in Delphi. In 1884 the German archaeologist Hans Pomtow had undertaken (in somewhat clandestine fashion) excavations at Delphi. A Franco-German enmity, in evidence in archaeology from the time of Winckelmann in the 1750s, and not helped by the Franco-Prussian War in the early 1870s, was now in full evidence regarding the honor of excavating Delphi. Nor were they the only countries interested. It was clear by 1887 that the Americans, willing to bear all the costs themselves, were also interested in Delphi.[43]

There was never any official link between the bill to reduce import tax on Greek currants and the convention to give the excavation of Delphi to the French, despite that both were adopted by the Greek parliament on the same day: 19 March 1887. But both bills failed to pass the last hurdle. The French Senate didn't ratify the French Parliament's currants bill, and, as a result, Tricoupis was "unable" to secure the Greek king's signature on the Delphi convention before its mandate passed. In the meantime, Hans Pomtow returned to Delphi in 1887 to conduct further, likely unauthorized, excavation.

Nothing more was done until 1889, and then, once again, the goad was foreign competition. The Americans in January 1889 began to ramp up their campaign to raise money for the excavation of Delphi. On 11 May 1889, the Archaeological Institute of America set out its official call for donations (their stirring words on Delphi provide the epigraph for this book). The French immediately wrote to the American secretary of state demanding assurances that the Americans would not gazump the French "right" to excavate the site. On 19 March 1890, the American secretary of state replied in diplomatic but firm terms that the Americans would not move unless they believed the French could not afford it, and that, given so much time had already elapsed, it seemed clear they couldn't. The race was on.[44]

On 28 April 1890 Tricoupis informed the French that the expropriation of the Castri village would cost 450, 000 francs, of which the Greeks would give only 60,000. On 11 June the French government made it clear they had the money. But in November 1890, Charilos Tricoupis lost power in Greek elections to Theodoros Deliyannis. At the same time, the long-suffering director of the French School in Athens, Foucart, who had spent the best part of a decade trying to secure the French excavation of Delphi, retired and was replaced by Theophile Homolle. These new players galvernized the pace of negotiations, not least because Deliyannis did not insist on linking Greek currants to Delphi since French vines had recovered and imports of Greek currants had declined substantially by 1893 to just 3,100 tons. Following some cosmetic changes to the deal (the French Parliament grumbled at paying so much to expropriate Castri and preferred to vote more money for the "excavation," which would, in reality, be used to move the village), the bill to make money available for the excavation passed in the French Parliament by 337 votes to 61 on 16 February 1891, was ratified by the Senate (despite grumbles that it made the French little better than "truffle hunters") on 4 March, and was signed into law on 8 March 1891. In Greece the agreement was signed by the king on 13 April and published on 6 May.[45]

But France's "Trojan War" was far from over. Homolle, the director of the French School, put his finger on it when claiming "the conquest of the polygonal wall will take three times as long and will cost no fewer assaults, labourers and schemes than the conquest of the walls of Troy."[46] The first problem, as ever, was the village of Castri (see fig. 12.3). Homolle had started gathering supplies for the excavation the moment the deal was published in Greece, and even set off to Delphi to mark out the excavation area that very month, in May 1891. But the Greek government was slow to put in place a commission to agree on prices with the locals. Athenian officials—thought to be less influenced by family ties than the local Phocian officials—were brought in, but the price still pushed at the ceiling of the 450,000 francs originally voted by the French Parliament. The villagers detailed further concerns about their new homes, but these were deftly sorted with small direct-cash payments (effectively, bribes) by the French administrator sent to oversee the move. His actions were deplored officially in France, but he, very realistically, understood there was no other way to keep the wheels in motion. Then the Greek election cycle got in the way in summer 1892. Tricoupis took back power and inaugurated his new government on 22 June 1892. The change of government meant there was a further delay in the payment of the Greek share of the expropriations. When Homolle went to start excavations in September 1892, he wrote, "as soon as the workshop was opened, the villagers assembled and the most excitable threw themselves at the workmen, took their tools out of their hands, claiming that, till they

Figure 12.5. A photo of the discovery of one of the Argive twins (propped up in the background), along with excavators and a uniformed soldier for their protection in the first years of the excavation (© EFA [La redécouverte de Delphes fig. 82])

were paid, no work was allowed." A gendarme, along with eleven armed soldiers, had to be provided to protect the workmen as they established the main arterial road to the site. A continued army presence, to protect the excavators, is visible in the photographs of the initial excavations (see fig. 12.5), and today's inscription depot at the site is still affectionately known as the "*stathmos*," because it occupies the site formerly used as the soldiers' headquarters.[47]

The first payment to villagers went out on 11 October 1892, four days after the inauguration of the excavation. It was a small, but solemn affair. Homolle outlined the honorable task ahead of them. A representative of the village of Castri/Delphi affirmed the village's now positive feelings about the excavation. French and Greek flags flew over the first wagons of earth carted away from the site. "The excavation would be," Tricoupis later wrote to Homolle, "époque making in the history of archaeology."[48] He was not wrong.

At noon, in the museum, I look again at the Charioteer. . . . You
try to hold on to the details. Then the analysis bothers you; you
have the impression that you are listening to a language not spoken
anymore. . . . We have worked like ants and like bees on these relics.
How close have we come to the soul that created them? I mean
this grace at its peak, this power, this modesty and the things that
the bodies symbolise. This vital breath that makes the inanimate
copper transcend the rules of logic and slip into another time . . ."

—George Seferis, *Dokimes*, vol. 2 (1981), trans. C. Capri-Karka

EPILOGUE: *Unearthing Delphi*

Ten years of discussion over negotiations to excavate Delphi gave way
in 1892 to almost ten years of excavation. The "Trojan War" for Delphi,
as the French like to label their long-lasting negotiations, now was to
become an epic Odyssey for its discovery. "La Grande Fouille," the "Big
Dig," lasted from 1892 to 1901 and would play a major part in a key era of
discovery about the ancient world. The French excavators wrote down
the day-to-day records of their quest in a journal that can be consulted
today (and now online) and that provides incredible insight not only
into the highs and lows of the excavations, nor simply into the careful
ways in which the original excavators pieced fragments of finds together
as they were discovered sometimes days and weeks apart, but also into
how, thanks to copious notes in the margins, subsequent generations of
researchers have added to this compendium, continually improving and
refining our understanding of the site.[1]

The first task had been to move the village of Castri, which was spread
over much of the Apollo sanctuary and further up the mountainside toward the stadium (see fig. 12.3). Théophile Homolle, director of excavations and director of the French School in Athens, calculated there were
one thousand building plots with three hundred owners, all of whom

Figure 13.1. A photo of the excavation in full progress, with the train tracks and wagons in use as the entrance to the Apollo sanctuary is cleared (© EFA [La redécouverte de Delphes fig. 77])

had to be moved to new homes on a site chosen about a kilometer to the west (see fig. 0.2). It must have been an odd sight as, on each side of the rocky crag of the Parnassian mountains that stretches out on Delphi's west side hiding it from the world, simultaneously one community was constructed and another demolished. Some inhabitants cried as they left the homes their parents and grandparents had lived and died in; others were surely happy at their good fortune—to be paid for their old homes and gifted the value of their new ones as well. But those initial years were not easy for the local inhabitants. The new village school was delayed, and so the children were taught by the local priests using the church that oversaw the village graveyard as a school.[2]

And the task of excavation was enormous. Homolle was assisted by a small team of archaeologists; by the most competent of work managers, Henri Convert; and by over two hundred workmen. Eighteen hundred meters of train track were laid crisscrossing the site on which fifty-seven wagons took the earth away as it was excavated (fig. 13.1). The tracks were laid at such a gradient that, when full of earth, a single workmen could use gravity to push them easily by hand away from the excavation toward the dumping area, and then packs of mules were used to pull them empty back up to the excavation area. In 1895 alone, 160,000 wag-onloads of earth were excavated (see fig. 13.2).[3]

Figure 13.2. An early photo of the excavation in progress with the Athenian stoa and temple terracing wall emerging from underneath the modern village of Castri (© EFA [La redécouverte de Delphes fig. 66])

The initial finds were impressive, even compared to some of the famous sculptures that had already come to light in earlier trial excavations (like the sarcophagus of Meleager discovered in 1842 or the Naxian Sphinx discovered in 1861). In the first two months of excavation, crucial inscriptions had come to light. In the first full season of 1893, the altar of the Chians; the rock of the Sibyl; and the treasury of the Athenians with its carved metopes, inscriptions, and recorded musical notation for the ancient hymns to Apollo were found. In 1894 the beautiful statue of the Roman Emperor Hadrian's onetime lover and treasured companion, Antinous (see fig. 11.1), was uncovered, as were the treasuries of the Cnidians and Sicyonians. These discoveries were headline news in a world hungry for more from the ancient world. The hymns from the Athenian treasury were played for the Greek king and queen on 15 March 1894, at the Odeon in St. Petersburg on 11 May, as far as Johannesburg later that year, and even at the conference organized by Pierre de Coubertin in 1894 at which it was decided to restage the ancient Olympic games. Plaster casts of finds such as the Naxian Sphinx and the statue of Antinous quickly made their way to exhibitions in Paris, engendering continued amazement at the quality, skill, and sheer beauty of ancient sculpture. Such reactions were further fueled by the discovery, on 28 April 1896, of the famous bronze Charioteer that is now the centerpiece of the modern Delphi museum (see plate 6).[4]

But not every day produced such finds. In 1895, despite moving 160,000 wagons of earth, nothing major was found. Nor did conditions at the site make excavation easy. Heavy rain frequently interrupted excavation, and considerable time at the end of each season had to be dedicated to constructing strong barriers to protect the site from rain, mud, and rockfalls. Winds so strong that they created dust storms could also blow up. The Greco-Turkish War interrupted excavation almost entirely in 1897. The journal bears witness also to a degree of exasperation among the French archaeologists that the local workmen claimed so many religious festivals as holidays, and the French correspondence shows ongoing difficulties in agreeing with members of the Greek Archaeological service present at the site about what constituted important finds and what could be ignored. The increasing number of VIP visits did not help the progress of the excavation, nor did the continued criticisms levied by journalists and other archaeologists, particularly the German archaeologist Hans Pomtow. Pomtow had already published his own book on Delphi following his early trial excavations during the ten-year-long negotiations for the site. Now he continued to doubt French ability to undertake the task; criticized Homolle's hands-on style; and when, despite all this, the French team published a significant number of results in 1898, his review in the *Berliner Philologische Wochenschrift* indicated that scholars should forgive Homolle his inaccuracies given the mass of work he was attempting to cover.[5]

By 1901, however, the main areas of the site had been uncovered. The wagons were shipped off to other French excavations on Delos in the Cyclades, and subsequently Thasos in the northern Aegean (although two can still be seen at Delphi today). The museum at the site that housed the finds, paid for by a Madame Iphigeneia Syngros, was inaugurated on 2 May 1903, and a big party was held to celebrate the end of the excavations. Five warships, three French and two Greek, were present in the harbor below; ten thousand locals were present in the area around the stadium; and a plethora of diplomats bore witness to the event in as fine an array of fashion as could be seen on the Champs Élysées. Homolle subsequently left, elevated to the position of director of the Louvre in France, and the dig house fell silent. Only the opening of the grand hotel "Apollo Pythia" in the new nearby village by 1906 gave an indication of the transformations still to come.[6]

When Homolle and his team left the dig site, their plan was to prepare its "definitive" publication in five volumes along the lines already established for Olympia (*Olympia: History, Architecture, Inscriptions, Statues, Small Objects*).[7] On the one hand, their excavation had been an incredible success: an extremely difficult dig that had returned to light the remains of one of the most important sanctuaries in the ancient world and produced some extraordinarily fine pieces of ancient sculpture alongside important architectural discoveries and endless inscriptions. Yet, on the other hand, there was a lingering feel of disappointment, which was in part inevitable. The excavation had been conducted with ancient literary descriptions of the site literally in hand, and its progression had intentionally mirrored that of Pausanias's second-century AD tour-guide visit to the sanctuary to ensure the highest probability of identifying all the monuments he mentioned. When all the wondrous objects Pausanias alluded to—particularly the temple sculpture and, even more disappointingly, the apparatus of the oracle (also the subject of other authors like Plutarch and Diodorus)—were not uncovered, naturally there was disappointment, and not only among the excavators.[8] As one critic grumbled in response to the 1901 Delphi display at the Universal Exhibition, "the impression is sad, the reality a long way from any concept of beauty, and there is nothing to do but rely on one's imagination."[9]

The disappointment felt at the lackluster state of the physical site of Delphi at the end of the big dig prompted its director, Théophile Homolle, to attempt the reconstruction of one of its most famous monuments: the treasury of the Athenians. Almost all the original pieces of the building had been found early on in the first full year of the excavations, and the inscriptions that covered its walls—particularly the hymns to Apollo, the earliest musical notation in Mediterranean history—quickly became world famous. In July 1902 Homolle wrote to the mayor of Athens, "For the Athenians of today, it would be a noble satisfaction to write their name alongside those who fought at Marathon and to inscribe, under the eloquent dedication which recalls one of the great events in Greek—and human—history, a new inscription which will, for future generations, be a memorial to their unwavering faith towards the great accomplishments, glory and courage of their ancestors."[10]

The municipal council of Athens immediately voted to give 20,000 drachmas for the project and made Homolle a citizen of the city. In 1903 Joseph Replat, a skilled architect, was tasked with the reconstruction, which he completed not only thanks to his architectural knowledge of how the ancient stones fitted together, but also, perhaps more importantly, thanks to the piecing together of the different inscriptions covering large numbers of blocks in the treasury's walls, and thus dictating the relationship of those blocks to the building's architecture. The story goes that Replat was so dedicated to his work at Delphi that, at the end of his active life, all he chose to exclaim was simply, "Delphi, adieu!"[11] The treasury was completed on 26 September 1906 and has remained one of the sanctuary's most impressive sights ever since (see fig. 5.4)

Yet much of the rest of the site was in chaos, with large depots of stones from the excavations piled helter-skelter. The museum, opened only in 1903, was leaking badly by 1906, and parts of the site were declared unsafe, not least thanks to the continued rockfalls from the Parnassian mountains above. In 1905 a series of massive rocks fell into the Athena sanctuary, and one of them—too big to move—still sits in the middle of it today, a continuing testament to the dynamic geology of the area (see plate 8). All these problems were the headache of the Greek Archaeological Service, which had taken over the running of the site, particularly the scholarly and diligent Antonios Keramopoullos and Alexandros Kondoleon. Keramopoullos published the first guide book to the site in 1912, and Kondoleon is remembered affectionately in the archives for his unique and unswerving dedication to Delphi, its preservation and study, which meant everything from chasing after soldiers who helped themselves to small museum exhibits, to subjecting new French scholars arriving at the site to a frosty reception until their skill and love for Delphi could be proven to Kondoleon's satisfaction.[12] But the French were not the only ones there: the German Hans Pomtow, active at Delphi before the dig big, and so critical of French efforts during it, returned on several occasions to conduct small excavations and publish finds and inscriptions (strictly in contravention of the French/Greek convention on the site).[13]

World War I brought a halt to work at Delphi, and despite its not being on a front line, made it once again a rather unsafe place thanks to increased local sectarian violence: one French scholar of the time recalled seeing three severed heads on display in the local town square. The 1920s saw the emergence of a new generation of French scholars at Delphi: Robert Demangel; George Daux; and Pierre de la Coste-Messelière, under the direction of Charles Picard as director of the French School, and guided by Emilie Bourguet, one of the surviving figures of the big dig after Homolle's death in 1925. When I first visited the library of the

French dig house at Delphi in 2006, I was intrigued to find an old colonial pith helmet propped on top of the bookshelves, which, I learned, belonged to one of the most colorful Delphic scholars of the 1920s generation: Pierre de la Coste Messelière, who was never seen without it while working on the site. De la Coste-Messelière was a marquis, descended from the family of Charles VII, and had fought in World War I as a mounted cavalry officer, for which he was awarded the Croix de Guerre. Following the war, he stumbled into the university lectures of Emilie Bourguet and become hooked on Delphi. Always immaculately dressed, pipe clenched in his teeth, he developed a love and sensitivity toward ancient sculpture that resulted in a number of crucial Delphic publications; he took to the battlefield again in World War II, was again awarded the Croix de Guerre, and later returned to work once again on the site (fig. 13.3).[14]

The 1920s also saw the reconstruction of a second Delphic monument: the altar of the Chians (see plate 2, fig. 1.3). Just as the treasury of the Athenians had been reconstructed with money put forward by modern Athens, so too the modern-day islanders of Chios paid for the

Figure 13.3. Pierre de la Coste-Messelière, smoking his pipe, examining sculpture from the tholos in the sanctuary of Athena at Delphi (© EFA [La redécouverte de Delphes fig. 124])

reconstruction of the altar. On 12 March 1920 the Greek minister of public education informed the director of the French School, Charles Picard, that 10,000 drachmas had been collected and deposited in a bank account, at his disposal for the rebuilding of the altar, and reconstruction began the next month.[15] Greek cities of the modern world had begun to stake their claim once again on ancient Delphi, ensuring their monuments would once again receive the respect they'd garnered so many centuries before. In the same vein, in May 1927 the Greek lyric poet and playwright Angelos Sikélianos and his wife, the American Eva Palmer, launched the first modern Delphic festival, which sought to re-create the ancient Pythian games with gymnastic contests and the performance of tragedy (in that year, Aeschylus's *Prometheus Unbound*), bringing the world once again to Delphi.[16] But we should not underestimate the ongoing difficulties in getting to and living at Delphi at this time. The road from Arachova was not yet dreamt of, the road up from the port of Itea was still only in rough condition (see fig. 0.1). To get there from Athens in 1933 meant a slow boat from Athens to Itea that arrived at three or four in the morning, then waiting till later in the day for one of the few taxis that made the journey up to Delphi. And upon arrival at the dig house or the site, there was no electricity, and locals were still found washing their clothing in the oracular Castalian spring.[17]

The scale of operations at Delphi increased dramatically in 1935, through design and necessity. During the year, plans were made to plant 6,500 pine trees around the site to make it more picturesque, although eyebrows were raised at introducing non-native vegetation to the area (see fig. 0.2). A new cycle of excavations had also just begun under an incoming generation of scholars who would become central figures in Delphic folklore: Pierre Amandry, Jean Bousquet, Jean Marcadé, Lucien Lerat, and Jean Pouilloux. But then, in December 1935, tragedy struck. A massive storm caused a rock- and mudslide that covered large sections of the site. In one stroke of nature's power, the big dig was partially wiped out. Delphi was, once again, hidden from view.[18]

The authorities were quick to act. In 1936 the French government made new resources available to dig Delphi out again. Back came the wagons from the original excavation; the train tracks—still visible today in places at Delphi—were oiled into operation, the wooden slides were reconstructed to help ferry material down toward the wagons, and work began. But this time the excavators dug deeper than the original ones had, focusing this time on uncovering Delphi's earliest history, whereas the earlier one had sought to uncover what Pausanias had seen in the second century AD. It was during these campaigns that Delphi began to give up more of its most closely guarded secrets: buried caches of ancient sculpture (including some from the early temple) and particularly the rare ivory and bronze sculptures that are now on display in the site's museum (see plate 5, fig. 4.2).[19]

The late 1930s were a busy time at Delphi. A new road from Arachova was built to the site in 1935, the road from Itea was improved, and excavations at the ancient port site were undertaken between 1936 and 1938. A new museum to house the expanding collection of finds opened in 1938. The French constructed a new dig house to cope with the larger number of people working on a regular basis, and it was inaugurated in April 1937 and promptly put to good use when a snowstorm kept everyone inside for five days. Work continued also on reconstructing other parts of the sanctuaries. Several of the columns of the round tholos structure in the Athena sanctuary were reconstructed, creating one of the most iconic (and yet, ironically, least understood) images of ancient Greece in the modern tourist literature (see plate 3). In 1938 work began on rebuilding several columns of the Apollo temple,[20] though not all offers of help were accepted. For instance, in the 1930s a rich American woman offered to pay for the rebuilding of the Naxian Sphinx upon its high column and was refused in large part because the lady wished to see a large elephant carved onto the Sphinx's supporting column, apparently the symbol of her favorite political party.[21]

World War II did not halt work at Delphi as completely as had World War I. Following the French armistice, some scholars were able to return, and even while Greece was involved in the fighting, work could still, just about, continue. The looming war clouds in 1938–39 meant that work on reconstructing the temple was postponed, and that the focus was changed to protecting the site and its contents. Some finds were dispatched for safe-keeping in Athens, but many were simply buried in the Delphi landscape. An excavated Roman underground tomb was put to use as a safety vault and hidden from public view. Massive holes were dug into the ground on the hillside, into which sculptures were lovingly placed covered in sheets and wrapping to protect them from the earth (fig. 13.4). A careful ledger was made of the exact position and contents of each underground deposit, so that, like squirrels with their food, the scholars could find them again when the time was right. The sad truth was that most were not exhumed again till long after the Greek civil war in 1952 (fig. 13.5). Delphi's treasures were once again consigned underground, this time for over a decade.[22]

Figure 13.4. Delphic statues are hidden underground in preparation for World War II (*BCH* 1944–45, vol. 68–69, pp. 1–4 fig. 5)

Figure 13.5. The excavators rejoice as Delphic sculptures are finally returned to the light in the early 1950s (© EFA/ J. Bousquet [La redécouverte de Delphes fig. 150])

During the war, hunger was the biggest problem for the local population and archaeologists. Parts of the site were given over to agricultural cultivation of foodstuffs, and chickens were kept around the French dig house. Inflation was rampant (in 1944 the government had issued a note for 100,000,000,000 drachma), and money, as a result, was pretty much disbanded as a viable system of exchange. Yet many scholars made Herculean efforts to return each season, taking trains, vans, bicycles, donkeys, and even walking on foot to reach their goal. To some, surely, returning to Delphi offered a sense of continuity in a world turned upside down, and without doubt a chance to escape the depressing reality of world events. But sometimes those events came to Delphi. In 1942 the Italian Black

Shirts camped nearby, used the Castalian spring as their water source, and the stadium as an arena for target practice. The French scholar Pierre Amandry, often resident at Delphi during the war, later scoffed that their aim must have been very poor, as not many of the ancient stones were harmed (fig. 13.6). On Easter 1943, the role of ancient Delphi as a reunion place of nations was reenacted when British forces met with Greek partisans to plan their resistance. A month later, however, the Italians were back, this time conducting "archaeology" while looking for weapons caches the British may have left behind.[23]

But Delphi's closest encounter with the brutal face of war, an experience with which it was not unfamiliar given the four Sacred Wars fought over it—not to mention its having been the focus of Persian and Gaulish

Figure 13.6. Pierre Amandry (with pipe in mouth), while excavating at Delphi, joins a group of Greek resistance fighters for a photo (© EFA [La redécouverte de Delphes fig. 147])

invasions in the ancient world—occurred in September 1943. Following the Italian surrender, German forces moved in to take control and were immediately attacked by Greek partisan forces hiding among the rocks in the area of Delphi. The German response was immediate, with a full battle taking place in and around the Delphic gymnasium and sanctuary of Athena. Pierre Amandry, resident at Delphi at the time, recounts that one hundred bodies were left among the olive groves surrounding the site as a result of the fighting (see fig. 0.2). That night he and the Greek site overseers, along with the local villagers, evacuated the site and withdrew up into the mountains, as centuries earlier, in 480 BC, ancient Delphians had done when the Persians attacked Delphi. In the mountains, they met with the partisan fighters, many of whom had been workmen on the excavation site before the war. The Greeks continued to resist German advances at the narrow pass of Delphi for two days, until the Germans retreated. Amandry and the locals came back down from the mountains, and, despite some ongoing shelling from German gunboats down by the port and several aerial bombardments, the Greek flag was raised at the ancient sanctuary and the church bells rung. Delphi had once again defeated its invaders.[24] Yet even Delphi could not withstand a ferocious renewed invasion the following year in the final phases of the war. Nor could it be unaffected by the bitter civil war that occupied Greece in 1947–49, which made travel to the site even more difficult since, once outside the zones patrolled by the government, travelers were at the mercy of the fighters asking first and shooting later or vice versa.[25]

On 10 July 1952, the many statues that had been hidden out of sight at the outset of the World War II were dug up and put back on display (see fig. 13.5). Following a decade of on-off conflict, there was much work to be done to put the site back in order, including everything from clearing the agricultural crops planted during the war and the general overgrown vegetation, to the recollating of site information following the theft and destruction of much of its archives, and the organization of the physical remains of the site to make it manageable and accessible once again to tourism.

But still Delphi retained a wonderful air of nonchalance. There were no barriers round the site, no tourist fee to enter: Delphi was still intrinsically part of the local community. Villagers on donkeys would use part of the sacred way to crisscross the mountainside; and at night the local lads would use the theater as a place to hang out, drink, sing and dance, including, according to one scholar's memoirs, "George the local hairdresser with his guitar," who could be found there on many occasions.[26]

All this changed in 1956 when electricity finally arrived at the museum, the road leading to the site was widened, and the site itself was enclosed, its access regulated. Tourism numbers began to increase substantially over the coming decades. Between Cyriac of Ancona in 1436 and the first excavations in 1892, just over two hundred people are recorded as having come to Delphi.[27] In July 1936 alone, there were 165. In July 1990, there were 77,900.[28] Delphi now welcomes over two million visitors a year. It is not surprising how much of the work at the site itself has been focused on preparing and maintaining it for such an onslaught, most recently, in 2004, with a new museum opening to chime in with the Olympic Games in Athens (see figs 0.1, 0.2).[29] It is a job never complete. Concern continues over how to protect the site from its increasing use; how to protect the tourists from the continuing rockfalls (the Kerna fountain was destroyed by a rockfall in 1980 and the stadium was closed to visitors in 2010 because of a serious rockfall in that area); and how to protect the area from the damage caused by the vibrations from the large number of buses each day that travel the road just outside the sanctuary and the damage caused by their petrol emissions to the ancient stones (a problem compounded by the acid produced by the local conifer trees).[30]

At the same time, excavation has continued, reflecting the changing priorities of archaeologists. There has been particular emphasis on the wider environment of the site; the importance of all types of finds rather than just star pieces of sculpture; and the full spectrum of Delphic history rather than simply its classical period heyday. In the 1970s, for example, the excavation of the Corycian cave was finally undertaken, with startling results, including the uncovering of fifty thousand figurine pieces (see fig. 1.2).[31] The quarries used to provide material for the sanctuary were also investigated, and in 1983, more systematic work began on the Christian-era village around the sanctuary. In the 1990s, during the last major excavation to take place inside the sanctuary, the ground underneath the Rhodian chariot on the temple terrace was investigated, solving lingering problems about Delphi's earliest development, and turning up a lion bone from a sixth century BC context—thought perhaps to be from one of the last lions in Greece.[32] And, of course, in the 1990s and early 2000s, the question of how the Pythian priestess was inspired was opened up again through the publication of research by geologists Hale and de Boer about Delphi's geological foundations.

People often ask me when I say I study the ancient world whether there is anything left to find. As well, on hearing that Delphi has been studied for over a hundred years, they ask whether there is anything more to say. The answer to both questions is yes. Not only because our techniques of investigation keep improving, allowing us to understand the material record in more depth and different ways, but also because age-old Delphic "enigmas" still need further study, and, perhaps most importantly, because our interests in Delphi continue to evolve motivating scholars to focus on new arenas and themes of investigation.[33] At Delphi, over the next decades, that interest, I think, will be in four main areas. First, the very early and very late eras of the site's occupation.[34] Second, the changing nature, systems, interests, and personalities of the city of Delphi itself, a city whose particular position as home to, and co-manager of such a famous sanctuary has not yet been fully understood.[35] Third, the relationship of the city of Delphi and its sanctuary with its immediate territorial neighbors as we seek to understand these relationships as well as the similarities and differences in the nature and experience of the different territories.[36] Lastly, the question—not only for Delphi but particularly for an archaeological site with so many stories to tell—of how best to display Delphi's rich history to the visitor and protect the site at the same time.[37] As such, it seems to me not only inevitable, but also welcome and important that Delphi continues to occupy, inspire, and surprise us for generations to come.

"Tell me, Euthydemus, have you ever been to Delphi?"

"Yes—certainly; twice."

"Then did you notice somewhere on the temple the inscription 'know thyself'?"

"I did."

"And did you pay no heed to the inscription, or did you attend to it and try to consider who you were?"

—Xenophon *Memorabilia* 4.2.24–25

CONCLUSION

The work to understand Delphi, as we have seen, continues unabated. In many ways, as a result, this book can be little more than a snapshot of where we are right now in our comprehension of the number of complex roles it occupied in the ancient Mediterranean world. What I hope the book has done, however, is to open our eyes to the fascinating nature of this small town and sanctuary clinging to the Parnassian mountains of Greece; its extraordinary place in ancient history; and the incredibly complex way in which such a position was achieved.

Delphi was lucky enough to have been (portrayed as) born great, to have achieved, greatness, and to have had greatness thrust upon it. Its oracle, as a preeminent connection to the gods in the context of a society constantly humming with interaction between the human and divine worlds, was, without doubt, a crucial part of Delphi's attraction and importance for large parts of the ancient world, especially in the archaic and classical periods. But Delphi's oracular reputation over a much longer period, and to an even wider Mediterranean world, owed as much to the ways in which the ancient writers chose to make use of the oracle as a device in their own narratives, as to the canny ways in which the stories of Delphi's oracular responses (and the process by which the oracle gave her responses) were developed, altered, reframed, and occasionally fabricated as part of the rich tapestry of literary, philosophical, theatrical, historical, religious, and polemical thought, argument, and writing that spanned the ancient world, and, as a result, ensured that the Delphic oracle became diffused, to various degrees at different times, into almost every branch of ancient life and understanding. In essence, the oracle at Delphi became for many a useful tool with which to think, argue, and explain, in the context of a constantly evolving world, and as such, its influence was always something more than the sum of the Pythia's responses.

And fundamental to understanding Delphi's story is the fact that the oracle was but one of a number of activities at the sanctuary, which, as a result, not only allowed Delphi to punch significantly above its weight in the ancient landscape, but also plugged Delphi into the ancient Mediterranean world in a bewildering number of ways. Fundamental to Delphi's continuing importance was its unusual management structure, placed as it was under the auspices of both a city and the Amphictyony. As a result, it was immune to domination by one city (well, at least some of the time), and was thus capable of acting as a resource for a wider congregation of cities and states. This meant it was also always a place of interest and importance to a wide community of Greeks who were in no small way responsible for it, and to whose authorities (and resources) Delphi could turn in times of need. Moreover, thanks to the intervention of the Amphictyony and the narratives of Sacred War, Delphi, despite being a city of little more than fifteen hundred citizens, controlled (to an unusually high degree) a vast swathe of sacred territory that, in later centuries, would evolve into being the property of the city rather than the god, thus turning Delphi into a place with fantastic resources at its deposal in contrast to its size. Coupled with this, in later centuries, it was in part thanks to the Roman misunderstanding of what the Amphictyony was—for the Romans, a "general council of the Greeks"—that the Amphictyony and Delphi continued to enjoy such a high level of attention from the Roman authorities as they sought both to control, and to reshape Greece from the first century BC onward. As a result of all these opportunities, effects, and misunderstandings, Delphi remained an independent entity for most of its history, enjoying a level of freedom (especially in the Roman era) of which many other important sanctuaries across Greece could only dream.

Yet Delphi also owed its preeminence to its own religious landscape. The worship of a plethora of divinities that continued to increase over time, coupled with multiple religious festivals at Delphi linked the worship conducted by Delphians of particular deities, particularly Apollo and Dionysus, not only to different physical parts of the ancient Mediterranean landscape, but also to the conduct of similar rites across Greece and the wider Mediterranean world. In turn, the flexible creation of festivals in response to investment by the leagues and powerful individuals of the Hellenistic and Roman periods meant Delphi's ritual landscape continued changing to keep pace with the society around it. Tied into its constantly evolving religious program was Delphi's ability to host (and reputation for hosting) athletic and musical games. Important from the sixth century BC, these competitions were, in a not insignificant way, responsible for ensuring Delphi's relevance throughout the Hellenistic and Roman periods, as they offered a forum for (at least some) monarchs, politicians, emperors, and philanthropists to engage with the competitive aspects of ancient Greek society that vast swathes of the Mediterranean society continued to find so enticing, and, at the same time, allowed Delphi to benefit by providing a convenient focus for financial investment in the sanctuary by those same groups.

In addition, Delphi's large sacred area, carved out of, and terraced into, the Parnassian mountainside provided an arena for display and competition by honoring the gods with a bewildering variety of monumental dedications, all of which, because they became the property of the god, had to remain in place. This was not unique to Delphi, as all sanctuaries received dedications in one form or another. But Delphi's other activities—its oracle, festivals, and games—not only called for such monuments to be offered (to thank the gods for an oracular response or celebrate victory in the games), but also ensured that a steady stream of people came to Delphi on a regular basis over the centuries.

As a result, the value of a permanent monument at Delphi, in a world in which large gatherings of people from different cities and states were rare occasions, became an obvious choice for much of the Mediterranean world. Moreover, as more and more dedications were set up in the sanctuary, its monumental landscape provided its own draw as a key space in which to be seen, to articulate identities and celebrate events, as well as the ideal space in which to oppose particular cities and individuals that had themselves previously invested in the sanctuary. All of this often propelled Delphi into the front line of commemoration for events that were themselves frequently at the epicenter of the tectonic power shifts in ancient Mediterranean history. Such constant dedicatory activity, combined with the difficulties (and opportunities) presented by the steep landscape and the seeming freedom dedicators had to design monuments in a vast array of architectural and artistic styles in response to their particular needs and the current vogues at Delphi, ensured that Delphi became a laboratory for the development of new styles (as well as a conservator of old ones), which, in turn, enabled the sanctuary to provide an even more attractive setting for dedicators looking to articulate their own identity and position in the ancient world.

It was the cumulative impact and the continued opportunities provided by this combined package of oracle, management, festivals, games and dedications that ensured Delphi was propelled to such prominence in the ancient world, and, in turn, changed Delphi into a place that continued to exert influence and hold symbolic importance long after some of those activities had waned (particularly its oracle).[1] In achieving the status of one of those rare sanctuaries that hosted periodos games and a number of other international festivals, a renowned oracle, and vast communities of dedications from around the Mediterranean world, Delphi became an important and useful place about which to talk, in which to be seen, through which to act, and often over which to hold sway, simply because it was Delphi. And as the Hellenistic world gave way to the might of Rome, Delphi's track record was good enough to ensure that the Delphians could capture the attention of Rome's politicians, emperors, and philanthropists, draw them into interacting with the sanctuary in a variety of ways, and put Delphi high on the list of places in which to invest as successive waves of interest toward Greece were generated within Roman Mediterranean society. And at the same time, because of its by now long and complex history, Delphi continued to be an attractive place for the great thinkers of the age, whose interest in, and attention to, Delphi once again ensured that the sanctuary was at the center of key debates, intellectual development, and changing world outlooks. As we saw at the beginning of this book, all this ensured that Delphi was still well known enough to be the appropriate setting for fictional novels in the third or fourth centuries AD; still important enough to be graced with expensive new structures in the early fourth century AD; and still so entrenched as to continue to be an important part of the developing Christian world of Greece in the fifth and sixth centuries AD.

This juggernaut of interacting activities, religious prominence, and unusual management structure of course gave Delphi not only a continually increasing social, political, economic, religious, and philosophical capital that ensured its survival and importance throughout the ancient world, but it also, in turn, made it a crucial sanctuary in the story of the modern rediscovery of Greece. For much of this time, the physical reality of Delphi has struggled to meet the expectations of its reputation. Slowly but surely, however, the ancient remains of Delphi have been resurrected so that, once again, in combination with Delphi's extraordinary reputation, they offer a continuing value to the modern world not totally unlike what Delphi offered in ancient times. Delphi is, for example, still a buzzword for modern notions of communication and access to knowledge, as well as for philosophical thought.[2] Its reputation as a place of international cooperation (however much we may want to nuance the reality of that reputation in the ancient Greek world and point instead to its origins in the Roman misinterpretation of Delphi and its Amphictyony) has ensured Delphi remains an ancient example for, and even yardstick of, our own modern attempts at international diplomacy and cooperation.[3] In 1995, the Hellenic Postal Service, for example, issued a commemorative set of stamps with the inscription: "Amphictyony, precursor of the United Nations." In 1977 the European Cultural

Centre was opened at Delphi with support from the Council of Europe, for the main purpose of reviving and continuing Delphi as a cultural and intellectual center of Europe and of the world, and it continues to host conferences on topics ranging from, for example, "Assessing Multilateralism in the Security Domain" (2005) to, in the same year, "Democracy, Ancient Drama and Contemporary Tragedy."[4] As part of the European Union border agreements in the 1990s, a series of walking routes was laid out that crisscrossed international borders to symbolize the new freedoms of the European Union. One of these, E4, was designed to go through Delphi.[5] And when you visit Delphi today, you cannot but be struck by the plethora of national flags standing prominently outside the site, or but be intrigued by the fact that modern Delphi is twinned with a town in Japan. What Delphi was, what it still is and will continue to be in the future, matters because we still value the ideas Delphi has come, over time, to embody.

Ultimately, it is in large part because Delphi continues to matter today that it is so important for us to continue to engage with the reality of ancient Delphi and attempt to understand how it came to have the reputation it does, a process I hope this book has contributed to, but which is by no means yet complete. And, in doing so, for me, what Delphi offers is, as a result, more than just an extraordinary story of success and survival. Scholars have argued that because Greece was never a dominant influence in the way Rome and Christianity have been, it has instead always been available to be used as a means of questioning the current values of society.[6] For me, there is no more perfect example than Delphi of Greece's role in keeping the ground insecure beneath our feet. It was a place in the ancient world that forced much of Mediterranean society to question its assumptions, interpretations, and identities (as the chapter epigraph from Xenophon's writings epitomizes). Just so, in the modern world, the unraveling story of Delphi's ancient reality forces us to question continually our own current position, progress, and expectations. The advice "know thyself" still rings true: Delphi, has, in many ways, never fallen silent.

GUIDE:

A Brief Tour of the Delphi Site and Museum

Here I pick out a few of the highlights of the site and museum at Delphi, which I would recommend you explore during your visit. If you want a full guide to the surviving remains on the site, the museum, and in the surrounding area, I recommend the *Guide de Delphes* vol. 1 (the site) and vol. 2 (the museum), produced by the French Archaeological School in Athens.

THE SITE:

The Approach (figs. 0.1, 0.2): Many today will approach Delphi by bus and be dropped off right outside the Apollo sanctuary. But if you have time, be sure to walk back along the road either toward the modern Delphi town or toward the Athena sanctuary. Go right around the bend till ancient Delphi is out of site, and then walk back. This gives a better sense of what the ancient approach to Delphi must have been like. Marvel as the sanctuary suddenly is revealed from its hiding place in the folds of the Parnassian mountains, and imagine how, when it was full of bronze, silver, gold, ivory, and marble, it must have sparkled in the sunlight and dazzled those arriving here.

The Athena Sanctuary (plate 3): This sanctuary is all too easy to miss and not normally included in the standard tour. But it is well worth visiting. Take note of how, unlike in the Apollo sanctuary where the temples of Apollo were built one on top of the other, in the Athena sanctuary several temples of Athena seem to have been built side by side. Notice too the enormous rock lying in the middle of the temple at the far end of the sanctuary: this is left over from the rockfall in 1905 that devastated the newly excavated sanctuary and is a bleak reminder of the precarious position of Delphi clinging to the mountainside. Notice, too, how the remaining columns of this temple have been reinforced with walls connecting the columns. The tholos round structure in the Athena sanctuary has become one of the most emblematic images of Delphi and of Greece: yet we do not know for sure what this temple was: it remains one of Delphi's many mysteries.

The Gymnasium (fig. 7.3): Again not often included in the standard tour, but worth visiting especially as it is connected to the Athena sanctuary. Practice a quick running race on the track at the top of the gymnasium and take note of the plunge pool below. It was on the site of the gymnasium that a church was built, which acted as the hostel for some of the first visitors to Delphi from the seventeenth century onward.

The Castalian Spring (fig. 0.2): It is difficult now to access the Castalian spring, as recent rockfalls have made the area unsafe, and the Greek archaeological service in charge of the site has cordoned the area off to visitors. But it was here in these waters that the Pythian priestess bathed on the days of consultation, and still today residents of the area talk of the "good water of Delphi," which is safe to drink. You can taste some of the Castalian water at the fountain running permanently by the entrance to the Castalian spring.

THE APOLLO SANCTUARY

The Entrance (fig. 6.2): After buying your ticket, the path takes you first to the Roman agora built outside the entrance to the sanctuary of Apollo proper. This agora (which we met in part III of this book) was the focus of much attention in the last centuries of Delphi's ancient existence, and was not only a "market," but also a place for tradesmen with small workshops, and a place in which Imperial statues were erected.

Walking through the agora, you go up some steps, and it is here that you enter the Apollo sanctuary proper. Notice the huge walls spanning left and right that comprised the boundary of the sanctuary constructed in the sixth century BC (see chapter 5). You are now at the beginning of the "sacred way"—again an anathema because this zigzag path dates only to the very last phases of Delphi's ancient life, when the path was created to serve the inhabitants living in the sanctuary. But it does connect some of the paths along which the Greeks would have moved through the sanctuary in the archaic, classical, Hellenistic, and Roman periods. Immediately on entering the sanctuary, you are witness to one of the greatest "keeping up with the Joneses" shows the sanctuary has to offer, although sadly little of it remains today. It was here that the Athenians built their statue group in honor of Marathon, and here that the Spartans choose to oppose Athenian domination of the sanctuary by building an even bigger statue group right next to it, as well as a stoa on the opposite side of the path (the huge foundations of which you can still see today). For more detail on this area, see chapters 6 and 7.

The Siphnian Treasury (plate 2, figs. 5.2, 5.3): It's easy in some ways to miss the Siphnian treasury nowadays as you continue up the modern pathway. All that remains are the lowest levels of the building. But this was once the most ornate treasury at Delphi, offered in the sixth century BC by the island of Siphnos after it had discovered silver and gold mines on the island. What remains of the fantastic sculpture that decorated this treasury can be seen in the museum at Delphi and is well worth spending some time over (see the Museum section of this guide for its sculpture, and chapter 5 for more detail on its construction).

The Athenian Treasury (fig. 5.4): Just around the corner from the Siphnian treasury is the rebuilt Athenian treasury. Dedicated after the Athenian victory at the battle of Marathon, this treasury was rebuilt with money from the modern city of Athens in the early twentieth century. Notice how it uses the natural inclination of the hillside to become even more imposing to the visitor: its south wall literally towers over you as you move up toward it. Notice too the remains of the inscription that covered the top level of the triangular plinth in front of it, alluding to the victory at Marathon (for more details, see chapters 5 and 6).

The "Aire" (plate 2): This is easy to walk past as you continue up toward the temple. As you continue along the sacred way path in the area directly opposite the Athenian stoa, you are in an open space known today as the "aire." Though it does not look it today, it was likely an important space at Delphi, not least because it is pretty much the only space within the Apollo sanctuary that was never built on. Instead, all the monuments around it hug an invisible roughly circular line keeping an open space at their center (the impression today is ruined somewhat by the modern sacred way path going straight through it). It was here, we think, that important parts of many of Delphi's religious festivals took place (see chapter 10 for more details on religious festivals).

The Chian Altar (fig. 1.3): As you walk up toward the temple, you pass the Chian altar, indeed it is fairly impossible to miss. Not least because of the inscription neatly set to face visitors as they approach the altar from below telling us that the Delphians gave the Chians "promanteia"—the right to consult the oracle first—in return for the Chians' dedicating the altar in the sanctuary in the sixth century (see chapter 5). The altar was in part reconstructed following a donation from the modern island of Chios in the twentieth century. As you pass the altar, look out also for the second inscription that runs along the top line of stone on the long side of the altar: another reminder that the Chians made this dedication.

Just before you pass by the Chian altar, you will see lots of stones lined up on your left, and also a series of structures on your right. The ones on your right are the remains of treasuries packed into this area, but you can also see one of the ancient "doorways" through the Apollo sanctuary boundary wall at this level (another indication that the modern sacred way was not the only way in and through this sanctuary). On the left, the neat lines of stones (many of them belonging to the temple of Apollo) were created by the archaeologists when excavating the sanctuary. If you wander through this area, you can peer down at different places to catch glimpses of some of the oldest buildings in the sanctuary dating to the seventh and early sixth century BC (see chapters 3 and 4), which have traditionally been associated with the mother goddess Gaia.

The Temple Terrace (fig. 1.3): The temple terrace is awash with monuments. To your right as you emerge up onto the terrace, having gone past the Chian altar, are the remains of many of the monuments associated with celebrating victory in the Persian Wars. If you search for it here, you can find the dark gray block of stone with the incomplete inscription that once belonged to the Salamis Apollo statue: potentially the first surviving inscription to mention the Hellenes, "the Greeks" (see chapter 6). Here too are the remains of the foundation of the Plataean serpent column. It was in this area that the last major excavations at Delphi were conducted, excavations that allowed us to understand some of Delphi's earliest history (including the maison noire discussed in chapters 2 and 3).

Straight ahead as you emerge onto the temple terrace are the monuments offered by the Sicilian tyrants in the early part of the fifth century BC (see chapter 6), as well as a number by later Roman dedicators. But most imposing is the temple of Apollo itself with its Corinthian-style ramp leading up to the front entrance of the temple. The temple you see is the one built in the fourth century BC (see chapter 7) and later restored by numerous Roman emperors. If you walk along the long side of it, you see the northern retaining wall and lots of travertine garnishing the wall (a telltale sign of the unstable geology of the area), which can also be glimpsed by going to the far end of the temple, aligning yourself with its foundation wall, and looking back. You will be able to see a strong bend in the line of the foundation blocks leading away from you that has been caused entirely by seismic activity over the centuries, forcibly buckling the once straight line of the temple's foundations (I thank Professor Iain Stewart who first pointed this out to me).

The Theater (plate 2): Taking the modern stairway (which leads you technically outside the boundary wall of the Apollo sanctuary), you climb to the north terrace of the Apollo sanctuary and reenter through its theater. This stunning piece of construction in such difficult terrain provided a permanent home for Delphi's famed musical contests as part of its Pythian games, and also served as the meeting place for the assembly of the polis of Delphi in the Roman period. It is also at this level that you get an excellent view of the temple, parts of the lower sanctuary and of the valley below Delphi.

The Stadium (fig. 11.2): It is a fairly long climb up to the stadium but well worth it. Due to recent rockfalls it has been closed off to visitors in recent years, but you can still get a good view of the whole structure by heading to the far end of the stadium and using the natural raised bank to look back at the ensemble. And on the way back, be sure to look out for the inscription set into the walls of the stadium, which describes an important ancient regulation for stadium use: that wine could not be taken out of the stadium (because it was sacred property used as part of the religious rituals undertaken before the athletic competitions).

THE MUSEUM

Outside the Museum (fig. 11.3): Before you take the ramp up to the museum entrance, look for the giant sarcophagus of Meleager, which was one of the earliest finds at Delphi, discovered in the period before the big dig (see chapter 12); it stands as testament to the wealth of Delphi in the second century AD (see chapter 11). The evidence suggests it was reused for an incredible fifteen further burials between the second and fifth centuries AD).

The Entrance (cover): Take a moment to look at Albert Tournaire's extraordinary 1892 drawing of Delphi at its height: it gives you a good sense of the packed nature of the Apollo sanctuary. All the items in the first room link to some of Delphi's earliest history, including the Cretan shields on display and the huge cauldrons (tripods).

Room III (figs. 3.1, 12.5): Greeting you in this room are the "Argive twins," often referred to as Cleobis and Biton. We know relatively little about the sculptures apart from the fact they seem to have been made in an Argive style and dedicated at the sanctuary early in the sanctuary's history. But many would like to believe they represent Cleobis and Biton, who helped their mother who in turn prayed to the gods to give them a great blessing, whereupon they died in their sleep. The god's explanation: it was a great blessing to die at the height of their prowess and fame as good sons.

Don't miss the "metopes" (carved stone squares) on the walls of this room. These were found in the Sicyonian treasury, which originally stood back to back with the Siphnian treasury. More precisely, they came from the floor of the Sicyonian treasury. As we saw in chapter 5, every piece of two previous Sicyonian monuments was dismantled and built into the foundations of the new Sicyonian treasury in the late sixth century BC. It is purely thanks to that preservation decision—these metopes were laid sculpted side down as floor tiles in the new treasury—that they have survived for us today.

Room IV (plate 5; fig. 4.2): Here, kept behind glass because of its fragility are the remains of the cache of dedications found buried beneath the sacred way in the vicinity of the aire. Many show signs of fire damage and seem to have been buried there as part of one or more reorganization of the sanctuary in the sixth and fifth centuries. The ivory and gold (chryselephantine) statues of, we think, Apollo are extremely rare. But to me the most incredible is the re-created silver bull statue on display in the room. Archaeologists and conservators have painstakingly re-created the hundreds of smashed and damaged fragments to offer us at least something of this wonderful dedication, offered by an Ionian dedicator in the sixth century BC (see chapters 4 and 5). Notice how the sheets of silver were fastened together using the strips of metals and hundreds of nails, covering a wooden frame.

Room V (figs. 4.1, 5.3, 5.4): This is for me the best room in the museum. As you enter, the marble door frame of the treasury of the Siphnians is on your right: the intricate marble work gives you a great sense of how beautiful and ostentatious this treasury must have been. Right next to it is the Sphinx of the Naxians. This would have stood near the Athenian treasury on the site and originally atop of a high column. But its height in the museum allows you to see the sculpture in much more detail. A beautifully sculpted piece from the sixth century BC (see chapters 4 and 5), the mystery of the creature that is the sphinx (part human, part animal, part bird), the sphinx mirrors the mystery of Delphi itself.

But perhaps most extraordinary in this room are the pedimental sculptures and frieze reliefs belonging to the treasury of the Siphnians.

These were the crowning achievement of the structure, carved in Parian and Naxian marble, the constituency of which allows for delicate and intricate carving without the danger of the marble shattering (which the Siphnian marble used for the walls of the treasury could just not compete with). Notice the incredibly complex carving of the "gigantomachy" scenes (the battle of gods and giants), and in particular, my favorite, the lion sinking his teeth into the fighters. But notice also the very obvious difference in carving style between the frieze on one wall and on the other (very obvious if you look at the horses' tails in the other frieze). Whereas the gigantomachy is carved in the round so that a wonderful 3-D effect is created from whichever angle you look, the horses' tails are simply drilled back into the stone at a straight angle. Scholars have often argued that two different sculptural teams were working on the frieze, and each seems to have responded to how their section of sculpture would have been seen. The gigantomachy was placed on the north side of the treasury—the side everyone walks past as they walk up the sacred way. As such, people could see this sculpture from a number of different angles. But the other frieze, on the south side, was right up against the sanctuary boundary wall and could only be seen from more of a distance and, so, responds to that by being sculptured in a technique that works best only from a frontal viewpoint.

Room VI (figs. 5.1, 7.1): In this room are displayed the remains of the pedimental sculpture of the temples of Apollo from the sixth and fourth centuries BC. Look, right by the entrance, for the fourth-century statue of Apollo, which once sat (Apollo is represented sitting almost hunched on his oracular tripod) in the middle of the east pediment of the temple. Likewise, look for the statue of the god Dionysus, which once adorned the west pediment of the same temple.

Room VII (fig. 5.4): This room contains the remaining metopes of the treasury of the Athenians. They all display the heroic labors of either Heracles or Theseus. These two heroes were brought together for the first time, here on the treasury of the Athenians at Delphi, in a single sculptural unit (i.e., in the same building). Heracles was a mythical hero well-known throughout Greece. He was also extremely popular as a sculptural subject at Delphi in the sixth and fifth centuries BC, not least because of the mythical story that he tried to take Apollo's oracular tripod from him. But Theseus was very much an Athenian hero. In bringing Heracles and Theseus together in this building, many scholars have argued that the Athenians were attempting to raise up Theseus to the kind of national, and international, renown that Heracles already enjoyed. They were in short trying to make Theseus a man as famous as Heracles, and, as a result, making a statement about the glory and importance of Athens in the ancient world.

Room VIII (fig. 5.4): Above all in this room, your eyes are drawn to the stones etched with writing. The marble blocks come from the wall of the treasury of the Athenians, and the inscriptions are the words and musical notations for a hymn sung in praise of Apollo as part of an Athenian festival procession (the Pythaïs) to the sanctuary in either 138 or 128 BC (see chapter 9). This hymn, when it was first discovered as part of the initial "big dig" at the sanctuary in the late nineteenth century quickly became world famous and was "played" in Greece and around the world.

Room XI (figs. 1.3, 2.1): This room contains a number of important sculptures, but particularly the "acanthus dancers." This monument, originally a high column placed on a base to the north of the temple terrace in the Apollo sanctuary, was topped by a number of carved dancers and acanthus leaves supporting a copy of the omphalos—the stone that sat in the temple at Delphi and supposedly marked the center of the world. It was erected, we think, in the fourth century BC by, it is often argued, the Athenians (see chapter 8).

Room XII (fig. 11.1): This room contains some of Delphi's Roman period history. Most striking is the statue of Antinous, dedicated at Delphi as part of the establishment of a religious cult to Antinous following his mysterious death in the Nile. The cult was established by the Roman emperor Hadrian in memory of his dear friend and onetime lover. But also visible in this room is the sculptured relief that went on the monument dedicated by the Roman general Aemilius Paullus after his stunning victory over Greek forces at the battle of Pydna in 168 BC. Paullus took over the monument the Greek commander had planned to dedicate at

Delphi, carved this war relief on to it alongside an inscription in Latin, and put a statue of himself on top (see chapter 9).

Room XIII (plate 6): This room contains Delphi's crown jewel: the original bronze Delphic charioteer found buried in the terrace just to the north of the temple. It was part of a much larger group: the charioteer stood in a bronze chariot with life-size bronze horses and a servant holding the reins. The image depicts the calm just before the start of a race in which this charioteer was the victor, thus giving the owner of the horses the right to put up a monument to his victory in the sanctuary. The owner in this case was the Syracusan tyrant Hieron, the occasion that of the Pythian games in the first half of the fifth century. The dedicating inscription for this monument also survives and shows that it was rededicated some years later by Hieron's successors on the occasion of their own victory (see chapter 6).

The find is fascinating because it is so rare to have original bronze statues from the Greek world. Bronze is a precious metal and most bronze sculptures were melted down at some point in antiquity so that their metal could be reused. It is only when the sculptures were hidden from view (either buried like the charioteer or at the bottom of the sea following a shipwreck) that they are likely to have survived to us today. Notice also the rich and expensive detailing of the charioteer's face: the inlaid teeth, eyes, and eyelashes, all in expensive and precious materials.

Room XIV (fig. 10.1): Don't leave without finding the bust of what is thought to be Plutarch that sits at the exit of the museum. As we saw in chapter 10, Plutarch was a priest of Apollo at the sanctuary and one of our most important sources for understanding the sanctuary, its festivals, and its oracle. Here, too, on display are some elements of Delphi's Christian history, particularly lamps decorated with Christian symbols. There is also a very useful 3D model of the Apollo sanctuary made by the Greek archaeological service.

IN THE MODERN TOWN OF DELPHI

If you have time, it is worth heading into the modern town of Delphi. In the entrance to the town hall on the main street, you can find another

3D model of the Apollo sanctuary created by the French excavators in the 1990s.

If you take the upper road and follow it around to the right, you will come across some miniature versions of the famous monuments from the sanctuary, in particular the Plataean serpent column (inscribed with the names of the city-states that fought in the Persian Wars) and the Messenian and Naupactian triangular column.

For the more adventurous, continuing on this road up the mountainside leads you eventually to the start of the ancient pathway that linked the sanctuary of Apollo to the Corycian cave 800 meters above Delphi on the high plateau of the Parnassian mountains (fig. 0.2).

ABBREVIATIONS

ABSA	*Annual of the British School at Athens*
Ael.	Aelian
VH	*Varia Historia (Various History)*
Aeschin.	Aeschines
In Ctes.	*Against Ctesiphon*
Aesch.	Aeschylus
Eum.	*Eumenides*
Agora	*The Athenian Agora: Results of excavations conducted by the American School of Classical Studies at Athens.* Princeton
AION(archeol)	*Annali di Archeologia e Storia Antica*
AJA	*American Journal of Archaeology*
AJPh	*American Journal of Philology*
Anth. Pal.	*Palatine Anthology*
Apollod.	Apollodorus
App.	Appian
Ill.	*Illyrian Wars*
Mith.	*Mithridatic Wars*

Apul.	Apuleius
Met.	*Metamorphoses*
Ar.	Aristophanes
Av.	*Aves (Birds)*
Eq.	*Equites (Knights)*
Nub.	*Nubes (Clouds)*
Plut.	*Plutus (Wealth)*
Vesp.	*Vespae (Wasps)*
Arist.	Aristotle
Ath. Pol.	*Constitution of the Athenians*
Pol.	*Politics*
Rh.	*Rhetoric*
Ath.	Athenaeus
Aul. Gell.	Aulus Gellius
BaBesch	*Bulletin Antieke Beschaving*
BCH	*Bulletin de Correspondance Hellénique*
BICS	*Bulletin of the Institute of Classical Studies*
Cae.	Caesar
B. Civ.	*Bellum Civile (Civil War)*
Callim.	Callimachus
Hymn 4	*Hymn to Delos*
Ia.	*Iambi*
C&M	*Classica et Mediaevalia: Revue Danoise de Philologie et d'Histoire*
Cic.	Cicero
Div.	*On Divination*
Font.	*For Fonteio*
CID	*Corpus des inscriptions de Delphes*
ClAnt	*Classical Antiquity*
Claud.	Claudian
IV *Cons. Hon.*	*De Quarto Consulatu Honorii Augusti*
Clem. Al.	Clement of Alexandria
Protr.	*Protrepticus (Exhortation)*
Cod. Theod.	*Codex Theodosianus*

CPh	*Classical Philology*
CQ	*Classical Quarterly*
CRAI	*Comptes-Rendus des Séances: Académie des Inscriptions et Belles-Lettres*
Dem.	Demosthenes
Dio Cass.	Dio Cassius
Dio Chrys.	Dio Chrysostom
Diod. Sic.	Diodorus Siculus
Diog. Laert.	Diogenes Laertius
Dion. Hal.	Dionysius of Halicarnassus
Ant. Rom.	*Antiquitates Romanae (Roman Antiquities)*
Eur.	Euripides
Andr.	*Andromache*
IT	*Iphigenia in Tauris*
Phoen.	*Phoenissae*
Euseb.	Eusebius
Praep. evang.	*Praeparatio evangelica (Preparation for the Gospel)*
FD	*Fouilles de Delphes*
FGrH	*Fragmente der griechischen Historiker* F. Jacoby. Berlin. 1923–
G&R	*Greece and Rome*
GRBS	*Greek, Roman and Byzantine Studies*
Heliod.	Heliodorus
Aeth.	*Aethiopica*
Hes.	Hesiod
Theog.	*Theogony*
Hdt.	Herodotus *Histories*
Hom. Hymn Apollo	*Homeric Hymn to Apollo*
Hom. Hymn Hermes	*Homeric Hymn to Hermes*
HSPh	*Harvard Studies in Classical Philology*
IG	*Inscriptiones Graecae*
JDAI	*Jahrbuch des Deutschen Archäologischen Instituts*
JHS	*Journal of Hellenic Studies*

JRS	*Journal of Roman Studies*
JRGZ	*Jahrbuch des Römisch-Germanischen Zentralmuseums*
Julian.	Emperor Julian (the Apostate)
Gal.	*Against the Galilaeans*
Or.	*Orations*
Just.	Justinus of Trogus
Epit.	*Epitome*
Juv.	Juvenal
Luc.	Lucan *De Bello Civile (On the Civil War)* or *Pharsalia*
Lucian	Lucian
Bis. Acc.	*Bis Accusatus (The Double Indictment)*
J. Conf.	*Jupiter Confutatus (Jupiter/Zeus cross-examined)*
J. Trag.	*Jupiter Tragoedus (Jupiter/Zeus rants)*
Philopat.	*Philopatris (The Patriot)*
Mart.	Martial
MDAI	*Istanbuler Mitteilungen (Deutsches Archäologisches Institut)*
MEFRA	*Mélanges de l'École française de Rome (Antiquité)*
MHR	*Mediterranean Historical Review*
NC	*Numismatic Chronicle*
Origen	Origen
C. Cels.	*Contra Celsus (Against Celsus)*
Paus.	Pausanias *Description of Greece*
Philoch.	Philochorus
Pind.	Pindar
Pyth.	*Pythian Odes*
Nem.	*Nemean Odes*
Pl.	Plato
Ap.	*Apology*
Chrm.	*Charmides*
Leg.	*Leges (Laws)*
Phdr.	*Phaedrus*
Resp.	*Respublica (Republic)*

Plin.	Pliny
HN	*Naturalis Historia (Natural History)*
Plut.	Plutarch
Mor.	*Moralia*
Vit. Aem	*Life of Aemilius Paullus*
Vit. Ant.	*Life of Anthony*
Vit. Demetr.	*Life of Demetrius*
Vit. Flam.	*Life of Flamininus*
Vit. Lyc.	*Life of Lycurgus*
Vit. Marc.	*Life of Marcellus*
Vit. Nic.	*Life of Nicias*
Vit. Num.	*Life of Numa*
Vit. Sol.	*Life of Solon*
Vit. Sull.	*Life of Sulla*
Vit. Them.	*Life of Themistocles*
Vit Thes.	*Life of Theseus*
Vit. Tim.	*Life of Timoleon*
Polyaenus	Polyaenus
Strat.	*Strategems*
Polyb.	Polybius *Histories*
Prudent.	Prudentius
RA	*Revue Archéologique*
REA	*Revue des Études Anciennes*
REG	*Revue des Études Grecques*
RFIC	*Rivista di Filologia e di Istruzione Classica*
SCI	*Scripta Classica Israelica*
SEG	*Supplementum epigraphicum Graecum*
SGDI	*Sammlung der griechischen Dialektinschriften* H. Collitz and Fr. Bechtel. Gottingen. 1899.
Syll³	*Sylloge Inscriptionum Graecarum* (third edition)
Simon.	Simonides
Soph.	Sophocles
OT	*Oedipus Tyrannus (Oedipus the King)*

Stat.	Statius
Theb.	*Thebai*
Silv.	*Silvae*
Strabo	Strabo *Geography*
Tac.	Tacitus
Ann.	*Annales*
Theopomp.	Theopompus Historicus
Thuc.	Thucydides *History of the Peloponnesian War*
Val. Max.	Valerius Maximus
Varro	Varro
Ling.	*De lingua Latina*
Verg.	Virgil
Aen.	*Aeneid*
Xen.	Xenophon
An.	*Anabasis*
Ap.	*Apology of Socrates*
Cyr.	*Cyropaedia*
Hell.	*Hellenica*
Mem.	*Memorabilia*
ZPE	*Zeitschrift für Papyrologie und Epigraphik*

KEY

Parke and Wormell + No. in bold: Oracular consultation reference number from Parke and Wormell 1956b.

Scott + No. in bold: Monumental dedication reference number from Scott 2010.

Jacquemin + No. in bold. Monumental dedication reference number from Jacquemin 1999.

Guide de Delphes + No. in bold: Monumental dedication reference number from Bommelaer 1991.

NOTES

PROLOGUE

1. Quote from the Memorandum of Justification for the Recommendation by United Nations International Committee on Monuments and Sites (ICOMOS) that Delphi be listed as a World Heritage site, 6 March 1986. Full text can be viewed online: http://whc.unesco.org/en/list/393/documents/ (1987 Advisory Body Evaluation)—last accessed 17.6.13.

2. Heliod. *Aeth*. For discussion of the novel, see: Feuillatre 1966, Hunter 1998.

3. Heliod. *Aeth*. 2.26–27; Pouilloux 1983, Weir 2004: 77–78, Baumbach 2008: 182.

4. For discussions of the veracity of Heliodorus's account: Feuillatre 1966: 45–70, Pouilloux 1984.

5. For discussion of the date of the *Aethiopica*: Bowersock 1997: 149–60, Baumbach 2008: 167.

6. E.g., Strabo 9.3.3.

CHAPTER I. ORACLE

1. "It happened just like at Delphi," e.g., Hdt. 7.111. Amandry argued that the earliest oracular consultation at Delphi may in fact have been the reading of the rustling of leaves from a laurel tree at Delphi (not just any laurel tree, but the one

that Daphne was transformed into when pursued by Apollo): Phylarchus *FGrH* 81F 32; Amandry 1950: 126–34.

2. Whereas at the oracular sanctuary of Dodona, questions and responses were often inscribed on lead tablets buried in the ground (and thus discoverable, and readable, today), at Delphi no such permanent records have survived, see Eidinow 2007. It is possible that archives of oracular responses were kept at Delphi: there is a *zygastron* referred to in inscriptions, but neither it, nor any responses, have ever been found: Flacelière 1961: 52.

3. Different accounts of same consultation: e.g., Thuc. 1.133–34 and Paus. 3.17.7 on Pausanias of Sparta. Different authorial styles: Herodotus's passion for oracles and his use of them in his narrative: Kindt 2003, Kindt 2006. For discussion of the "use" of the Delphic oracle in other Athenian sources: Bowden 2005: 40–87. On the use of oracle stories in Pausanias: Habicht 1988, Elsner 2001, Elsner 2004, Hutton 2005a, Juul 2010. See also on the use of oracles in later literature: Busine 2005: 26–28.

4. All ahistorical accounts of oracle responses before fifth century BC, e.g., Fontenrose 1978: 11–195. Impossible to write a history after the fourth century BC: Parke and Wormell 1956a: 244. Middle path: Parke and Wormell 1956b: xxi.

5. The first Pythia was Phemonoe (meaning literally "prophetic mind"): Hes. Frag. 226; Strabo 9.3.5. Aristonice was Pythia at the time of the battle of Salamis in the fifth century BC: Hdt. 7.140. Periallus was the Pythia whom Cleomenes of Sparta bribed: Hdt. 6.66.

6. Plut. *Mor.* 405C. See Flacelière 1961: 42. By the third century AD, however, the post had become associated with the "priestly" families of Delphi: de la Coste-Messelière 1925: 83–86.

7. Chosen for life: Flacelière 1961: 42. See Roux 1976: 69. House to live in: *FD* III 5 50; Amandry 2000: 19. Multiple Pythias: Plut. *Mor.* 414B.

8. Diod. Sic. 16.26. See Flacelière 1961: 41. Pythia previously married: Parke and Wormell 1956a: 34.

9. Plut. *Mor.* 388E; Flacelière 1961: 39, Roux 1976: 175–76. Possibility of "special" consultations at other times: Price 1985: 134.

10. The lot oracle: Amandry 1939a, Amandry 1950: 25–36, Flacelière 1961: 39. Possibly a jar of black and white beans, the color indicating yes or no, selected at random by the Pythia: Price 1985: 132. These "lots" may have been kept in, and indeed consulted from, the tripod in which the Pythia was said to sit: Lucian *Bis. Acc.* 1. See also the early consultation by the Thessalians at Delphi about the

choice of their king, which was said to have been performed with a lot oracle: Plut. *Mor.* 492A.

11. Amandry 1984c, Picard 1991: 261. See also Graf 2005.

12. Washing: Schol. Vet. on Eur. *Phoen.* 224. The Castalia was cleaned and fenced off in the third century BC: Colin 1899: 567. Burning barley: Plut. *Mor.* 397A. Only laurel wood was used on the sacred hearth: Parke and Wormell 1956a: 26. See Flacelière 1961: 43, Fontenrose 1978: 224.

13. Plut. *Mor.* 435B, 437B, 438A. See Parke and Wormell 1956a: 30. Plutarch intimates that, occasionally, huge efforts were made to ensure the goat shuddered, including pouring a good deal of cold water over the animal: Plut. *Mor.* 438B. At the same time, Plutarch goes on to show how this bending of the rules led to an unsatisfactory consultation in which the Pythia's voice was odd, ending with everyone running from the temple in fear and the Pythia dying a few days later.

14. Chian promanteia: Inscribed in the third century BC, when the Chians undertook a refit of their dedication (first made in the late sixth century BC): Courby 1927: 124. Several consulters with promanteia, see Eur. *Ion* 908.

15. *CID* I 8. See Parke and Wormell 1956a: 32, Flacelière 1961: 48.

16. *CID* I 13; Amandry 1950: 245 (XVI). For discussion: Parke and Wormell 1956a: 31–32. The Sciathus inscription also says that it costs one Aeginetan stater for "consultation by 2 beans," which is the best evidence for the existence of a lot (or "bean") oracle at Delphi.

17. Asclepiads: *FD* III 1 394 1.22–33.

18. Waiting area: Flacelière 1961: 40. Proxenos: Eur. *Ion* 228. See Sourvinou-Inwood 1990: 15. It is not unlike the practice in the Gulf States today, such as in the United Arab Emirates, where a local, native partner is needed if a foreigner or foreign business wishes to engage in any business venture in the country.

19. Daux 1949c, Parke and Wormell 1956a: 32–33.

20. Plut. *Mor.* 385A, 378D.

21. See Hdt. 8.37; Plut. *Mor.* 388E; Plut. *Vit. Sull.* 12; *Vit. Tim.* 8; Fontenrose 1978: 226–27, Price 1985: 135. Elsewhere in the temple it was said there were busts of Homer and Hesiod, as well as Pindar's iron seat and numerous other precious dedications: Flacelière 1961: 58.

22. E.g., Parke and Wormell 1956a: 28.

23. Initial temple publication: Courby 1927. See (reprinted) discussions in: Amandry 2010b, Amandry 2010a. Latest plan: Amandry 2000: 20–21, Amandry and Hansen 2010: 315–21 (figure 18.19).

24. Painted by the Codrus painter, supposedly showing Aegeus before the Pythia or Themis: Fontenrose 1978: 204, Lissarrague 2000. This impression of the consultation is favored by Fontenrose 1978: 223.

25. There were two priests of Apollo in second–first centuries BC (*SGDI* 1684–2343), but three by first century AD: Amandry 2000: 18. Bowden thinks there was only one in classical times, drawn from among the leading families of Delphi: Bowden 2005: 14. It seems local Delphians may also have been selected by lot to accompany the priests during parts of the consultation process: Plut. *Mor.* 438B; Parke and Wormell 1956a: 30.

26. Prophetes: Hdt. 8.36, Eur. *Ion* 413–16. Hosioi: the earliest mention of these officials is in the second century BC. There were five hosioi in Plutarch's day: *Mor.* 292D; Parke 1940. Women responsible for flame: Plut. *Mor.* 385C. Parke and Wormell argue that these were women who had "ceased from marital relations" and may have been the group from which a Pythian priestess was picked. Tending the flame was thus a kind of preselection round for being chosen as the Pythia: Parke and Wormell 1956a: 36. Plutarch also mentions a group of "versifiers": "there used to be [men who would sit around the oracle] weaving hexameters and metres and rhythms extemporaneously as vessels for the oracles," Plut. *Mor.* 407B. For more on personnel: Roux 1976: 54–63.

27. Fontenrose 1978: 218.

28. Asking the question: Eur. *Andr.* 1104; Schol. Ar. *Plut.* 39. Providing answer in oral and written form: Eur. *Ion* 100; Hdt. 1.48; *IG* II² 1096. See Parke 1940, Parke and Wormell 1956a: 33, Price 1985: 136.

29. Amandry 1950: 129–30. Callimachus tells us she wore a bay-leaf crown and also held a bay sprig in her hand: Callim. *Ia.* 4.26–27.

30. Fontenrose 1978: 198–200.

31. See Parke and Wormell 1956a: 19–20.

32. Diod. Sic. 16.26.

33. "Delightful fragrance": Plut. *Mor.* 437C. Debate among friends: Plut. *Mor.* 432C–438D. Calm and peaceful: Plut. *Mor.* 759B. Bad consultation: Plut. *Mor.* 438B.

34. Strabo 9.3.5. Luc. 5.165–74; Fontenrose 1978: 208. The occasion of the consultation is that of Appius Claudius in 48 BC (see later chapters), and though the Pythia "rages," her response is still clear and coherent. Pausanias 10.24.7. Lucian *Bis.Acc.1.* John Chrysostom *The Homilies on the First Epistle to the Corinthians* 29.1.

35. Pl. *Phdr.* 244A–245C, 265A–B. See Amandry 1950: 41–56, Flacelière 1961: 50, Fontenrose 1978: 204. "Intelligible and satisfying": Parke and Wormell 1956a: 22.

36. Homolle, director of the original excavations at Delphi 1892–1901, is quoted as saying in 1894, "the temple, on which so much hope had rested, has been a great deception": Broad 2006: 87.

37. Oppé 1904.

38. Price 1985: 139.

39. Parke and Wormell 1956a: 39. See also Dodds 1951: 70, Lloyd-Jones 1976.

40. E.g., Maurizio 1995.

41. Dempsey 1918.

42. Holland 1933.

43. The stone block: Bourguet 1914: 249, Parke and Wormell 1956a: 29. It was recently used as the center of an "oracle-consultation" scene in the movie *Driving Aphrodite / Life in Ruins*. It has, over time, been recognized as carrying the tomb of Dionysus, as the base for the tripod, and as having nothing at all to do with the temple. In reality, it seems to be a stone block originally from the temple that received its curious markings only so it could be made use of as an olive press in the last phase of the ancient settlement at Delphi in the sixth century AD: Hansen 2009: 115–20.

44. For an introduction to the general geology of the landscape at Delphi: Péchoux 1992.

45. De Boer and Hale 2000, de Boer, Hale, and Chanton 2001, de Boer, Hale, and Spiller 2002. See Broad 2006.

46. Price 1985: 131. See the discussion in Maass 1997: 1–19.

47. Respected: Rosenberger 2001: 65–126. Oracles were, as Mary Douglas put it, not "a poor man's whiskey, used for gaining conviviality and courage against daunting odds": Douglas 1966: 69. Numerous sites: e.g., Parke 1967, Parke 1985, Curnow 2004, Struck 2005, Johnston 2008, Stonemann 2011. For Dodona: Eidinow 2007. For oracles of the dead: Ogden 2001.

48. Paus. 2.24.1–2. For description of this sanctuary see: Vollgraff 1956.

49. See Dillery 2005, Flower 2008.

50. Eidinow 2007: 27.

51. Xen. *Mem.* 1.1.6–9.

52. Evans-Pritchard 1937. See Whittaker 1965.

53. See the scorn in later writers about how Croesus had mishandled his interaction with the oracle: Xen. *Cyr.* 7.2.17. On Herodotus and Croesus: Herodotus

1.46.2; Crahay 1956, Kindt 2003, Barker 2006, Kindt 2006. See how Herodotus also has Croesus misunderstand happiness as not being solely dependent on material possessions in his meeting with Solon of Athens: Herodotus 1.29–32; Osborne 2009: 204.

54. Bowden 2005: 22. See also Price 1985: 144. Some examples of personal questions with equal leeway: "is it advantageous for me to sail/farm/go abroad": Plut. *Mor.* 386C.

55. It provided what has been termed "resistance" for the oracle to any accusation of falsehood: Parker 2000: 78–80.

56. Plut. *Mor.* 407E.

57. Johnston 2005: 301.

58. Parker 2000: 78. See Cleomenes in Sparta received an ambiguous oracle about his impending invasion of Argos. Making his own interpretation of it, he decided not to attack. When he was later put on trial in Sparta for his withdrawal, he defended himself by explaining his reasoning, which was determined sufficient to acquit him of all charges: Hdt. 8.77.

59. Advisor: Xen *Mem.* 1.4.15; Hdt. 1.157.3. There is no clear case of disobedience to a specifically solicited oracular responses recorded in the surviving sources: Parker 2000: 76.

CHAPTER 2. BEGINNINGS

1. *Hom. Hymn Apollo* lines 281–93. For discussion of the *Homeric Hymn to Apollo*, see Parke and Wormell 1956a: 107, Fontenrose 1959: 13, Miller 1986.

2. *Hom. Hymn Apollo* 300–304.

3. Alcaeus F 142 West; Davies 2007: 49–50.

4. See Roux 1976: 19–34.

5. Anaxandra *FGrHist.* 404 F 5; Callim. frag. 86–89; Plut. *Mor.* 417F–418B. See also Parke and Wormell 1956a: 7.

6. Ephorus *FGrHist.* 70F 31B; see Strabo 9.3.11: its purpose was to "summon humanity to civilization and rebuke it" See Parke and Wormell 1956a: 378.

7. Amandry 1950: appendix XCVI.

8. Simon. frag. 26a; Fontenrose 1959: 15.

9. Strabo 9.3.3; Fontenrose 1959: 410–11.

10. E.g., Strabo 9.3.12; Paus. 10.6.1.

11. Pind. frag. 55.

12. See Paus. 10.6.6; 10.7.2; 2.7–8; Morgan 1990: 145, Luce 2008: 429.

13. Strabo 8.6.14; Paus. 10.5.6; Ephorus *FGrHist* F150; Parke and Wormell **314.**

14. See Amandry 1950: 196–200; appendix XCVI, Parke and Wormell 1956a: 11 n.28. The argument often ran that Dionysus's followers were women, thus explaining the choice of a female oracular priest at Delphi: Parke and Wormell 1956a: 11. Dionysus's tomb was supposedly inside the temple of Apollo at Delphi (earliest source third century BC): Philoch. *FGrHist* 328 f7. By Plutarch's time at the latest (first century BC), Dionysus ran Delphi for three months each winter: Plut. *Mor.* 388E.

15. Parke and Wormell 1956a: 13. For the argument that the Sibyl was active much earlier in the archaic and classical period: Pollard 1960.

16. Paus. 10.6.1–4 and Plin. *HN* 7.203.

17. Pind. frag. 54; Plut. *Mor.* 409E–410A; Strabo 9.3.6. In early Greek maps, Delphi occupied the exact center of the world, like Jerusalem in maps of medieval Christendom: Parke and Wormell 1956a: 1.

18. Heraclitus frag. 93. See "Delphi, most famous of the clefts of ancient Greece, owed its name to this mythical image. 'Delphi' signifies in fact the female generative organ": Eliade 1962: 21, see Richter 1994.

19. Centre of the Earth: Aesch. *Eum.* 39; Soph. *OT* 897. Cronus stone: Hes. *Theog.* 498–500; Paus. 10.24.6. Voice or "omphe" of the gods: Apollod. *FGrHist* 244f 94-99. Pytho's tomb: Varro *Ling.* 7.17. Virgil thought the oracular tripod, not the omphalos, was Pytho's tomb: Verg. *Aen.* 3.92. For discussion of the "archaic omphalos," see Bousquet 1951. For the discussion on where in the temple of Apollo it was placed: Amandry 1992b. For a recent scientific investigation of the properties of the omphalos as an optical transforming device known as a space-inverting anamorphoscope (which has the effect of reflecting the world around it in such as a way as to "condense" its surroundings, making it look like it is warping the world around it and acting as its center): Kuckel 2010.

20. For discussion, see Sourvinou-Inwood 1979.

21. Single narrative: e.g., Dempsey 1918. Narrative roles: e.g., Miller 1986. A similar initiative, as we saw in the last chapter, has occurred in understanding the stories of Delphic oracular responses in literature. Comparison with other myth cultures: e.g., Fontenrose 1959.

22. For the *Homeric Hymn to Apollo* as confirming Delphi's universal, Panhellenic status, see Clay 1989.

23. See Miller 1986: 73–75, 81, 107. Some scholars go further and seek to tie parts of the *Hymn* to historical events. For example, the Lelantine War (late eighth

century BC) should be seen as a reason for the rejection of the Lelantine plain as an oracular site by Apollo, and the First Sacred War (early sixth century BC) should be seen as the outcome of the Delphic authorities not obeying Apollo's final warning/ prophecy not to engage in hubris. See Malkin 2000: 72. For both these events, see chapters 3 and 4. But tying the *Hymn* so closely to such events, of course, requires taking a particular stance about the date of the *Hymn*'s first appearance, as well as of the date (and indeed historicity) of the events themselves.

24. See Malkin 2000. For discussion of Delphi's role in, and the nature of Greek colonization, see the next chapter.

25. See Amandry 1950: 214, Sourvinou-Inwood 1987: 231.

26. See Sourvinou-Inwood 1979: 251.

27. The most notable of the myths is Heracles' fight with Apollo over the oracular tripod, which comes about as a result of Heracles having fought off a number of others keen to take the sanctuary: Fontenrose 1959: 28, 401. But, as we shall see throughout this book, Delphi is also the subject of numerous conflicts for its ownership in the ancient world.

28. Aristotle told a story of a man called Hegesippus, who first went to the oracle of Zeus at Olympia to ask a question, and then to Apollo at Delphi where he asked only, "Does the son agree with the father?" Arist. *Rh.* 2.23.12 (1398 b 34). Hegesippus had effectively played Delphi off against Olympia, as Apollo at Delphi could hardly not agree with his father Zeus. The same story is told of king Agesipolis of Sparta on the question of whether to invade Argos, in Xen. *Hell.* 4.7.2.

29. See Defradas 1954: 148, Morgan 1990. Indeed, the later literary sources will claim that Delphi's oracle was fundamental to the establishment of the oracle at Olympia (once again establishing its superiority over it): Parke and Wormell 1956a: 367. Similarly, in Strabo (9.3.12), the autochthonos nature of the Delphians is stressed, thus intimating their eternal association with the region, see Kyriakidis 2011: 86. Nevertheless, the myths fail to elucidate how Delphi is linked to other parts of the territory of Phocis, which it had to have been (in practical, economic terms if nothing else): McInerney 2011: 97.

30. The dragon was called Pytho e.g., Simon. frag. 26a. It is also suggested that the name Pytho came from the cry of the paean song encouraging Apollo to shoot the unnamed monster: Ephorus *FGrHist* 70F 31b (Strabo 9.3.12).

31. Graf 2009: 52.

32. See Larson 2007: 87–99.

33. For the etymology of Apollo, see Nagy 1994. He connects it to "*apeileo*": to "make a boastful promise or threat."

34. See Roux 1976: 35–52, Davies 1997. While many point to the equal worship of Dionysus at Delphi, and while it is not impossible that this god was worshiped at Delphi from its earliest existence, there is no archaeological proof for worship of Dionysus at Delphi until the fourth century BC. As a result, Dionysus's role at Delphi will be considered in later chapters, along with that of the host of other deities worshiped at Delphi.

35. De La Coste-Messelière and Flacelière 1930.

36. Plut. *Mor.* 420C; *FD* III, 5, 25, col. III, A, 1.3–4 (*CID* II 62 IIIA.4). For discussion on whether this was a new sanctuary or the first attestation of a very old one: Dempsey 1918: 4, de La Coste-Messelière 1936: 63, Amandry 1950: 202–204, Sourvinou-Inwood 1987: 221.

37. For the initial excavation: Radet 1992. For the lion muzzle: Picard 1991: 7.

38. For the detailed publication of the cave: Touchais 1981. For the pottery: Picard 1991: 243.

39. Mycenean finds at the Corycian cave: Lerat 1984.

40. For discussion of the Delphic site in this period: Perdrizet 1908: 5–7, Amandry 1938: 305–307, Themelis 1983, Morgan 1990: 107. For the tomb: Bommelaer 1991: 15. For a wider discussion of Mycenaean Delphi and the surrounding area, see Müller 1992b, Müller 1992a, Luce 2011b: 306–10. For recent discussions on the nature and location of settlement across the Pleistos valley at this time: Skorda 1992b, Luce 2011b: 315–19.

41. Evidence for Gaia worship: Demangel 1926: 13–28. Deposited at later time: Lerat 1935.

42. Demangel 1926: 36, Bommelaer 1991: 48.

43. See Forrest 1957: 171, Morgan 1990: 107, Bommelaer 1991: 15.

44. Initial accounts of excavations: Luce 1992. Full report: Luce 2008. See also a summary of the arguments in Rolley 2002, Luce 2011b: 310–12. Pottery: Luce 2008: 438. Contact with Thessaly: Lerat 1961: 352–57, Morgan 1990: 108.

45. Luce 2008: 85–94, Luce 2011b: 312–15. See also Amandry 1938, Amandry, Lerat and Pouilloux 1950.

46. For discussion, see Morgan 1990: 106, 112, Luce 2008: 26–27, 29–50 (maison noire), 83. Theopomp. *FGrHist* 115F 193 [219] indicates that the first dedications at Delphi were tripods and cauldrons. See Jacquemin 1999: 37.

47. For a recent discussion of the (inverse) development of the settlements of Medeon and Delphi in Phocis during the Iron Age through to the eighth century BC: Luce 2011a.

48. Osborne 2009: 16.

49. For a wider discussion of eighth century BC change, see Snodgrass 1980, Morgan 1990: 5–20, Sourvinou-Inwood 1993, Osborne 2009: 66–162.

50. For the increasingly different political attachments of Delphi and Kalapodi, and thus their difference trajectories of development, see recently: McInerney 2011.

51. For discussion of the low level of elaboration at Olympia and Delphi in this early period, see Morgan 1990. For discussion of the comparative elaboration of "polis" sanctuaries: Alcock and Osborne 1994, de Polignac 1995. For debate over the appropriateness of the "Panhellenic" label, see Scott 2010: 260–64.

52. For discussion, see Morgan 1990: 112–27. For recent work on Kalapodi, see Felsch 2007, McInerney 2011.

53. Starting late eighth century BC: Morgan 1990: 134. For a comparison of the development of divination and cult at the sanctuaries of Delphi and Didyma in the eighth century BC: Morgan 1989. Long history of oracle at Delphi stretching back to second millennium BC: Bommelaer 1991: 19.

54. E.g., Snodgrass 1980: 120, Snodgrass 1986: 53–54. See Morgan 1993.

55. Note that some dedications from the west seem to have arrived before there is any evidence for Delphic involvement in colonization in the west: d'Agostino 2000: 79.

56. Luce 2008: 29–50.

57. See Parke and Wormell 1956a: 312, Miller 1986: 105, Bommelaer 1991: 18. The stories involving Delphi and the heroes of the Homeric cycle grow in the literary sources during the classical and Hellenistic period. In the *Odyssey*, King Agamemnon is said to have consulted the oracle (Parke and Wormell **19**), but also, later, to have planted a plane tree at Delphi to commemorate his visit (Plin. *HN* 16.238). In the Hellenistic period, Agamemnon's visit was said to have been the moment of the foundation of the cult of Dionysus at Delphi: Parke and Wormell **408**. It is interesting to note that later literary sources claim Homer himself consulted the Delphic oracle about his own birthplace: Parke and Wormell **317, 318, 319**. The oracle's response was later said to have been inscribed onto the base of a statue of Homer, which stood in the front section of the temple of Apollo at Delphi: Parke and Wormell 1956a: 394. Similarly, Hesiod (writing in the same

period) was also later said to have consulted the oracle at Delphi about his fate: Parke and Wormell **206.**

58. It was initially thought that Delphi, in contrast, did not receive the more personal kinds of dedications seen at Perachora (although such items were dedicated at the Corycian cave). The most recent excavations, have started to turn up more and more personal objects: Luce 2008: 212. Delphi, it seems, acted both as a local place for personal cult activity and, increasingly, for more state-level interaction.

59. See Morgan 1990: 142–46.

CHAPTER 3. TRANSFORMATION

1. Burning of the maison noire: Luce 2008: 47. Not the entire settlement: Lerat 1938, Lerat 1961: 330–38.

2. The Phlegyians: *FGrHist* 3 F 41e and *FGrHist* F 70, 93 (mid-fifth century–fourth century BC); Luce 2008: 48–49. Diod. Sic. (4.37.1) records another raid on Delphi, this time by the Dryopes (date uncertain). Neeft argues that an earthquake may have caused the destruction instead: Neeft 1981.

3. For the development of the relationship between Delphi and Medeon, see recently: Luce 2011a. Sadly much of the material evidence for the development of the Itean plain and other settlements like Medeon is still not widely available.

4. For further discussion, see: Morgan 1990: 115–26, Luce 2011b, Luce 2011a, McInerney 2011, McInerney (forthcoming). For discussion in particular on the north-south trade corridor: Kase, Szemler, Wilkie, and Wallace 1991.

5. Picard 1991: 243.

6. This is, however, unlikely. Tripod dedications, often identical to the ones at Delphi, are known from a variety of sites in the eighth century BC, many of which never had an oracle: Bommelaer 1991: 15–16.

7. Inception last quarter eighth century: e.g., Morgan 1990: 134. Problems of such a link: e.g., Osborne 2009: 192.

8. Luce 2008: 437. At the same time, of course, later literary sources claim the oracle was fully involved in a number of well-known Greek myths stretching far back in time: Kings Codrus and Aegeus of Athens consulted; famously, the family of Oedipus of Thebes as well as the Thebes's rulers during the era of "the seven against Thebes"; King Oenomaus of Pisa; Orestes of the Atreus family; Io the nymph priestess of Hera seduced by Zeus; Jason who sought the Golden Fleece; Trophonius and Agamedes who were associated with the early building of the

temple of Apollo at Delphi; Neoptolemus, the son of Achilles; and Heracles the demigod. As well, the oracle at Delphi was said to have given responses concerning Orpheus the son of Apollo, told the Epidaurians to worship Asclepius, identified the shoulder bone of the hero Pelops, set up the oracle at Olympia and the oracle of Trophonius at Lebadea, and been involved in the establishment of the shrine of Apollo Pythaios at Argos: Parke and Wormell 1956a: 297–318, 340–51, 367–68.

9. For further discussion, see Osborne 2009: 153–95.

10. See Morgan 1990: 155–61, 184–85.

11. Rejecting all accounts: e.g., Fontenrose 1978. Here, I have followed the list of fake and historical oracles in Morgan 1990: 186–90. Examples of "fakes": involvement of the Delphic oracle in encouraging the Dorian invasion of Greece, and the Ionian migration: see Parke and Wormell 1956a: 55–57. Also consultations that link the oracle to authorizing the beginning of the Olympic games (Parke and Wormell **485; 486**); the city of Aegion asking who were the better Greeks and being told that they were not in the reckoning (Parke and Wormell **1**). Plut. *Mor.* 492A–B claims that the Thessalians consulted a "lot" oracle at Delphi when choosing Aleuas the Red as king.

12. In terms of individual consultations, the first more reliable consultation is that of Archilochus, the poet from Paros in the seventh century BC on the issue of his prospects for begetting children, and, later on, about what to do during hard financial times: Parke and Wormell **231, 232;** Parke and Wormell 1956a: 396.

13. Parke and Wormell **29, 21, 217–21.**

14. Tyrtaeus frag. 5 (West) repeated in Plut. *Vit. Lyc.* 6, and Diod. Sic. 7.12.5.

15. Process, oaths, land: Parke and Wormell **222, 539, 561.** Warning: Parke and Wormell **222**

16. Commencement: Parke and Wormell **296.** Improve fortunes: Parke and Wormell **363, 297, 299.**

17. Maximize chances: Parke and Wormell **365.** Conduct during war: Parke and Wormell **364**: it is ironic here that the oracle is supposed to have told Sparta to use trickery to take Messenia and to have warned the Messenians to beware Spartan trickery! Salvation: Parke and Wormell **298, 366, 367.**

18. The oracle advised them to bring the bones of Orestes back to Sparta: Parke and Wormell **32, 33.**

19. Lion and eagle oracle: Parke and Wormell **7.** Aetion oracle: Parke and Wormell **6.** Oracle to Cypselus: Parke and Wormell **8.**

20. Parke and Wormell **12.** For discussion of this early involvement between Athens and Delphi: Daux 1940: 40–41.

21. Parke and Wormell **51.** In addition, by the mid-sixth century BC, literary sources relate that Gyges also asked the oracle who was the happiest man alive (expecting to be told himself) and instead was told it was an Arcadian, Aglaus of Psophis: Parke and Wormell **244;** Parke and Wormell 1956a: 384–85. For a recent discussion of Delphi's relationship with the east: Wörrle 2000.

22. Parke and Wormell **50.** See Paus. 10.16.1–2. Strabo is the only ancient source to mention the construction of a treasury by Gyges at Delphi (Scott **4**).

23. See discussion in Morgan 1990: 172–82.

24. Parke and Wormell 1956a: 115, Londey 1990.

25. See Parke and Wormell's characterization of the oracle as "opportunistic," especially in political issues (as opposed to more impartial or conservative in religious issues): Parke and Wormell 1956a: 418.

26. Malkin 1989: 150.

27. Parke and Wormell **370, 371, 384.** For discussion of the Lelantine War, see Forrest 1957: 160–64, Salmon 1984: 67–70, Morgan 1990: 167–68.

28. See Osborne 1998, Osborne 2009: 122. For a recent discussion of colonization, and ways of approaching the relationship between colony and mother-city, see Scott 2012.

29. Ephesus: Parke and Wormell **234.** Aegae: Parke and Wormell **225.** Gela: Parke and Wormell **410, 3.** Pausanias on Archias of Corinth: Parke and Wormell **2.** Strabo on Croton and Syracuse: Parke and Wormell **229.**

30. Thera: Parke and Wormell **37, 38, 40** (believed by the Therans); Battus: Parke and Wormell **39.** See also Parke and Wormell **41.**

31. Other literary sources: Pind. *Pyth.* 4.9; Diod. Sic. (Parke and Wormell **71**); Paus. 10.15.7. Inscriptional evidence: *SEG* 9.72 (Sacred laws: Parke and Wormell **280**); Meiggs and Lewis 1988: No. 5 (granting citizenship to Therans on basis of original agreement at time of colonial foundation).

32. Parke and Wormell **46, 47, 525, 526, 568.**

33. Morgan 1990: 176. Yet for recent arguments for the lack of desire for a relationship between the colony and Delphi (as opposed to the desire for such a relationship on the part of the mother city), see: Davies 2009, Jacquemin 2011.

34. E.g., Thuc. 1.38.2 and 6.1.6 on the close relationship between Corinth and its colonies in the fifth century BC and on its willingness to provide military support on the basis of its role in their foundation.

35. Defradas 1954.

36. Forrest 1957, Snodgrass 1980: 120, Snodgrass 1986: 53–54. For the debate on where the stories of colonial consultations were shaped, see: Murray 2001: 31–34.

37. See the review of previously scholarly opinion in Malkin 1987: 18–22.

38. Parke and Wormell 1956a: 78, Malkin 1987: 7, 17–81, Morgan 1990: 171–78.

39. Callinus of Ephesus: see Malkin 1987: 19. Dorieus of Sparta: Malkin 1987: 78–81, Morgan 1990: 171–78.

40. Forrest 1957: 174. See Malkin 1987: 89–91, Osborne 2009: 193–94, Aurigny 2011. For the later take-up of Delphi as a place of crucial importance particularly for the development of identity among the western colonies after Phocaean intervention in the sixth century BC: d'Agostino 2000: 82–85. For a recent discussion on the importance of colonization for the identities of relevant communities, emphasizing the local emergence of Delphic colonial oracular consultation stories rather than their development at Delphi: Giangiulio 2010. For a very different view, emphasizing the lack of connection between Apollo Pythios and colonial foundations involving the oracle (as opposed to the stress put on Apollo by the mother city), see: Davies 2009, Jacquemin 2011.

41. In addition, Parke and Wormell argue for the oracle establishing something of a moral code by this time: Parke and Wormell 1956a: 382–84. Despite its religious conservatism, the oracle by this time seems also to have been responsible for directing the foundation of the Apollo Pythios cult in other places (like Athens: Parke and Wormell **541**); regulating the occasion of sacrifice for other divinities (Aphrodite around Attica: Parke and Wormell **212**); and even authorizing the worship of new divinities to the Epidaurians: Damia and Auxesis: Parke and Wormell **10, 11.**

42. Le Roy 1967: 21–28, Morgan 1990: 132. See de La Coste-Messelière 1936, Dinsmoor 1950. For the latest excavation, and suggestion of an early sixth century date: Luce 1992: 704, Luce 2008: 95–117. There is also evidence for an early temple in the Athena sanctuary at roughly the same time, although its dimensions and form are uncertain: Demangel and Daux 1923: 38–39. Some scholars have seen a Corinthian influence in the design of this early temple: Østby 2000: 241.

43. Luce 1992: 697, 700–701, Luce 2008: 51–60, 61–78.

44. Morgan 1990: 16, 137, 183.

45. Scott 2010: 45.

46. Luce 2008: 412.

47. Thessaly may have offered a life-size statue at Delphi in the first half of the seventh century (Paus. 10.16.8): Jacquemin **333**; Scott **1**. Cypselus's treasury: Scott **2**; Jacquemin **124**. It was in Cypselus's treasury that the offerings of King Gyges of Lydia were kept.

48. Jacquemin 1999: 32, Scott 2010: 42.

49. Items found include a bronze horse from northern Greece in the Corycian cave 700–650 BC, rings and buttons near the Athena sanctuary from the Balkans. For Olympia finds: Kilian-Dirlmeier 1985, Luce 2008: 413–15.

50. Vatin 1977, Luce 2008: 411–26, Scott 2010: 41–45. For discussion of their identification as Cleobis and Biton: Parke and Wormell 1956a: 378–80.

51. See Pouilloux 1976, Lerat 1980: 102.

52. Luce 2008: 418. Pind., *Pyth.* 5, talks of a "treasury of the Cretans," which has never been found and was increasingly thought to have been made up. But the collected nature of their offerings in the eighth and seventh centuries BC may possibly open the debate again over the existence of some kind of early treasury structure: Roux 1962, Jacquemin 1999: 289. For further discussion of Cretans at Delphi: Perdrizet 1908: 2, Guarducci 1946.

53. Scott **10**. For discussion, see Courby 1927: 186–87, de La Coste-Messelière 1936: 63–78, Bommelaer 1991: 229.

54. See Luce 2008: 429–36. Equally note the convergence between the oracle's minimal role in new foundations around the Black Sea and the lack of offerings from that area.

55. No Cretan tripods at Olympia: Rolley 1977: 103. Indeed at Olympia, Cretan weapons appear that seem to have been dedicated by Crete's enemies. Delphi may have been the sanctuary for Cretans to dedicate in, Olympia for its enemies: Rolley 1977: 146. As well, Sparta seems to have dedicated more often at Olympia in the seventh century than at Delphi, despite its close relationship with the oracle: Picard 1991: 161. For more on the differences between Olympia and Delphi down to the seventh century BC, see Morgan 1990. For the archaic and classical periods, see Scott 2010.

56. See Roux 1979: 3, Morgan 1990: 185, Luce 2008: 434. Unless you count a story in Plut. *Mor.* 492A–B that the Thessalians used an early form of lot oracle at Delphi when selecting their King Aleuas the Red (and even then it is noticeable that it is not the Pythian oracle they are interacting with). Pausanias also later claimed the first monumental dedication at Delphi was from Larissa in Thessaly

in the late eighth century BC (Paus. 10.16.8; Jacquemin **333**; Scott **1**), but this may have been dedicated only in the sixth century BC: Jacquemin 1999: 51.

CHAPTER 4. REBIRTH

1. Crisa was powerful enough for the sea gulf to the south to have been known as the Crisaean Gulf (Thuc. 1.107.3). Strabo (6.1.15) believed Crisa had also established a colony at Metapontum in southern Italy. Where was Crisa? It has never been identified archaeologically: some suggest it's the settlement of Moulki on the plain near the coast (see map 3): Morgan 1990: 136. See also Dor, Jannoray, van Effenterre, and van Effenterre 1960. Crisa as the town hampering Delphi should not be confused with Cirrha (although the name is sometimes used in the ancient sources for Crisa), which was the port town where ancient pilgrims arrived en route to Delphi throughout its history, or with the name Castri which was given to the modern village built on top of Delphi in the medieval period after Delphi's abandonment in the seventh century AD. See Rousset 2002b: 218.

2. Oracle response: Aeschin. *In Ctes.* 3.108 (Parke and Wormell **17**). See also the version in Diod. Sic. 9.16 (Parke and Wormell **18**). Length of war: Callisthenes *FGrHist* 124 f1. Leaders of expedition: Parke and Wormell 1956a: 103. Introduction of hellebore: Parke and Wormell 1956a: 104–105.

3. For a recent résumé of the details, along with discussion of the existence of an earlier festival at Delphi, which the Pythian games superseded: Weir 2004: 11–16.

4. Robertson 1978. For previous scholarly discussion of the war, see in particular Forrest 1956. See also Jannoray 1937, Sordi 1953, Defradas 1954. The surviving evidence for the war is best catalogued in Davies 1994. See "the fantasy of the Crisa war cannot be exorcised, instead it will continue to haunt the dreams of historians": Càssola 1980: 422.

5. Although some have argued for involvement of the Amphictyony from the mid-seventh century BC: Parke and Wormell 1956a: 103.

6. See Mosshammer 1982. Pausanias (10.7.2–5) also reports that the oldest competition was for the singing of hymns to Apollo, with harp, flute, and athletic competitions added in 586 BC.

7. See Strabo 9.3.10; Paus. 10.7.2. For discussion of the difficulties in ascertaining the origins and precise development of the games from the ancient sources: Morgan 1990: 136. Davies in particular argues that the origins of Delphi's local games were later elaborated in order not only to compete with, but also to ally the

increasing number of polis and sanctuary games in the first half of the sixth century BC, and particularly those of the periodos circuit: Olympia, Delphi, Isthmia, and Nemea: Davies 2007: 56–65.

8. See McInerney 1999. Indeed McInerney argues that the Sacred War may have been provoked by Delphi as part of an intentional land grab: McInerney 1999: 105. See Rousset 2002a: 281.

9. Bandit stories: Robertson 1978: 44. Change in favoritism of the oracle: See Forrest 1956. Cretan influence: Guarducci 1946, Davies 1994: 204. Heracles and tripod images: Parke and Boardman 1957.

10. First perimeter wall: Luce 1992: 694, Luce 2008: 79–81, Bommelaer 2011: 14–19. Temple dated to same period: Luce 2008: 98–104. Major elaboration of the roof in 575 BC of a preexisting temple: Billot 1977, Jacquemin 1999: 30, 222.

11. Scott 2010: 52. See also Bommelaer 1991: 19, Morgan 2003: 113, Hall 2007: 276–90. The war may have been encouraged by rival factions within Delphi itself: Dovatour 1933. Provoked by Delphi: McInerney 1999: 105. The war as the result of regional rather than "interregional" tensions and interests: Morgan 1990: 136.

12. For the importance of the Thessalian-Isthmus corridor to Thessalian policy: Kase and Szemler 1984.

13. The tyrants of Corinth are said to have plotted actively against the Sicyonian tyrant: Forrest 1956: 37. Sicyon may have later been attacked for its role in the war at Delphi by Corinth's ally Miletus: Salmon 1984: 227.

14. The Alcmaeonids had been significantly tainted by the Cylon affair in Athens: Cylon, was the would-be tyrant of Athens in the late seventh century, whom the oracle had supposedly supported, but whom the Alcmaeonids had taken upon themselves to kill. In doing so they committed religious sacrilege, and so subsequently had to be punished for their crime: Forrest 1956: 39–42.

15. Luce 1992: 704. The annexation of this vast stretch of land (150–200 sq km) as sacred land was a game changer in Delphi's history. The degree to which this vast area was controlled by the city from the sixth century BC through to the Hellenistic period has no real likeness in the Greek world. The control can be demonstrated archaeologically: the area of Cirphis extending down from Delphi toward the sea has revealed no surviving remains indicating any kind of settlement from this period, in striking contrast to the rest of the region, a fact only plausible if the entire area had been off limits at that time as sacred land: Rousset 2002b: 239. As a result, control over the sacred land made Delphi something of a unique case in the ancient world, and enabled this small city to punch

significantly above its weight in comparison to other Greek cities; see Rousset 1996. The inclusion of Delphi under the auspices of the Amphictyony also put Delphi on a different track from other regional sanctuaries in Phocis, some of which demonstrate strong degrees of anti-Thessalian activity at exactly this time, e.g., Kalapodi: McInerney 2011: 101–102.

16. Importance of symbolic capital in sixth century: Osborne 2009: 231. Prizes at games: see Valavanis 2004. At Delphi, it was a wreath made out of laurel branches.

17. Development of cultural homogeneity: see Snodgrass 1986. For the use of Corinthian pottery at Delphi in this period: Luce 2008: 421. For sculpture and coinage: Osborne 2009: 234–54.

18. See Parke and Wormell 1956a: 99–100.

19. Original focus around sanctuary of Demeter Anthela: Sanchez 2001: 44. Change in composition after annexation of Delphi: Lefèvre 1998: 16. See Tausend 1992.

20. Range of purpose: see Sanchez 2001: 44–50. Prototype European Union: see Tenekides 1931, Daux 1957a, Daux 1957b, Sordi 1957, Tenekides 1958, Amandry 1979. Old boys' club: Hammond and Griffith 1979: 452. Recent consensus: Sanchez 2001: 44–51, 468–77, Lefèvre 2011. See Daux 1975: 350–54. Of varying interest to Greeks over time: see Lefèvre 1996. Absence in the fifth century BC (and from Herodotus): Sanchez 2001: 27, Hornblower 2007. For discussion of its existence and purpose in late Hellenistic and Roman times: Daux 1975.

21. Convincing rest of Amphictyony: Sanchez 2001: 488. New range of raw materials: Jacquemin 1993.

22. Difficulties in knowing: see Lefèvre 1998: 51. No permanent secretariat: Davies 1998: 11, Lefèvre 1998: 193. Reality: Davies 1998: 10–11.

23. The primary bodies in the administration of the city of Delphi were its *ekklesia* (assembly), its *boule* (council), and its *prytaneis* (magistrates), among whom was the eponymous archon (chief magistrate) of the city. It is thought that it was primarily the prytaneis who liaised with the Amphictyony and handled sanctuary management: Arnush 1991: 11–45. All three bodies had places to meet within the city, with many scholars arguing that the bouleuterion (meeting place of the boule) was within the Apollo sanctuary, and the prytaneion very close to it. In later centuries (Hellenistic and Roman times), the theater within the sanctuary was used for meetings of the city's assembly, and the council of damiourgoi

(a particular class of citizen) came to have considerable influence: Heliod. *Aeth.* 4.19; Vatin 1965: 227, Weir 2004: 51.

24. Tension between Delphic city and Amphictyony: Lefèvre 1998: 51, Weir 2004: 53–55. On the responsibility of the city for particular events, and on its constitution (Aristotle wrote a treaty on the constitution of the Delphic polis, which is now lost): Roux 1970, Roux 1979: 61, Bommelaer 1991: 24, Jacquemin 1995b, Lefèvre 1998: 44–45.

25. New cults may also have begun at this time at Delphi, like that of Neoptolemus. The stories associating the death of Neoptolemus with Delphi are varied, evoked perhaps to explain the emergence of a cult place in his honor within the Apollo sanctuary that is well known by the fourth century BC: Downie 2004: 152–217.

26. See Parke and Wormell 1956a: 108–109.

27. Questions about plague: Diog. Laert. 1.110; Parke and Wormell **13**. See Bowden 2005: 110–11. Solon's consultations: Parke and Wormell **15** and **16**. For Solon's (later) popularity and sources, see: Osborne 2009: 204–11. For more on Solon, see: Blok and Lardinois 2006, Lewis 2006.

28. Golden statues at Delphi: Plut. *Vit. Sol.* 25. *Exegetai pythochrestoi*: Parke and Wormell 1956a: 110–11.

29. Parke and Wormell **326**. See Bowden 2005: 114.

30. Early Athenian treasury Jacquemin **85**; Scott **7**; see Scott 2010: 49.

31. See Parke and Wormell 1956a: 110.

32. Cypselus, tyrant of Corinth, had offered the sanctuary's first treasury (see the last chapter), as well as numerous other dedications, and been heavily involved with the oracle. His tyrant son, Periander, continued to follow in his father's footsteps, perhaps with the dedication of a delicate and exquisitely carved ivory chest, fragments of which have been found buried in the sanctuary: Carter 1989.

33. Jacquemin **435, 434**; Scott **19, 20**.

34. Scott 2010: 53–54. For more on the tholos and monopteros: de La Coste-Messelière and Picard 1928: 191–92, de La Coste-Messelière 1936: 52–54, 79 , Partida 2000: 90.

35. Paus. 10.7.7. The chariot may even have been displayed inside the monopteros: de La Coste-Messelière 1936: 79 n.3. The chariot and stadium races in this period would have taken place in the plain below the sanctuary, as there was no room for them on the steep hillside. While the stadium races would later

take place in the stadium built into the hillside, the chariot races for the games, throughout the sanctuary's history, took place on the plain below: Bommelaer 1991: 10.

36. Although there are some notable Corinthian dedications during this period, including one of the chryselephantine statues found in the burial underneath the sacred way (now on display in the museum): Luce 2008: 412.

37. Pausanias 5.16.5. See Salmon 1984: 227, Carter 1989: 374, Arafat 1995, Snodgrass 2001.

38. Oracle responses concerning Adrastus: Parke and Wormell **24**. Using spoils on games: Schol. Pind. *Nem.* 9.20. See Parke and Wormell 1956a: 121.

39. For the tendency of the ancient sources concerning Delphi's interactions with tyrants increasingly to rebrand the sanctuary as antityrannical in periods when tyranny was no longer a positive political option, as noted in the last chapter, see: Parke and Wormell 1956a: 121, Malkin 1989: 149. Some tyrants, though, in the period 600–550 BC, received more useful responses, especially when they were portrayed as seeking atonement for their sins, e.g., Pythagoras, tyrant at Ephesus, who sought a method of alleviating famine brought on his city by is own impiety: Parke and Wormell **27**.

40. This story too is argued to be a later creation, perhaps from the fifth century, given that all the rival competitors to Delphi in Croesus's competition were Delphi's real-life competitors for oracular consultation in the fifth century BC (Abar, Dodona, Amphiarius at Oropus, Lebadeia, Didyma, Ammon at Siwa), when a story underlining Delphi's preeminence would have been welcome: Parke and Wormell 1956a: 132. Although Herodotus notes that other sanctuaries received dedications following this process as well (e.g., the oracle of Amphiarius at Oropus: Hdt. 1.49–52), perhaps indicating that Delphi was not the only one to get the question right, but simply the one Croesus chose to use.

41. For discussion of Croesus's offerings: Parke 1984, Flower 1991.

42. See Flower 1991: 67–68. Croesus may even have named one of his grandchildren Pythios after the oracle: Parke and Wormell 1956a: 139.

43. Parke and Wormell **53**. Croesus went on to make Sparta his allies, an introduction possibly made by Delphi itself as the oracle told the Spartans to go to Croesus when they needed gold: Parke and Wormell **56**. Croesus asked several other questions as well: Would he rule for a long time (Parke and Wormell **54**), which received an equally ambiguous answer: "Till a mule becomes king of Persia." He is also said to have asked about how to cure his dumb son (Parke and Wormell **55**).

44. Further gifts to and from Delphi: Hdt. 1.54. See Kurke 2011: 58. For discussion of Croesus's actions: Parke and Wormell 1956a: 135.

45. Glaucus: Parke and Wormell **35, 36**. Aesop: Parke and Wormell **58**. For discussion of Aesop as a test case of Delphic greed: Parke and Wormell 1956a: 398, Kurke 2011: 59–74.

46. Parke and Wormell 1956a: 331–39.

47. Prevalence of Dionysus in oracular accounts: Parke and Wormell 1956a: 331. Importance of Dionysiac cult and activity at Delphi: Roux 1976: 176. E.g., consultation of the oracle in the Hellenistic period by various guilds of Dionysiac actors: Parke and Wormell **349**. See subsequent chapters for detailed discussion of Dionysus's role at Delphi.

48. See Malkin 1987: 79.

49. Heracleia Pontice: Malkin 1987: 73–76. Chersonesus: Bowden 2005: 120.

50. Scott **22**; Le Roy 1967: 70–76. In a site on a steep hillside, and in which over 80 percent of the roofs were of yellow Corinthian clay, the presence of a different roofing clay and style would have been very noticeable: Scott 2010: 51. In addition, in the 540s BC, Cyrene, founded thanks to an oracle from Delphi, would turn back to the oracle to ask for help during a period of political turmoil and for which the oracle helped appoint a mediator, Demonax of Mantinea: Malkin 1989: 139, Scott 2012: 14–44.

51. Scott **11, 12, 17**. For discussion: Scott 2010: 49.

52. Scott **23** and **32**. For discussion: Scott 2010: 50.

53. Bouleuterion: Scott 2010: 48–49. Cnidian Treasury: Scott **33**. Scott 2010: 47. Naxian Sphinx: Scott **21**; Scott 2010: 46.

54. Hdt. 2.134–35; Scott **9**. Plutarch, in the first century AD, recounts how his friends were outraged that a dedication from a courtesan could have been accepted in a sanctuary like Delphi: Plut. *Mor.* 401A.

55. The discovery and initial report of the burial: Amandry 1939b, Amandry 1977, Picard 1991: 191–226, Luce 2008: 415.

CHAPTER 5. FIRE

1. Also to be included in the Delphic "portfolio" is the 150–200 km of "sacred land"—the territory around Delphi declared sacred following the "First Sacred War"—which Delphi administered. In the second half of the sixth century BC, there seems to have been a specific magistrate in charge of it, who may also have had a role in running the Pythian games: Rousset 2002a: 212, 285 and inscription 33 (550–25 BC).

2. For the ancient sources on the fire, see Hdt. 2.180; 5.62.2–3; Paus. 10.5.13. For the melting of Croesus's dedications: Parke and Wormell 1956a: 143.

3. Hdt. 2.180. Herodotus chooses to use the word "*automatos.*"

4. Scott 2010: 56–60. For a recent discussion of the new boundary walls, see: Bommelaer 2011: 19–25.

5. For the stone quarries that fed the building programs at Delphi, see: Amandry 1981a: 714–21, Bommelaer 1991: 245–47.

6. Davies 2001a: 213.

7. Cost of temple rebuilding: the daily pay for an Athenian juryman was approximately half a drachma (by the end of the fifth century BC), whereas a skilled hoplite could expect a drachma. There were 6,000 drachmas in a talent. See Burford 1969: 109. Contribution from Egypt: Parke and Wormell 1956a: 143–44.

8. De La Coste-Messelière 1946: 285.

9. Schachter 1994: 295–98.

10. Polycrates of Samos: Parke and Wormell **67**. Archesilaus III of Cyrene: Hdt. 4.163; Parke and Wormell **69** and **70**. See also Malkin 1989: 139, Parker 2000: 92.

11. Pactyes: Hdt. 1.157.2–160; Parker 2000: 92–93. Cnidians: Hdt. 1.174.4; Parke and Wormell **63**.

12. Parke and Wormell **75, 76, 77, 78**.

13. Murder of Cylon: Hdt. 5.71; Thuc. 1.126; Osborne 2009: 202. Alcmaeon: see Hdt. 6.125. Parke and Wormell 1956a: 144. For the Alcmaeonids and Delphi: Daux 1940: 42–44.

14. Factions in Athens: Osborne 2009: 268. Peisistratus achieving power in Athens: Hdt. 1.59–64; Arist. *Ath. Pol.* 13–17.

15. Claiming exile the entire time: Hdt. 6.123. Cleisthenes as archon: Lewis 2009: 53, Osborne 2009: 269.

16. Miltiades the Elder: Parke and Wormell **60, 61**. Parke and Wormell 1956a: 145. Megacles and Apollo *Ptoios*: *IG* I^3 1469; Schachter 1994: 291, Athanassaki 2011: 263. Schachter argues that this sanctuary was chosen in order to gain Theban support for the Alcmaeonids, who had traditionally supported Peisistratus: Schachter 1994: 293.

17. No dedications at Delphi, see Osborne 2009: 269. Cult of Apollo Pythios in Athens: Colin 1905. Later dedication of an altar to Apollo Pythios and the twelve gods: Meiggs and Lewis 1988: No. 11. Peisistratus responsible for burning the temple of Apollo: Schol. Pind. *Pyth.* 7.9b (*FGrHist* 628 F 115).

18. Contractors unable to finish: Parke and Wormell 1956a: 144–46. It is suggested that the Alcmaeonids may have used the money from the contract to bolster their campaign to overthrow the Peisistratids in Athens, and subsequently returned with their own cash to complete the temple: Parke and Wormell 1956a: 146.

19. Hdt. 5.61. They may also have been responsible for designing the theme of the pedimental sculpture (which was without doubt completed by Athenian sculptors): Knell 1998: 50–51, Athanassaki 2011: 250.

20. Hdt. 5.63.1; 5.90; 6.123; Parke and Wormell **79**; Parke and Wormell 1956a: 147.

21. Part of wider negotiations: Parke and Wormell 1956a: 147. Attractive to Sparta: Osborne 2009: 277. Four separate campaigns: Hdt. 5.63–76.

22. Hansen 1992: 146–49.

23. As argued by Boëthius 1918. See Zahrnt 1989, Athanassaki 2011: 250. It also reflected the established of a permanent sacred way for visitors to Delphi from Athens: a processional route, which, especially at the time of the Pythian games, the Athenians knew as the *Pythais*: Roux 1976: 174.

24. Reuse of stones: Jacquemin 1999: 232. Boundary walls: Levi 1988. Sacred Way: Roesch 1984: 187–88, Jacquemin 1999: 32–33, Scott 2010: 24.

25. Area later to be occupied by stadium as work and living area for craftsmen: de La Coste-Messelière 1946: 283, Aupert 1977: 243, Aupert 1979: 17–20. Area of later theater established for worship of Dionysus?: de La Coste-Messelière 1969: 747. Area above temple terrace used for worship of Poseidon: Scott 2010: 61.

26. Expansion: Demangel and Daux 1923: 65, Jacquemin 1999: 28. Temple sculpture: Poulsen 1908: 337–41, Demangel and Daux 1923: 15. Another structure was also built at this time in the Athena sanctuary, possibly celebrating the worship of Athena and Artemis: Roux 1989: 62–63.

27. See Roux 1976: 184–95. See also the map with some of the sanctuaries to these divinities and heroes, which we can pinpoint in Jacquemin 1999: Planche 1.

28. See Roux 1976: 196–206.

29. Roux 1976: 165. See also: Maass 1997: 76–88, Amandry 2000. The Labyadai, a phratry (civic unit of the polis) at Delphi, known through an inscription dating to the fourth century BC, had to participate in fifteen sacred banquets a year, in addition to rituals for their own cults, as well as those of the city as a whole and those of the Amphictyony celebrated at Delphi: Rhodes and Osborne 2003: No. 1.

30. Scott **57**. See Thuc. 1.13.6; Daux 1958b: 252, 285, Jacquemin 1999: 72, 85, 142, 248, 252.

31. Reuse of old boundary walls: Structures Scott **42, 43, 47, 49.** See Partida 2000: 119, 129–30, 195. New Sicyonian treasury: Scott **50.** See Laroche and Nenna 1990. Compare the more desultory treasury built at Olympia by the Sicyonians in the same period: Scott 2010: 163–69.

32. Siphnian story: Hdt. 3.57; Parke and Wormell 1956a: 150–51. The Gigantomachy relief: de La Coste-Messelière and Picard 1928: 126, 143. For discussion of the decisions taken regarding the Siphnian treasury in the context of the wider issues surrounding the degree of control dedicators at Delphi had over where their dedications were placed and what they looked like, see Scott 2007, Scott 2010: 62–65.

33. New treasuries: Scott 2010: 68–69. For the importance of Croton in the West in this period: Dunbabin 1948: 355–63. For Etruscan desire to link itself more closely with the Greek world (a goal now achievable through a presence at Delphi): Briquel 1984: 218, 220–21. Name change of Corinthian treasury: Plut. *Mor.* 400D-F for Delphi agreeing, but Olympia refusing; *FD* III 3 153–54 (inscription 153 is dated to 540 BC and confirms the name change to "Corinthian treasury," and 154 is a promanteia inscription from mid-fifth century BC confirming it is the Corinthians who have the right to skip the oracle queue).

34. Siphnian question to oracle: Parke and Wormell **65** and **66.** Outcomes: Hdt. 3.57.3; Paus. 10.11.2.

35. Hdt. 5.66.2. See Parke and Wormell 1956a: 147.

36. Cleomenes's interventions in Athens: see Hdt. 6.106–107; Lewis 2009: 54. Cleisthenes's reforms: see Hdt. 5. 63–76; Osborne 2009: 278–79.

37. Pythia picking ten heroes: Parke and Wormell **80**; Parke and Wormell 1956a: 148, Bowden 2005: 95. See also Hdt. 5.66, 6.131; Arist. *Ath. Pol.* 21.6. Fighting against the Boeotians and Chalcidians: Meiggs and Lewis 1988: No. 15. Sanctioning a fighting force: Bowden 2005: 98–99.

38. Thebes: Parke and Wormell **81**; Parke and Wormell 1956a: 148-9. Aeginetans: Parke and Wormell **82**; Hdt. 5.89.2.

39. See Scott 2010: 68–69. For the craftsmen dedication: Homolle 1909: 54. For the Chian altar: Amandry 1986: 209, 218. It had a dedicating inscription along its top edge facing visitors as they approached the temple (*FD* III 3 212) carved into a layer of black Chian stone. For the Phocian oracular consultation and subsequent dedication of shields (they dedicated half their booty at Delphi

and half at the sanctuary of Apollo at Abae): Hdt. 8.37; Parke and Wormell **68**; Parke and Wormell 1956a: 157.

40. The Athenians in particular seem to have dedicated a particular kind of figurine at the cave, which, while similar to those dedicated at and near the Acropolis in Athens, are different to those found in the Apollo and Athena sanctuaries below. Athenians it seems were making dedications specifically tailored to their intended location of dedication within the Delphic complex: Picard 1991: 245, Luce 2008: 413.

41. See Hdt. 5.74–75; Osborne 2009: 278.

42. In contrast, the dedication of the Chian altar is often interpreted as a strong statement by Chios that it intended to defy Persia: it was tying its trousers to the Greek mast by dedicating at Delphi: Hdt. 6.8, 15–16, 20, 31.

43. Hdt. 6.49.

44. Hdt. 6.66; Parke and Wormell 1956a: 94–98, 160–61. Demaratus would return to Greece as an advisor to King Xerxes of Persia, in particular advising him not to underestimate the Spartans at Thermopylae.

45. Consultation after the battle: Parke and Wormell **90.** Treasury: Amandry 1998, Neer 2004, Scott 2010: 78–79. Statue group alongside the treasury and inscription: *FD* III 2 1; Audiat 1930, Audiat 1933: 61. Shields and inscription on the temple: *FD* III 4 190; Paus. 10.19.4.

46. See Osborne 2009: 312.

47. Pind. *Pyth.* 7. See Parke and Wormell 1956a: 150. For the conciliatory tone: Athanassaki 2011: 236–45. The "learning curve" for the Alcmaeonids is clear. In Pind. *Pyth.* 8, also probably commissioned by the Alcmaeonids, but written sometime in the decade before Megacles's win (and Pind. *Pyth.* 7), the Alcmaeonids' own role in constructing the Apollo temple at Delphi is made clear: Hubbard 2011: 362.

48. Debates in Athens: Thuc. 1.93.3. Argos: Parke and Wormell **92.** Crete: Parke and Wormell **93.** Spartans: Parke and Wormell **100.** Delphians: Parke and Wormell **96.** This is the explanation for the cult of the winds worshiped at Delphi: Roux 1976: 200. The altar for the cult was situated inside the sanctuary of Thyia, location of the latter uncertain, but probably near the Castalian fountain: Jacquemin 1992b.

49. Parke and Wormell 1956a: 165.

50. Hdt. 8.3; Xen. *Hell.* 6.4.30; Diod. Sic. 11.14.2; Paus. 10.8.7; Parke and Wormell 1956a: 172. These heroes subsequently became the focus of cult practice at Delphi: Roux 1976: 196–67.

51. Hdt. 7.163.2.

52. Hdt. 9.42.2; Parke and Wormell **98;** Bowden 2005: 35.

53. Original response: Parke and Wormell **94.** Second question and response: Parke and Wormell **95;** Hdt. 7.139.5–144; Parker 2000: 87. See Bowden 2005: 100–103.

54. Thucydides' argument: Hdt. 8.51.2. The decree: Meiggs and Lewis 1988: 23, Bowden 2005: 104–105, Lagogianni-Georgakarakos and Buraselis 2009: 74–77.

55. The historian Robert Parker argues that Delphi's prestige was never higher than in the immediate aftermath of the Persian Wars: Parker 2000: 98.

56. Hdt. 7.132; Rhodes 2007: 34. A fourth century BC copy survives: Rhodes and Osborne 2003: No. 88.21–51.

57. Parke and Wormell **102.**

58. Osborne 2009: 312.

CHAPTER 6. DOMINATION

1. Oracle's response: Parke and Wormell **104.** Euchidas' run: it is about a 125-mile round trip: Parke and Wormell 1956a: 176.

2. Oath to dedicate at Delphi, see Hdt. 7.132. Amphictyonic statue group at Delphi: Paus. 10.19.1. Price on Ephialtes' head: Parke and Wormell 1956a: 178.

3. Statue: Hdt. 8.151; Paus. 10.14.5. Statue base: Block inv. 1198 (formerly *FD* III 1 2). See Laroche and Jacquemin 1988, Bommelaer 1991: 169.

4. Asking Pythia if Apollo was satisfied: Hdt. 8.121–22; Parke and Wormell **105.** In an effort to deny the accusation of Medism, show off their pro-Greek credentials, and retell history in the process, the Aeginetans also seem to have put up a monument at Marathon to commemorate that victory, even though they had had no role in the battle: Jacquemin 1999: 251.

5. E.g., the Preparethians and the Epidaurians: Scott 2010: 83–84.

6. Commemoration at other sanctuaries: Hdt. 9.81. Pausanias hijacking column: Thuc. 1.132; Bonner and Smith 1943: 2. Punishment of Pausanias: the Plataeans demanded that Sparta should be fined one thousand talents for Pausanias's misdemeanor, and that Pausanias should remove the inscriptions: Thuc. 1.132; Diod. Sic. 11.33; Plut. *Mor.* 873C; Roux 1979: 54. Serpent column inscription: Meiggs and Lewis 1988: No. 27.

7. Carystians: Hdt. 9.30–31; Jacquemin 1999: 261. Alexander's pro-Persian role?: Hdt. 8.142 and 9.44–45. The style of his offering (a large statue of himself) would, without doubt, have looked particularly inappropriate to the

anti-tyrannical city-states of Greece: Hammond and Griffith 1979: 103. For a wider discussion of the relationship between Macedon and Delphi: Miller 2000.

8. Refusing Themistocles' dedications was later explained by way of the fact that Themistocles would soon find himself chased out of Athens and into the Persian court, whose acceptance of him might have been more difficult if he had been allowed by the Pythia to dedicate victory offerings from a Persian defeat. In reality, however, the Pythia's choice is still not fully understood: Paus. 10.14.5; Parke and Wormell **106**; Parke and Wormell 1956a: 177. Arguing against Sparta's proposal: Plut. *Vit. Them.* 20.3.

9. The attachment between the Western Greek world and Delphi (and Olympia) in this period is striking: the other periodos sanctuaries—Isthmia and Nemea—do not receive any Western dedications in this period: Jacquemin 1999: 252. Gelon's offerings: Scott 2010: 88–91.

10. Croton's tripod: Jacquemin 1999: 173. Hieron's victory dedications: Hieron offered a victory column next to Gelon's for his victory at the battle of Cumae (474 BC), a statue of himself on the temple terrace, and a statue base in the southern half of the sanctuary: Bommelaer 1991: 188, Rougement 1991. Charioteer dedication: *FD* III 4 452. Reinscription by Polyzalus: Rolley 1990, Adornato 2008. Cyrene dedication: Valavanis 2004: 202.

11. See Fontenrose 1988: 128. We have a surviving inscription from the mid-fifth century BC with a list of those who gave hospitality to the theoroi on their journeys: Daux 1968: 629–30. It is interesting to note the balance of responsibility between the city and the Amphictyony for the organization. The city sent out the theoroi: *CID* 10.45–46; Sourvinou-Inwood 2000: 16. But the Amphictyony were responsible for getting the sanctuary in order (*CID* IV 1: 380 BC), and both groups could create new events in the Pythian games.

12. Hoplitodromoi race: Fontenrose 1988: 126. Painting: Plin. *HN* 35.9.58. In the first competition a man called Timagoras apparently beat Panainus, the brother of the famous sculptor Pheidias. Mime and pantomime: Valavanis 2004: 194–95.

13. Pind. *Pyth.* 1, 4, 5, 6, 7 (alongside *Pyth.* 2 and 3 also most probably for chariot races). Also commemorated by Pindar were winners in the wrestling, the hoplite race, running races, and flute-playing competition. The iron chair in which Pindar sat and sang his hymns when he visited Delphi was dedicated inside the temple of Apollo after his death: Paus. 10.24.5. A religious cult was established in 442 BC to Pindar after his death, at the behest of the Delphic oracle, and the choice portion of sacrifice was set aside for the spirit of the poet and could be

claimed by his descendants: Paus. 9.23.3; Parke and Wormell **119;** Parke and Wormell 1956a: 399, Johnston 2005: 284.

14. For the various versions of Neoptolemos's death and their discrepancies, see Parke and Wormell 1956a: 315–18. The Aenianes at Delphi: Paus. 10.24.4, 6. The cult tomb of Neoptolemus at Delphi: Pouilloux and Roux 1963: 102–23, Pouilloux 1984. Neoptolemus fighting to protect Delphi: Roux 1976: 197.

15. The oracle was involved in this period in setting up honors for historical individuals, such as Orrhippus of Megara, the athlete who had been the first to run naked at the Olympics (720 BC). His tomb in his home city carried an inscription saying the monument had been set up with Delphic approval: Parke and Wormell **89.** Several other such instances of Delphic involvement with the establishment of honors are known: Parke and Wormell 1956a: 352–57.

16. Parke and Wormell **114.**

17. Parke and Wormell **113:** the sources also explain this consultation as the Athenians seeking relief from plague. The oracle was also involved c. 460 BC in the affairs of the Praxiergidae, an Attic *genos*: *IG* I³ 7.

18. Vogt 1998, Bowden 2005: 52–56.

19. See "even if the practical influence of the Pythia in Greek politics had begun to wane, the accumulated fame of Delphi had a momentum which carried it triumphantly through the 5th century BC": Parke and Wormell 1956a: 180.

20. Bousquet 1943, Colonna 1984, Jacquemin 1999: 121–22. The dedication in this case was associated with an oracular consultation that had guided them to victory: Parke and Wormell **128.**

21. Jacquemin 1999: 192–93.

22. New layout of the north section of the sanctuary at this time: Pouilloux 1960, Bommelaer 1992b. Pausanias's description of the paintings: Paus. 10.25.1–29. For discussion: Kebric 1983. For discussion of the lesche: Pouilloux 1960: 123, Scott 2010: 94.

23. Treasury in Athena sanctuary: Amandry 1984b: 191. Stoa: for dating see Walsh 1986. For discussion of purpose: Kuhn 1985, Hansen 1989. Athenian palm tree and Athena: Amandry 1954: 300, Miller 1997: 39. New statue group at entrance to sanctuary: Jacquemin 1999: 190–91. This collection was added to with monuments also from individual Athenians: a horse statue, for example, from the Athenian general Callias: Scott 2010: 96. At the Corycian cave, too, there was a massive influx of Athenian pottery in this period, making up 50 percent of the material found there: Luce 2008: 413. For a recent study of worship and dedication at the cave in the period 500–450 BC: Volioti 2011.

24. Parke and Wormell 1956a: 184.

25. Parke and Wormell **121** and **154.** Why did the Amphictyony allow such domination, or were they powerless to prevent it? For discussion of the Amphictyony in the fifth century BC, including the possibility that it was largely inactive: Bowden 2003. For the assertion that the Amphictyony continued to be active: Daux 1975, Sanchez 2001: 27, 80–110. It is curious, that, at some point around the mid-fifth century, we know from surviving inscriptions that Athens actually made an alliance with the Amphictyony, as if they were another city-state: *IG* I³ 9; Roux 1979: 45.

26. "Spartan" approach to monument building: Thuc. 1.10; Cartledge 2002: 194, Low 2006. Spartan action at Delphi: Thuc. 1.112.5.

27. Hdt. 1.51–53; Prontera 1981: 256.

28. Parke and Wormell 1956a: 186.

29. The Apollo "Sitalcas" statue, standing fifteen and a half meters high: Diod. Sic. 16.33.1; Paus. 10.15.1–2. Its date of dedication is, however, disputed. For its dedication now in the fifth century BC: Jacquemin 1999: 15, 47. For its dedication in the fourth century BC: Bommelaer 1991: 187.

30. This monument is associated with Thessalian victory over Athens at the battle of Tanagra (Thuc. 1.107): Daux 1958a.

31. Scott 2010: 101. Gaia and Themis statues: de La Coste-Messelière and Flacelière 1930.

32. Thurii: Parke and Wormell **131, 132;** Schol Ar. *Nub.* 332. Amphipolis: Thuc. 4.102; Polyaenus *Strat.* 6.53; Parke and Wormell **133;** Malkin 1987: 81–84.

33. Religious officials: *IG* I³ 131.9–11 and *IG* I³ 137.3–5; First Fruits decree: *IG* I³ 78; Plut. *Mor.* 408C; Plut. *Vit. Nic.* 13.5–6; Hdt. 5.63.1, 5.66.2–3; Thuc. 5.16.2; Paus. 3.4.3–4; Mylonas 1961: 127, Cavanaugh 1996: 62. See Parke and Wormell **164, 165.**

34. Thuc. 1.25; Parke and Wormell **136.** See Parke and Wormell 1956a: 188, Parker 2000: 89.

35. Bommelaer 1992a: 293, Scott 2010: 101–103.

36. Des Courtils 1992: 244–51. For this idea that Delphi was an incubator, or laboratory, for sculptural styles and ideas (as well as a conservator of styles and ideas): Croissant 2000: 347.

37. Thuc. 1.118; Parke and Wormell **137.**

38. Parke and Wormell 1956a: 190. Corinth suggests using Delphi to bankroll Sparta's campaigns: Thuc. 1.121.3, 1.143.1. A new Spartan base at Heraclea in Trachis banned to outsiders: Thuc. 3.92; Parke and Wormell **159.**

39. Bribery by King Pleistonax of Sparta: Thuc. 5.16.2; Parke and Wormell **160.**

40. E.g., Eur. *Andr.* 1085ff, 1161ff. Ar. *Eq.* 197, 999. See also Soph. *OT* 711.

41. Fontenrose 1978: 95–117, Moret 1982, Shapiro 1996: 110–12, Bowden 2005: 59–60.

42. Agreement of 423 BC: Thuc. 4.118.1. Agreement of 421 BC: Thuc. 5.18.2.

43. Arcadia: Parke and Wormell **163.** Thasos and Neapolis: Thuc. 1.28.2.2; Pouilloux 1954: 178–92. Delian exiles: Thuc. 5.32.1; Parke and Wormell **161, 162;** Parker 2000: 95. Recovery from plague: Parke and Wormell **125;** Paus. 1.3.4; Bowden 2005: 111. Note that the oracle also advised Cleonae on how to save themselves from the plague in this period: Parke and Wormell **158.**

44. Traveling to Delphi through Boeotia territory: Parke and Wormell 1956a: 197–98. Aristophanes' lament: Ar. *Av.* 188. Euripides: E.g., Eur. *Ion* 369ff, 436ff, 859ff. See Dougherty 1996. See also the parody of Delphic oracles in Ar. *Vesp.* 158-60; *Plut.* 1–55.

45. Possible consultation leading up to Sicilian expedition: Parke and Wormell **166** (Plut. *Mor.* 403B). Supporting Sparta: Parke and Wormell **169** and **170.**

46. One possible dedication by an Athenian supporter (Corcyra) at this time: Scott 2010: 109. Spartan dedications: Bommelaer 1981: 22, Scott 2010: 104–108. For discussion of the problems of the archaeology of this area: Pouilloux and Roux 1963: 3–68.

47. Plut. *Vit. Nic.* 13.3. This was, according to Plutarch, dismissed at the time by the Athenians as a story invented by the Syracusans.

48. Parker 2000: 93.

49. Pl. *Chrm.* 164e–165a; see Bowden 2005: 70. See the relation of these maxims to Socrates' claim that the oracle had told his pupil no one was wiser than Socrates, a response Socrates attributed to the fact that he knew nothing in comparison to most people who thought they knew it all: Parke and Wormell **134** (see also a later version: **420**). Pl. *Ap.* 20e–21a; Xen. *Ap.* 14. For the date of the pupil's consultation: Parke and Wormell 1956a: 402–404.

50. Parke and Wormell 1956a: 387–89.

CHAPTER 7. RENEWAL

1. Parke and Wormell 1956a: 404.

2. Xen. *An.* 3.1.5–7. Half-tithe of spoils: Xen. *An.* 5.3.5. Note that Xenophon later described the oracle as an "advisor," through which "we learn what we ought to do and what not" Xen. *Cyr.* 1.6.46; *Mem.* 1.4.15.

3. The classicist Michael Arnush argues that a series of events from the Peloponnesian War through to Alexander the Great contributed to diminishing the importance of international political pilgrimage to the oracle specifically at Delphi (rather than oracles altogether): Arnush 2005: 105–106. Ceasing consultation over arbitration: Parker 2000: 89, 101, Arnush 2005: 105. Arbitration over Leuke: Parke and Wormell **178**. Even earlier end: Parke and Wormell 1956a: 188.

4. King Agis: *FD* III 4 196; Diod. Sic. 15.54.1; Parke and Wormell 1956a: 203. Lysander: Parke and Wormell 1956a: 204–207.

5. Julian. *Or.* 5.159b (written c. 360 AD); Parke and Wormell **572**; Parke and Wormell 1956a: 324, Bowden 2005: 205.

6. Phaselis: *CID* I 8. Skiathos: *CID* I 13.

7. Ascelpiads: *CID* I 11. Asclepiads of Cos and Cnidus highlighting their special honors: *CID* I 12. It was said that an Asclepiad from Cos was buried in the area of Delphi's hippodrome and had been involved in the Amphictyony's efforts to free Delphi from Crisa during the First Sacred War in the sixth century BC: Bousquet 1956: 579–93, Roux 1976: 197. Honors to individuals: the Athenian Callias claimed in the inscription accompanying his Pythian victory statue that he had secured a full spread of wins at all the periodos games—those of Olympia, Delphi, Isthmia, Nemea—even though the Olympic victory was actually achieved by another member of his family: *FD* III 1 510; Bousquet 1992. For Gorgias: Scott 2010: 111.

8. Parke and Wormell 1956a: 209.

9. Delphi population: Homolle 1926, Rousset 2002a. Population cramped into Delphi: Rousset 2002a: 50. Isolated and yet powerful: Rousset 2002a: 46.

10. Paus. 10.23.9; Rousset 2002a: 205.

11. Roux 1979: 70–77, Bommelaer 1991: 24.

12. Delphi in Plato's ideal state: Pl. *Resp.* 427b–c. It should be noted that Plato thus envisages a role for Delphi that is more religious than political, see Parker 2000: 82–85. Delphi in Plato's later work: Pl. *Leg.* 759c6–d1, 759d1–e1, 828a1–5, 856d2–e3, 865a3–b2, 913d4–914a5. See Parke and Wormell 1956a: 405, Bowden 2005: 84–86.

13. Labyadai: *CID* I 9 (fourth century BC Labyadai text); *CID* I 9bis (older Labyadai text). See also Rhodes and Osborne 2003: No. 1. Amphictyonic statement of responsibility for Pythian games: *CID* I 10 and *CID* IV 1. For discussion, see Roux 1979, Lefèvre 2002b: 5, 36. Number of other Amphictyonic laws: *CID* IV 2, 3, 4.

14. Narrative of First Sacred War, see Davies 1994: 201. Dionysius of Syracuse: Diod. Sic. 15.13.1. Iphicrates: Diod. Sic. 16.57.2. Earthquake: Parke and Wormell 1956a: 214, Amandry and Hansen 2010: 147–51, Scott 2010: 114. Jason of Pherai: Xen. *Hell.* 6.4.30 Parke and Wormell 1956a: 210–12.

15. Later oracles: Parke and Wormell 1956a: 220. Oracles prophesying Spartan downfall at Leuctra: Parke and Wormell **254.** Wall rebuilding: Hansen 1960, Amandry 1981a: 691, Jacquemin 1991b. The massive polygonal terracing wall of the temple was probably also deformed as a result of the earthquake and rockslide: Amandry and Hansen 2010: 151.

16. Amphictyony from the start: Roux 1979: 137–49, Lefèvre 1996: 121–26. Discussions pre-Leuctra whether Sparta should engage Thebes or play the Panhellenic "card" and lead the reconstruction at Delphi: Xen. *Hell.* 6.4.2; at the peace conference in summer 371 BC before Leuctra, participants decided to set up bureaucratic body, the naopoioi, to lead the reconstruction and a fund-raising scheme: Bourguet 1903: 9, Parke and Wormell 1956a: 214–16. See also Sordi 1957: 41–48, 67. Note that in 368 BC, Dionysius of Syracuse wrote to Athens rather than Delphi asking how the temple rebuilding was progressing: *Syll*³ 159; Rhodes and Osborne 2003: No. 33.

17. Argive monument: Bommelaer 1971a, Bommelaer 1971b. For the monument, see also Salviat 1965. Dedications crumbling: Plut. *Mor.* 397F.

18. This dedication was perhaps the first monumental articulation of the new confederacy: Delphi had once again acted as a petri dish for the creation of identity: Scott 2008. The inscription: *FD* III 1 6. This is despite the fact that the actual role of the Arkadians at Leuctra was minimal at best. The Arkadians may have later decided to attach themselves to this victory as the clearest way of announcing the Confederacy's anti-Spartan credentials: Scott 2008.

19. Theban treasury: Partida 2000: 196–98. Thessalian monument: Jacquemin 1999: 128.

20. Jacquemin 1999: 220.

21. The Theban general Epaminondas was later said to have received a warning from the oracle about how his life would end: Parke and Wormell **258.** As well, the Athenian general Callistratus consulted the oracle on his chance of returning from exile to Athens, but was killed following his return (later said to have been because he misunderstood the oracle's response): Parke and Wormell **259.**

22. The Tarentines, Lipareans, and Corcyrians all reinscribed their dedications: Jacquemin 1999: 76, Scott 2010: 122. This was not only happening at Delphi. In

Athens, the Athenians chose to reinscribe the oath of Plataea at this point, which included the promise to dedicate a tithe of booty from those who had sided with the Persians during the Persian Wars (which included Thebes) at a time when Athens was vying with Thebes for supremacy in Greece: Rhodes and Osborne 2003: No. 88.21–51, Rhodes 2007.

23. Naxians: Amandry 1940/1: 60–63. Siphnians: Valavanis 2004: 210.

24. Xen. *Hell.* 7.1.27. See Parke and Wormell 1956a: 220, Parker 2000: 88, Bowden 2005: 79.

25. For the initial work carried out in preparation for the rebuilding (the establishment of foundations, the decision about reusing stone blocks, the cutting of new stone in local quarries: Amandry and Hansen 2010: 157–82.

26. Lowering of interest: the "Law of Cadys": Homolle 1926. Astycrates: *FD* III 5 15–18. See Parke and Wormell 1956a: 221–22, Buckler 1985, Bommelaer 1991: 24. Theban promanteia: *Syll³* 176.

27. The affair of Crates and Orsilaus: Arist. *Pol.* 1303b.37; Plut. *Mor.* 825B; Ael. *VH* 11.5; Homolle 1926: 95–96, Parke and Wormell 1956a: 221, Roux 1976: 192. See also the legislation from this period for murder at Delphi: *CID* IV 4. The tholos in the Athena sanctuary: Lerat 1985, Laroche 1992.

28. For a recent discussion of the dating of the Third Sacred War: Deltenne 2010.

29. Parke and Wormell **261.** Parke and Wormell 1956a: 223–25.

30. Temporary set up for oracle: in 352 BC, surviving inscriptions relate that a contractor was paid to build a "shelter" for those consulting the oracle: *Syll³* 247. Destruction of inscriptions: Sanchez 2001: 173–76. Building defensive walls: Diod. Sic. 16.25.1; Amandry 1981a: 741, Maass 1997: 68–79.

31. Phocians going back on their promises: Parke and Wormell 1956a: 227. Melting down of objects: Jacquemin 1999: 238, Scott 2010: 124–25. Total value: Diod. Sic. 16.56.6.

32. Parke and Wormell 1956a: 227.

33. Changes in ritual practice at Athens: *IG* II² 4969.1–3; *SEG* 21 519.4–10; *IG* II² 333.24–26; *IG* II² 1933.1–3. See Bowden 2005: 123. The consultation over sacred land at Eleusis: Parke and Wormell **262**; Rhodes and Osborne 2003. No. 58; *IG* II² 204. Delphi's response: *FGrHist* 328 F 115. See Bowden 2005: 88.

34. The festival: Roux 1976: 178. Safely making it home: Plut. *Mor.* 249E.

35. Dionysus worship attested in fourth century BC, see Roux 1976: 176. The Dionysion: Jacquemin 1999: 29. One inscribed dedication speaks of the "mania"

of Dionysus: Daux and Bousquet 1942–43: 26. Paean: Croissant 1996: 128. Statue: Paus. 10.32.1; Bommelaer 1991: 210.

36. Athenian sculptors: Paus. 10.19.4; Croissant 2003: 144–46, 176. Macedonian influence: Croissant 1996: 128. Athenian influence: Croissant 1996: 136. See Stewart 1982. Breadth of worship at Delphi: see Parke and Wormell 1956a: 330–38, Scott 2010: 142.

37. Diod. Sic. 16.57; Strabo 9.3.8.

38. *Syll*³ 633; Parker 2000: 89.

39. See Diod. Sic. 16.23–60; Paus. 3.10.2, 10.2.2.

40. Breakup of cities: Parke and Wormell 1956a: 229–33. Curse on those who touched the money: Aeschin. *In Ctes.* 114. Removal of sculpture: *CID* II 34 II.56–62.

41. Philip's representatives on the lists: Daux 1957b: 100. Promanteia and statue: Jacquemin 1999: 39. Common Peace: Diod. Sic. 16.60.3.

42. Athens's disillusionment with Delphi: cf. Dem. 5.25; Parke and Wormell 1956a: 233–35. Hated of Philip: see Dem. 19.327; 9.32.

43. E.g., Dem. 21.51–52; 43.66. See Bowden 2005: 56–58.

44. No contractors or suppliers for the rebuilding came from Thessaly, even though the Thessalians presided over the Amphictyonic council. But the Peloponnesians contributed the largest sum to the rebuilding, were involved on the commission for reconstruction and as suppliers and contractors, even though they had meager representation on the Amphictyonic council: de La Coste-Messelière 1974: 208, Roux 1979: 105–11, Davies 2001a. Thanks to the preserved accounts, we also get a feeling for the way in which the Delphian authorities liked the construction processes to proceed and how they negotiated with their contractors: Feyel 1993, Feyel 2006, Amandry and Hansen 2010: 461–94. For discussion of the accounts, see Roux 1979, Bousquet 1988, Bousquet 1989, Davies 1998, Davies 2001b, Bommelaer 2008. In turn, the collaboration of skilled workmen at Delphi from different arenas has recently been argued to have aided innovative creation of architectural features and the resulting spread of those innovations back into different communities around Greece: Partida 2011.

45. Small donations: Anaxis of Phocaea gave just one obol (and it cost four obols to inscribe one hundred letters): *CID* II. 4 col. III.13; Weir 2004: 77. Clearistus of Carystus: *CID* II 1 col II.26–30; Weir 2004: 77.

46. Although from the start, Phocis was not always able to meet their annual quota: in 344 BC, almost immediately after reparation payments began, the

Phocians only managed to pay thirty talents rather than the full sixty: *FD* III 5 14, II.12–14; Arnush 1991: 20. Rearrangement of sanctuary: Courby 1927: 202, Pouilloux 1960: 17–32, 49–60, 109–20, 153, Amandry 1981a: 688, 692, Amandry and Hansen 2010, Scott 2010: 118.

47. Remaking of dedications: *CID* II 79 A 1; 81A; 93; 102 II A; 107; 108. The stadium inscription: *CID* I 3; Fontenrose 1988: 128.

48. Odysseus's mishap: Paus. 10.8.8. The gymnasium: Jannoray 1953, Pentazos 1992a. Honors for Aristotle: *FD* III 1 400 (335 BC); Fontenrose 1988: 137. List of victors: *FD* III 5 59B. Aristotle was also said to have consulted the oracle about whether to become a philosopher, to have dedicated a monument at the sanctuary to his friend Hermias, and to have written a study (now sadly lost) of the constitution of the city of Delphi: Bowden 2005: 86. Parke and Wormell do not believe that Aristotle consulted the oracle: Parke and Wormell 1956a: 406.

49. Demeter at Anthela: *CID* II 80; 82 Currency: *CID* II 75; Raven 1950, Bommelaer 1991: 35. The Athena sanctuary: Le Roy 1977: 271.

50. Cyrenean contribution to temple rebuild: *CID* II 4 III.11; 26.4–12; Cyrenean and Rhodian dedications: Scott 2010: 127–29.

51. Roux 1979: 30–33, Croissant 1996: 134, Croissant 2003: 180.

52. Aeschines' speech: Aeschin. *In Ctes.* 115–23. Turning to Philip: Parke and Wormell 1956a: 235–37.

53. Consultation: Parke and Wormell **265.** Demosthenes' comment: recounted by his rival Aesch. *In Ctes.* 130. See Parker 2000: 96. For the commemoration by Philip of his victory at Chaeronea, and the violence of the battle as revealed by the skeletons buried at the site: Ma 2008.

54. Daux 1949a: 259–60, Jacquemin 1999: 60.

CHAPTER 8. TRANSITION

1. Daochos dedication: Jacquemin and Laroche 2001. For Thessalian associations with Neoptolemus: Downie 2004: 217. *Tamiai*: *CID* IV 9; Roux 1979: 55, Davies 2001a: 213. Soon after their creation, the Amphictyony seems to have delegated financial decisions also entirely to the treasurers not just for the rebuilding but for all the Amphictyony's business: Roux 1979: 191. Philip's Hellenic league: Miller 2000: 271. Philip returning to oracle: Parke and Wormell **266–67.**

2. Response to Philip: Parke and Wormell **266–67.** See Parker 2000: 88. Olympias's involvement: Parke and Wormell 1956a: 238. The knife: Just. *Epit.* 9.7.13. *Para Alexandrou*: *CID* II 77; Lefèvre 2002a: 73–74.

3. Parke and Wormell 1956a: 240.

4. Parke and Wormell **270**. See also another later story of a Delphic oracle concerning Alexander: Parke and Wormell **269.**

5. Alexander's dealing with embassies from sanctuaries: Alexander also did not make any efforts to revive the use of the oracle at Delphi for mainstream political consultations, which had ceased after the middle of the century, in contrast to his efforts to revive dormant oracles at other sites, like Didyma: Morgan 1989: 29, Arnush 2005: 105-106. New temple at Delphi: Diod. Sic. 17.103.4, 18.4.5; Parke and Wormell 1956a: 242. Theban treasury: Parke and Wormell 1956a: 241-42.

6. For a study of the use of the civic honor of proxenia as a political tool by Boeotia and Athens in diplomatic relations: Gerolymatos 1986. Collective promanteia for the Aetolians: *SEG* 17.230; Arnush 2000: 300-301. This is in the context of a substantial growth in the numbers of such awards during the fourth century BC: only four honorific decrees are known from the city of Delphi before 373 BC, but between 373 and 300 BC, there are ninety-nine: Empereur 1981. Delph's risk taking: Arnush 2000: 307.

7. There seems to have also been a certain degree of tension within the city: inscriptions dating to 330-27 BC detail the sums collected from the rental of a number of properties (eleven houses, a farm, a garden, and nineteen plots of land) that had previously been confiscated from members of the city, a number of whom had been exiled from Delphi following the Third Sacred War and many of whom were confirmed as still in exile and living in Athens in 363 BC: *CID* II 67-72; Rousset 2002b: 230, Rousset 2002a: 205-10.

8. Representatives "not seated": *CID* II 102 col. I A.4-17; col. II A.24-33. The crown: *FD* III 5 58.4-8 (money set aside), *CID* II 97.5-6 (money redistributed); Marchetti 1977, Arnush 2000: 302-303, Marchetti 2011: 144-49.

9. In 321-20BC five proxeny decrees were issued, one for Patron of Elateia in Phocis: Daux 1933: 69-70, Arnush 2000: 297-300, 307. Phocis stopped paying its fine circa 322-21 BC: Arnush 1991: 20.

10. Acanthus column: *FD* III 4 462 (attribution to Athens is debated): Pouilloux and Roux 1963: 122-49.

11. Parke and Wormell **274**; See Bowden 2005: 133.

12. For the towers: Skorda 1992b: 54-56, Maass 1997: 27, 70, Weir 2004: 77. Diod. Sic. (2.136) tells the story of a philosopher from Eretria who was attacked en route to Delphi in the late fourth/early third century BC. Rousset has argued

that these towers were probably constructed for the surveillance of isolated pieces of territory and the exploitation of land rather than for safeguarding against attack: Rousset 2002b: 236.

13. For the inscriptions: Empereur 1984. Ambryssian inscription: Roux 1976: 184. For the cult of Pan and the Nymphs at the cave: Pasquier 1977, Amandry 1984a. For the incredible collection of offerings (including 25,000 knuckle bones) found at the cave from the sixth through the beginning of the second century BC: *BCH* Suppl. 9 (1984); Picard 1991: 241–61.

14. Parke and Wormell 1956a: 244. Indeed one of those local questions at the end of the fourth century—on the issue of childlessness—shows how active the mythology surrounding Delphi must have been. The children begotten following the consultation were named Delphis and Pytho: Parke and Wormell **334**. More widely, Parke and Wormell also argue that no private individual inquiries from outside the local region are known (with the exception of Cicero) between the end of the fourth century BC and the first century BC: Parke and Wormell 1956a: 407.

15. See Paus. 10.18.5; Plut. *Mor.* 401D.

16. "Sanctimonious humbug": Parke and Wormell 1956a: 252. Oracle's decline in the Hellenistic period: Parke and Wormell 1956a: 244, Parker 2000: 87, 102. Oracles for Hellenistic kings as rehashings of older responses: e.g., Parke and Wormell **431** (to Attalus I of Pergamon rehashing that given to Cypselus). Demetrios Poliorcetes as an oracle: Plut. *Vit. Demetr.* 11–13; Parke and Wormell 1956a: 245.

17. Oracle helping create a long-term and more glorious history of Messenia to cover over its centuries under Spartan domination: Parke and Wormell 1956a: 248–53. Hellenistic cities also continued to use the oracle for moral leverage, particularly in securing recognized rights of asylia (sacred protection) e.g., *Syll*³ 635b. Foundation of new sanctuaries: Parke and Wormell 1956a: 371–74.

18. Parke and Wormell **331, 332**. Parke and Wormell 1956a: 326.

19. Tarquinius Superbus: Parke and Wormell **438, 439**. Rome consulting before the fall of the city of Veii, fourth century BC: Parke and Wormell **440**. Camillus's dedication at Delphi (a gold mixing bowl, placed in the treasury of the Massalians in the Athena sanctuary, and melted down by Phocians in Third Sacred War): Diod. Sic. 14.93.2; Livy 5.21.2. Consultation during the Samnite War: Parke and Wormell **352**. Involvement in process of Magna Mater transfer: Parke and Wormell **356**; and Asclepius: Parke and Wormell **353**.

20. Aetolians: Flacelière 1937: 41–42, 49–50, Parke and Wormell 1956a: 254. Power over Delphi: see Plut. *Vit. Demetr.* 40.7–8. Flacelière argues that their occupation of Delphi took place soon after the battle of Ipsus in 301 BC, which created a power vacuum in mainland Greece: Flacelière 1937: 57. Later, the text of a treaty between the Aetolians and Boeotians seems to have been erected at Delphi: Flacelière 1937: 58–59, 67.

21. Control over council: Flacelière 1937: 49–50. The Amphictony council was still functioning (it recognized the games in Alexandria in honor of Ptolemy Soter in 279 BC), as was the city of Delphi (it established a convention with Pellana during the 280s: *FD* III 1 486). Indeed the third century BC would be the city's most diplomatically active century: 326 honorific decrees were given out between 279–200 BC compared to 141 in the period 400–279 BC: Jacquemin 1999: 78. Failure of war to "free" Delphi: Just. *Epit.* 24.1.1; Paus. 10.37.5. See Bourguet 1911: 488. Aetolian victory dedication: Jacquemin 1999: 63.

22. See Paus. 10.22–24; Just. *Epit.* 24.6–8. See also reference to Gauls in Callim. *Hymn* 4.183–85. For numbers: Flacelière 1937: 103.

23. Leave things as they are: Parke and Wormell **329.** Successful defeat of the invasion: Parke and Wormell 1956a: 255. For more on the Gaulish invasion and later celebration by the Aetolians of its defeat: Nachtergael 1977.

24. Diod. Sic. 5.32.5; Strabo relates that the gold taken from Delphi supposedly traveled as far as Toulouse: Strabo 4.1.13.

25. Sources for war: Segre 1929. Delight at Delphi's survival: Cos: *Syll*[3] 398 1.1–25; Honors for helping with return of the money: *Syll*[3] 405, 406, 416, 417, 418, and *FD* III 1 189 (all 275–71 BC). Gaulish shields on the temple: Paus. 10.19.4. The Gaulish invasion became a mental marker in history: Polybius used it as a point around which to date less important events (e.g., Polyb. 1.6.5, 2.20.6), and Cicero refers to it as the moment when the Gauls set out to "plunder Pythian Apollo and the oracle of the whole world" Cic. *Font.* 14.30.

26. Phocian statue: Jacquemin **402.** Aetolians as saviors: Flacelière 1937: 93, 98, 112, 258, Parke and Wormell 1956a: 258–59, Jacquemin 1999: 256. Place in Amphictyonic records: Flacelière 1937: 113.

27. The Aetolians erected a monument to their victory at the other sanctuary around which their koinon was based, at Thermon, but their commemoration at Delphi was, understandably, more vocal than anywhere else: Flacelière 1937: 107–108. For discussion of the west stoa: Amandry 1978: 751–81, Amandry 1981a: 729–32, Bousquet 1985, Bommelaer 1991: 218–19, Perrier 2011.

28. Female Aetolia: Courby 1927: 288–91, Bommelaer 1991: 223, Partida 2009: 296. The placement of this monument on the west end of the temple terrace (as opposed to the east end, which had been popular since the time of the Persian Wars) suggests that the west stoa (which opened onto the west end of the temple terrace) also performed the function of some kind of major (ceremonial?) access point to the sanctuary from the city, rather than being simply a dead-end annex to the sanctuary as it often appears on modern maps: Perrier 2011: 48. Statue base on temple terrace: Courby 1927: 291–99. Statues of chiefs: Paus. 10.15.2; Statue of general: Paus. 10.16.4.

29. The same picture holds true for Delphian awards of promanteia as well: Pouilloux 1952, Arnush 2005: 108–109.

30. Athenians: Jacquemin 1999: 229. Chians: Amandry 1986: 205–18, Bommelaer 1991: 173–75. Later stele erected around the altar: Jacquemin 1999: 223. Rearrangement of sanctuary: Bommelaer 1991: 146.

31. Soteria: Flacelière 1937: 107, Roux 1976: 201, Fontenrose 1988: 137, Bommelaer 1991: 29. New popularity for Delphi: Fontenrose 1988: 137, Valavanis 2004: 222. Lists of those giving hospitality to the Delphic theoroi sent out to announce the games are substantial in this period: Plassart 1921, Daux 1980: 120–122. At some point in the third century BC, new powers were endorsed for the protection of people at Amphictyonic meetings, Pythian or Soterian festivals, giving magistrates full powers to prosecute anyone committing an offence: CID IV 51.

32. Hellenistic kings' focus on Delos and Samos: Bommelaer 1991: 22, Jacquemin 1999: 78. Although Sostratus of Cnidus did put up statues of Ptolemy II and Arsinoe II at Delphi 275–70 BC: Jacquemin 120, and a statue of Seleucius II (246–26 BC) was erected by an unknown dedicator near the statue of Aetolia at the west end of the temple terrace: Jacquemin 515; Bommelaer 1991: 225. Absences of Western Mediterranean: Jacquemin 1999: 74–78.

33. For the same argument regarding the attraction of Delphi and Delos during the archaic period (but in reverse), see: Roux 1984. See Jacquemin 1999: 256.

34. Jacquemin 386, 386. See Bousquet 1952a.

35. FD III 4 178; Paus. 10.16.6; Courby 1927: 312.

36. Grants from the Amphictyony: CID IV 12; Flacelière 1937: 120–22. Symbiosis of Apollo Patroos and Apollo Pythios in Athens: Daux 1940: 262, Parke and Wormell 1956a.

37. Plut. Vit. Marc. 8; Parke and Wormell 1956a: 270.

38. Flacelière 1937: 179–89. Possible alliance with Athens: IG IX 1² 176—date disputed, see discussion in Flacelière 1937: 190. For a broader view of the complex

military and political maneuvers of this period: Walbank 1981, Malcolm Errington 2008.

39. See Flacelière 1937: 208, 227, 228.

40. One large festival: the Aetolian invitation to the world to come and celebrate their Soteria: *IG* IX I² 194a. Their declaration of its isoPythian status: Fontenrose 1988: 137. See Bommelaer 1991: 29. Stadium refitting: Bommelaer 1991: 215. See Valavanis 2004: 190. See also to records of works before the Pythia in c. 250 BC (for discussion on date see *CID* IV p. 24): *CID* II 139; *CID* IV 57; Pouilloux 1977, Le Graff 2010.

41. Athens: *Syll³* 408; Chios: *Syll³* 402; Tenos: *FD* III 1 482; Cycladic city: *FD* III 1 481; Smryna *FD* III 1 483. For discussion of the dating, which is argued to be either from original institution of the Soteria c. 274 BC, or from its reorganization c. 242 BC: Flacelière 1937: 125, 135–48, Parke and Wormell 1956a: 259. The lists of Soteria participants and winners were also now being inscribed and publicized in the sanctuary: e.g., *CID* IV 31, 42, 45, 47, 48, 53, 55 (participants) and *CID* IV 61, 67, 73, 75, 79, 84, 89 (winners) during the period 270–20 BC (participants come from mostly before 242 BC and winners mostly after). One of these victor lists was inscribed on the reverse side of a stele originally placed inscribed and placed in the sanctuary in the fifth century BC: Jacquemin 1999: 226.

42. Individual Aetolian dedications all date from after the middle of the century: Jacquemin 1999: 64. Invention of two column monument: Flacelière 1937: 266, Partida 2009: 274–96. Aristaineta: Jacquemin **297**; Charixenus: Jacquemin **298**. The Aetolian Lycus also dedicated in the sanctuary 250–25 BC, alongside other anonymous Aetolians: Jacquemin **299, 300;** Bommelaer 1991: 235–36.

43. Lamius: Jacquemin **296**.

44. Jacquemin **388**.

45. *CID* IV 85 (Syll 3 523). This inscription also banned campfires in the sanctuary and was accompanied by another inscription banning visitors from bathing in the small fountain in the southwest corner of the temple terrace: Maass 1997: 29. For discussion of the Attalid stoa: Flacelière 1937: 270, Roux 1952, Roux 1987.

46. See Jacquemin 1999: 256.

47. Aetolian dominance at Delphi: See Flacelière 1937: 245–56. Statue of Aetolian general: Jacquemin **187**. Granting of asylia: Thebes: *CID* IV 70. Apollo Ptoios: *CID* IV 76; Boiotian sanctuary: *CID* IV 77.

48. Interaction Athens and Delphi: Flacelière 1937: 272. Athenian monument update: statues were added for Antigonus I of Macedon, Ptolemy III of Egypt,

and Athens's own Demetrius Poliorcetes. The tribes of Antigonids and Deme-triads were suppressed by 200 BC (another example of how Athens sought to keep pace with events, although its statues at Delphi do not seem to have been removed): Jacquemin 1999: 228.

49. Achaean league: see Polyb. 4.25.8; Flacelière 1937: 294, Parke and Wormell 1956a: 260. Aratus buried as a hero: Parke and Wormell **358.** Men from Sardia: *Syll*³ 548; Arnush 2005: 108.

50. Response to Romans requesting gifts: Parke and Wormell **354.** Response indicating greater victory: Parke and Wormell **355.**

51. Parke and Wormell 1956a: 275.

52. *FD* III 4 21–24; Flacelière 1937: 298–304.

53. Flacelière 1937: 309–40. The Delphians set up a statue of an anonymous Aetolian at this time as well: Jacquemin **207.**

CHAPTER 9. A NEW WORLD

1. The role of the Aetolian governor at Delphi: see *IG* IX 1² 174; Roussel 1926, Daux 1936a: 215–20, Pouilloux 1980: 282. For their rights to keep herds on public land: *Syll*³ 553A; *FD* III 4 175.

2. Decline in visitors to Corycian cave: Empereur 1984: 340. Proxenia: Parke and Wormell 1956a: 261. Proxenia: *Syll*³ 585; Arnush 2005: 110.

3. Territory: Rousset 2002b: 240. Theoroi: about thirty Delphians are sent away as theoroi in the middle of the second century BC: Daux 1949b: 27–30. Sa-tyrus of Samos: *FD* III 3 128; Weir 2004: 108. He was given an honorary statue by the Amphictyony in the sanctuary as well: Jacquemin **053.** Ai Khanoum: Taplin 1989: 2. Statues: *CID* IV 99 (statues of Antiocheia and Antiochus III). Eques-trian statue: Jacquemin **494.** The statue personifying the people of Antiocheia is argued to have been in a new style—youthful and energetic—to complement a renewed era of civic iconography: Biard 2010.

4. Declaration of freedom: Polyb. 18.46.5. Dedications by Flaminius: Plut. *Vit. Flam.* 12.11–12. Delphic statue: *Syll*³ 616. Delphi's honoring of Flaminius: Jacquemin **191.** A portrait head of Flamininus has been tentatively identified in the sanctuary excavations at Delphi: *FD* IV Album p. 40; Chamoux 1965, Picard 1991: 111. There are, however, some notes of not outright approval for the Roman victory over Philip, detected by some scholars in oracular responses said to be from the period e.g., Parke and Wormell **357;** Parke and Wormell 1956a: 276.

5. Proxeny decrees for those in Flaminius's army e.g., *Syll*³ 585.

6. Antiochus's forces: Livy 26.11.5. His declaration of freedom: Flacelière 1937: 356–59.

7. Daux 1936a: 225–26.

8. There are a series of oracles from this period that threaten Rome with all manner of misfortunes if does not retire from Greece. Only one is attributed to the Delphic oracle, and all seem to have been composed by supporters of Antiochus in the short period between his triumphant arrival in Delphi and his eventual defeat in 189 BC: Parke and Wormell 1956a: 276–77.

9. Glabrio confiscating properties: seventy properties were taken belonging to fifty-nine different owners, forty-six of which were Aetolian, and they were in turn given to "the god and the city": Daux 1936a: 10, 229, Michaud 1977, Rousset 2002a: 250–69, Rousset 2002b: 232. Changes to sacred land: Rousset 2002a: 226. Letter to Delphians: Roussel 1932: 7–10.

10. *CID* IV 103. Statue: Jacquemin **143**; See Michaud 1977. The Amphictyony were also quick to put up a statue of Glabrio in the sanctuary: Jacquemin **019**.

11. Problems with Amphissa: Daux 1936a: 257. Tussle for power within Delphi: see *Syll³* 613A; Habicht 1987.

12. Another Roman general, P. Cornelius Scipion (Scipio Africanus) was tasked with dealing with the Aetolians and seems to have, with Athenian help, ensured a truce at this point, leaving Glabrio free to deal with Antiochus: Daux 1936a: 257. Scipio himself also seems to have dedicated an offering in the sanctuary at Delphi at this time: Jacquemin **420**. Defeat of Antiochus: Eckstein 2008: 344.

13. Albinus's reply: *CID* IV 104. Reform of Amphictyony: see Holleaux 1930: 39, Habicht 1987: 61. Some of the leading families in Athens, acting as ambassadors for the Amphictyony, were prominent in this reorganization. One of the Amphictyonic ambassadors, Nicostratus, was even honored with a statue and inscription in the sanctuary by the Amphictyony (much, probably, to the chagrin of the city of Delphi, whose plan to achieve complete control over the sanctuary, Habicht argues, he had thwarted): *Syll³* 613 A; Habicht 1987: 62.

14. For the Romaia festival, which included processions, sacrifices, a banquet, and gymnastic competitions: Roux 1976: 205. Glabrio's statues base and its inscriptions: Daux 1936a: 262. The letter of Livius Salinator: *CID* IV 105 (*Syll³* 611); Daux 1936a: 231.

15. Delphians dependent on Aetolian business: Daux 1936a: 269. The Delphians even erected a statue to the Aetolian general Pantaleon in the period

186–72 BC: Jacquemin **187.** Rome leaving: Eckstein 2008: 346. For more detail on the complicated politics of this period down through to the 170s BC at Delphi: Reinach 1910, Habicht 1987.

16. *FD* III 3 237, 299. For discussion of the building of the theater, which was not finished until the Imperial period: Daux 1936a: 686–95, Roux 1976: 165–75, Bommelaer 1991: 206–10. In fact nearly all major construction at Delphi in this period is related to the musical and athletic festivals: Bommelaer 1991: 22.

17. Asylia for Eumenes: *CID* IV 107. Statue by Aetolians: *FD* III 3 230; Courby 1927: 275–89, Jacquemin and Laroche 1986: 785. Statue by the Amphictyony: Jacquemin **035.** A little later, the Aetolians placed a statue of King Prusias II of Bithynia atop a monumental column, also on the temple terrace: *FD* III 4 76; Courby 1927: 262–65, Jacquemin and Laroche 1986: 786–88. The statue seems to have been surrounded by a ring of bronze "spikes," perhaps to keep birds from landing and defecating on it and the plinth: Perrier 2008. Jacquemin characterizes these statue dedications as the last acts of a dying koinon: Jacquemin 1999: 64. In the following century, the Delphians would continue the relationship with Bithynia by honoring King Nicomedes III with a statue (94 BC), the decision to erect it inscribed on the column of Prusias: *FD* III 4 77.

18. *Syll*³ 631.4–6. The festival took place in October, and included a procession from the sacred aire to the temple: Roux 1976: 203. There were probably many more such "mini" festivals for which evidence has not survived: Amandry 2000: 17.

19. Rousset 1996: 46. During the second century BC, the bringing-in of outsiders to settle Delphic disputes, not just with neighbors, but also within their own polis, would become a common feature of the political scene: Daux 1936a: 473–82, Gauthier 2000.

20. End of Aetolian use of the sanctuary: Daux 1936a: 276. Amphictyony's jibe: Habicht 1987: 60.

21. Colonisation by Paros: Parke and Wormell **429;** Parke and Wormell 1956a: 243, 246, 277. Eudocus's statue: Jacquemin **250bis.**

22. Daux 1936a: 301.

23. Careful diplomatic line, see Polyb. 25.3. Use of Delphi: Polyb. 27.1–2.

24. Sacrificing at Delphi: *FD* III 4 75; Livy 42.40.8; Polyb. 25.3.1; Daux 1936a: 315. Perseus using Delphi as a center of propaganda: Polyb. 25.3.2; Plut. *Vit. Aem.* 28, 36. He also asserted his right to two Macedonian votes on the Amphictyonic council, first given to Philip after the Third Sacred War in the fourth century BC: *CID* IV 108.

25. Parke and Wormell **430**. A statue was also erected in the sanctuary in his honor: Jacquemin **349**; Jacquemin, Laroche, and Lefèvre 1995.

26. Eumenes' embassy to Rome: Daux 1936a: 317. His attempted murder by Perseus: Polyb. 22.18.4; Livy 42.15–17; Plut. *Mor.* 489E.

27. Rome's grievances against Perseus: Parke and Wormell 1956a: 260. Their inscription at Delphi: *Syll³* 643 (*FD* III 4 75); Livy 42.40; Daux 1936a: 320–25. The details of the inscription tallies with what the literary sources tell us Eumenes II reported to the Roman Senate: Livy 42.13.5, 9.

28. See Bousquet 1981.

29. Jacquemin **418**; *FD* III 4 36; Plut. *Vit. Aem.* 28.2; Laroche and Jacquemin 1982: 207–12, 15–18. For the frieze: Kähler 1965, Picard 1991: 124–26. For the monument: Bommelaer 1991: 235, Jacquemin 1999: 239.

30. Eckstein 2008: 342, 349, 365, 381.

31. That close relationship between Pergamon and Rome continued. In 133 BC, Attalus III would, on his death without an heir, gift Pergamon and its territories to Rome.

32. *Syll³* 671–72 /*FD* III 3 328. Eumenes II gave one talent for his festival, and Attalus II gave 18,000 drachmas (three talents) for his. The rituals involved a torchlight procession from the gymnasium, and the victors of competitions were awarded money rather than laurel wreaths: Roux 1976: 205, Bommelaer 1991: 216, Rousset 2002a: 226.

33. Erecting a statue of Attalus at Delphi: *FD* III 3 121; Jacquemin **149**. Other statues of Eumenes II and Attalus II were erected in the sanctuary by unknown dedicators at this time (e.g., Jacquemin **505**) and placed within the stoa of Attalus complex; Jacquemin and Laroche 1986: 788–89. Delphi honoring Attalus's artists: *Syll³* 682.

34. Definite action by Amphictyony in this period: Daux 1936a: 350. Arbitration over Lamia: *CID* IV 110. Honoring Hegesandros of Athens 150 BC: *CID* IV 112, who was also honored by the Delphians: Jacquemin **170**. Rearrangement of Amphictyony: Daux 1936a: 352.

35. See Parke and Wormell 1956a: 261.

36. Mummius celebrates at Delphi: Polyb. 39.6.1. Shrinking world of Delphi: Daux 1936a: 483.

37. Arbiters of land dispute: *FD* III 2 130 col. II; Rousset 1996: 46. Revival of Pythaïs: Daux 1936a: 532–40, Mikalson 1998: 269–70. See Strabo 9.2.11. Celebration of 138/7 BC: *Syll³* 696. Celebration of 128/7 BC: *Syll³* 697–99. Celebration of

106/5 BC: *Syll³* 771. Celebration of 98/7 BC: *Syll³* 728. See Daux 1940: 37, Parke and Wormell 1956a: 262–63. Hymns: Bélis 1992: 131–35.

38. CID IV 114 (completed with help of copy of the decree inscribed in Athens: *IG* II² 1132.94; Spawforth 2012: 152). See also additional letters inscribed in Athens, which accompanied this decree: CID IV 115, 116.

39. The Delphians honored them for their performance in 128 BC: *FD* III 2 47. Amphictyony honors in 125 BC: *FD* III 2 69, *CID* IV 117. The date of 125 has been disputed and some argue for a date of 117 BC: Spawforth 2012: 152. Restatement in 112 BC?: *CID* IV 120 (*FD* III 2 70). The Roman Senate became involved because there was a dispute between the guild members of Athens and those of Isthmia, which was finally resolved by the Roman Senate in favor of Athens: Daux 1936a: 355–69. It seems the guild members of Isthmia and Nemea, perhaps as a last attempt at gaining favor, or perhaps in recognition of the Roman decision, put up a statue at Delphi in 112 BC of the Roman P. Cornelius Lentulus: Jacquemin **474**; Pomtow 1914: 302–303. The Amphictyony also put a statue up for Antipatrus of Athens in 130 BC (*CID* IV 113), and the Delphians honored the guild members of Athens in 106 BC and again in 97 BC with statues as well: *FD* III 2 48 and *FD* III 2 48.

40. *CID* IV 117.11–14. See Daux 1936a: 369, Spawforth 2012: 152.

41. Dating to 117 BC: Rousset 2002a: 131–32. Inscribing Amphictyonic attendance: Daux 1936a: 372. The account: *CID* IV 119: contains the letter to the Amphictyony from the Roman proconsul, the lists of attendance at the emergency Amphictyonic session, the report of the Amphictyony, the accounts of moneys lost, the redefining of the sacred land of Apollo, the reparations made to the Delphian whistle-blowers, and the accounts of restitution made to the god.

42. These inscriptions make clear first that the sacred land could be used for the grazing of animals belonging to Pythian Apollo, and second, that there was a distinction between the sacred land controlled by Delphi (which could not be used except for the god's benefit) and land controlled by the city, which could be apportioned to, and cultivated by, its residents. In turn this land was split into public territory run by the city, and private plots: *CID* IV 108, 119; Rousset 2002b: 227–28, 230. The territory of Delphi was "a mosaic, composed of private properties, public territories and sacred domains" (my translation): Rousset 2002b: 234.

43. See Daux 1936a: 372–84, 699–707, Parke and Wormell 1956a: 278, Rousset 2002a: 131.

44. Daux 1936a: 386.

45. See Parke and Wormell 1956a: 278.

46. Jacquemin **183, 184.** Inscription in Greek: *FD* III 1 526. Inscription in Latin: *Syll³* 710B. Unusual use of bilingual honors: Vatin 1967. Rufus in turn made an offering in the sanctuary (Jacquemin **421),** as did a family relation: Jacquemin **422.**

47. Roman law copied at Delphi: *FD* III 4 37; Daux 1936a: 601. A copy of this law has also been found in Cnidus: Hassall, Crawford and Reynolds 1974: 195–209. During this period, 91–89 BC, Rome was also beset with its own social war, see Crawford 1978. Kidnappers near Delphi: *FD* III 1 457; Parke and Wormell 1956a: 278.

48. Stadium refitting: Bommelaer 1991: 215. Alexandros: *FD* III 2 48. Eastern Locrians: Jacquemin **340.** Antipatros: *Syll³* 737; Weir 2004: 109. He also received a statue in the sanctuary put up and paid for by the Delphians: Jacquemin **146.**

49. Daux and Bousquet 1942–43: 113–25, Roux 1976: 181, Partida 2009: 302.

50. For Sulla's difficult position and need for military funds: Diod. Sic. 38.7; Plut. *Vit. Sull.* 12, 19; Paus. 9.7.5; App. *Mith.* 54, 122. See Daux 1936a: 398. Sulla and the consultation of the oracle: Parke and Wormell 1956a: 280. Sulla and the gold statue of Apollo: Plut. *Vit. Sull.* 29; Stat. *Silv.* 5.3.293. For discussion of the degree to which Romans thought of plundering sanctuaries outside their own territory as religious sacrilege, see Pape 1975: 37, Jacquemin 1999: 239.

51. The silver bowl appears several times in Delphic inscriptions between the sixth and first centuries BC e.g., *FD* III 5 63 and *FD* III 3 224; Bourguet 1897: 489. Sulla reapportioning Theban land: Parke and Wormell 1956a: 279.

52. For the impact of Sulla on the way Rome related to Greece: Kallet-Marx 1995. The Soteria festival, started by the Aetolians in 279 BC, may also have fallen by the way side by this time: Nachtergael 1977: 376–78. Delphi was, however, also used by the pro-Sulla camp. The nearby city of Chaeronea, for example, put up honors in the sanctuary at Delphi in this period for a Thracian chief who had been sent to fight for Sulla against Mithridates: Daux 1936a: 401.

53. Parke and Wormell **434** (see **154**). Sulla executed all Athenians, even those who sought refuge in Athens's main sanctuary on the acropolis: Paus. 1.20.7

54. Polygnota: *FD* III 3 249–50; Daux 1936a: 405–406, Weir 2004: 81. Flaccus in Greece: Daux 1936a: 406.

55. Damage visible on the remains of the temple: Reinach 1910, Courby 1927: 116. The fire seems to have taken place in the same year as the one that consumed the temple of Jupiter Capitolinus in Rome (Dion. Hal. *Ant. Rom.* 4.62).

56. See App. *Ill.* 4; Plut. *Vit. Num.* 9; Daux 1936a: 392, Parke and Wormell 1956a: 278–79.

57. Amphictyony active: *CID* IV 127 (dated to end second century BC/beginning first century BC); Giovanni 1978: 64–72. For the picture of Amphictyonic activity in this period: Sanchez 2001: 420. Repairs to temple earlier: Weir 2004: 93. Spartan consultation: *FD* III 1 487. Other Greek cities seem to have been similarly indebted to this individual, as the same monument carries other inscribed thanks: *FD* III 1 488–96; Spawforth 2012: 191. See Diod. Sic. 16.57.4 "the Spartans, even today, continued to consult Delphi on matters of great weight." Cicero: Parke and Wormell **435**; Parke and Wormell 1956a: 283, 407–408, Flacelière 1977. No more oracles in verse form: Cic. *Div.* 1.19.37.

58. E.g., *FD* III 3 11: The sale to Pythian Apollo of a slave called Heraclea for the price of two mines of silver, guaranteeing Heraclea's right to be free and independent. Each of these manumissions mentions the archon at Delphi in the year it was inscribed, as well as the parties and a series of witnesses to the contract. See Daux 1936a: 15–60, Parke and Wormell 1956a: 261–62. The manumissions will be published as a collection in the fifth volume of the *Corpus des Inscriptions de Delphes*. At present, see: Lejeune 1939.

59. Down to 190 BC: Daux 1936a: 220. After 167 BC: Daux 1936a: 269, 491–95, McInerney 2011: 98. We should not understand these manumissions as a statement of the rejection of slavery, in fact they were the "motor" of enslavement, because a slave had to buy his or her freedom, providing the master with money to purchase another slave. As well, the master could impose conditions on the soon-to-be-freed slave, for example, that they return each year to put a fresh crown on their master's statue in the sanctuary.

60. Caesar: Parke and Wormell 1956a: 283. Caes. *B Civ.* 3.56. Calenus is also mentioned in a surviving Delphic inscription: *FD* III 1 318. Consultation by Censorinus: Parke and Wormell 1956a: 408. He was clearly a religious enthusiast: he was also initiated into the Eleusinian mysteries: Beard, Price, and North 1998: 152–53, Spawforth 2012: 144. Response to Censorinus: Parke and Wormell **436**; Val. Max. *De Miraculis* 1.8.10. Anthony and Delphi: Plut. *Vit. Ant.* 23; Daux 1936a: 409. Offer to repair the temple: Plut. *Vit. Ant.* 23.4; Pelling 1988: 176. Dispatch of sacred embassy and renewal of friendship: Spawforth 2012: 148, 149.

CHAPTER 10. RENAISSANCE

1. Nicopolis: Strabo 7.7.6. In later years, Nicopolis would dedicate a statue in the Apollo sanctuary at Delphi: *FD* III 1 542 (end first century AD). The first attested epimeletai (under Tiberius), and their immediate successors, would also happen to be from the city: Pouilloux 1980: 284–87. Augustus and the Amphictyony: Parke and Wormell 1956a: 283. Epimeletai: Sanchez 2001: 529, Weir 2004: 56. There had been informal epimeletai appointments under the Aetolians. The surviving inscriptions record epimeletai from the time of Tiberius to the end of second century AD: Pouilloux 1980: 282. For discussion of the reorganization of the Amphictyony, see Daux 1975: 354–55, 9.

2. Discussion over the letter E: Plut. *Mor.* 384-394. Livia's offering: Plut. *Mor.* 385F; Jacquemin 1999: 75.

3. Spawforth 2012: 147. See Agora XVI 337.7–8.

4. "Lively interest" in Olympia: see Spawforth 2012: 164. No need for oracles: see Strabo's description of Delphi and its current poor state in the early first century AD: 9.3.6–8. Chryselephantine statue: e.g., Langenfeld 1975: 247–48. Strabo's description of Zeus at Olympia: Strabo 8.3.30.

5. Privileged position of Greece in Roman world: Barrow 1967: 2. Roman misunderstanding of the Amphictyony: Plin. *HN* 35.35.59. See Spawforth 2012: 160–61.

6. Robert 1929: 37, Weir 2004: 109.

7. Only Delphi and Amphictyony dedications: Jacquemin 1999: 79. Athens honoring Augustus: Jacquemin **079.**

8. Barrow 1967: 2–3.

9. Tiberius: Amphictyony: *CID* IV 136. City of Delphi: Jacquemin **200.** Agripinna Major: *CID* IV 133.

10. Statue of Poppaeus: Jacquemin **189.** For discussion of the accompanying inscription and the "saving" referred to, see Eilers 2001. Statue of Theocles: Jacquemin **197** (while in post); Jacquemin **198** (when retired). Epimeletai from Nicopolis: Pouilloux 1980: 293.

11. Amphictyony: Jacquemin **031** (Caligula), *CID* IV 137 (Drusilla). Koinon: Jacquemin **008,** *IG* VII 2711.

12. Measures of L. Iunius Gallio: *FD* III 4 286 (AD 52); Pouilloux 1971: 377. Unbroken chain of Imperial communication: see Jacquemin 1999: 274, Weir 2004: 88. Publicly inscribing Claudius's letter on the temple: Weir 2004: 89.

13. Claudius statues: Jacquemin **155, 156.** Statue of Claudius erected in the third century AD by the city of Delphi (reusing a base originally set up in the sanctuary by Pharselis): Jacquemin **157.** Claudius as magistrate at Delphi: *SEG* 51.607; Spawforth 2012: 235. The eponymous archon was a member of the city of Delphi's prytaneis, a board of nine magistrates tasked with overseeing the city's role in administering the Delphic sanctuaries, as well as the money given to the sanctuary by the Amphictyony and ruling as judicial magistrates over the city: Arnush 1991: 11–15.

14. Secretary of the Archives: Weir 2004: 51, 55. Stars of stadium and theater: Jacquemin 1999: 79. Theater refurbishment: Picard 1991: 129, Partida 2009: 306. All this during a time, when, as has been recently highlighted, most cities in Greece were cobbling together both private and public funds to continue hosting their festivals: Camia 2011: 73. Competitions for Maidens: *FD* III 1 534; Weir 2004: 138.

15. Musical competitions had to be inserted into the games at Olympia for him: Spawforth 2012: 236. Declaring freedom of Greece: Barrow 1967: 2–3.

16. Reorganizing the Amphictyony: Jacquemin 1999: 229. Statue of Nero: *CID* IV 138 (end AD 54). Agrippina Minor (AD 54–55): Jacquemin **144.** Nero's consultation of the oracle: Parke and Wormell **461;** Parke and Wormell 1956a: 283.

17. Settling soldiers on sacred land: Dio Cass. 62.14.2; Dio Chrys. 31.148; Paus. 10.7.1; Rousset 2002a: 275. Removing statues: Plin. *HN* 34.36. Pliny is at pains to point out that this still left over three thousand statues at Delphi. For descriptions of Nero's collection in the Domus Aurea (Golden House) in Rome: Tac. *Ann.* 15.45, 16.23. Removing a statue from Amphictyonic dedication: Jacquemin 1999: 228.

18. Parke and Wormell **597, 243.** This story also signifies how prevalent, by the time of Nero, the understanding that the Pythia was inspired by vapors must have been (even though the first time it is mentioned in the sources is the first century BC in Diodorus Siculus: see chapter 1).

19. Weir 2004: 133.

20. Titus/Domitian statue: *Syll*³ 817; Spawforth 2012: 238. Statue: Jacquemin **201** Domitian inscription: *Syll*³ 821A; *FD* III 4 120; Haussoullier 1882: 451, Jacquemin 1999: 75.Where it was placed, see Weir 2004: 153, Spawforth 2012: 238. What Domitian was repairing: Weir 2004: 93. Plaque from the Cnidian treasury: Courby 1927: 219.

21. Difficult times for Rome: Weir 2004: 151. Domitian's involvement in procession between Athens and Delphi: Weir 2004: 149–50. Letter from Domitian to Delphi: *Syll*³ 821C.2–3; Sanchez 2001: 450–51, Spawforth 2012: 238. Publication and copying of the games: Weir 2004: 166.

22. *Agonothetes*: these officials had been part of the Soteria festival in the third century BC, but not the Pythian: *FD* III 4 125–28. Return to local control: Sanchez 2001: 529, Spawforth 2012: 56–58.

23. Statue of Domitian by temple: *FD* III 4 444. Thought originally to be for Augustus, this has now been disproved: Jacquemin and Laroche 1986: 785–88. For discussion, see Courby 1927: 277–81. For the niche, *Guide de Delphes* **528**; Bommelaer 1991: 171. See Weir 2004: 94, 153.

24. Additions to the gymnasium: Pouilloux 1980: 289, Bommelaer 1991: 73, 76, Weir 2004: 101–103. New library and dining room: Weir 2004: 101. The new colonnade more likely belonged to the Hadriannic period (AD 117–38). Peristyle house: *Guide de Delphes* **299**. Rebuild of Pythia's house: *Syll*³ 823A. Discussion: Bousquet 1952b: 28–29.

25. Dio Chrysostom: Parke and Wormell **462**. Nerva: Jacquemin **185**; Trajan: *CID* IV 149. A citizen of Delphi even erected a statue to Matidia Minor, half-sister of the Empress Sabina and wife of the Emperor Hadrian: Jacquemin **256**. Amphictyony honors proconsul of Asia: *CID* IV 143; City of Delphi honors proconsul: Jacquemin **154**.

26. Amphictyony honoring an agonothetes: Jacquemin **055**; wife of the epimelete: Jacquemin **174**; Agonothetes: Jacquemin **175**; Grammarian Jacquemin **179**. Gortyn: Jacquemin **304**. Hypata: *Syll*³ 925B. Sophists: Jacquemin **470–71**. Memmia Lupa: Bommelaer 1991: 101, 210. Statue: Jacquemin **258**.

27. Letters: *FD* III 4 287–88; *FD* III 4 301. This was perhaps a Delphic initiative to draw the emperor into communication with the sanctuary: Flacelière 1976. Balancing the books: Barrow 1967: 4.

28. *FD* III 4 290–99; Rousset 2002a: 145, Rousset 2002b: 219, Weir 2004: 50. It is interesting that in these inscriptions the land in question—the sacred land that for centuries could not be cultivated on pain of displeasing Apollo—is referred to simply as the territory of Delphi. It seems that parts of Delphi's sacred history—by the Roman corrector, at least—are being forgotten: Rousset 1996: 47. As a result, the city of Delphi now has full control over a vast area of land it could exploit, divide, and sublet, allowing it much more financial muscle in comparison to most major central Greek cities: Rousset 2002b: 241.

29. Dio Cass. 69.2.5. The status of a corrector, established first under Trajan, evolves over the course of the second and third centuries AD. Established first as a position to help (and control) free cities over which the proconsul of a province had no authority (like Delphi), by the third century AD, the same individual

could be proconsul and corrector (e.g., Cn. Claudius Leonticus who is known at Delphi), suggesting the evolution of a greater degree of control over free cities during this time: Vatin 1965: 136–43.

30. Lamprias: *SEG* 1.181; Jones 1971: 10. *Homonoia: Syll³* 843. In the late second century AD, citizens of Chaeronea would be made citizens of Delphi: *Syll³* 824. Plutarch's Roman citizenship: *Syll³* 829A; Barrow 1967: 12. Traveling and education: Plutarch was asked when in Sardis for his advice on how to carry out public duties, for which he wrote a treatise on the precepts of government: Plut. *Mor.* 798A–825F; Barrow 1967: 132. Friends with Sosius: Plut. *Vit. Thes.*; Barrow 1967: 41. His brother's son: Apul. *Met.* 1.2.

31. First visit to Delphi: Barrow 1967: 30. Roles at Delphi: Barrow 1967: 31. See also *Syll* 3 829A (as epimelete supervising the erection of a statue in honor of the Emperor Hadrian). Procurator: Jones 1971: 33–34. Plutarch also held a series of offices in his home town of Chaeronea, and was a *boeotarch* for Boeotia: Barrow 1967: 13. Friendship with Nigrinus: Barrow 1967: 36–40, Jacquemin 1991a: 217. Portrait bust: Jacquemin **106**; *CID* IV 151. There is also a surviving bust (on display at the museum at Delphi), which has been identified with Plutarch: Picard 1991: 135.

32. See Mossman 1997, Pelling 2002.

33. Plut. *Mor.* 384D. See Barrow 1967: 32.

34. Plut. *Mor.* 384D–394C.

35. Ibid., 394D–409D.

36. Ibid.,. 409E–438E.

37. Particularly in comparison to the claim of Juvenal that the oracle had fallen silent, and rival claims in other Roman literature: Juv. 6.555. Contrast Mart. 9.42 and Stat. *Theb.* 3.474.

38. Ignorant guides: e.g., Plut. *Mor.* 386B, 400D. See Jacquemin 1999: 263–64; 269–70. Rhodopis: Plut. *Mor.* 401A. For confusion and discussion over the meaning of dedications, such as the frogs and water snakes of the Corinthians and Axes of Tenedus: Plut. *Mor.* 399F–400D.

39. Memory at Delphi: Jacquemin 1991a: 218–20. Treatises on dedications: Jacquemin 1991a: 221–22. Corycian cave: Jacquemin 1984b, Jacquemin 1999: 270.

40. Division of year between Apollo and Dionysus: Plut. *Mor.* 388E; Roux 1976: 175. Pythia: see Roux 1976: 171–73. The traditional laurel wreath prize for victors would be swapped, probably in the time of Hadrian, for a prize of apples (which were supposed to be a special kind of Delphic apple—obtained by mixing an apple and quince tree) to evoke Delphi's Cretan ancestry: Perrot 2009.

41. Another festival seems only to have been begun by the Hypatians in the second century AD, in honor of Neoptolemus at Delphi: Heliod. *Aeth.* 2.34; Pouilloux 1983: 274–76.

42. Roux 1976: 206, Bommelaer 1991: 23.

43. Theoxenia: Paus. 9.23.3. See the calendar in Bommelaer 1991: 29. For discussion of the Theoxenia: Hoyle 1967: 84. For the involvement of the worship of Neoptolemus as part of the Theoxenia: Downie 2004: 155. Worship of Dionysus: Plut. *Mor.* 365A; Hoyle 1967: 84–85, Roux 1976: 180.

44. Thyades of Delphi and Athens: Plut. *Mor.* 249E; Hoyle 1967: 91–92, Roux 1976: 178. Herois: Roux 1976: 168–69. Charila: Plut. *Mor.* 293D–F; Hoyle 1967: 86–87, Roux 1976: 169–71.

45. Septerion: Roux 1976: 166–68. Dispute over festivals: Bommelaer 1991: 30, 146. Plut. *Mor.* 417F–418D.

46. Only one priestess: Plut. *Mor.* 414B. The banality of questions now asked of the oracle: Plut. *Mor.* 386C, 407D, 408C (whether to purchase a slave, about one's job, whether to get married, go on a journey, risk a loan, etc.), see Parke and Wormell 1956a: 393–94. But, there seem to have been people, known as exegetai, on hand in the sanctuary whose role was to instruct those not familiar with the consultation or sacrificial procedure on how to do it (suggesting that people were coming to consult). And even at the end of the third century AD, jokes circulated in Athenaeus's writings about how Delphians always had a sacrificial knife in their hands ready to perform ritual (at a price) at any moment: Ath. *Deipnosophists* 173D–E; Jacquemin 1991a: 221.

47. The families: the Memmii, Babbii, and Gellii occupied key positions in the Delphic polis: Jacquemin 1991a: 217. Dramatis personae list, which includes members of the Memmii and Mestrii families: Inv. 3569 (unpublished); Weir 2004: 54.

CHAPTER 11. FINAL GLORY?

1. Letters from Hadrian: *FD* III 4 300; 301. See Flacelière 1971, Weir 2004: 168–73. Statue of Hadrian from Amphictyony: *Syll*[3] 829 A (*CID* IV 150). The city of Delphi's statue: *Syll*[3] 829 B.

2. Honors for Memmius: Vatin 1965: 65–73. Hadrian putting Prudens in charge: *Syll*[3] 830. Archon of city: See *Syll*[3] 836: Delphic honors for a Catillius Macer Nicaieus, whose inscription proclaims that Hadrian was archon in that year. Questions for oracle: Parke and Wormell **465**; *Anth. Pal.* 14.102. This is

despite the fact that some biting texts survive from this period complaining about the uselessness of oracles, e.g., Oenomaus of Gadara complaining about the oracle of Apollo at Clarus in Asia Minor: Parke and Wormell 1956a: 286. Statue for Hadrian: *Syll*[3] 835B.

3. Jacquemin **252**; Jacquemin 1991a: 229.

4. Coins: Bommelaer 1991: 36. Coins with Corycian cave: Weir 2004: 104.

5. For the series of Delphic coins with Antinous: Blum 1913, Roux 1976: 200, Jacquemin 1991a: 229. The cult statue: indeed the incredibly good condition of the statue on its discovery during the major excavation of Delphi at the end of the nineteenth century has prompted scholars to think the cult was not left to fail after the death of Hadrian in AD 138, but continued to be cared for (and thus function) for a long time afterward. See Picard 1991: 133.

6. Columns for running track: Bommelaer 1991: 76. It's uncertain whether new baths were also added to the gymnasium precinct in this period or slightly later: Bommelaer 1991: 73. Roman agora: Weir 2004: 95–96. One of the workshops in this area—a glass manufacturer—dates to the second and third centuries AD. Asclepieion: Bommelaer 1991: 233.

7. Changes to tradition: *CID* IV 152; see Vatin 1965: 7–21, Jacquemin 1999: 275. For reorganization of the territory belonging to Delphi, see: Vatin 1965: 74–127, 157–95, Ferrary and Rousset 1998, Rousset 2002a: 231. For discussion of the damiourgoi, and the degree to which this constituted a new part of the civic system at Delphi: Vatin 1965: 232–40. Correspondence between Hadrian and Delphi: *FD* III 4 302, 303, 304, 305, 306, 307, 308. For the "peace of the universe" letter (*FD* III 4 307) see Flacelière 1971: 175.

8. *FD* III 4 302 (*CID* IV 152), col. II.3–6. For Nero's rearrangement, see the previous chapter and Jacquemin 1991a: 229.

9. See Jacquemin 1991a: 230. The comparison between the Amphictyony and modern international organizations will be discussed in the conclusion.

10. Aim of the Panhellenion: see Spawforth and Walker 1986: 104. Requirement for membership: Spawforth and Walker 1985: 81–82, Romeo 2002: 21, 31. Delphi original heart of Panhellenion: Romeo 2002: 24–25. Report of Senate: *FD* III 4 78 col II.1–6; Daux 1975: 355–58, Sanchez 2001: 434–35, Spawforth 2012: 252. Panhellenion at Athens: Spawforth and Walker 1985: 82–100.

11. *Syll*[3] 835 A; Jacquemin **311**.

12. Coins: Bommelaer 1991: 36, Weir 2004: 173–75. Statue of Antoninus Pius: *CID* IV 161; Jacquemin 1999: 75.

13. See Weir 2004: 113. The philosophical maxims of Delphi ("know thyself," etc.) were visible at Delphi from the fifth century BC. But the earliest mention of the story in which the Seven Sages were said to have been responsible for inscribing the Delphic them onto the temple is in Diodorus Siculus, writing in the first century BC (Diod. Sic. 9.10.4). See also Dio Chrys. 72.12; Paus. 10.24.1. Once again, Delphi's Roman world audience seems to be augmenting and rearticulating Delphi's history and as a result its place and role within the Mediterranean world.

14. Aulus Gellius: Aul. Gell. 12.5.1. For the full list of attested philosophers at Delphi during this period, see Weir 2004: 115–16. The city of Delphi erected a statue in honor of a sophist from Byblus (in Lebanon) at the end of the second century AD: *FD* III 3 244; Ephesus put up a statue of the Sophist Soterus circa AD 150: *FD* III 4 265; Hypata erected a statue of a Sophist at around the same time: *CID* IV 158; and a group of disciples erected a monument for T. Flavius Phoinix of Hypata during the second century AD: Jacquemin **471**. Some statues from this period of individuals rendered in "philosopher-like" style, yet without identification as such through an inscribed base, were also found during the excavation of the site: Picard 1991: 135.

15. E.g., Amphictyony honoring agonothetes with statues in the second century AD: Jacquemin **023, 027.** Argos erected a statue in AD 176 to M. Aurelius Ptolemaius, a victorious poet, which they placed in their centuries'-old dedication, the Argive semicircle at the southeast corner of the Apollo sanctuary: *FD* III 1 89; Bommelaer 1991: 115. Nicomedia (in Bithynia in Asia Minor) erected a statue to one of its Pythian musical victors during the Antonine period: Jacquemin **375.**

16. Ancyra: Jacquemin **064.** Myra: *FD* III 1 548. Sardis: Jacquemin **429, 430, 431.**

17. A well-known tradition in the Roman world was to make copies of classical Greek works of art in order to export them around the empire. This seems to have been going on at Delphi, too, in this period: some remains of casts (particularly heads) have been found at the site: Picard 1991: 131.

18. Herodes Atticus: Graindor 1930. Building at Delphi: Weir 2004: 110–11. Stadium: Aupert 1979, Amandry 1981a: 720–21, Bommelaer 1991: 215–17. Statues of Herodes Atticus, his wife, and Polydeucion put up by the city of Delphi: *FD* III 3 66; 71; Jacquemin **188.** Statues set up by Herodes Atticus and his family: Jacquemin o**88, 89, 90, 91, 92, 95.**

19. Confirming independence of the sanctuary: *FD* III 4 313. Lengthy correspondence, e.g., *FD* III 4 328. For further discussion: Pouilloux 1971: 380.

20. For general discussion of these burial areas: Maass 1997: 70–73. Underground crypt: Bommelaer 1991: 221. Sarcophagus: Zagdoun 1977: 107–32, Bommelaer 1991: 41, Picard 1991: 130.

21. Spartan theopropos: *FD* III 1 215; Galen: Parke and Wormell **463**; Parke and Wormell 1956a: 409.

22. Lucian *J. Conf.* 12; *J. Trag.* 6, 28; *Philopat.* 5; *Phal.* 1, I–II, 2, 9. See Parke and Wormell 1956a: 286–87.

23. Pausanias saw Antinous: Juul 2010: 15. Age: Habicht 1988: 12–13. His genre of writing: Habicht 1988: 2.

24. On the debate around the nonsurvival of an original eleventh book: Juul 2010: 16.

25. Indeed they decided to excavate in the same order as Pausanias recounted his visit to Delphi so that they could make the best use of the text in identifying the many monuments Pausanias described: Amandry 1992a: 75, Radet 1992: 144.

26. Criticism of von Wilamovitz Moellendorff: Juul 2010: 17. Difficulties of using Pausanias for archaeology: see Lacroix 1992, Jacquemin 2001.

27. Goal of Pausanias's narrative: Habicht 1988, Elsner 2001: 18, Elsner 2004: 262, Hutton 2005b, Hutton 2005a. Pausanias's focus: Daux 1936b: 179, Heer 1979: 288, Alcock 1996: 250. Nothing after 260 BC: Daux 1936b: 173, Habicht 1988: 23, 134–35, Weir 2004: 105. For discussion of the implications of his agenda for his description of different sites: Heer 1979: 280–300; Bommelaer 2001; Pretzler 2007: 8; Scott 2010: 229–33.

28. Not read in antiquity: Habicht 1988: 1. See "it is indeed a blessing that what this loner achieved can still be read today": Habicht 1988: 27. Spluttering Hellenism: Habicht 1988: 25.

29. Stadium: Bommelaer 1991: 216–17. Sacred land: Paus. 10.37.5

30. Response of Septimius: *FD* III 4 329; Pouilloux 1971: 380. Restoration of temple: *FD* III 4 269, 270, 271; Weir 2004: 93. Archaeological evidence for restoration of the temple at this time: Bommelaer 1991: 101, 181. They may also date to the period of Emperor Julian the Apostate well over a century later: Amandry 1989. See also Rousset 2002a: 280.

31. M. Junius Mnaseas: *FD* III 1 553; Jacquemin 1991a: 218. Statues by Delphians of family members: Jacquemin **259, 260**. Important officials: M. Aurelius Niciades (the last of the epimeletai known in the surviving records although

the position certainly continued) *Syll*[3] 874B (also honored by the Amphictyony *FD* III 6 96), see Pouilloux 1980: 293. Tib. Claudius Callippianus (proconsul of Achaea): Jacquemin **160**; and G. Publius Proculeianus: *FD* III 4 473. The proconsul of Asia would also be honored jointly by the Amphictyony and the city of Delphi in AD 225–50: Jacquemin **058.**

32. Statues of Leonticus: Jacquemin **244, 245, 246, 247, 248.** See *FD* III 4 269–71. On Leonticus and his status, see: Vatin 1965: 143, 153–56. Roman agora: this is an area not yet fully published or understood, with a mix of Roman and early Christian period housing: Bommelaer 1991: 89, 236–37.

33. Clement of Alexandria: Clem. Al. *Protr.* l.c.; Parke and Wormell 1956a: 288. Origen: Origen *C. Cels.* 3.25, 7.3. Indeed Porphery, writing in the third century AD, now credits Delphi with being the first oracle to sanction sacrifice using ox, pig, and sheep in the earliest days of Greek civilization, strengthening Delphi's claim to historic and cultic significance: Parke and Wormell **536**; Parke and Wormell 1956a: 364.

34. Hypatians: Heliod. *Aeth.* 2.34; Pouilloux 1983: 274–76, Weir 2004: 59. Expansion of Pythian games: for the full list of new games, see Weir 2004: 179–80. Wide variations in the games at different places, e.g., the Pythian festival at Perinthus copied Delphi in having no cash prizes, but the games at Ancyra made financial awards to its victors: Weir 2004: 176. Expansion not known at Delphi: Weir 2004: 176.

35. Publicity through the minting of coins in host cities: Weir 2004: 194. Wider change in emperor worship: Mitchell 1990, Mitchell 1993: 221, Weir 2004: 177. Pythian festival at Thessalonike: Weir 2004: 198. For a description of the atmosphere in the mid- to late second century AD at the games: Weir 2004: 124–29. Decline in numbers AD 217–59: Weir 2004: 130.

36. Rise of Apollo Helios: Weir 2004: 89, 210. "Third century crisis" for the empire, see Mennen 2011.

37. Gordian III: *FD* III 4 274. Gallienus: Jacquemin **168.** Valerian: Jacquemin **204.** Gallienus seems to have engaged in correspondence with the sanctuary (although only fragments of the inscribed letter survived (to do with Pythian games): Vatin 1965: 250. Claudius Gothicus: Jacquemin **167.** Carus: Jacquemin **153,** *Syll*[3] 897. This statue base was seen by Cyriac of Ancona in the fifteenth century; Jannoray 1946: 259–61.

38. Eastern baths: Bommelaer 1991: 196. Sinope: Jacquemin **440.** Mercenaries: Jacquemin **472.**

39. Last dual Amphictyonic and Delphic statue: Jacquemin 1991a: 231. Last Amphictyonic statue of Philiscus: Jacquemin **051**; *FD* III 4 273. Last known record: *FD* III 2 161; Jacquemin 1991a: 231, Jacquemin 1999: 79. Debate over ability to act: see Daux 1975, Weir 2004: 59.

40. Claudius: *Syll³* 801 A (Jacquemin **157**); Pharsalians: Jacquemin **389**. See Jacquemin 1999: 230. Athenian treasury: *FD* III 2 142; Bousquet 1942–43: 124–26, Weir 2004: 90. For a wider assessment of this period of Roman history: Mitchell 2007.

41. Meetings of damiourgoi: Weir 2004: 54. Statues of philosophers: Picard 1991: 138.

42. For the wider history of this period, see Harries 2012.

43. Last major building project: Bousquet 1952c: 660. Inscription from AD 319: *SEG* 12.266; Weir 2004: 54. Menogenes' role in Athens: Bousquet 1952c: 653–57. This donation is accepted officially by the damiourgoi; the Amphictyony are not even mentioned: Bousquet 1952c: 657, Ginouvés 1955. Donation used for: Bousquet 1952c: 660, Bommelaer 1991: 196. It is perhaps at this time (or slightly later) that the stoa and terrace of Attalus is completely reconstructed so as to serve as a massive cistern for the baths: Bommelaer 1991: 191–92, Etienne 1996: 183.

44. Vatin 1962: 229. The remains of the serpent column from Delphi still stand today in the middle of Constantine's hippodrome in Istanbul, flanked by obelisks taken from Egypt, one in the fourth century AD and one in the tenth century AD. One of the golden serpent heads from the Plataean column is on display in the Istanbul Archaeology Museum. Constantine may have chosen this monument in particular because of its ongoing memorialization of the clash between East and West: Jung 2006: 378–81, Spawforth 2012: 273.

45. *Syll³* 903A; *Syll³* 903B.

46. Roman agora: Bommelaer 1991: 89. The stylobate of the north portico is composed entirely of reused material: Weir 2004: 94. Place for Imperial statues: Weir 2004: 94.

47. Dalmatius: Jacquemin **165**. Hadrian: Jacquemin **169**.

48. Statue for Flavius Constantius: Vatin 1962: 232–35. Reuse of base: Jacquemin 1999: 230.

49. See Freeman 2009: 215.

50. Reassurance of Delphic cult liberty, following complaint received: Vatin 1965: 253–64, Pouilloux 1980: 294.

51. Euseb. *Praep. Evang.* 5,16; Parke and Wormell 1956a: 287.

52. Parke and Wormell **475;** Barrow 1967: 36.

53. See Prudent. *Apotheosis* 438; Parke and Wormell **518;** Parke and Wormell 1956a: 288–89.

54. For Julian's defense of Delphi: Julian *Or.* 6.188a; *Gal.* 198c. The irony is that not a single inscription from Delphi survives praising Julian: Vatin 1962: 235. Julian's inquiry of the oracle: Parke and Wormell 1956a: 290. The last response: Parke and Wormell **476.** Consultation not at Delphi but Daphne: Vatin 1962: 236–37.

55. Amandry and Hansen 2010: 145–47.

56. Jacquemin **203;** Jacquemin 1999: 79.

57. Meritt 1947, Vatin 1962: 240–41.

58. Vatin 1962: 240.

59. Ibid., 241.

CHAPTER 12. THE JOURNEY CONTINUES

1. Claud. 4.2.5; IV *Cons. Hon.* 144 (AD 398); Parke and Wormell 1956a: 290. The city was well-known enough to catch the attention of the Emperor Theodosius II in 424 AD: *Cod. Theod.* 15.5.4; Vatin 1962: 229. For a discussion of the image of Delphi in Christian texts: Déroche 1986: 153–59. Discussion of slow absorption of pagan beliefs, see Spieser 1976.

2. Gymnasium: Pentazos 1992a. Habitation around Apollo sanctuary: Déroche 1986: 143–45. Perimeter of Apollo sanctuary: in particular the buildings to the south of the Apollo sanctuary employed parts of the Sicyonian treasury in their masonry. The number of baths is also high, perhaps due to the ease of accessing water sources at the site: Déroche 1986: 143–45, Déroche 1996: 184–86.

3. Redevelopment of northern sector of Apollo sanctuary: Laurent 1899: 271, Bommelaer 1991: 101, Déroche 1996: 183. Development of Apollo sanctuary into commercial center: Bommelaer 1991: 92. For the development of habitation around the south of the Apollo sanctuary: Bommelaer 1991: 237, Maass 1997: 74–75. For the Roman agora: Daux 1965: 1049, Amandry 1981a: 724. Sacred way: Déroche 1986: 130–37, Picard 1991: 192. And indeed the name "sacred way" has no ancient precedent at all. It was probably constructed in order to allow access for wagons to the heart of the site: Déroche 1996: 183.

4. Pagan motifs in fifth-century Christian architectural fragments: Laurent 1899: 207, 269–71. See Déroche 1992. Delphians trying to attract Christian worshipers, see Dyggve 1948.

5. Organic growth of Christian worship at Delphi: Spieser 1976: 317. No basilica before AD 450: Déroche 1986: 115.

6. Basilica to the west: Daux 1960: 752–55, Déroche 1986: 15-33. Basilica in the gymnasium: Déroche 1986: 34–57, Bommelaer 1991: 73–4. Basilica in the sanctuary: Déroche 1986: 58–91. For the basilica to the west (basilica "of the new village"): the ornate mosaic floor was discovered and excavated in 1959–60. Its foundations had been partly ruined when the new village of Castri was constructed in the nineteenth century. The structure seems to have originally employed reused blocks from the Apollo sanctuary, including parts of a monument dedicated by the Boeotians in the fourth century BC. The mosaic is now on display outside the museum at Delphi: Daux 1960: 752–55, Bommelaer 1991: 237–38.

7. Position of basilica inside Apollo sanctuary: Déroche 1986: 89. Rich and ornate style: Déroche 1986: 91. See Spieser 1976: 316–17, Taplin 1989: 16, Bommelaer 1991: 24. Basilica for the bishop is located on the spot of the later church of Saint-Nicholas (which survived in the modern village of Castri until the excavations in the later nineteenth century): Bommelaer 1991: 44. Mosaic underneath chapel of St George: Goffinet 1962, Bommelaer 1991: 237.

8. There are also a large number of tombs from this period in the area around Delphi: Déroche 1986: 145. For the Christianization of Olympia (the workshop of Pheidias became the Christian basilica rather than the temple of Zeus): Spieser 1976: 324. Nondestruction of temple of Apollo: Déroche 1986: 127, 146.

9. Déroche 1986: 135–37, 143, Bommelaer 1991: 101–102.

10. Lamp with Christ and snake: Dyggve 1948: 9–28, Goffinet 1962: 260. St. George mosaic: Goffinet 1962, Bommelaer 1991: 237.

11. Contraction of area covered by inhabitants: Déroche 1996: 186–88. Plague of Justinian and invasion: Déroche 1986: 147, Déroche 1996: 186.

12. Defensive wall across the gymnasium: Bommelaer 1991: 44. Final layer showing abandonment: Déroche 1986: 149–50, Déroche 1996: 187.

13. Colin 1981: 531, Hellmann 1992: 20. For this period of Delphic rediscovery, see also: Déroche 1986: 163–67, Maass 1997: 232–36.

14. Taplin argues the name Castri to have come from the Latin *castra*, echoing the village's survival within the ancient "fortification" walls surviving from the old settlement and sanctuary of Delphi. From the time of the Fourth Crusade through to 1460, Castri belonged to the Dukes of Salona (old Amphissa): Taplin 1989: 16–17.

15. While the physical location of Delphi had been forgotten, the legend of Delphi's oracle had not. In Shakespeare's *A Winter's Tale* the oracle of Delphos is an island—often thought to have been Delos: Taplin 1989: 18.

16. Humanist movement: Stonemann 2010: 25. Suspicion of Eastern Orthodox church: according to Pope Innocent III (AD 1160–1216), the Greeks were "worse than Saracens": Etienne and Etienne 1992: 23.

17. Best sellers: Stonemann 2010: 22–23. For Cyriac's goals, see the surviving fragments of Cyriac's *Commentary on Ancient Things*; Etienne and Etienne 1992: 26. Cyriac's task: as observed by Francesco Filelfo (AD 1398–1481); Stonemann 2010: 27.

18. Hellmann 1992: 15, 20, Mulliez 2007: 134–35.

19. Stonemann 2010: 36.

20. Important period for interest in ancient Greece, see Stonemann 2010: 38–80, Constantine 2011: 3–6. Use of the term "archaeology": see the preface to Spon's work on epigraphy *Miscellanae eruditae antiquitatis*; Etienne and Etienne 1992: 38, Constantine 2011: 7–33. Reflections on the gymnasium: volume II, 51, in J. Spon 1678 *Voyage d'Italie, de Dalmatie, de Grèce et du Levant, fait aux années 1675 et 1676* (three volumes), G. Wheler 1682 *A Journey into Greece*; Mulliez 2007: 135.

21. Society of Dilettanti: Letter to Horace Mann, 14th April 1783; Stonemann 2010: 120–21. Use of inscriptions: Stonemann 2010: 108.

22. The call: J. Stuart and N. Revett 1762–1816 *The Antiquities of Athens* (four volumes); Stonemann 2010: 122. See Soros 2006. Stones of the temple terrace wall: Stuart and Revett *The Antiquities of Athens* (volume IV, 7); Hellmann 1992: 21.

23. For examples of the scornful reaction to the gusto Greco, see Sir William Chambers 1759 *Treatise of Civil Architecture*; Stonemann 2010: 116, 121. For the English translation of Winckelmann's key text by H. Fusseli and published in 1765, see *Reflections on the Painting and Sculpture of the Greeks: With Instructions for the Connoisseur, and an Essay on Grace in Works of Art*. See Schnapp 1996: 260–64, Constantine 2011: 106–42. Richard Chandler 1776 *Travels in Greece or an Account of a Tour Made at the Expense of the Society of Dilettanti* (pp. 264–71); Hellmann 1992: 21.

24. Hellmann 1992: 20. See also Jacob Spon in the epigraph to this chapter.

25. See Edward Clarke 1818 *Travels I–VIII;* Otter 1825, Stonemann 2010: 154. Painting: see Tsigakou 1981: 29. Mapping Greece: W. M. Leake 1821 *The*

Topography of Athens; 1824 *Journals of a Tour in Asia Minor*; 1830 *Travels in the Morea I–III*; 1835 *Travels in Northern Greece*; 1846 *Peloponnesiaca*.

26. See, "Antiquity is a garden that belongs by natural right to those who cultivate its fruits," Captain de Verninac Saint Maur, commander of expedition to bring the Luxor obelisk to Paris; Stonemann 2010: 165.

27. William Gell 1827 *The Itinerary of Greece, Containing One Hundred Routes in Attica, Boeotia, Phocis, Locris and Thessaly* (his drawings are in the British Museum). George Hamilton and Henry Raikes: Amandry 1981b, Hellmann 1992: 25–31. Sir William Hamilton and Lord Nelson: Dyson 2006: 160, Stonemann 2010: 169.

28. Argument between Elgin and the Dilettanti: Stonemann 2010: 177. See St. Claire 1984. Byron at Delphi: Hellmann 1992: 31.

29. Borst 1948, Eliot 1967, Hellmann 1992: 31–35.

30. Pierre Augustin Guys 1771 *Voyage litteraire de la Grèce ou lettres sur les Grecs anciens et moderns, avec un parallèle de leurs moeurs*; see Constantine 2011: 151–87. War of Independence: see Etienne and Etienne 1992: 85.

31. Sarcophagus of Meleager: Pentazos 1992b: 55. First complete description of site: Hellmann 1992: 16, 36. F. Thiersch 1840 *Über die Topographie von Delphi* in *Abb. Der philo.-philolog. Classe der königl. Bayerischen Akademie der Wissenschaften* III, I, 1–74. Visit of King Otto and Queen Amelie: Hellmann 1992: 36, Stonemann 2010: 244. See also L. Ross 1851 *Wanderungen in Griechenland im Gefolge des Königs Otto und der Königin Amalie, mit besonderer Rücksicht auf Topographie und Geschichte*. Petition for small museum: Pentazos 1992b: 55. Illegal to give as a dowry: Mulliez 2007: 138.

32. Andréas Moustoxydis: Pentazos 1992b: 55. See also A. Moustoxydis 1834 *Ionios Anthologia* I, 151–78. Prince Hermann: Mulliez 2007: 136. See also Prince de Pukler Muskau 1840 *Entre l'Europe et l'Asie. Voyage dans l'Archipel, traduit de l'Allemand par Jean Cohen* I, 50–64.

33. Stoll 1979: 229–33, Hellmann 1992: 16, 40, Mulliez 2007: 137.

34. The call to repair the village: Pentazos 1992b: 56–58. Dimos Frangos: Mulliez 2007: 138.

35. Curtius 1843, Hellmann 1992: 16.

36. Interest in Olympia: see Kyrieleis 2007. Lecture by Curtius: Stonemann 2010: 253–64.

37. Kyriakos Pittakos: Pentazos 1992b: 60. French school in Athens: its aims, at its foundation, was to provide an opportunity for scholars to read ancient texts

in situ, but also to provide a broader base for humanist, philhellenic, artistic, archaeological, philological, and political interaction between France and Greece: Stonemann 2010: 251. Committee of Antiquaries: Skorda 1992a: 61–64.

38. Skorda 1992a: 64–67.

39. The 1870s, see Hellmann 1992: 50. Dealing with Dimos Frangos: Amandry 1992a: 106, Skorda 1992a: 68. In essence, they paid for one house one-tenth of the money raised by the Greek Archaeological Society for the expropriation of the whole site in 1872. The property's real value was more like one hundred drachmas.

40. Request at the Congress of Berlin: Skorda 1992a: 68. 1880 excavation: Amandry 1992a: 78. 1881 agreement: Amandry 1992a: 81, Mulliez 2007: 138.

41. American and British Schools: see Thomas 1988: 174. Greek Archaeological Society: Amandry 1992a: 141, Dassios 1992: 129.

42. Amandry 1992a: 82–93, 112.

43. Greek enthusiasm for the deal: see Hellmann 1992: 52. French, German, and American enthusiasm for Delphi: Amandry 1992a: 95–102, Hellmann 1992: 53, see also Constantine 2011: 133.

44. Amandry 1992a: 104–109.

45. Ibid., 1992a: 110–16, Kolonia 1992: 194.

46. Etienne and Etienne 1992: 105.

47. Homolle 1893: 185; Amandry 1992: 118–22; Jacquemin 1992: 178; Mulliez 2007: 141.

48. Amandry 1992a: 122.

EPILOGUE

1. Delphi as important part of wider investigation into ancient world, see Mulliez 2007. Among many other claims to fame, the site has been particularly important for our understanding of the development of archaic sculpture: Croissant 2000: 338–41.See For the journal of the big dig, see Jacquemin 1992a. To see the original journals online: http://www.efa.gr/Documentation/Arch_man/doc_arch_man_ligne.htm.

2. Construction and destruction: see Bommelaer 1991: 24, Amandry 1992a: 140. Use of church as school: Kolonia 1992: 195, Mulliez 2007: 141.

3. Jacquemin 1992a: 163, Radet 1992: 144–46.

4. Pre-excavation finds: Hellmann 1992: 42, 49. Initial inscriptions: now Rhodes and Osborne 2003: No. 1. Sculptural finds: Jacquemin 1992; Kolonia 1992: 196; Mulliez 2007: 145–47.

5. Radet 1992.

6. Bommelaer, Pentazos and Picard 1992: 205–207, Jacquemin 1999: 281.

7. Bommelaer, Pentazos, and Picard 1992: 205. In reality, the excavations reports have continued unabated right into the twenty-first century: The archaeological excavation of Delphi has been published in the *Fouilles de Delphes* series (still in separate tomes: I. History of the City of Delphi (nothing has yet appeared in this one); II. Topography and Architecture; III. Epigraphy; IV. Sculpture; V. Small objects), with inscriptions republished in the *Corpus d'inscriptions de Delphes* (4 volumes), alongside countless journal articles and several edited volumes (including *BCH Supplement* volumes), combined with a larger number of monographs focusing on different aspects of the sanctuary, its architecture, inscriptions, and art. For a general (but now out-of-date) overview, see: Bommelaer 1991: 9–11. The original Olympia publication series (*Olympia*) has also been greatly expanded by two new series of excavation reports *Olympia Bericht* and *Olympia Forschungen*, alongside an equal number of articles, edited volumes, and monographs.

8. See Croissant 2000: 333.

9. Kolonia 1992: 201. The excavators grumbled "that not even the little finger of any fourth century BC temple sculpture had been found": Radet 1992: 147, Croissant 2000: 334.

10. Archives of the Ephoria of Delphi; Kolonia 1992: 201.

11. Bommelaer, Pentazos, and Picard 1992: 210–11.

12. Keramopoullos 1912.

13. See also Emilie Bourguet's magisterial early synthesis of the sanctuary: Bourguet 1914. See also Bommelaer, Pentazos and Picard 1992: 205–10, 213, 219. For Pomtow's continuing publications, see, for example: Pomtow 1909, Pomtow 1918.

14. Bommelaer, Pentazos, and Picard 1992: 219, 226–27. Perhaps the most crucial of de La Coste-Messelière's publications are: de La Coste-Messelière and Picard 1928; de La Coste-Messelière 1931; de La Coste-Messelière 1936; de La Coste-Messelière 1957. He was also responsible for one of the first attempts to create maps for different chronological periods of the sanctuary's life: de La Coste-Messelière 1969.

15. See Replat 1920, Amandry 1986.

16. Precious moments of the performance of Aeschylus's *Prometheus Unbound* from the festival survive on film: Taplin 1989: 18. This festival led in turn to the

foundation of the Greek National Theatre and to the first performances at the ancient theater of Epidaurus.

17. Bommelaer, Pentazos, and Picard 1992: 222, 227, 229.

18. Ibid., 227, 231, Jacquemin 1999: 294.

19. Amandry 1939b, Amandry 1945, Bommelaer, Pentazos, and Picard 1992: 233–41.

20. For a wonderful sense of the site and its local inhabitants in the 1930s, see the picture book of Delphi created by Pierre de la Coste Messelière and George de Miré published in 1943: de Miré and de la Coste-Messelière 1943.

21. Jacquemin 1999: 293 note 75.

22. Demangel 1944–45, Bommelaer, Pentazos and Picard 1992: 244.

23. Bommelaer, Pentazos, and Picard 1992: 245–46.

24. P. Amandry in ibid., 1992: 244–47.

25. See accounts of Lucien Lerat, George Roux, and Jean Pouilloux in Bommelaer, Pentazos, and Picard 1992: 249–51.

26. Personal account of Eric Hansen, in Bommelaer, Pentazos, and Picard 1992: 253.

27. Hellmann 1992: 18–19.

28. Bommelaer, Pentazos, and Picard 1992: 264.

29. See Mulliez 2007: 153.

30. Bommelaer, Pentazos, and Picard 1992: 256, 264.

31. Amandry 1981b, Jacquemin 1984a, Picard 1991: 241–61.

32. Luce 1992: 693.

33. As noted by Bommelaer in the 2008 edition of the French journal *BCH*, in relation to the inscriptions of the fourth century BC temple rebuilding, very little of our understanding of these accounts is fixed. Instead, our understanding of them is changing all the time: Bommelaer 2008: 223.

34. In the 1996 showcase volume of the work of the French School in Athens, it is indicative of the developing interest in the town's Christian era that a section was dedicated to Delphi at the end of antiquity: Déroche 1996. There is still no published volume in the excavation reports on this time in Delphi's history, although the first *Fouilles de Delphes* volume is expected soon: Déroche, Pétridis, and Badie (forthcoming).

35. Equally indicative is that in the same showcase volume (Etienne 1996), Delphi was not mentioned as an example in the section "The Space of the City." This

is soon to be in part rectified with the anticipated publication of N. Kyriakidis *Delphon politeia: Etude d'une communauté politique (VI–I. siècle avant J.C.).*

36. This area has been the focus of recent work, particularly by Rousset 2002a. But we still only have a basic understanding of how the landscape around Delphi was used, perceived, and experienced. See the recent work on different aspects of this experience in Kyriakidis 2011, McInerney 2011, McInerney (forthcoming).

37. For a recent consideration of the issues regarding display at the museum of Delphi: Partida 2009. For recent publications utilizing new digital technologies to produce three-dimensional computer graphics of the site: Bommelaer 1997. For a recent consideration of what a Christian and Byzantine tour of Delphi might look like: Dimou and Pétridis 2011.

CONCLUSION

1. "Delphi became a bank of social capital," McInerney 2011: 96.

2. E.g., for modern politics: Tsoukalis and Emmanoulidis 2009.

3. See Delphi's confirmation (quoted in the introduction to this book) as a World Heritage Site thanks to its "enduring mission to bring together men and women who otherwise remain divided by material interests." Full text can be viewed online: http://whc.unesco.org/en/list/393/documents/ (1987 Advisory Body Evaluation)—last accessed 17.6.13. The literature on comparisons between Delphi, its Amphictyony, and modern-day international organizations like the European Union and United Nations continues to increase, despite a number of calls (including in this book) for caution over such comparisons: Tenekides 1931; Daux 1957; Tenekides 1958; Amandry 1979; Zepos 1979. "Delphi was also the centre of meetings of the Amphictyonic league (the nearest equivalent to the UN for the isolated ancient Greek city-state)": Toubis 2007: 58–59.

4. http://www.eccd.gr/ : last accessed 17.6.13

5. http://www.era-ewv-ferp.com/index.php?page_id=29: last accessed 17.6.13.

6. See also Taplin 1989: 33.

BIBLIOGRAPHY

Adornato, G. (2008) "Delphic Enigmas? The *gelas anasson*, Polyzalos and the Charioteer Statue," *AJA* 112: 29–56.

Alcock, S. (1996) "Landscapes of Memory and the Authority of Pausanias," in Bingen, J., ed. *Pausanias Historien*, 241–67. Geneva.

Alcock, S. E., and Osborne, R. eds. (1994) *Placing the Gods: Sanctuaries and Sacred Space in Ancient Greece*. Oxford.

Amandry, P. (1938) "Vases, bronzes et terres cuites de Delphes," *BCH* 62: 305–31.

———. (1939a) "Convention religieuse conclue entre Delphes et Skiathos," *BCH* 63: 183–219.

———. (1939b) "Rapport préliminaire sur les statues chryséléphantines de Delphes," *BCH* 63: 86–119.

———. (1940–41) "Dédicaces delphiques," *BCH* 64–65: 60–75.

———. (1945) *Note sur l'aire delphique*. Athens.

———. (1950) *La mantique apollinienne à Delphes: Essai sur le fonctionnement de l'oracle*. Paris.

———. (1954) "Notes de topographie et d'architecture delphiques IV. Le palmier de bronze de l'Eurymédon," *BCH* 78: 295–315.

———. (1977) "Statue de taureau en argent," *BCH Suppl. 4: Etudes delphiques*: 272–93.

———. (1978) "Consécration d'armes galates à Delphes," *BCH* 102: 571–86.

Amandry, P. (1979) "L'Amphictionie delphique," in Zepos, J., ed. *Symposium: L'idée delphique en l'Europe*, 123–36. Athens.

———. (1981a) "Chronique delphique 1970–81," *BCH* 105: 673–769.

———. (1981b) *L'Antre corycien (BCH Supp. 7)*. Paris.

———. (1984a) "Le culte de Pan et des Nymphs à l'Antre Corycien," *BCH Suppl. 9: L'Antre Corycien II*: 395–426.

———. (1984b) "Notes de topographie et d'architecture delphiques VIII. Eléments d'architecture archaïque et classique," *BCH* 108: 177–98.

———. (1984c) "Os et Coquilles," *BCH Suppl. 9: L'Antre Corycien II*: 347–80.

———. (1986) "Chios and Delphi," in Boardman, J., and Vaphopoulou-Richardson, C. E., eds., *Chios: A Conference at the Homereion in Chios 1984*, 205–32. Oxford.

———. (1989) "La ruine du temple d'Apollon à Delphes," *Bulletin de la Classe des Lettres de l'Academie Royale de Belgique* 75: 26–57.

———. (1992a) "Fouilles de Delphes et raisins de Corinthe: Histoire d'une négociation," in Picard, O., ed., *La redécouverte de Delphes*, 77–128. Paris.

———. (1992b) "Où étiat l'omphalos?," in Bommelaer, J. F., ed. *Delphes: Centenaire de la "Grande fouille" réalisée par l'Ecole française d'Athènes (1892–1903)*, 177–205. Leiden.

———. (1998) "Notes de topographies et d'architecture delphiques X. Le 'socle marathonien' et le trésor des Athéniens," *BCH* 122: 75–90.

———. (2000) "La vie religieuse à Delphes: Bilan d'un siècle de fouilles," *BCH Suppl. 36: Delphes: Cent ans après la Grande fouille. Essai de bilan*: 9–21.

———. (2010a) "La ruine du temple d'Apollon à Delphes," in Amandry, P., and Hansen, E., eds., *Fouilles de Delphes II 14: Le temple d'Apollon du IVième siècle*, 13–29. Paris.

———. (2010b) "Recherches sur la cella du temple de Delphes," in Amandry, P., and Hansen, E., eds., *Fouilles de Delphes II 14: Le temple d'Apollon du IVième siècle*, 73–84. Paris.

Amandry, P., and Hansen, E. (2010) *Fouilles de Delphes II 14: Le temple d'Apollon du IVième siècle*. Paris.

Amandry, P., Lerat, L., and Pouilloux, J. (1950) "Chronique des fouilles: Delphes," *BCH* 74: 319–32.

Arafat, K. W. (1995) "Pausanias and the Temple of Hera at Olympia," *ABSA* 90: 461–73.

Arnush, M. F. (1991) *The Chronology of Delphi in the Late Fourth and Early Third Centuries* BC—*An Epigraphic and Historical Analysis*. London.

———. (2000) "Argead and Aetolian Relations with the Delphic Polis in the Late Fourth Century BC," in Brock, R., and Hodkinson, S., eds., *Alternatives to Athens: Varieties of Political Organization and Community in Ancient Greece*, 293–307. Oxford.

———. (2005) "Pilgrimage to the Oracle of Apollo at Delphi: Patterns of Public and Private Consultation," in Elsner, J., and Rutherford, I., eds., *Pilgrimage in Graeco-Roman and Early Christian Antiquity*, 97–110. Oxford.

Athanassaki, L. (2011) "Song, Politics and Cultural Memory: Pindar's Pythian 7 and the Alcmaeonid Temple of Apollo," in Athanassaki, L., and Bowie, E., eds., *Archaic and Classical Choral Song: Performance, Politics and Dissemination*, 235–68. Berlin.

Audiat, J. (1930) "Le dédicace du trésor des Athéniens à Delphes," *BCH* 54: 296–321.

———. (1933) *Fouilles de Delphes II 2: Le trésor des Athéniens*. Paris.

Aupert, P. (1977) "Un édifice dorique archaïque à l'emplacement du stade," *BCH Suppl. 4: Etudes delphiques*: 229–45.

———. (1979) *Fouilles de Delphes II: Le stade*. Paris.

Aurigny, H. (2011) "Le sanctuaire de Delphes et ses relations extérieures au VII siècle av. J.C.: Le témoninage des offrandes," *Pallas* 87: 151–68.

Barker, E. (2006) "Paging the Oracle: Interpretation, Identity and Performance in Herodotus' History," *G&R* 53: 1–25.

Barrow, R. H. (1967) *Plutarch and His Times*. London.

Baumbach, M. (2008) "An Egyptian Priest at Delphi: Calasiris *"as theios aner"* in Heliodorus' Aethiopica," in Dignas, B., and Trampedach, K., eds., *Practioners of the Divine: Greek Priests and Religious Officials from Homer to Heliodorus*, 167–86. Cambridge, Mass.

Beard, M., Price, S.R.F., and North, J. A. (1998) *Religions of Rome*. Cambridge.

Bélis, A. (1992) *Les Hymnes à Apollon (CID III)*. Paris.

Biard, G. (2010) "Diplomatie et statues à l'époque hellenistique: À propos du décret de l'Amphictionie pyléo-delphique CID IV 99," *BCH* 134: 131–51.

Billot, M. F. (1977) "Note sur une sima en marbre de Delphes," *BCH Suppl. 4: Etudes delphiques*: 161–77.

Blok, J., and Lardinois, A. eds. (2006) *Solon of Athens: New Historical and Philological Approaches*. Leiden.

Blum, G. (1913) "L'Antinoos de Delphes," *BCH* 87: 323–39.

Boëthius, A. (1918) *Die Pythaïs. Studien zur Geschichte der Verbindungen zwischen Athen und Delphi.* Uppsala.

Bommelaer, J. F. (1971a) "Le monument de Lysandre à Delphes," *REG* (*Actes de l'Association*) 84: xxii–xxvi.

———. (1971b) "Les navarques et les successeurs de Polyclète à Delphes," *BCH* 95: 43–64.

———. (1981) *Lysandre de Sparte: Histoire et traditions.* Paris.

———. (1991) *Guide de Delphes: Le site.* Paris.

———. (1992a) "Monuments argiens de Delphes et d'Argos," *BCH Suppl. 22: Polydipsion Argos: Argos de la fin des palais mycéniens à la constitution de l'état classique*: 265–305.

———. (1992b) "Observations sur le théâtre de Delphes," in Bommelaer, J. F., ed. *Delphes: Centenaire de la "Grande fouille" réalisée par l'Ecole française d'Athènes (1892–1903)*, 277–300. Leiden.

———. (1997) *Marmaria: Le sanctuaire d'Athéna à Delphes.* Paris.

———. (2008) "À nouveau les comptes de Delphes et la reconstitution du temple d'Apollon au IVe siècle av. J. C.," *BCH* 132: 221–55.

———. (2011) "Delphica 2: Les périboles de Delphes," *Pallas* 87: 13–38.

Bommelaer, J. F., Pentazos, E., and Picard, O. (1992) "De la Grand Fouille à la mission permanente," in Picard, O., ed. *La redécouverte de Delphes*, 205–87. Paris

Bonner, R. J., and Smith, G. (1943) "Administration of Justice in the Delphic Amphictyony," *CPh* 38: 1–12.

Borst, W. (1948) *Lord Byron's First Pilgrimage.* New Haven.

Bourguet, E. (1897) "Inscriptions de Delphes," *BCH* 21: 477–96.

———. (1903) "Inscriptions de Delphes," *BCH* 27: 5–61.

———. (1911) "Monuments et inscriptions de Delphes," *BCH* 35: 456–91.

———. (1914) *Les ruines de Delphes.* Paris.

Bousquet, J. (1942–43) "Inscriptions de Delphes," *BCH* 64–65: 124–36.

———. (1943) "Les offrandes delphiques des Liparéens," *REA* 45: 40–48.

———. (1951) "Observations sur l'omphalos archaïque' de Delphes," *BCH* 75: 210–23.

———. (1952a) "Dropion, roi des Péones," *BCH* 76: 136–40.

———. (1952b) *Fouilles de Delphes II: Le trésor de Cyrène.* Paris.

———. (1952c) "La donation de L. Gellius Menogenes à Delphes et les thermes de l'est," *BCH* 76: 653–60.

———. (1956) "Inscriptions de Delphes," *BCH* 80: 547–97.

———. (1981) "Le roi Persée et les Romains," *BCH* 105: 407–16.

———. (1985) "L'hoplothèque de Delphes," *BCH* 109: 717–26.

———. (1988) *Etudes sur les comptes de Delphes*. Paris.

———. (1989) *Corpus des inscriptions de Delphes II: Les comptes du quatrième et du troisième siècle*. Paris.

———. (1992) "Deux épigrammes Grecques," *BCH* 116: 585–606.

Bowden, H. (2003) "The Functions of the Delphic Amphictyony before 346 BCE," *SCI* 22: 67–83.

———. (2005) *Classical Athens and the Delphic Oracle*. Cambridge.

Bowersock, G. (1997) *Fiction as History: From Nero to Julian*. Berkeley.

Briquel, D. (1984) *Les Pélasges en Italie: Recherches sur l'histoire de la légende*. Paris.

Broad, W. J. (2006) *The Oracle: The Lost Secrets and Hidden Messages of Ancient Delphi*. New York.

Buckler, J. (1985) "Thebes, Delphoi and the Outbreak of the Third Sacred War," in Roesch, P., and Argoud, G., eds., *La Béotie antique*, 237–46. Paris.

Burford, A. (1969) *The Greek Temple Builders at Epidauros*. Liverpool.

Busine, A. (2005) *Paroles d'Apollon: Pratiques et traditions oraculaires dans l'antiquité tardive (II–VI siècles)*. Leiden.

Camia, F. (2011) "Spending on the Agones: The Financing of Festivals in the Cities of Roman Greece," *Tyche* 26: 41–76.

Carter, J. B. (1989) "The Chests of Periander," *AJA* 93: 355–78.

Cartledge, P. (2002) *Sparta and Lakonia: A Regional History, 1300–362* BC, 2nd ed. London.

Càssola, F. (1980) "Note sulla guerra Crisea," in Fontana, M. J., Piraino, M., and Rizzo, F., eds., *Miscellanea di studi classici in onore di E. Manni vol. II*, 413–39. Roma.

Cavanaugh, M. B. (1996) *Eleusis and Athens: Documents in Finance, Religion and Politics in the Fifth Century* BC. Atlanta.

Chamoux, F. (1965) "Un portrait de Flaminius à Delphes," *BCH* 89.

Clay, J. S. (1989) *The Politics of Olympus: Form and Meaning in the Major Homeric Hymns*. Princeton.

Colin, G. (1899) "Institut de Correspondance Hellenique," *BCH* 23: 561–83.

Colin, G. (1905) *Le culte d'Apollon Pythien à Athènes*. Paris.

Colin, J. (1981) *Cyriaque d'Ancône: Humaniste, grand voyageur, et fondateur de la science archéologique*. Paris.

Colonna, G. (1984) "Apollon, les Etrusques et Lipara," *MEFRA* 96 (2): 557–78.

Constantine, D. (2011) *In the Footsteps of the Gods: Travellers to Greece and the Quest for the Hellenic Ideal*. London.

Courby, M. F. (1927) *Fouilles de Delphes II 1: La terrasse du temple*. Paris.

Crahay, R. (1956) *La littérature oraculaire chez Hérodote*. Paris.

Crawford, M. (1978) *The Roman Republic*. Sussex.

Croissant, F. (1996) "Les Athéniens à Delphes avant et après Chéronée," in Carlier, P., ed. *Le IVe siècle av. JC Approches historiographiques*, 127–39. Paris.

———. (2000) "La fouille de Delphes et l'histoire de la sculpture grecque," *BCH Suppl. 36: Delphes: Cent ans après la Grande fouille. Essai de bilan*: 333–47.

———. (2003) *Fouilles de Delphes IV 7: Les frontons du temple du IVe siècle*. Paris.

Curnow, T. (2004) *The Oracles of the Ancient World: A Comprehensive Guide*. London.

Curtius, E. (1843) *Anecdota Delphica*. Berolini.

D'Agostino, B. (2000) "Delfi e l'Italia tirrenica: Dalla protostoria alla fine del periodo arcaico," *BCH Suppl. 36: Delphes: Cent ans après la Grande fouille. Essai de bilan*: 79–86.

Dassios, P. (1992) "Les péripéties de la Convention vues de Grèce (1881–1891)," in Picard, O., ed. *La redécouverte de Delphes*, 129–43. Paris.

Daux, G. (1933) "Notes de chronologie delphique," *BCH* 57: 68–97.

———. (1936a) *Delphes au IIe et au Ier siècle: Depuis l'abaissement de l'Etolie jusqu'à la paix romaine, 191–31 av. JC*. Paris.

———. (1936b) *Pausanias à Delphes*. Paris.

———. (1940) "Athènes et Delphes," *HSPh Suppl. 1: Studies in Honor of W. S. Ferguson*: 37–69.

———. (1949a) "Inscriptions de Delphes inédites ou revues," *BCH* 73: 248–93.

———. (1949b) "Listes delphiques des Théarodoques," *REG* 42: 1–30.

———. (1949c) "Un règlement cultuel d'Andros," *Hesperia* 18: 58–72.

———. (1957a) *Amphictyony: An International Organisation in Antiquity*. Sather Lectures, Berkeley.

———. (1957b) "Remarques sur la composition du conseil Amphictionique," *BCH* 81: 95–120.

———. (1958a) "Dédicace thessalienne d'un cheval à Delphes," *BCH* 82: 329–34.

———. (1958b) "Notes de lecture: Le trésor de Marseille à Delphes," *BCH* 82: 360–64.

———. (1960) "Chronique des fouilles 1959," *BCH* 84: 617–868.

———(1965) "Chronique des fouilles: Delphes," *BCH* 89: 899–908.

———. (1968) "Notes de Lecture," *BCH* 92: 625–32.

———. (1975) "Les empereurs romains et l'amphictionie pyléo-delphique," *CRAI*: 348–62.

———. (1980) "Trois remarques de chronologie delphique (III et IIe siècle avant J.C.)," *BCH* 104: 115–25.

Daux, G., and Bousquet, J. (1942–43) "Agamemnon, Télèphe Dionysos Sphaleô-tas et les Attalides," *RA* 20: 19–40.

Davies, J. K. (1994) "The Tradition about the First Sacred War," in Hornblower, S., ed. *Greek Historiography*, 193–212. Oxford.

———. (1997) "The Moral Dimension of Pythian Apollo," in Lloyd, A. B., ed. *What Is a God? Studies in the Nature of Greek Divinity*, 43–64. London.

———. (1998) "Finance, Administration and Realpolitik: The Case of Fourth-Century Delphi," in Austin, M., Harries, J., and Smith, C., eds., *Modus Operandi: Essays in Honour of Geoffrey Rickman*, 1–14. London.

———. (2001a) "Rebuilding a Temple: The Economic Effects of Piety," in Mattingly, D. J., and Salmon, J. B., eds., *Economies beyond Agriculture in the Classical World*, 209–29. London.

———. (2001b) "Temples, Credit and the Circulation of Money," in Meadows, A., and Shipton, K., eds., *Money and Its Uses in the Greek World*, 117–28. Oxford.

———. (2007) "The Origins of the Festivals, Especially Delphi and the Pythia," in Morgan, C., and Hornblower, S., eds., *Pindar's Poetry, Patrons and Festivals: From Archaic Greece to the Roman Empire*, 47–70. Oxford.

———. (2009) "Pythios and Pythian: The Spread of a Cult Title," in Malkin, I., Constantakopoulou, C., and Panagopoulou, K., eds., *Greek and Roman Networks in the Mediterranean*, 57–68. London.

De Boer, J. Z., and Hale, J. R. (2000) "The Geological Origins of the Oracle at Delphi, Greece," in Mcguire, J., ed. *The Archaeology of Geological Catastrophes*, 399–412. London.

De Boer, J. Z., Hale, J. R., and Chanton, J. (2001) "New Evidence for the Geological Origins of the Ancient Delphic Oracle (Greece)," *Geology* 29.8: 707–10.

De Boer, J. Z., Hale, J. R., and Spiller, H. A. (2002) "The Oracle at Delphi: A Multi-Disciplinary Defence of the Gaseous Vent Theory," *Journal of Toxicology* 40: 189–96.

De La Coste-Messelière, P. (1925) "Inscriptions de Delphes," *BCH* 49: 61–103.

———. (1936) *Au Musée de Delphes. Recherches sur quelques monuments archaïques et leur décor sculpté.* Paris.

———. (1946) "Les Alcméonides à Delphes," *BCH* 70: 271–89.

———. (1969) "Topographie delphique," *BCH* 93: 730–58.

———. (1974) "Les naopes à Delphes au IVe siècle," *Mélanges helléniques offerts à G. Daux,* 199–211. Paris.

De La Coste-Messelière, P., and Flacelière, R. (1930) "Une statue de la terre à Delphes," *BCH* 54: 283–92.

De La Coste-Messelière, P., and Picard, C. (1928) *Fouilles de Delphes IV 2: Art archaïque (suite): Les trésors "ioniques."* Paris.

De Miré, G., and De La Coste-Messelière, P. (1943) *Delphes.* Paris.

De Polignac, F. (1995) *Cults, Territory and the Origins of the Greek City-State* (2nd ed.). Trans. J. Lloyd. Chicago.

Defradas, J. (1954) *Les thèmes de la propagande delphique.* Paris.

Deltenne, F. (2010) "La datation du débout de la troisième guerre sacrée. Retours sur l'interpretation des comptes de Delphes," *BCH* 134: 97–116.

Demangel, R. (1926) *Fouilles de Delphes II 3: Sanctuaire d'Athèna Pronaia: Topographie du sanctuaire.* Paris.

———. (1944–45) "Aspect de guerre du musée de Delphes," *BCH* 68-9: 1–4.

Demangel, R., and Daux, G. (1923) *Fouilles de Delphes II 3: Sanctuaire d'Athèna Pronaia: Les temples en tuf et les deux trésors.* Paris.

Dempsey, T. (1918) *The Delphic Oracle: Its Early History, Influences and Fall.* Oxford.

Déroche, V. (1986) *Etudes sur Delphes paléochrétienne (Mémoire de l'EfA).* Athens.

———. (1992) "Les chapiteaux ioniques d'époque Romaine et tardives à Delphes," in Bommelaer, J. F., ed. *Delphes: Centenaire de la "Grande fouille" réalisée par l'Ecole française d'Athènes (1892–1903),* 301–15. Leiden.

———. (1996) "Delphes à la fin de l'Antiquité," in Etienne, F., ed. *L'espace grec: 150 ans de fouilles de l'EFA,* 183–87. Paris.

Déroche, V., Pétridis, P., and Badie, A. (Forthcoming) *Delphes de l'antiquité tardive. Le secteur au sud-est du péribole (FD II).* Paris.

Des Courtils, J. (1992) "L'architecture et l'histoire d'Argos dans la première moitié du Ve siècle av. JC," *BCH Suppl. 22: Polydipsion Argos: Argos de la fin des palais mycéniens à la constitution de l'etat classique*: 241–51.

Dillery, J. (2005) "Chresmologues and manteis: Independent diviners and the problem of authority," in Johnston, S. I., and Struck, P., eds., *Mantike: Studies in Ancient Divination*, 167–232. Leiden.

Dimou, K., and Pétridis, P. (2011) "La redécouverte de Delphes protobyzantine," *Pallas* 87: 267–81.

Dinsmoor, W. B. (1950) *The Architecture of Ancient Greece: An Account of Its Historic Development.* London.

Dodds, E. R. (1951) *The Greeks and the Irrational.* Berkeley.

Dor, L., Jannoray, J., Van Effenterre, H., and Van Effenterre, M. (1960) *Kirrha: Etude de préhistoire phocidienne.* Paris.

Dougherty, C. (1996) "Democratic Contradictions and the Synoptic Illusion of Euripides' *Ion*," in Ober, J., and Hedrick, C. W., eds., *Demokratia: A Conversation on Democracies, Ancient and Modern*, 249–70. Princeton.

Douglas, M. (1966) *Purity and Danger: An Analysis of the Concepts of Pollution and Taboo.* London.

Dovatour, A. (1933) "Un fragment de la constitution de Delphes d'Aristote," *REG* 46: 214–23.

Downie, S. M. (2004) *The Political Uses of Hero Cult at Olympia and Delphi.* Ann Arbor.

Dunbabin, T. J. (1948) *The Western Greeks: The History of Sicily and South Italy from the Foundations of the Greek Colonies to 480* BC. Oxford.

Dyggve, E. (1948) "Les traditions cultuelles de Delphes et l'église chrétienne," *Cahiers archeologiques* 3: 9–28.

Dyson, S. (2006) *In Pursuit of Ancient Pasts: A History of Classical Archaeology in the Nineteenth and Twentieth Centuries.* New Haven.

Eckstein, A. (2008) *Rome Enters the Greek East 230–170* BC. Oxford.

Eidinow, E. (2007) *Oracles, Curses and Risk among the Ancient Greeks.* Oxford.

Eilers, C. (2001) "C. Poppaeus Sabinus and the Salvation of the Greeks," *ZPE* 134: 284–86.

Eliade, M. (1962) *The Forge and the Crucible* (trans. S. Corrin). Chicago.

Eliot, C. (1967) "Lord Byron, Early Travelers and the Monastery at Delphi," *AJA* 71: 283–91.

Elsner, J. (2001) "Structuring 'Greece': Pausanias' Periegesis as a Literary Construct," in Alcock, S., Cherry, J. F., and Elsner, J., eds., *Pausanias: Travel and Memory in Roman Greece*, 3–20. Oxford.

———(2004) "Pausanias: A Greek Pilgrim in the Roman World," in Osborne, R., ed. Studies in Ancient Greek and Roman Society, 260–85. Cambridge.

Empereur, J.-Y. (1981) *CID: Décrets de la cité de Delphes*. Athènes.

———. (1984) "Inscriptions," *BCH Suppl. 9: L'Antre Corycien II*: 339–46.

Errington, R. Malcolm (2008) *A History of the Hellenistic world: 323–30* BC. Oxford.

Etienne, R., ed. (1996) *L'Espace Grec: 150 ans de fouilles de l'EFA*. Paris.

Etienne, R., and Etienne, F. (1992) *The Search for Ancient Greece*. London.

Evans-Pritchard, E. E. (1937) *Witchcraft, Oracles and Magic among the Azande*. Oxford.

Felsch, R.C.S. (2007) *Kalapodi II: Ergebnisse der Ausgrabungen im Heiligtum der Artemis und des Apollon von Hyampolis in der antiken Phokis*. Mainz am Rheim.

Ferrary, J.-L., and Rousset, M. D. (1998) "Un lotissement de terres à Delphes au IIe siècle après J.C.," *BCH* 122: 277–342.

Feuillatre, E. (1966) *Etudes sur les Ethiopiques d'Héliodore. Contribution à la connaissance du roman grec*. Paris.

Feyel, C. (1993) *Recherches sur les entrepreneurs de travaux mentionnés dans les comptes de Delphes et d'Epidaure. École pratique des hautes études*. Paris.

———. (2006) *Les artisans dans les sanctuaires grecs aux époques classique et hellénistique à travers la documentation financière en Grèce*. Paris.

Flacelière, R. (1937) *Les Aitoliens à Delphes*. Paris.

———. (1961) *Greek Oracles*. London.

———. (1971) "Hadrien et Delphes," *CRAI*: 168–86.

———. (1976) "Trajan, Delphes et Plutarque," in Chamoux, F., ed. *Etudes sur l'antiquité grecque offert à André Plassart par ses collègues de la Sorbonne*, 97–104. Paris.

———. (1977) "Ciceron à Delphes?," *BCH Suppl. 4: Etudes delphiques*: 159–60.

Flower, H. I. (1991) "Herodotus and the Delphic Tradition about Croesus," in Flower, M. A. and Toher, M., eds., *Georgica: Studies in Honour of G. Cawkwell*, 57–77. BICS Suppl.

Flower, M. A. (2008) *The Seer in Ancient Greece*. Berkeley.

Fontenrose, J. (1978) *The Delphic Oracle: Its Responses and Operations with a Catalogue of Responses*. London.

———. (1988) "The Cult of Apollo and the Games at Delphi," in Raschke, W. J., ed. *The Archaeology of the Olympics*, 121–40. Wisconsin.

———. (1959) *Python: A Study of Delphic Myth and Its Origins*. Los Angeles.

Forrest, W. G. (1956) "The First Sacred War," *BCH* 80: 33–52.

———. (1957) "Colonisation and the Rise of Delphi," *BCH* 6: 160–75.

Freeman, C. (2009) *A New History of Early Christianity*. Yale.

Gauthier, P. (2000) "Les institutions politiques de Delphes au II siècle avant J. C.," *BCH Suppl. 36: Delphes: Cent ans après la Grande fouille. Essai de bilan*: 109–39.

Gerolymatos, A. (1986) *Espionage and Treason: A Study of the Proxenia in Political and Military Intelligence Gathering in Classical Greece*. Amsterdam.

Giangiulio, M. (2010) "Collective Identities, Imagined Past and Delphi," in Foxhall, L., Gehrke, H.-J., and Luraghi, N., eds., *Intentional History: Spinning Time in Ancient Greece*, 121–36. Stuttgart.

Ginouvés, R. (1955) "Sur un aspect de l'évolution des bains en Grèce vers le IV siècle de note ère," *BCH* 79: 135–52.

Giovanni, A. (1978) *Rome et la circulation monétaire en Grèce au IIe. s. av. J.C.* Basel.

Goffinet, E. (1962) "L'Eglise Saint Georges à Delphes," *BCH* 86: 242–60.

Graf, F. (2005) "Rolling the Dice for an Answer," in Johnston, S. I., and Struck, P., eds., *Mantike: Studies in Ancient Divination*, 51–98. Leiden.

———. (2009) *Apollo*. London.

Graindor, P. (1930) *Un milliardaire antique: Hérode Atticus et sa famille*. Cairo.

Guarducci, M. (1946) "Creta e Delfi," *Studi e Materiali di Storia delle Religioni* 19–20: 9–31.

Habicht, C. (1987) "The Role of Athens in the Re-Organisation of the Delphic Amphictyony after 189 BC," *Hesperia* 56: 59–71.

———. (1988) *Pausanias' Guide to Ancient Greece*. Los Angeles.

Hall, J. M. (2007) *A History of the Archaic Greek World ca. 1200–479 BCE*. Oxford.

Hammond, N.G.L., and Griffith, G. (1979) *A History of Macedonia vol. II: 550–336 BC*. Oxford.

Hansen, E. (1960) "Les abords du trésor de Siphnos à Delphes," *BCH* 84: 387–433.

———. (1992) "Autour du temple d'Apollon," in Bommelaer, J. F., ed. *Delphes: Centenaire de la "Grande fouille" réalisée par l'Ecole française d'Athènes (1892–1903)* 125–66. Paris.

Hansen, E (2009) "Trois notes d'architecture delphique," *BCH* 133: 113–52.

Hansen, O. (1989) "Epigraphica bellica on the dedication of the Athenian portico at Delphi," *C&M* 40: 133–34.

Harries, J. (2012) *Imperial Rome* AD *284 to 363: The New Empire*. Edinburgh.

Hassall, M., Crawford, M., and Reynolds, J. (1974) "Rome and the Eastern Provinces at the End of the Second Century B.C." *JRS* 64: 195–220.

Haussoullier, B. (1882) "Inscriptions de Delphes," *BCH* 6: 445–66.

Heer, J. (1979) *La personalité de Pausanias*. Paris.

Hellmann, M.-C. (1992) "Voyageurs et fouilleurs à Delphes," in Picard, O., ed. *La redécouverte de Delphes*, 14–54. Paris.

Holland, L. B. (1933) "The Mantic Mechanism at Delphi," *AJA* 37: 201–14.

Holleaux, M. (1930) "Le consul M. Fulvius et le siege de Samé," *BCH* 54: 1–41.

Homolle, T. (1909) *Fouilles de Delphes IV 1: Monuments figurés et sculpture: Art primitif: Art archaïque du Péloponnèse et des iles*. Paris.

———. (1926) "La loi de Cadys sur le prêt à intérêt," *BCH* 50: 3–106.

Hornblower, S. (2007) "Did the Delphic Amphictyony Play a Political Role in the classical Period?," *MHR* 22: 39–56.

Hoyle, P. (1967) *Delphi*. London.

Hubbard, T. (2011) "The Dissemination of Pindar's Non-Epincian Choral Lyric," in Athanassaki, L., ed. *Archaic and Classical Choral Song: Performance, Politics and Dissemination*, 347–64. Berlin.

Hunter, R. ed. (1998) *Studies in Heliodorus*. Cambridge.

Hutton, W. (2005a) *Describing Greece: Landscape and Literature in the Periegesis of Pausanias*. Cambridge.

———. (2005b) "The Construction of Religious Space in Pausanias," in Elsner, J., and Rutherford, I., eds., *Pilgrimage in Graeco-Roman and Early Christian Antiquity*, 291–317. Oxford.

Jacquemin, A. (1984a) "Céramic des époques archaïque, classique et hellénistique," *BCH Suppl. 9: L'Antre Corycien II*: 27–156.

———. (1984b) "Lampes," *BCH Suppl. 9: L'Antre Corycien II*: 157–66.

———. (1991a) "Delphes au IIe siècle après J.C: Un lieu de la mémoire grecque," in Said, S., ed. *Hellenismos: Quelques jalons pour une histoire de l'identité grecque*, 217–31. Leiden.

———. (1991b) "Les chantiers de Pankratès, d'Agathôn et d'Euainétos au péribole du sanctuaire d'Apollon à Delphes," *BCH* 115: 243–58.

———. (1992a) "En feuilletant le *Journal de la Grande Fouille*," in Picard, O., ed. *La redécouverte de Delphes*, 149–79. Paris.

———. (1992b) "Thyia et Castalie," in Bommelaer, J. F., ed. *Delphes: Centenaire de la "Grande fouille" réalisée par l'Ecole française d'Athènes (1892–1903)*, 167–75. Leiden.

———. (1993) "Répercussions de l'entrée de Delphes dans l'Amphictionie sur la construction à Delphes à l'époque archaïque," in Courtils, J., and Moretti, J. C., eds., *Les grands ateliers d'architecture dans le monde Egéen du VIe siècle av. JC*, 217–25. Paris.

———. (1995) "Une femme sous influence: L'echo des discordes delphiques chez Hérodote," *Ktema* 20: 30–36.

———. (1999) *Offrandes monumentales à Delphes*. Paris.

———. (2001) "Pausanias, le sanctuaire d'Olympie et les archéologues," in Knoepfler, D., and Piérart, M., eds., *Editer, traduire, commenter Pausanias en l'an 2000*, 283–300. Geneva.

———. (2011) "Adieu l'apoikia, adieu le Pythien! Que reste-t-il d'Apollon Pythios après la fondation de la colonie?," *Pallas* 87: 205–22.

Jacquemin, A., and Laroche, D. (1986) "Delphes: Piliers votifs ," *BCH* 110: 783–89.

———. (2001) "Le monument de Daochos ou le trésor des Thessaliens," *BCH* 125: 305–32.

Jacquemin, A., Laroche, D., and Lefèvre, F. (1995) "Delphes, le roi Persée et les Romains," *BCH* 119: 125–36.

Jannoray, J. (1937) "Krisa, Kirrha et la première Guerre Sacrée ," *BCH* 61: 33–43.

———. (1946) "Inscriptions delphiques d'époque tardive," *BCH* 70: 247–61.

———. (1953) *Fouilles de Delphes II: Le gymnase* Paris.

Johnston, S. I. (2005) "Delphi and the Dead," in Johnston, S. I., and Struck, P., eds., *Mantike: Studies in Ancient Divination*, 283–306. Leiden.

———. (2008) *Greek Divination*. Oxford.

Jones, C. P. (1971) *Plutarch and Rome*. Oxford.

Jung, M. (2006) *Marathon und Plataia: Zwei Perserschlachten als "lieux de mémoire" in antiken Griechenland*. Gottingen.

Juul, L. (2010) *Oracular Tales in Pausanias*. Odense.

Kähler, H. (1965) *Der Fries vom Reiterdenkmal des Aemilius Paullus in Delphi*. Berlin.

Kallet-Marx, R. (1995) *Hegemony to Empire: The Development of the Roman Imperium in the East from 148–62* BC. Berkeley.

Kase, E., Szemler, G. J., Wilkie, N., and Wallace, P. W. (1991) *The Great Isthmus Corridor Route: Vol 1: Explorations of the Phokis-Doris Expedition.* Iowa.

Kase, E. W., and Szemler, G. J. (1984) "The Amphiktyonic League and the First Sacred War: A New Perspective," in Harmatta, J., ed. *Proceedings of the VII Congress of the International Federation of the Societies of Classical Studies vol. I,* 107–16. Budapest.

Kebric, R. B. (1983) *The Paintings in the Cnidian Lesche at Delphi and Their Historical Context.* Leyde.

Keramopoullos, A. (1912) *Topographia ton Delphon.* Athens.

Kilian-Dirlmeier, I. (1985) "Fremde Weihungen in griechischen Heiligtümern vom 8. bis zum Beginn des 7. Jahrhunderts v. Chr.," *JRGZ* 32: 215–54.

Kindt, J. (2003) The Delphic Oracles: A Poetics of Futures Past between History, Literature and Religion. Ph.D. Dissertation, University of Cambridge.

———. (2006) "Delphic Oracle Stories and the Beginning of Historiography: Herodotus' *Croesus logos*," *CPh* 101: 34–51.

Knell, H. (1998) *Mythos und Polis.* Darmstadt.

Kolonia, R. (1992) "L'écho de la fouille," in Picard, O., ed. *La redécouverte de Delphes,* 194–202. Paris.

Kuckel, P. W. (2010) "Ancient omphalos at Delphi: Geometrically a space-inverting anamorphoscope," *Archaeometry* 53: 387–95.

Kuhn, G. (1985) "Untersuchungen zur Funktion der Säulenhalle in archaischer und klassischer Zeit," *JDAI* 100: 169–316.

Kurke, L. (2011) *Aesopic Conversations.* Princeton.

Kyriakidis, N. (2011) "'De l'importance de ne pas être phocidien' Enjeux politiques et identitaires des récits des origines delphiques," *Pallas* 87: 77–93.

Kyrieleis, H. (2007) "Olympia: Excavations and Discoveries at the Great Sanctuary," in Valavanis, P., ed. *Great Moments in Greek Archaeology,* 100–17. Los Angeles.

Lacroix, L. (1992) "À propos des offrandes à l'Apollon de Delphes et du témoinage de Pausanias: Du réel à l'imaginaire," *BCH* 116: 157–76.

Lagogianni-Georgakarakos, M., and Buraselis, K. (2009) *Athenian Democracy Speaking through Its Inscriptions.* Athens.

Langenfeld, H. (1975) "Die Politik des Augustus und die griechische Agonistik," in Lefèvre, E., ed. *Monument Chiloniense: Kieler Festschrift für Erich Burke*, 228–59. Amsterdam.

Laroche, D. (1992) "La tholos de Marmaria," in Bommelaer, J. F., ed. *Delphes: Centenaire de la "Grande fouille" réalisée par l'Ecole française d'Athènes (1892–1903)*, 207–23. Brill.

Laroche, D., and Jacquemin, A. (1982) "Notes sur trois piliers delphiques," *BCH* 106: 191–218.

———. (1988) "Une base pour l'Apollon de Salamine à Delphes," *BCH* 112: 235–46.

Laroche, D., and Nenna, M. (1990) "Le trésor de Sicyone et ses foundations," *BCH* 114: 241–84.

Larson, J. (2007) *Ancient Greek Cults: A Guide*. London.

Laurent, J. (1899) "Delphes Chrétien." *BCH* 23: 206–79.

Le Graff, L. (2010) "A propos d'une erreur du comptabilité dans le compte de Dion," *BCH* 134: 117–19.

Le Roy, C. (1967) *Fouilles de Delphes II: Les terres cuites architecturales*. Paris.

———. (1977) "Pausanias à Marmaria," *BCH Suppl. 4: Etudes delphiques*: 247–71.

Lefèvre, F. (1996) "L'Amphictionie pyléo-Delphique au IVe siècle," in Carlier, P., ed. *Le IVe siècle av. JC approches historiographiques*, 121–26. Paris.

———. (1998) *L'Amphictionie Pyléo-Delphique: Histoire et institutions*. Paris.

———. (2002a) "Alexandre et l'Amphictionie en 336/5 ," *BCH* 126: 73–81.

———. (2002b) *CID IV: Documents Amphictioniques*. Paris.

———. (2011) "Quoi de neuf sur l'Amphictionie?," *Pallas* 87: 117–31.

Lejeune, M. (1939) *Observations sur la langue des actes d'affranchissement delphiques*. Paris.

Lerat, L. (1935) "Trouvailles Mycéniennes à Delphes," *BCH* 59: 329–75.

———. (1938) "Fouilles de Delphes (1934–5)," *RA* 11–12: 183–227.

———. (1961) "Fouilles à Delphes à l'est du Grand Sanctuaire (1950–57)," *BCH* 85: 316–66.

———. (1980) "Trois boucliers archaïques de Delphes," *BCH* 104: 93–114.

———. (1984) "Epoque mycénienne," *BCH Suppl. 9: L'Antre Corycien II*: 3–26.

———. (1985) "Les 'enigmes des Marmaria,'" *BCH* 109: 255–64.

Levi, M. A. (1988) "Il mondo di Delfi," in Mactoux, M.-M., and Geny, E., eds., *Mélanges P. Lévêque*, 219–28. Paris.

Lewis, J. (2006) *Solon the Thinker: Political Thought in Archaic Athens*. London.

Lewis, S. (2009) *Greek Tyranny*. Bristol.

Lissarrague, F. (2000) "Delphes et la céramique," *BCH Suppl. 36: Delphes: Cent ans après la Grande fouille. Essai de bilan*: 53–67.

Lloyd-Jones, H. (1976) "The Delphic Oracle," *G&R* 23: 60–73.

Londey, P. (1990) "Greek Colonists and Delphi," in Descoeudres, J. P., ed. *Greek Colonists and Native Populations*, 117–27. Oxford.

Low, P. A. (2006) "Commemorating the Spartan War Dead," in Powell, A., and Hodkinson, S., eds., *Sparta and War*, 85–109. Swansea.

Luce, J. (1992) "Travaux de l'Ecole française en Grèce en 1991: Delphes," *BCH* 116: 686–704.

———. (2008) *L'aire du pilier des Rhodiens (fouille 1990–1992) à la frontière du profane et du sacré (FD II 13)*. Paris.

———. (2011a) "Delphes et Médéon de Phocide à l'Age du fer," *Pallas* 87: 60–76.

———. (2011b) "La Phocide à l'âge du fer," in Mazarakis Ainian, A., ed. *The "Dark Ages" Revisited*, 305–30. Volos.

Ma, J. (2008) "Chaironea 338: Topographies of Commemoration," *JHS* 128: 72–91.

Maass, M. (1997) *Das antike Delphi: Orakel, Schätze und Monumente* (2nd ed.). Darmstadt.

Malkin, I. (1987) *Religion and Colonisation in Ancient Greece*. Leiden.

———. (1989) "Delphoi and the Founding of Social Order in Archaic Greece," *Metis* 4: 129–53.

———. (2000) "La fondation d'une colonie Apollienne: Delphes et *l'Hymne Homérique à Apollon*," *BCH Suppl. 36: Delphes: Cent ans après la Grande fouille. Essai de bilan*: 69–77.

Marchetti, P. (1977) "A propos des comptes de Delphes sous les archontats de Theon (324/3) et de Caphis (327/6)," *BCH* 101: 133–45.

———. (2011) "Quelques aspects trop souvent négligés des comptes de Delphes: De l'amphictionique nouveau aux couronnes d'Olympias," *Pallas* 87: 133–50.

Maurizio, L. (1995) "Anthropology and Spirit Possession: A Reconsideration of the Pythia's Role at Delphi," *JHS* 115: 69–86.

Mcinerney, J. (1999) *The Folds of Parnassos*. Austin.

———. (2011) "Delphi and Phokis: A Network Theory Approach," *Pallas* 87: 95–106.

———. (Forthcoming) "Making Phocian Space: Sanctuary and Community in the Definition of the Polis," in Beck, H., and Funke, P., eds., *Greek Federal States and Their Sanctuaries*, Cambridge.

Meiggs, R., and Lewis, D. (1988) *A Selection of Greek Historical Inscriptions to the End of the Fifth Century* BC (rev. ed.). Oxford.

Mennen, I. (2011) *Power and Status in the Roman Empire, AD 193–284*. Leiden.

Meritt, B. (1947) "The Persians at Delphi," *Hesperia* 16: 58–62.

Michaud, J.-P. (1977) "Nouvelle inscription de la base de M.Acilius," *BCH Suppl. 4: Etudes delphiques*: 125–36.

Mikalson, J. (1998) *Religion in Hellenistic Athens*. Berkeley.

Miller, A. M. (1986) *From Delos to Delphi: A Literary Study of the Homeric Hymn to Apollo*. Leiden.

Miller, M. (1997) *Athens and Persia in the Fifth Century* BC. Cambridge.

Miller, S. G. (2000) "Macedonians at Delphi," *BCH Suppl. 36: Delphes: Cent ans après la Grande fouille. Essai de bilan*: 263–81.

Mitchell, S. (1990) "Festivals, Games and Civic Life in Roman Asia Minor," *JRS* 80: 183–93.

———. (1993) *Anatolia: Land, Men and Gods in Asia Minor. Volume 1: The Celts in Anatolia and the Impact of Roman Rule*. Oxford.

———. (2007) *A History of the Later Roman Empire* AD *284–641*. Oxford.

Moret, J. M. (1982) "L'"Apollonisation" de l'imagerie legendaire d'Athènes dans le second moitié du Ve siècle," *RA*: 109–36.

Morgan, C. (1989) "Divination and Society at Delphi and Didyma," *Hermathena* 147: 17–42.

———. (1990) *Athletes and Oracles: The Transformation of Olympia and Delphi in the Eighth Century* BC. Cambridge.

———. (1993) "The Origins of Pan-Hellenism," in Marinatos, N., and Hägg, R., eds., *Greek Sanctuaries: New Approaches*, 45–61. London.

———. (2003) *Early Greek States beyond the Polis*. London.

Mosshammer, A. (1982) "The Date of the First Pythiad—Again," *GRBS* 23: 15–30.

Mossman, J. ed. (1997) *Plutarch and His Intellectual World*. Swansea.

Müller, S. (1992a) "Delphes et sa région à l'époque mycénienne," *BCH* 116: 445–96.

———. (1992b) "Delphes mycénienne. Un réexamen du site dans son contexte régional," in Bommelaer, J. F., ed. *Delphes, Centenaire de la "Grande Fouille" réalisée par l'École française d'Athènes (1892–1903)*, 67–83. Strasbourg.

Mulliez, D. (2007) "Delphi: The Excavation of the Great Oracular Centre (1892)," in Valavanis, P., ed. *Great Moments in Greek Archaeology*, 134–57. Los Angeles.

Murray, O. (2001) "Herodotus and Oral History," in Luraghi, N., ed. *The Historian's Craft in the Age of Herodotus*, 16–44. Oxford.

Mylonas, G. (1961) *Eleusis and the Eleusinian Mysteries*. Princeton.

Nachtergael, G. (1977) *Les Galates en Grèce et les Sôtèria de Delphes. Recherches d'histoire et d'épigraphie hellénistiques*. Brussels.

Nagy, G. (1994) "The Name of Apollo: Etymology and Essence," in Solomon, J., ed. *Apollo: Origins and Influences*, 3–7. Tuscon.

Neeft, C. W. (1981) "Observations on the Thapsos Class," *MEFRA* 93: 7–88.

Neer, R. T. (2004) "The Athenian Treasury at Delphi and the Material of Politics," *ClAnt* 23: 63–94.

Ogden, D. (2001) *Greek and Roman Necromancy*. Princeton.

Oppé, A. P. (1904) "The Chasm at Delphi," *JHS* 24: 214–40.

Osborne, R. (1998) "Early Greek Colonisation: The Nature of Greek Settlements in the West," in Fisher, N., and Van Wees, H., eds., *Archaic Greece: New Approaches and New Evidence*, 251–70. London.

———. (2009) *Greece in the Making c.1200–479* BC (2nd ed.). London.

Østby, E. (2000) "Delphi and Archaic Doric Architecture in the Peloponnese," *BCH Suppl. 36: Delphes: Cent ans après la Grande fouille. Essai de bilan*: 239–62.

Otter, W. (1825) *Life and Remains of Edward Danielle Clarke*. London.

Ozenfant, A. (1939) *Journey through Life: Experiences, Doubts, Certainties, Conclusions*.

Pape, M. (1975) *Griechische Kunstwerke aus Kriegsbute und ihre öffentliche Aufstellung in Rom von der Eroberung von Syrakus biz zur augusteischen Zeit*. Hamburg.

Parke, H. W. (1940) "A Note on the Delphic Priesthood," *CQ* 34: 85–89.

———. (1967) *Greek Oracles*. London.

———. (1984) "Croesus and Delphi," *GRBS* 25: 209–32.

———. (1985) *The Oracles of Apollo in Asia Minor*. London.

Parke, H. W., and Boardman, J. (1957) "The Struggle for the Tripod and the First Sacred War," *JHS* 77: 276–82.

Parke, H. W., and Wormell, D. E. (1956a) *The Delphic Oracle Vol. I: The History*. Oxford.

———. (1956b) *The Delphic Oracle Vol. II: The Oracular Responses*. Oxford.

Parker, R. (2000) "Greek States and Greek Oracles," in Buxton, R., ed. *Oxford Readings in Greek Religion*, 76–108. Oxford.

Partida, E. (2000) *The Treasuries at Delphi: an Architectural Study*. Jonsered.

——. (2009) "From Hypaethral Depots to Hypaethral Exhibitions. Casting Light on Architecture and Society in 4th–3rd Century BC Delphi," *MDAI* 124: 273–324.

——. (2011) "The Nexus of Inter-Regional Relations Established by Creators and Artisans in the Ancient Sanctuary and Town of Delphi," *Pallas* 87: 223–42.

Pasquier, A. (1977) "Pan et les Nymphs à l'Antre Corycien," *BCH Suppl. 4: Etudes delphiques*: 365–87.

Péchoux, P.-Y. (1992) "Aux origines des paysages de Delphes," in Bommelaer, J. F., ed. *Delphes: Centenaire de la "Grande fouille" réalisée par l'Ecole française d'Athènes (1892–1903)*, 13–38. Leiden.

Pelling, C. (1988) *Plutarch: Life of Anthony*. Cambridge.

——. (2002) *Plutarch and History*. Swansea.

Pentazos, E. (1992a) "Le Gymnase," in Bommelaer, J. F., ed. *Delphes: Centenaire de la "Grande fouille" réalisée par l'Ecole française d'Athènes (1892–1903)*, 225–32. Leiden.

——. (1992b) "Les premiers signes d'intéret en Grèce," in Picard, O., ed. *La redécouverte de Delphes*, 55–60. Paris.

Perdrizet, P. (1908) *Fouilles de Delphes V 1: Monuments figurés: Petits bronzes, terres-cuites, antiquités diverses*. Paris.

Perrier, A. (2008) "La moisson et les pigeons. Note sur l'assise sommitale du pilier de Prusias à Delphes," *BCH* 132: 257–70.

——. (2011) "Le portique dit 'des Etoliens' à Delphes. Bilan et perspectives," *Pallas* 87: 39–56.

Perrot, S. (2009) "Pommes agonistiques à Delphes: Réflexions autour du cognassier sacré d'Apollon," *BCH* 133: 153–68.

Picard, O. ed. (1991) *Guide de Delphes: Le musée*. Paris.

Plassart, A. (1921) "La liste des théorodoques," *BCH* 45: 1–85.

Pollard, J. (1960) "Delphica," *ABSA* 55: 195–99.

Pomtow, H. (1909) "Studien zu den Weihgeschenken und der Topographie von Delphi V," *Klio* 9: 153–93.

——. (1914) "Zur delphischen Archontentafel des III Jhdts.," *Klio* 14: 265–320.

——. (1918) "Delphische Neufunde II," *Klio* 15: 1–77.

Pouilloux, J. (1952) "Promanties collectives et protocole delphique," *BCH* 76: 484–513.

Pouilloux, J. (1954) *Recherches sur l'histoire et les cultes de Thasos I: De la fondation de la cité à 196 av. JC.* Paris.

———. (1960) *Fouilles de Delphes II: La région Nord du sanctuaire de l'époque archaïque à la fin du sanctuaire.* Paris.

———. (1971) "Delphes et les Romains," *REA* 73: 374–81.

———. (1976) "Cypriotes à Delphes," *Report of the Department of Antiquities Cyprus*: 158–67.

———. (1977) "Travaux à Delphes à l'occasion des Pythia," *BCH Suppl. 4: Etudes delphiques*: 103–23.

———. (1980) "Les épimélètes des amphictions: Tradition delphique et politique romaine," *Mélanges de literature et d'epigraphie latines d'histoire ancienne et d'archaeologie. Hommage à la memoire de Pierre Wuilleumier,* 281–300. Paris.

———. (1983) "Delphes dans les éthiopiques d'Heliodore," *JS*: 259–86.

———. (1984) "Roman Grec et realité: Un episode delphique des Ethiopiques d'Heliodore," in Walter, H., ed. *Hommages à Lucien Lerat* 691–703. Paris.

Pouilloux, J., and Roux, G. eds. (1963) *Enigmes à Delphes.* Paris.

Poulsen, F. (1908) "Recherches sur quelques questions relatives à la topographie de Delphes," *Bulletin de l'Académie des Sciences et Lettres de Danemark* 6: 337–46.

Price, S.R.F. (1985) "Delphi and Divination," in Easterling, P. E., and Muir, J. V., eds., *Greek Religion and Society,* 128–54. Cambridge.

Prontera, F. (1981) "Gli Alcmeonidi a Delfi: Un ipotesi su Erodoto I, 51, 3–4," *RA*: 253–58.

Radet, G. (1992) "La Grande Fouille vue par un contemporain," in Picard, O., ed. *La redécouverte de Delphes,* 144–48. Paris.

Raven, E.J.P. (1950) "The Amphictionic Coinage of Delphi 336–334 ," *NC* 10: 1–22.

Reinach, T. (1910) "Delphes et les Bastarnes," *BCH* 34: 249–330.

Replat, J. (1920) "Note sur la restauration partielle de l'autel de Chios à Delphes," *BCH* 44: 328–53.

Rhodes, P. J. (2007) "Impact of the Persian Wars on Classical Greece," in Bridges, E., Hall, E., and Rhodes, P. J., eds., *Cultural Responses to the Persian Wars: Antiquity to the Third Millienium,* 31–45. Oxford.

Rhodes, P. J., and Osborne, R. (2003) *Greek Historical Inscriptions.* Oxford.

Richter, J. (1994) *Sacred Geography of the Ancient Greeks.* Albany.

Robert, L. (1929) "Décrets de Delphes," *BCH* 53: 34–41.

Robertson, N. (1978) "The Myth of the First Sacred War," *CQ* 72: 38–73.

Roesch, P. (1984) "La base des Béotiens à Delphes," *CRAI*: 177–95.

Rolley, C. (1977) *Fouilles de Delphes V 3: Les trépieds à cuve clouée.* Paris.

———. (1990) "En regardant l'Aurige," *BCH* 114: 285–97.

———. (2002) "Delphes de 1500 à 575 BC—Nouvelles données sur le problème 'ruptures et continuité,'" in Kyrieleis, H., ed. *Olympia 1875–2000 125 Jahre Deutsche Ausgrabungen*, 273–79. Mainz.

Romeo, I. (2002) "The Panhellenion and Ethnic Identity in Hadrianic Greece," *CPh* 97: 21–40.

Rosenberger, V. (2001) *Griechische Orakel: Eine Kulturgeschichte.* Darmstadt.

Rougement, G. (1991) "Delphes et les cités Grecques d' Italie du sud et de Sicile," in Carratelli, G. P., ed. *La Magna Grecia e I grandi santuari della madrepatria*, 157–92. Taranto.

Roussel, P. (1926) "Les épimélètes Aitolians à Delphes," *BCH* 50: 124–34.

———. (1932) "Delphes et l'Amphictionie après la guerre d'Aitolie," *BCH* 56.

Rousset, M. D. (1996) "Territoire de Delphes et terre d'Apollon," in Etienne, F., ed. *L'Espace Grec: 150 ans de fouilles de l'EFA*, 45–49. Paris.

———. (2002a) *Le territoire de Delphes et la terre d'Apollon.* Paris.

———. (2002b) "Terres sacrés, terres publiques et terres privées à Delphes," *CRAI*: 215–41.

Roux, G. (1952) "La terrasse d'Attale I à Delphes," *BCH* 76: 141–96.

———. (1962) "Pindare, le prétendu trésor des Crétois et l'ancienne statue d'Apollon à Delphes," *REG* 75: 366–80.

———. (1970) "Les Prytanes de Delphes," *BCH* 94: 117–32.

———. (1976) *Delphes, son oracle et ses dieux* Paris.

———. (1979) *L'Amphictionie, Delphes et le temple d'Apollon au IVe siècle.* Paris.

———. (1984) "Politique et religion: Delphes et Délos à l'époque archaïque ," in Harmatta, J., ed. *Proceedings of the VII Congress of the International Federation of the Societies of Classical Studies vol. I*, 97–105. Budapest.

———. (1987) *La terrasse d'Attale I (FD II).* Paris.

———. (1989) "Problèmes delphiques d'architecture et d'épigraphie," *RA*: 23–64.

Salmon, J. B. (1984) *Wealthy Corinth: A History of the City to 338 BC.* Oxford.

Salviat, F. (1965) "L'offrande Argienne de l'"hémicycle des rois' à Delphes et l'Héraclès Béotien," *BCH* 89: 307–14.

Sanchez, P. (2001) *L'Amphictionie des Pyles et de Delphes: Recherches sur son rôle historique, des origines au IIe siècle de notre ère.* Stuttgart.

Schachter, A. (1994) "The Politics of Dedication: Two Athenian Dedications at the Sanctuary of Apollo Ptoieus in Boeotia," in Osborne, R., and Hornblower, S., eds., *Ritual, Finance, Politics: Athenian Democratic Accounts Presented to David Lewis* 291–306. Oxford.

Schnapp, A. (1996) *The Discovery of the Past*. London.

Scott, M. C. (2007) "Putting Architectural Sculpture into Its Archaeological Context: The Case of the Siphnian Treasury at Delphi," *BABesch* 82.2: 321–31.

———. (2008) "Constructing identities in Sacred Inter-State Space: The Case of the Arcadian Monument at Delphi," in Menozzi, O., Di Marzio, M., and Fossataro, D., eds., *SOMA 2005: Proceedings of the IX Symposium on Mediterranean Archaeology*, 431–38. Oxford.

———. (2010) *Delphi and Olympia: The Spatial Politics of Panhellenism in the Archaic and Classical Periods*. Cambridge.

———. (2012) *Space and Society in the Greek and Roman Worlds*. Cambridge.

Segre, M. (1929) "Il sacco di Delfi e la leggenda dell'Aurum tolosanum," *Historia* 8: 592–648.

Shapiro, H. (1996) "Athena, Apollo and the Religious Propaganda of the Athenian Empire," in Hellstrom, P., and Alroth, B., eds., *Religion and Power in the Ancient Greek World*, 101–13. Uppsala.

Skorda, D. (1992a) "Les projets d'expropriation 1963–1881," in Picard, O., ed. *La redécouverte de Delphes*, 61–71. Paris.

———. (1992b) "Recherches dans la vallée du Pléistos," in Bommelaer, J. F., ed. *Delphes: Centenaire de la "Grande fouille" réalisée par l'Ecole française d'Athènes (1892–1903)*, 39–66. Leiden.

Snodgrass, A. M. (1980) *Archaic Greece: The Age of Experiment*. London.

———. (1986) "Interaction by Design: The Greek City-State," in Renfrew, C., and Cherry, J. F., eds., *Peer-Polity Interaction and Socio-Political Change*, 47–58. Cambridge.

———. (2001) "Pausanias and the Chest of Kypselos," in Elsner, J., Cherry, J. F., and Alcock, S., eds., *Pausanias: Travel and Memory in Roman Greece*, 127–41. Oxford.

Sordi, M. (1953) "La prima guerra sacra," *RFIC* 81: 320–46.

———. (1957) "La fondation du collège des naopes et le renouveau politique de l'Amphictionie au IVe siècle," *BCH* 81: 38–75.

Soros, S. ed. (2006) *James "Athenian" Stuart: The Rediscovery of Antiquity*. New Haven.

Sourvinou-Inwood, C. (1979) "The Myth of the First Temples at Delphi," *CQ* 29: 231–51.

———. (1987) Myth as History: The Previous Owners of the Delphic Oracle," in Bremmer, J. N., ed. *Interpretations of Greek Mythology*, 215–41. London.

———. (1990) "What Is Polis Religion?," in Murray, O., and Price, S.R.F., eds., *The Greek City from Homer to Alexander*, 295–322. Oxford.

———. (1993) "Early Sanctuaries: The Eighth Century and Ritual Space: Fragments of a Discourse," in Marinatos, N., and Hägg, R., eds., *Greek Sanctuaries: New Approaches*, 1–17. London.

———. (2000) "What Is Polis Religion?," in Buxton, R., ed. *Oxford Readings in Greek Religion*, 13–37. Oxford.

Spawforth, A. (2012) *Greece and the Augustan Cultural Revolution*. Cambridge.

Spawforth, A., and Walker, S. (1985) "The World of the Panhellenion I: Athens and Eleusis," *JRS* 75: 78–104.

———. (1986) "The World of the Panhellenion II: Three Dorian Cities," *JRS* 76: 88–105.

Spieser, J. M. (1976) "La Christianisation des sanctuaries païens en Grèce," in Jantzen, U., ed. *Neue Forschungen in griechischen heiligtümern* 309–20. Tübingen.

St. Claire, W. (1984) *Lord Elgin and the Marbles* (2nd ed.). Oxford.

Stewart, A. (1982) "Dionysos at Delphi: The Pediments of the Sixth Temple of Apollo and Religious Reform in the Age of Alexander," in Barr-Sharrar, B., and Borza, E. N., eds., *Studies in the History of Art Vol. X: Macedonia and Greece in Late Classical and Early Hellenistic Times*, 205–27. Washington.

Stoll, H. (1979) *Entdeckungen in Hellas. Reisen deutscher Archäologen in Griechenland, Kleinasien und Sizilien*. Berlin.

Stonemann, R. (2010) *Land of Lost Gods: The Search for Classical Greece*. London.

———. (2011) *The Ancient Oracles: Making the Gods Speak*. London.

Struck, P. (2005) *Mantike: Studies in Ancient Greek Diviniation*. Leiden.

Taplin, O. (1989) *Greek Fire*. London.

Tausend, K. (1992) *Amphiktionie und Symmachie. Formen zwischenstaatlicher Beziehungen im archaischen Griechenland*. Stuttgart.

Tenekides, C. (1931) "L'Amphictyonie de Delphes et la Ligue de Corinthe, dans leurs affinités avec la Société des Nations," *Revue Générale de l'Académie de droit international public*: 5–20.

———. (1958) "L'Amphictyonie delphique. Légende et réalité," *Annuaire de l'Association des auditeurs et des anciens auditeurs de l'Académie de droit internationale de La Haye* 90/II: 145–55.

Themelis, P. (1983) "Delphi and the Surrounding Region during the Eighth and Seventh Centuries BC (in Greek)," *Annuario* 61: 213–55.

Thomas, C. (1988) "The Modern Rediscovery of Ancient Greece," in Thomas, C., ed. *Paths from Ancient Greece*, 168–86. Leiden.

Toubis, M. (2007) *Greece: A Journey through History and Civilisation*. Athens.

Touchais, G. (1981) "Le matérial néolithique," *BCH Suppl. 7: L'Antre Corycien (I)*: 95–172.

Tsigakou, F.-M. (1981) *The Rediscovery of Greece: Travellers and Painters of the Romantic Era*. New York.

Tsoukalis, L., and Emmanoulidis, J. (2009) *The Delphic Oracle in Europe: Is There a Future for the European Union?* Oxford.

Valavanis, P. (2004) *Games and Sanctuaries in Ancient Greece: Olympia, Delphi, Isthmia, Nemea, Athens*. Athens.

Vatin, C. (1962) "Les empereurs du IVe siècle à Delphes," *BCH* 86: 229–41.

———. (1965) *Delphes à l'époque imperiale (Mémoire)*. Athens.

———. (1967) "Les monuments de M. Minucius Rufus à Delphes," *BCH* 91: 401–407.

———. (1977) "Couroi Argiens à Delphes," *BCH Suppl. 4: Etudes delphiques*: 13–22.

Vogt, S. (1998) "Delphi in der attischen Tragödie," *Antike und Abendland* 44: 30–48.

Volioti, K. (2011) "Travel Tokens to the Korykian Cave near Delphi: Perspectives from Material and Human Mobility," *Pallas* 86: 236–85.

Vollgraff, W. (1956) *Le sanctuaire d'Apollon Pythéen à Argos*. Paris.

Walbank, F. (1981) *The Hellenistic World*. Harvard.

Walsh, J. (1986) "The Date of the Athenian Stoa at Delphi," *AJA* 90: 319–36.

Weir, R. (2004) *Roman Delphi and Its Pythian Games*. Oxford.

Whittaker, C. (1965) "The Delphic Oracle: Belief and Behaviour in Ancient Greece—And Africa," *Harvard Theological Review* 58: 21–47.

Wörrle, M. (2000) "Delphes et l'Asie Mineure: Pourquoi Delphes?," *BCH Suppl. 36: Delphes: Cent ans après la Grande fouille. Essai de bilan*: 157–65.

Zagdoun, M. A. (1977) *Fouilles de Delphes IV 6: Monuments figurés: Sculpture, reliefs*. Paris.

Zahrnt, M. (1989) "Delphi, Sparta und die Rückführung der Alkmeoniden," *ZPE* 76: 297–307.

INDEX

Note: Illustrations, including maps, are indicated with **bold** page numbers.

Acanthus: dedications by, 137

Acanthus column, 299; as Athenian dedication, 166, 344n10; elements in museum, 299

access to Delphi, 45, 136; adyton as restricted space, 18; dangers to travelers, 73, 196; modern transportation and, 277, 278; trade routes and, 52

Achaea: and financial tribute to Rome, 209, 211; Roman province of, 169, 205, 207, 209, 227, 235, 243, 255

Achaia: pottery from, 53

Achean League and Achean War, 193

Actium, battle of, 203

Adrastus, 83

adyton, 18–19, **19,** 24

Aegean Islands: dedications from, 110

Aegina: dedications by, 120–21; as potential Persian ally, 110, 111–12, 120–21; Temple of Aphaia at, 255

Aegospotamoi, battle of, 139–40; Spartan dedication to victory at, **129,** 137, 147, 156, 219

Aemilius Paullus, 190–91, 196, 299–300; column, frieze, and statue erected by, **191,** 299; location of statue and column of, **16**

Aeschines, 71, 160–61

Aeschylus, 33–34, 126, 277

Aesop, 85

Aethiopica (Heliodorus), 1–2, 6, 236

Aetion, 57

Aetolia, 165–66; Aetolian style, 176; Attalids as ally of, 177, 180; control over Delphi, 169–76, 179, 180, 183, 185, 186; dedications from, 172, 176, 351n17; as enemy of Macedon, 178, 180; and manumissions at Delphi, 200; military victories, 171–74; murder of Delphi's ambassadors to Rome, 187; Prusias II and, 351n17; Soteria festival and, 175–76; statue of the personification of, 172; withdrawal from Delphi, 188

Afghanistan, visitor from, 184

Against Ctesiphon (Aeschines), 71

Agamemnon, 318n57

Agesilaus of Sparta, 142

Agis of Sparta: dedication by, 141

Aglaus of Psophias, 321n21

agonothetes (president of games), 213, 214, 229, 358n22, 362n15; Plutarch as, 216

agora, Roman, **129**, 226, 236, 241–42, 246, 292, **Plate II**

agriculture: cultivation of sacred land, 71–72, 73, 75, 80, 151, 161, 169; grazing on sacred land, 353n42; near Delphi, 143; at site during W.W.II, 280

Agrippina Major, 207, 209–10

Agrippina Minor, 210

Ai Khanoum, visitor from, 184

aire, 173, 294, 297, **Plate II**

Alcaeus, 33

Alcesippeia, 188, 220

Alcesippus of Calydon, 188, 220

Alcetas, 219

Alcmaeon, 72

Alcmaeonids, 75, 98–100, 109, 113; and reconstruction of temple, 100; and Second Sacred War, 131–32

Alexander I of Macedon, 122, golden statue of, 151

Alexander the Great of Macedon, 164–65; death of, 166; Delphi and defiance of, 165–66; relationship of Amphictyony with, 165–66

Alexandrus, 197

Altar of Chians, 176, 272, 294, 332n19, 333n42; discovery and excavation of, 272; dismantled, 246; location of, 16; reconstruction of, 276–77; repair and inscription of, 173

Alyattes of Lydia, 58, 83; dedications by, 151

Amandry, Pierre, 277, **281**, 281–82

Amasis, pharaoh of Egypt, 96

ambiguity of oracle, 110, 120–21, 179, 201, 314n58; Christian criticism of, 233; as defense against powerful consultants, 29, 84–85; and deliberation or interpretation, 28–30; and differing reports in literary sources, 60; Nero's consultations and, 210–11; and Persian war, 114, 116–17; and reputation, 30; in response to Croesus, 28–29, 83–85, 328n43; and retroactive interpretation of response, 163–64; unambiguous responses to consultations, 134

American excavations at Delphi, 266

American School of Classical Studies, 264

Ammon, chariot sculpture of, 160

Ammon, sanctuary in Egypt, 165

Amphictyony, 15, 71–72, 75, 337n25; and access to the oracle, 90; Aetolia and the, 171–72, 175, 178; and Alexander the Great, 165; as arbitrator in conflicts, 192; and Asclepieion shrine, 226; Attalids and the, 177; Augustus and reorganization of, 203, 205–6, 207; and city of Delphi, 159, 186–87; composition of, 77, 235; and construction at Delphi, 75, 92, 94, 103, 113, 146, 157, 159, 162; control and management of Delphi by, 73, 77–80, 95, 180, 184, 186–87, 286, 288–89, 350n12; currency minted by, 159, **159**, 199; declining power and influence of, 132, 192–93, 238–39; dedications by, 120, 155, 185, 188, 207–10, 214, 238, 349n3, 350n12; and defense of Delphi, 78, 150, 161, 178; and Delian league, 122; First Sacred War and, 144–45; as "general council of Greece," 205–6; Hadrian's reorganization and, 226–27; internal conflict at Delphi and, 148; legal decrees by, 144; membership in, 77, 82, 154–55, 171–72, 175, 178, 210, 216, 226–27, 235, 351n24; members honored with dedications, 350n12; military force organized by, 161; Nero and the, 209–10; Phocia and, 154–55, 171; Phocians fined by, 149–50, 154, 156, 159; Plutarch as member of, 216; and political independence of Delphi, 130; purpose of, 77–78, 144, 205–6; Pythian games and, 123–24; and rebuilding of Delphi, 94, 103, 146, 157, 159, 162, 340n16; responsibilities of, 144; Romans and role of, 226–28, 286–87; and scandal at Delphi, 195–96; Thessaly and, 82, 210, 227; and war against Crisa, 71–72, 75

Amphipolis, 133

Amphissa, 52, 152, 161–62, 170, 186, 188, 215; dedications at Delphi, 162

Anaxandridas, 219

Ancyra, 229

Andos, 132

Andromache (Euripides), 135

Androsthenes, 153

Anecdota Delphica (Curtius), 261

Anthony, 201–2; and political value of Delphi, 201–2

Antigonus II of Macedon, 178

Antinous, 233, 272, 299; cult at Delphi, 104, 224, 299; dedication of statue of, 224, **225,** 272, 299; discovery and excavation of statue dedication, 272

Antiocheia: dedications from, 184

Antiochus III: dedications honoring, 184; "liberation" of Delphi by, 185; Roman defeat of, 185–86, 192

Antipatrus of Eleuthernai, 197, 206

Antoninus Pius, 228, 233

Apollas, 219

Apollo: ambiguity and Apollo Loxias, 29; divination and, 29, 40; and establishment of Delphi, 31–33; as god of colonization, 63; linked to Imperial cult of Rome, 237–38; and order *vs.* chaos, 39–40; purification of, 35; sites considered for oracle of, 32, 51. *See also* Apollo sanctuary at Delphi; Temple of Apollo

Apollo, or The Oracle at Delphi (1891), 22

Apollonia in Illyria: dedications from, 110–11

Apollonius, 219

Apollo Patroos, 175

Apollo Ptoios, sanctuary of, 96, 99, 104, 116, 178

Apollo Pythios: dual nature of, 41–42

Apollo sanctuary at Delphi, 69; Asclepieion shrine within, 226; Cleisthenes and dedication of, 82; entrances to, 294; evidence of cult activity buried in, 48; habitation at site of, 366n3; location of, **Plate I**; perimeter wall and boundary of, 74–75, 87, 293; photos of location, 3; reconstruction depicting dedications at entrance to, 129; reconstruction of, **16,** 278; Roman agora adjacent to, 292; "sacred way" in, 246; Temple Terrace, **16,** 102, 295, **Plate II.** *See also* Pythia; Temple of Apollo

Apollo's arrival via chariot, pedimental sculpture, 101

Appius Claudius Censorinus, 200

apples, Delphic, 259n40, 359n40

Aratus of Achea, 179

arbitration: by the Amphictyony, 192; Pythia and, 58, 135–36, 138, 140, 174; by Roman corrector at Delphi and, 215

Arcadia: Arcadian confederacy, 135–36, 146; dedications by, 146–47; Sparta as enemy of, 57, 146

archaeological excavation: "big dig" (1892–1901), 42, 267–74, 277; at Corycian cave, 283–84; De le Coste-Messelière and, 275–76; and European appropriation of antiquities, 255–56; French, 43, 251, 263–67, 275–78 (*see also* "big dig" *under this heading*); German scholarship and, 252, 257, 261, 263; Greek support of, 257–58, 261–67, 274, 276–77; Homolle and, 265–66, 266–71, 273–75, 313n36; Leake's maps and, 254; literary sources and expectations, 42, 233–34, 254, 256–57, 274; mudslide over excavated area, 277; Müller's, 258; of oldest buildings at site, 294–95; Pomtow and, 265–66, 273, 275; in progress, **270, 271;** Raike's maps and, 254; relocation of Castri and, 259–60, 267, 269–70; Replat and site reconstruction, 274–75; Spon and Wheler expedition, 251, 253; Stuart and Revett expedition, 251; war and interruption of, 272, 275, 278–82

Archesilaus III of Cyrene, 97

Archesilaus IV of Cyrene, 123, 125

Archilochus of Paros, 320n12

architecture: Corinthian-style elements, 295; cultural homogeneity and temple, 77; and definition of community identity, 133; development of style vocabulary, 82, 342n44; domestic residences, 214; Doric style, 113; evolution of Greek architectural vocabulary, 82; Ionic style, 87, 105, 224, 226; mythology and identification of earliest structure at site, 41–42; style experimentation and Delphic identity, 133, 288; terracing and engineering, **16,** 45, 94, 102

archives: at Temple of Cybele, 141

Argive twins, 67, 296; discovery and excavation of, **268**

Argos, 48, 133; Agesilaus and Spartan attack on, 142; Argive statues, **Plate II**; consultation of the oracle by, 114; dedications by, 67, **129**, 133, 146, 362n15; divination at, 24; and purification of Apollo, 35

Arioborzanes, 147

Aristaineta, 176

Aristocles of Carystus, 156

Aristocrates, 197

Aristonice, 116–17, 310n5

Aristophanes, 25, 135, 136

Aristotle, 159, 167, 316n28, 343n48

Arkadia: dedications by, 129, 340n18

Artemis, 103

Artemisium, 120

Asclepiads, 17, 141–42; shrine within Apollo sanctuary, 226

Asclepius, 154, 169, 226, 320n8, 339n7; Amphictyony and shrine within Apollo sanctuary, 226; cult in Rome, 169; cult practices at Delphi, 154; inscription of the Aesclepiads, 17, 104, 141–42, 339n7

Aspis (Hesiod), 72

Astycrates, 148, 154

asylia (religious sanctuary), 168, 174–75, 178, 188, 345n17; Delphi and declarations of, 188

ateleia (exemption from consultation tax), 174

Athena: dedications depicting, 128. *See also* Athena sanctuary

Athena Nikephoros, sanctuary in Pergamon, 188

Athena sanctuary, 94–95, 159; 4th c. Temple in, **Plate III**; 6th c. Temple in, **Plate III**; altars in, **Plate III**; Amphictyony and, 103; Doric treasury, **Plate III**; and gymnasium at Delphi, 158–59; Hadrian statue dedication in, 224; location of, **Plate I**; Massalian treasury, 105, **Plate III**; rebuilding of, 103, 278, 292; reconstruction of, 278, **Plate III**; repurposing of treasury, 159; tholos in, 149, 278, 292, **Plate III**

Athenian dedications, 128–29, 166, 336n23; acanthus column, 166, 299, 344n10; palm tree, **16,** 128; reconstruction depicting entrance to Apollo sanctuary, 129; spatial monopolization and, 128–30; statue groups, 113, 120, **129**, 174, 293; stoa, **Plate II**; updating of, 172–73, 178. *See also* Athenian treasury

Athenian treasury, **115**; architectural style of, 112–13; discovery and excavation of, 272; inscriptions on, 194, 293–94; as pawnshop, 239; rebuilding of, 293; site and construction, 293

Athens, 66, 75, 81, 100, 109; Aegospotamoi, battle of, 139–40; and Aetolian Soteria festival, 176; Alcmaeonids and rule of, 98–101, 109–10; Amphictyony and honors for, 194–95; boycott of Pythian games, 155–56, 166; Chaeroneia, defeat at, 161–62; consultation of the Pythia by, 136, 178; control of Delphi, 126–27; Crisans, war with, 71–72; dedications at Delphi (*see* Athenian dedications; Athenian treasury); Delian league and, 126; and domination of sanctuary space, 130, 132; First Fruits Decree, 133; independence of, 178; interpretation of "wooden wall" oracle, 117; and Marathon, 112–13, 129, 137, 293–94; Parthenon in, 251–52; peace agreements, 135; and Philip II of Macedon, conflict with, 155, 160; Philip V's plan to annex, 184; political structure of, 98; preeminence of, 129–30; Pythia and protection of, 137; and rebuilding of Delphi, 156; relationship with Delphi, 81, 102, 134–36, 174–75, 178, 193–94, 204; Rome and, 204; Sparta as political/military rival of, 100–102, 111, 130–32, 134–35, 137, 139–40, 147; Sulla's siege of, 198–99; symbolic association with Delphi, 102; Thebes as rival, 148

athletic competitions, 4, 72, 73, 364n34; Capitoline games in Rome, 213; dedications honoring victories, 123, 188, 197, 214, 238, 300; at Delphi (*see* Pythian games); funding of, 72, 83; Isthmain games, 184; Nero as competitor in, 209–10; Nikephoria games, 188; Olympics, 204, 207; periodos circuit of, 76, 209, 229, 288, 324n7, 339n7;

and reputation of Delphi, 287; revival of Olympics during 19th century, 272; at Sicyon, 83; of Soteria festival, 173, 175–76; at Thessalonike, 237; women as competitors in, 209; as worship of Emperor, 237

Attaleia, 192, 220

Attalus I, 186–87

Attalus II, 192; and First Macedonian War, 180; statue of, location, 16; stoa dedicated by, 177

Attica, 66; pottery from, 53

Augustus, 220; dedications to sanctuary at Delphi, 203–4; herm dedicated by Athens in honor of, 206–7; and oversight of Delphi, 203

Aulus Gellius, 229

Aurelia Julia Sotia, 240

Aurelius Niciadas, M., 207, 363n31

Aurelius Ptolemaius, M., 362n15

Avidius Nigrinus, C., 215–16

Avidius Quietus, T., 214

Bassae, Temple of, 254

baths, Roman, 213–14, 236, 238, 240, 246, 336n2, 361n6, 365n43, 366n2, **Plate II**; location of, **158**

battles: Actium, 203; Aegospotamoi, 137, 139–40, 147, 156, 219; Chaeroneia, 155, 161–62, 165; Magnesia, 186; Mantinea, 147; Marathon, 112–13, 129, 137, 160, 178, 293–94; Philippi, 201; Plataea, 117; Pydna, 190, 193, 299–300; Salamis, 117, 120

bias: and consultation via sealed jars, 151–52; Delphic oracle as biased, 151, 161

"big dig" (1892–1901), 42, 267–74; online records of, 269

Birds (Aristophanes), 25

bison, statue portrait of, 174

Bithynia, 251n17

"Black house" *(maison noire),* 45, 49, 51, 64, 74

Black Sea settlements, 132

Boeotia: and access to Delphi, 136; Athens as enemy of, 110, 136; cauldrons from, 67; consultation of the oracle, 86; dedications by, 160, 174, 177, 207–8; Perseus

of Macedon and, 189; pottery from, 53; proxenia and, 344n6; sanctuaries in, 178

border disputes, 188; and community identity, 59; Delphi's boundaries and, 193–94, 215; Roman arbitration of, 215

bouleuterion, 87, 143, 326n23

boundaries: Delphi's, 59, 186; of sanctuary in Delphi, 64, 66, 195–96. *See also* border disputes; walls

Bourguet, Emilie, 275

Bousquet, Jean, 277

Brennus, 170

bribes, 25, 100–101, 111–12, 114–16, 134, 141

British School, 264

bronze: Antiocheian dedications, 184; bull, 67–68, 300; Charioteer, 123, 272, 300; colossal Apollo statue in sanctuary, 132; "E," 204, 217; embellishment on Gigantomachy frieze, 107; palm trees, 107, 128, 137; serpents on Plataean column, 121; temple, legendary, 36; tripods, 45, 48; value in ancient world, 300; vessels used in oracle consultation, 151–52; weapons, 44; wolf, 131

Brutus, 201

bulls, statues of, 122; bronze, 68; silver, 88, **89,** 297

burial: of cult objects during rituals, 221; of dedications, 44, 88–90, **89,** 123, 278–79, 297, 300, 328n36, **Plate V**; dromos tomb, 44; Meleager sarcophagus, 231–32, 257; Mycenaean cult figures as funerary items, 44; necropolis of Delphi, 230–32; of oracle responses, 310n2; in sanctuary as honor, 119, 339n7

Byron, George Gordon Lord, 256–57; graffiti signature at Delphi, **256**

Caesar (Julius), 200, 201

calendar, 173, 220, 226. *See also* festivals at Delphi

Caligula, 207–8

Callinus of Ephesus, 62–63

Callisthenes, 159

Camillus, 168, 175

Caphis, 197

Caracella, 235

Caristanius Julianus, 214

Carthage, 170, 179–80, 184, 190, 193

Carus, 238, 239

caryatids, **106**, 106–7

Carystus: dedications, 122, 156

Cassius, 201

Castalian fountain, 13, 245, 277, 292; location of, **Plate I**; photos of location, 3; statuary dedications at, 132

Castri, 249; earthquake damage at, 262–63; before excavation, **259, 260**; Gell's drawing of, **254**; museum proposed at, 257; negotiations with residents, 262–64, 266–67, 269–70; relocation and archaeological excavation, 259–60, 267, 269–70

ceramics: Athenian vase painting, 135; cultural homogeneity and, 77; as dedications, 66; depictions of Delphi in, 135; krater depicting murder of Neoptolemus at Delphi, 125; lamps found in Corycian cave, 219; Neolithic shards, 43; shift from Thessalian to Corinthian style, 45; Thapsos ware, 47

Chaeroneia: battle of, 155, 161–62, 165; as Plutarch's home city, 215, 216

Chalcis, 56, 59

Chandler, Richard, 253

Chapel of Gaia, 68

Chapel of St. George, 248

Charila festival, 221

Charioteer of Delphi, 123, 300, Plate **VI**; buried with earthquake rubble, 156; discovery and excavation of, 272; location of, 16

chariots: Ammon depicted in, 160; chariot racing during Pythian games, 124–25; as dedications, 123, 160. See also Charioteer of Delphi

Charixenus, 176

chasm, 20, 22, 23

Chersonesus, 86

Chios, 15; altar dedication by, 16, 173, 176, 246, 272, 276–77, 294, 332n19, 333n42; and promanteia, 173, 294; updating of dedications by, 172–73

chresmographeion (waiting area), 17

chresmologoi (oracle-tellers or seers), 25

Christianity, 6, 11; basilicas at Delphi, 247–48; Christian period artifacts, 248, 300; Church on gymnasium site, 292; and decline of Delphi, 239–40; Julian the Apostate and, 243; oracles as continuing institution during, 236, 243–44; and prohibition of paganism, 245; research on Christian-era Delphi, 372n34; schism of, 250; statues of Christian emperors in pagan sanctuary, 242–43; and tolerance of paganism, 243–44; use of pagan motifs or symbols, 247, 248

Chrysostom Dios, 214

Chyselephantine sculpture, 205; dedication by Corinth, 88, 90, 297, **Plate V**

Cicero, 199–200

Clarke, Edward, 253

Claudian, 245

Claudius, 207; as archon of Delphi, 208–9; correspondence with Delphi, 208; dedications honoring, 208

Claudius Callippianus, Tib., 364n31

Claudius Gothicus, 238, 239

Claudius Leonticus, Cn., 235

Claudius Marcellus, 175

Clazomenae, 108, 140

Clearchus, 184

Clearistus of Carystus, 156

Cleisthenes of Athens, 98–99

Cleisthenes of Sicyon, 72, 75, 82–83

Cleisthenes the Alcmaeonid, 109–10

Clement of Alexandria, 236

Cleobis and Biton (Argive twins), **67**, 296

Cleomenes of Sparta, 109, 111–12

Cnidian lesche, 128, 160, 192, **Plate II**; houses built on site of, 246

Cnidos, 87, 97–98, 128; lesche dedication by, 128, 160, 192, **Plate II**; statue of Dionysus dedicated by, 153; treasury, 212, 272

Cobon, 112

coins, 77, 123, 199; Amphictyony and minting of, 159, **159**, 199

Collier, John, 22; Priestess at Delphi by, Plate IV

colonization, 59–63; Apollo as god of, 63; community identity and, 322n40;

founding of Delphi, 38; oracle and advice on settlement, 86, 89, 97, 111, 132–33, 140, 188

columns: Aemilius Paullus dedication, **16,** 190–91, **191,** 196, 299; Aetolian two-column style dedications, 178; Agis of Sparta's dedication, 141; of Apollo sanctuary, rebuilding, 278; of Athena sanctuary, rebuilding, 278, 292; Athenian omphalos dedication and, 160, 299; of Athenian treasury, 113; caryatid, 106–7; Gelon's tripod, 123; graffiti inscribed on, **256;** ionic, 224–25; Naxian lion dedication, 87, 147; omphalos and tripod dedication, **16;** Plataean serpent dedication, **16,** 121–22, 151, 240–41, **241,** 295; Rhodian chariot of Helios dedication, 160; of running track, 224–26

Committee of Antiquaries, 262

community identity: architectural style and, 133; Attalids and cultural, 177; colonization and, 322n40; and cultural homogeneity among the Greeks, 77; dedications and definition of, 133, 167, 177, 288, 322n40, 340n18; of Delphi, 143; Hellanes (Greeks) as shared, 120; pan-Greek interaction at sanctuaries, 76–77; Persian War commemoration and collective "Hellanes," 121–22; self-definition and, 54, 59

Constantine the Great, 240–41, 365n44

Constantius Chlorus, 240

construction at Delphi: during Aetolian control of Delphi, 176; Amphictyony and, 75, 92, 94, 103, 113, 146, 157, 159, 162; and architectural innovation, 342n44; contracts for, 93, 95, 100; domestic architecture, 45, 49, 51, 64, 74; during Domitian's reign, 213; earliest structure at site, 41–42; financing of, 95–96, 100, 113, 156, 188, 199, 235, 331n18; after fire of 548, 94–98; legendary, 32; materials used in, 36, 87, 95, 100, 102, 106, 113, 224–26, 235, 246, 298 (*see also* reuse of materials *under this heading*); rebuilding projects, 94, 102–3, 146, 156, 157, 159, 162, 278, 292, 293, 340n16; reuse of materials, 102–3, 104, 246, 366n2;

during Roman Imperial governance, 236; stadium, 235; stone quarries in area, 95, 235, 285; tamiai (treasurers) instituted for oversight, 163; temple, 87, 95, 100, 113, 246; terracing and site engineering, 45, 92–93, 102, 156, **Plate II**

consultation of the Pythia: ambiguity of responses, 28–30, 60, 84–85, 110, 114, 117, 120–21, 134, 136, 163–64, 179, 201, 210–11, 233, 314n58, 328n43; annual calendar and, 13; Athenian, 151, 198; colonization and, 61, 63, 86, 89, 97, 111, 132–33, 140, 188; communication of response to consultant, 19–20, 27–28; decline in, 183, 204–5, 221–22, 336n19; exemption from tax, 174; fabrication or appropriation of, 164, 168; "fake" oracles and, 55, 320n11; fees for, 16–17, 85, 141, 174, 210; "forced" prophecy, 20–21, 311n13; framing of questions for, 26–28, 83–84, 139, 142; as male privilege, 17; orientation of Pythia and consultant, 18; Plutarch on, 218; and political deliberation, 26–27, 29, 54–56; process of, 17–20, 360n46; promanteia and, 15; religious contexts of, 24–26; research and authentication of evidence, 55; Roman, 199–201, 204–5, 210–11, 214; sacrifice and, 15, 17–21, 364n33; "shopping" for favorable responses, 84, 142, 316n28; sources describing, 10–11; Sparta and, 130–31; temple architecture and, 18; verse responses to, 19, 27–28, 200, 218, 312n26; via tin inscriptions in sealed jars, 151–52

Convert, Henri, 271

Corcyra, 133

Core: sanctuary at Eleusis, 151–52

Corinth, 45–46, 47–48, 52, 56, 57, 66, 70; Chyselephantine statue dedication by, 328n36, Plate **V**; conflict with Sicyon, 325n13; petition to rename Cypselus's treasury, 108; Rome and destruction of, 193; sanctuary at, 165; treasury of, 66, 108, 327n32, **Plate II**

Cornelius Scipion, P. (Scipio Africanus), 350n12

correctors (Roman), 215, 358n29

correspondence with Delphi: Claudius and, 208; Domitian and, 212–13; Gallienus and, 208, 364n37; Hadrian and, 223–24, 226; Trajan and, 215

Corycian cave, 53, 183, 234; archaeological excavation of, 283–84; artifacts found in, 43, 219, 345n14; as home of serpent, 35; inscriptions at, 167; modern visitors to, 301; photos of, **3, 14**; Raikes and discovery of, 255; terra-cotta lamps found in, 219

Corycians, 86–87

Cos, 171

Coubertin, Pierre de, 272

craters, **125,** 157

Craterus, niche of, 246

Crates, 148–49

Crete: consultation of the oracle by, 114; decline of influence at Delphi, 74; and founding of Delphi, 38; and purification of Apollo, 35; relationship with Delphi, 69; shields as dedications, 296; smaller offerings as dedications from, 68, 69

Crisa, 31–32, 71–72, 77, 324n1

Croesus of Lydia, 17, 26–30, 83, 97, 314n53, 328n43; consultation of the Pythia by, 28–29, 83–85, 328n43; dedications to Delphi, 84–85, 93–94; golden lion dedication, 84, 93, 151; mixing bowls dedicated by, 84, 93, 151, 198

Croton, 108; dedications from, 123

cultivation of sacred land, 71–72, 73, 75, 80, 151, 161, 169

cults: Antinous Propylaius at Delphi, 104, 224, 299; calendar of sacrifices at Delphi, 104; during Christian era, 242; Domitian and traditional religious observances, 212–13; evidence of, 48; gods worshipped at Delphi, 2, 103–4; Imperial cult of Rome at Delphi, 220; mingling of secular and sacred activities, 64–65, 74; oracle as authority on, 86, 89; provenance of dedicated objects, 49. *See also Specific gods*

cultural homogeneity among the Greeks, 77

currants, tax on export crop, 265–67

currency: Hadrian and Delphic coinage, 224

curses: of the Alcmaeonids, 98–99, 109; and cultivation of sacred land, 235; on looted Delphic treasures, 154, 170–71, 199; on the Phocians, 154; and violation of asylum, 98

Curtius, Ernst, 261

Cybele, 141

Cylon, 58, 80, 98, 325n14

Cyme, 97, 140

Cyprus, 67–68; dedications from, 110

Cypselus, 57, 66, 83, 108, 327n32

Cyrene, 60–61, 97; treasury dedicated by, 160, **Plate II**

Cyriac of Ancona, 249–51, 283

Cyrus, 85, 139

damiourgoi, government of Delphi by, 226, 239–40, 326n23, 365n43

dancers originally part of Acanthus column dedication, 166, 299

Daochus of Thessaly, 163, 166

Dardani, 199

Daux, Georges, 192–93, 275

de Boer, Jelle, 23, 284

dedications, 53; as advertisement of dedicators' reputation, 121–23, 127–28, 132, 137, 142, 146, 174, 288; archaic style implemented in, 167–68; armor or shields as, 111, 112, 113; athletic victors honored with, 123, 188, 197, 214, 238, 300; burial of, 44, 88–90, **89,** 123, 278–79, **279, 280,** 297, 300, 328n36, **Plate V**; civic, in sanctuary, 162; and civic identity of donors, 108, 111, 167, 287–88; and community identity, 120, 133, 167, 177, 288, 322n40, 340; contemporary studies and records of, 167; by Delphians for member of their families, 235–36; destruction of, 151, 154–55; "dying" with dedicators, 146; as evidence of relationship of communities to Delphi, 49, 66–69; and favoritism of oracle, 82–85; as historical record, 122, 133–34, 137, 146, 147, 160, 167–68; inscriptions and rededication of monuments, 147; and interaction with sanctuary, 65–66; linked with fate of dedicators, 137; military victories commemorated with, 16, 120–23, 127–29, **129,**

133, 137, 147, 156, 160, 167, 178, 190, **191,** 193, 210–11, 219, 238–39, 293–95, 299–300; "monument war" and, 146–47; Nero and removal of, 210; omens seen at Delphi, 137, 165; painted embellishment of, 128; poets honored with, 197, 362n15; as political statements, 333n42; as propaganda, 189–90, 351n24; as property of the gods, 105, 195; as proxy for political control or pre-eminence, 129–32; refused by Delphi, 122, 335n8; reorganization and repositioning of, 173; repurposing of, 105, 131, 190, 212, 239, 297; as restitution for transgression, 81; "spatial monopolization" of sacred site and, 113, 127–28, 140–41, 146–47; "style" and attributed provenance of, 68, 86–87, 105; theft of, 170–71, 195, 199; updating of, 172–73, 174, 178. *See also Specific donors or monuments*

defense of Delphi: Aetolians and, 170–71, 180; Amphictyony and, 78, 150, 178; fortress-like walls constructed, 150, 249; against the Gauls, 170–71; lack of Delphian army, 161, 187, 196; landscape as natural, 3; neutrality and shared responsibility for, 72; Phocians and, 170–71; Sparta and, 131; supernatural, 116–18, 125–26, 170; vulnerability and, 70, 134, 196

Defradas, Jean, 62

De la Coste-Messeliere, Pierre, 183, 275–76, **276**

Delian league, 122, 126

Deliyannis, Theodoros, 266–67

Delos, 136; excavation of, 263; sanctuary of Apollo at, 173

Delphi, 103, 134; abandonment of, 249; archeological evidence of cult practice at, 44; as the "center of the world," 30, 36, 49, 86, 120, 122, 315 (*see also* omphalos); city's role in management of sanctuary, 144, 159, 186–87, 238, 284, 286, 288–89, 326n23, 350n12, 357n13; civic government of, 326n23, 343n48; civic structures of, 143; as cosmopolitan community, 104–5, 184, 209; as cultural rather than financial power, 206; decline of, 193, 200–201,

235–36, 239–40; defense of, 142–45, 166, 187, 196, 199; disappearance of, 249; economic dependence on sanctuary, 143; founding of, 31–33, 38, 133–34; habitation of, 44–45, 94; *Homeric Hymn to Apollo* on origin of, 31–33; as information hub, 27–28, 38, 62, 218; internal conflict in, 148; landscape and setting of, 2–4, 291; meaning of name, 36; modern, 3, 300–301; neutrality or autonomy of, 65, 135–36, 186–87, 188, 215, 235, 286–87; oracle at (*see* Pythia); as "Panhellenic," 65; and political rivalry between Athens and Sparta, 111, 134–35; political value of, 201–2; population of, 142–43, 208, 249; relationship with Amphictyony, 159, 186–87; Rome and, 184, 200, 235–36, 286–87; sacked by northern tribes, 199; strategic value of, 75, 134; territorial boundaries of, 186

Delphiens, 263

Delphus, 35–36

Demangel, Robert, 275

Demaratus of Sparta, 109, 111–12

Demeter: First Fruits dedication at sanctuary of Eleusis, 133; sanctuaries dedicated to, 77–78, 151–52, 159, 174

Demetrius, war of, 178

Demetrius Poliorcetes, 168

demigods, Delphi as worship site for, 103–4

democracy, 98, 109, 133

Demonax of Mantinea, 97

Demosthenes, 155, 160–61

Dempsey, T., 23

Déroche, Vincent, 247

Description of Greece (Pausanias), 233–34, 254

Dio Chrysostom, 214

Diodorus Siculus, 13, 72, 131–32, 151, 154, 170–71

Dionysius of Syracuse, 144–45

Dionysus: Delphi as cult site, 13, 18, 35, 36, 86, 104, 152–53, 197, 220–21, 313n43, 315n14, 317n34, 318n57, 329n47; Dionysiac guild of Athens, 194; sanctuary at Thebes, 178; sculpture on Temple of Apollo pediment, **153,** 153–54; Thyades celebration in Parnassian mountains, 152, 220–21 divination. *See* oracles; Pythia

Dodona, 24, 310n2

Dolonchi of the Chersonesus, 99

dolphins, 32

Domitian, emperor of Rome, 211–12; dedication honoring, 213; and traditional religious observances, 212–13

dragon of Delphi, 32, 34

Dragoumis, Stephanos, 265

Dropion of Paeonia, 174

Drusilla, 207

earthquakes, 295; and collapse of walls, 145, 177; and disruption of oracle, 145, 147, 242–43; mudslide over "big dig" excavation, 277; protection of site from, 283; reconstruction after, 148; and relocation of Castri residents, 262–63; structures and dedications damaged by, 156, 212

Echecrates of Thessaly, 13

economics: archaeology as international business, 265–66; costs of reconstruction after fire, 95–96; currency, 77, 159, **159**, 199; Delphi as cultural rather than financial power, 206; Delphi as resource poor site, 38; donations and support of Delphi, 156, 192; evidence of economic crisis in Greece, 148; fees or price of oracle consultation, 16–17, 85, 141, 174, 210; festivals and, 188; oracle as business, 33, 70, 85, 96–97, 143, 187, 360n46 (*see also* fees or price of oracle consultation *under this heading*); purchase of offering goods, 16–18; Pythian games as enterprise, 236–37; Roman financial administrators at Delphi, 215; and secular habitation of Delphi, 143; of slavery and manumissions, 355n58, 355n59; tax to consult oracle, 85; trade, 46–48, 52–53, 68

Egypt, 173, 176; control of Greek territories by, 184; support of Delphi by, 96

Elatea, 161

Eleusis, 161

Elgin, 256

Elis, 140

"E" (mysterious inscription), 203–4, 217–18

entryways into sacred space, 66, 103, 242, 246, 294, 347n28

Ephialtes, 120

Ephorus, 35, 72

Epidamnus, 133

Epidaurus, 165

epimeletai (overseers), 183, 203, 207, 356n1; Delphians as, 213

Epirus, 173; dedications by, 175, 177

Eponymous, 178

Etruscans, 123, 127

Euboea: pottery from, 53

Euchidas of Palatea, 119

Eudamus of Nicopolis, 207

Eudocus, 188

Eumeneia festival, 192, 220

Eumenes II of Pergamon, 185–86; dedication at Delphi, 188; monument erected honoring, 192; Perseus and attempted murder of, 189; relationship with Delphi, 187–88; as Roman ally, 192; statue of, location, 16

Eumenides (Aeschylus), 15

Euripides, 25, 34–35, 135, 136

Eurylochus, 72

Eurymedon, 128

Eusebius, 11, 242–43

Evans, Arthur, 43

Evans-Pritchard, Edward, 26

exegetai pythochrestoi (interpreters of sacred law and ritual), 81

feathers and beeswax, temple of, 36

festivals at Delphi, 152, 351n18; 20th century revival of, 277; adjustments to Delphic festival calendar, 173; Alcesippeia, 188, 220; Athenian Pythaïs, 194–95, 204, 299; Attaleia, 192, 220; Charila, 221; Dodekais, 204, 212–13; Eumeneia, 192, 220; Herois, 221; monthly, 220; Plutarch on religious calendar, 219–20; and reputation of Delphi, 287; Romaia, 187, 220, 350n14; Sebasta, 220; Septerion, 221; Soteria, 173, 175–76, 220, 348n41, 354n52; Theoxenia, 220. *See also* Pythian games

fines, 149–50, 154, 159, 196

fire: Athenian Pythaïs festival and, 194; Delphi as hearth of Greece, 119–20, 122; at Delphi extinguished by northern tribes, 199; and destruction at Delphi, 51, 64, 90, 93–94; reconstruction after fire of 548, 94–98; sacred hearth in Delphi, 15, 17, 19, 194, 312n26

First Macedonian War, 180

First Punic War, 175

First Sacred War, 71–74; Amphictyony and, 144–45; literary tradition and, 160

Flavius Aristotimus, T., 224

Flavius Constantius, 242

"forced" prophecy, 20–21, 311n13

Forrest, George, 62, 63

"fortune telling," 30

Foucart, Paul, 263, 264, 266

Fountain spring, 262

Fourth Sacred War, 161–62

Frangos, Dimos, 260, 263, 264

fraud, oracle as, 22–23, 27–28

French School in Athens, 262, 263, 264, 266, 267, 269, 275, 277, 369n37, 372n34

Fufius Calenus, Q., 200, 355n60

Fulvius Nobilior, M., 187

Gaia, 33–35, 39, 41, 44, 87, 104, 132, 295; "Chapel of Gaia," 68; Delphi as cult site, 102, 132, 295; Demeter, sanctuaries dedicated to, 77–78

Galba, 210

Galen, 232

Gallienus, 208, 238, 364n37

games. See athletic competitions

Gauls, invasion of, 170–71, 346n25

Gell, William, 253, 255; drawing of Castri by, **254**

Gellius Menogenes, L., 240

Gelon of Gela, 114, 116, 122–23; dedications by, 151

geography of Delphi: aerial views, **2, 3**; earthquakes, 145, 156, 170, 212, 242–44, 262, 340n15; and explanations for inspiration of the Pythia, 23–24, 242–43, 284; and isolation of Delphi, 38, 143; map of Delphi and immediate surroundings, **xvi**; pine trees planted, 277; research on, 373n36; rock falls, 275, 283, 292, **Plate VIII.** See also earthquakes

George I, King of Greece, 262

Gephyraei, 202

German Archaeological Institute, 261

Germany: attack on Delphi during W.W.II, 282

Giantomachy (Siphnian treasury), 107, 298

Giantomachy (Temple of Apollo), 102

glass, 68, 361n6

Glaucus, 85

goats, sacrifice of, 15, 20–21

gods worshipped at Delphi, 2, 103–4, 287. See also Specific gods

gold: Alexander I of Macedon, golden statue of, 122, 151; Croesus and dedications of, 83–84, 93, 151; "E," 204, 217; lion, 84, 93, 151; mines of Siphnos, 105–6; on palm tree dedications, 121, 128, 137; Perseus, golden statue planned by, 190; tripod of Plataean serpent column, 121, 151, 228; vessels as dedications, 84, 175; vessels used in oracle consultation, 151–52

Gordian III, Emperor, 237, 238

Gorgias of Sicily, 142

Gortyn, 214

grammarian, dedication honoring, 214

Great Rhetra (Spartan constitution), 56

Greco-Turkish War, 272

Greek Archaeological Society, 258, 261–62, 263, 264; administration of Delphi site, 275

Greek Civil War (1947–49), 282

Guide de Delphes, 291

Guys, Pierre Augustin, 257

Gyges of Lydia, 58, 321n21

gymnasium, 157–59, 292; baths, library, and dining room constructed, 213–14; Christian church constructed on site, 292; construction on site of, 245–46; graffiti inscribed on columns, **256**; location of, **Plate I**; reconstruction illustrating, **158**; running track, 213, 224–25

gymnasium complex, 213–14

Hadrian, 215, 299; consultation of the oracle by, 224; and cult of Antinous Propylaius, 104, 224; and Delphi, 222, 223–28; and government of Delphi by damiourgoi, 226, 239–40; Panhellenion, 227–28, 234; statue of, 223–24, 242

Hale, first name, 284

Hamilton, Gavin, 252

Hamilton, George, Earl of Aberdeen, 255

Hamilton, William, 255

Heliodorus, 1–2, 6, 236

Helios, Rhodian statue of, location, 16, 160

Helladic periods, 43

Heracleia Pontice, 24, 86

Heracles, 74, 104, 108, 113, 298–99, 316n27, 320n8

Herculaneum, 252

Hermes: cult practices at Delphi, 154

Herodes Atticus, 229–30, **231**, 235, 362n18

Herodotus, 18, 26–27, 56, 58, 60–61, 63; on Alcmaeonids, 98; on construction of temple, 100; consultations mentioned in, 85; on dedications, 87–88; on fire of 548 BC, 94; on Peisistratids, 99; on Persian Invasion, 116; on Siphnians, 105–6, 108

heroes: at battle of Marathon, 129; Delphi and identification of, 179; Delphi as worship site for, 104, 110, 125–26; ghostly warriors, 112, 116; tribal heroes of Athens selected by Delphic oracle, 113

Herois festival, 221

Hesiod, 31, 38–39, 72, 318n57

Hieron of Syracuse, 123, 125, 300, 335n10

Hippias, 100–101, 109, 111–12

history: dedications at Delphi as public historical record, 133–34, 137, 147, 160, 167–68; oracle and creation of history for Messenia, 168, 345n17; revision or retelling at Delphi, 147, 160, 167–68

hoax, oracle as, 22–23, 27–28

Homer, 224, 318n57

Homeric Hymn to Apollo, 40, 69, 72, 143; on origins of Delphi, 31–33, 38

Homolle, Theophile, 265–66, 266–71, 273–75, 313n36

horses, sculptures of, 123, 184, 190, 239, 298, 300, 323n49

hosioi, 19

Hypata, 213

Hyperboreans, 13, 33, 102

Iliad (Homer), 49

Iliupersis painter, crater decorated by, **125**

Illyria, 144–45, 199

impiety: accusations of, 160–61

inscriptions: about Amphictyony, 144; archaeological excavation of, 258; on Athenian treasury, 194, 293–94; bilingual, 196; at Corycian cave, 167; discovery and excavation of, 272; 18th century enthusiasm for, 252; as evidence of economic crisis in Greece, 148; graffiti inscribed on columns, **256**; imperial correspondence, 208, 226; letter form evolution seen in, 157–58; of manumissions, 200, 355n59; in museum, 299; of musical notation, 194, 299; prohibited activities, 348n45; on reserved theater seats, 214; on stadium, 157–58, 296; on temple of Apollo, 208, 211–12, 215; on walls, 157–58, 200, **201, 252**

Ion (Euripides), 136

Ionians, 89

Ion of Samos, 147

Iphicrates, 145

Iphigenia at Tauris (Euripides), 34–35

iron, dedications of, 58, 65, 83; chair of Pindar, 311n21, 335n13; spits of Rhodopis, 87–88, 219

Isagoras, 109

Isocrates, 72

Isthmia: Isthmian games, 184, 209; sanctuaries at, 76, 121

Itean plain, 95; aerial photo of, 2; settlement of, 52, 319n3

Iunius Gallio, L., 208

Jason of Pherai, 145

Johnston, Sarah I., 29

Julian, emperor, 141; defense of Delphi by, 366n54

Julian the Apostate, 243

Julius Caesar, 200
Julius Prudens, C., 223
Junius Mnaseas, M., 235

Kalapodi, 46–48, 318n50, 318n52, 326n15
Kalligas, P., 262
Keramopoullos, Antonios, 275
Knights (Aristophanes), 25, 135
koinons, 169, 207–8
Kondoleon, Alexandros, 275
Koumoundouros, Alexandros, 264–65

Labydai, 144
Laconia, 66, 69
Lamius the Aetolian, 176
lamps: Christian period artifacts, 300
landscape, 2–4; 19th painting and enthusiasm
    for, 253–54. *See also* geography of Delphi
laurel: as intoxicant, 22; oracular powers
    linked to, 20, 21, 22, 309n1; temple of, 36;
    and worship of Apollo, 15, 18, 19; wreaths
    as prize in games, 73, 221, 259n40, 326n16,
    359n40
law: Amphictyony and decrees, 144; Delphi
    as legislative authority, 341n27; Delphi
    as site of manumissions, 200, 355n59;
    Delphi's role in Plato's ideal state, 143–44;
    legal contracts and construction projects,
    95; oracle as authority and judge, 89, 97,
    127, 136, 166
Leake, William Martin, 254
Lelantine War, 59
Lerat, Lucien, 277
lesche, Cnidian, 128, 160, 192, **Plate II**
Letter to Philip (Speusippos), 72
Leuctra, 145, 340n18
Leuke, 140
lions: bone found during excavation, 284;
    Croesus's golden lion dedication, 84, 93,
    151; on fragment of Minoan vessel, 42;
    Naxian lion dedication, 87, 147
Liparians, 127
literary sources: archeological evidence
    contrasted with, 48; and archeological ex-
    pectations, 42, 233–34, 256–57; and dating
    of events, 37–38; evidence for Sacred Wars

in, 72–73, 160; and evidence of consulta-
    tion process, 11; reliability of, 22. *See also*
    Specific authors
Livia, 203–4, 217–18
Livius Salinator, G., 187
Locris, 160–61; dedications by, 176–77, 197;
    manumissions at Delphi, 200; tribute of
    maidens to Troy, 168
lot oracle, 13, 24–25, 141, 310n10, 311n16,
    320n11, 323n56
Lucan, 21
Luce, Jean Marc, 51, 54
Lucius Mummius, 193
Lucius Cornelius Scipio Asiaticus, 199
Lucius Verrus, 233
Lydia, 70, 151. *See also* Croesus of Lydia
Lysander, 137, 141, 146

Macedon, 178, 180, 188–89. *See also* Alexan-
    der I of Macedon; Alexander the Great of
    Macedon; Perseus of Macedon; Philip II
    of Macedon; Philip V of Macedon
"madness" of the Pythia, 21–22
Maedi, 199
Magna Mater, 169
Magnesia, battle of, 186
maison jaune, 64, 74
maison noire, 45, 49, 51, 64, 74
maison rouge, 64, 74
Malkin, Irad, 59
management of Delphi: Aetolian, 169–76,
    175, 179, 180, 183, 185, 186; Amphictyony
    and, 71–80, 73, 184, 186, 238, 286; city of
    Delphi and, 144, 159, 186–87, 238, 284,
    286, 288–89, 326n23, 350n12, 357n13; and
    neutrality, 286; Phocian, 154–55; as po-
    litical issue, 79–80; by prytaneis, 357n13;
    and reputation and influence in ancient
    world, 288–89; Roman, 194–96, 213, 226;
    Spartan, 130–31, 134–37, 142
Manius Acilius Glabrio, 185–86
manteis (oracle-tellers or seers), 25
Mantinea, battle, 147
manumissions: inscriptions at Delphi, 200,
    355n59

maps: Delphi and immediate surroundings, **xvi**; Delphi and the Aegean, **xv**; Delphi and the Mediterranean, **xiv**; Leake's maps of Greece, 254; Raike's maps of Parnassian landscape, 254

Marathon, battle of, 112–13; dedications commemorating, 129, 137, 160, 178, 293–94

Marcadé, Jean, 277

Marcus Aurelius, 215, 230, 232, 233

Mardonius, 116

Massalians, 104–5; dedications from, 110

maxims of Delphi, 138

Medeon, 52

Megacles, 98–99, 113, 125

Megarians, 137

megaron (room of consultation), 18

Megera, 86

Meleager sarcophagus, 231–32, **232**, 296

Melisseus, 219

Memmia Lupa, 214

Memmius, 223

Messenia, 180; oracle and creation of history for, 168, 345n17; triangular column, miniature of, 301; war with Sparta, 57, 320n17

Mestrius Florus, L., 215

metallurgy. *See Specific metals*

metopes, 297; in Museum at Delphi, 297, 298; relief sculpture on Athenian treasury, 113, 272, 298; shields hung from Apollo temple, 113, 160, 171; on tholos, 82; visual experience of scenes in, 82

Midas of Phrygia, 58

Miltiades the Elder, 99

Minoan rhyton, 42

Minucius Rufus, M., 196

Mithridates, 197, 198–99

modern use of site, 283

monopteros, 82, 105

Montholon, le Compt de, 265

Moralia (Plutarch), 216–20

mosaics, 247–48, 367n6

Moustoxydis, Andréas, 258

Moüy, le Compt de, 264, 265

Müller, Carl, 258

museums: 2004 opening of new, 283; construction of, 278; and electrification at site, 283; tour of exhibits, 296–300

music: competitions, 4, 72–73, 173, 184, 188–89, 287, 357n15; construction of theater at Delphi, 188; fees for performances, 206; hymn inscribed in Athenian treasury, 272; inscription of musical notation, 194, 299; performances at Delphi, 189, 197, 206; and reputation of Delphi, 287

Mycenae: excavation of, 263

Mycenaean period, 44–45

Myra, 229

Naupactian triangular column, 301

Naxian Sphinx, 87, 88, 147, 297, **Plate II**; plaster cast exhibited in Paris, 272; reconstruction plan for, 278

Naxos, 87. *See also* Naxian Sphinx

Nemea, 76

Nemean (Pindar), 125

Neolithic occupation of Delphi, 43

Neopolis, 136

Neoptolemus, 174; cult of, 104, 125–26, 157, 163, 236–37; in Heliodorus, 1

Nero: as competitor in Pythian games, 209, 211; and consultation of the Pythia, 210–11; dedications removed from Delphi by, 210–11; honored by Amphictyony, 209–10

Nerva, 214

Nicates, son of Alcinus, 195

Nicias, 25

Nicopolis, 203, 205, 207

Nicostratus: dedication honoring, 350n12

Nigrinus, 215–16

Nike of Gelon, 151

Nikephoria games, 188

Octavian, 201–2

Odysseus: association with Delphi site, 158–59

Odyssey (Homer), 49

offerings: altars for burning sacrificial, 94; pelanos (cakes) as, 16; smaller or sacrificial,

26, 47, 67–68; trade and, 53; treasuries and storage of, 66. *See also* dedications

oikos (room of consultation), 18

Olympia, 67, 69, 108, 112, 140, 165; archaeological excavation of, 261; dedications at, 82–83, 332n31; excavation of, 263; games at, 166; Roman interest in, 204–5, 207; Sicyonian focus on, 332n31

Olympias (Myrtale), 164, 165

omens: and celebration of Pythaïs festival, 194; Delphi consulted to interpret, 161; divination and natural events, 24–25, 309n1; reported at Delphi, 137, 148, 165; and Sulla's raiding of treasuries at Delphi, 197–98

omphalos, 36; Athens column dedication, 166; as the "center of the world," 18, 36, 166, 299; Hellenistic/Roman version of, 37; in museum, 299; as optical device, 315n19; and tripod, location of, 16, 18

On the Embassy (Aeschines), 71

Oppé, A. P., 22

oracles: authority and competition among, 39–40; as continuing institution during Christian era, 236, 242–43; at Delphi (*see* Pythia); discover of "lost," 145; at Dodona, 24, 310n2; "fortune telling," 30; interpretation of natural phenomena, 24, 309n1; lot oracle, 13, 24–25, 141, 310n10, 311n16, 320n11, 323n56; manipulation of, 142; manteis (oracle-tellers or seers), 25; Plutarch on "obsolescence of," 218; political leaders as, 168; religious contexts for, 24–26, 54–55; as "sense-making mechanism," 30

Orestiea (Aeschylus), 33–34

Oribasius, 243

Origen of Alexandria, 236

Orneates of the Argolid, 167

Orrhippus of Megara, 336n15

Orsilaus, 148–49

Osborne, Robin, 46, 59–60, 117

Otto, King of Greece, 257, 262

Ottoman Empire, 250–51, 263–64; Greece independence from, 257

Ovid, 169

Pactyes, 97

Paean (Pindar), 36, 125

painting: competition at Delphi, 124; crater decorated by Iliupersis painter, **125**; embellishment of dedications, 128

Palmer, Eva, 277

palm tree dedications, 16, 121, 128, 137

Pan, 167

Parallel Lives (Plutarch), 216

Parke, Herbert, 11–12, 140, 164, 167, 183

Parnassus, Mount, 31, 34

Parnassus (hero), 35

Paros, 188

Parthenon, 251–52, 255–56; Elgin's removal of marbles from, 255

Pausanias (historian and geographer), 60, 83; and archeological expectations, 42, 233–34, 363n25; English translation of works, 254; on founding of Delphi, 35–36; on inspiration of the Pythia, 21; on rivalry among oracles, 39–40; on Siphnians, 108

Pausanias (Spartan general): attempted "hijack" of Plataean dedication by, 121, 126, 334n6

Peisistratids, 98–101

Peisistratus, 25

pelanos (cakes) as offerings, 16

Peloponnesian War, 136–38

pochora, 46–47, 49

Pergamon, 184, 192

Periallus (Pythia involved in bribery), 112, 310n5

Periander, 83, 327n32

Pericles, 131

periodos circuit, 76, 209, 229, 288, 324n7, 339n7

perirrhanterion, 82

"peristyle house," 214

Perseus of Macedon, 189; Delphi used for propaganda by, 189–90, 351n24

Persia, 97–98, 112; Cyrus and, 139; peace negotiations at Delphi, 147; Philip II of Macedon and plans to attack, 163; as threat to Greek city states, 114. *See also* Persian Wars

Persians (Aeschylus), 126

Persian Wars: consultations of Delphic oracle during, 112–17; dedications commemorating, 117–18, 121–22, 295; Delphi suspected of treason during, 114–17, 119; and reputation of Greek cities, 117–18; Thebes as Persian ally, 160

Phaselis, inscription of, 141

Pheidias, 205

Phemonoe, 310n5

Phi figurines, 44

Philip II of Macedon, 154–55; Athens and, 155, 160, 161; consultation of the Delphic oracle by, 163–64; death of, 163–64; dedications honoring, 155, 162; Hellenic league based in Delphi, 163; victory at Chaeroneia over Athens and Thebes, 161–62

Philippi, battle of, 201

Philip V of Macedon, 179, 180; annexation of Greek territories by, 184; death of, 188; invasion of Pergamon by, 186; as Roman ally, 185

Philiscus of Abydus, 147

Philiscus (Roman governor of Thessaly), 238–39

Philodamus, 152

Philomelus, 149, 164

philosopher, bust of, 217, 300, 362n14

philosophy at Delphi, 138, 229, 362n14

Phlegyians, 32, 51

Phocis, 148; accused of sacrilege by Thebans, 149; control of Delphi by, 154–55; dedications from, 111, 167, 169, 171; destruction of dedications to finance war, 151, 154; fine levied on, 154, 156, 159; and incorporation of Delphi, 130–31, 130–32; manumission inscriptions at Delphi, 200; proxeny granted to, 165–66; restored to Amphictyony, 171

phratries, 144, 331n29

Phrygians, 68

Phylacus, 104, 170

Picard, Charles, 275, 277

Pindar, 35, 36, 73, 124–25

Pittakos, Kyriakos, 161–62

plagues, 85, 136, 212, 221

Plataea: battle of, 117

Plataean serpent column, 121–22, 151; Constantine's removal of, 240–41, 365n44; destruction of elements, 151; location, 16; miniature of, 301; Pausanias and attempted "hijack" of, 121, 126, 334n6; remnants at Delphi, 295

Plataikos (Isocrates), 72

Plato, 143–44

Pliny, 35–36

Plutarch: as agonothetes and member of Amphictyony, 216; on ambiguity of oracle, 29; bust of "philosopher type" identified with, 217, 300; on calendar of religious events at Delphi, 219–21; Chaeroneia as home of, 215–16, 359n30; on consultation of the Pythia, 18–21, 311n13; on Delphi as cult site, 41–42, 104, 218–21; on Dionysian festivals at Delphi, 152, 220–21; and fate of dedicators, 137; honored with dedications, 216; Moralia, 216–20; on mysterious "E," 204, 217–18; on Nero, 209; on obsolescence of oracles, 218; Parallel Lives, 216; on pneuma and inspiration of Pythia, 20–21, 23, 357n18; as priest of Apollo, 222, 223, 229, 300; and reputation of Delphi, 229; on selection and number of Pythias, 12; on verse response of Pythia, 218, 312n26; visits to sanctuary at Delphi, 215–16

poetry: dedications honoring poets, 197, 362n15; Pythia and verse responses to consultation, 19, 27–28, 200, 218, 312n26

Polemon of Ilion, 219

political roles of oracle: and adaptability, 59; as antityrannical or prodemocratic voice, 83, 328n39; in arbitration, 58, 133, 135–36, 138, 140, 168, 174; in colonization, 59–63; and control of Delphi as political issue, 70, 79–80, 122, 201–2; declining, 168, 336n19; and favoritism or bias, 148; interpretation as opportunity for political deliberation, 26–27, 29, 54–56; legitimation of rulers, 141; "management consultant," 30, 55, 57; in Plato's ideal state, 143–44; and propaganda, 189–90; and proxenia as political tool, 344n6; rulers as oracles in their own right, 168; and support of cult sites by political communities, 47; support of reform or innovation, 54–59, 81, 109–10

politics: Alcamaeonid/Peisistratid rivalry, 98–101, 110; Amphictyony as "general council of Greece," 205–6; Athenian, 98–101, 109–10, 111–12, 113–14; and civic community of Delphi, 134; dedications as political statements, 146–47, 190; Delphi as neutral or independent, 65, 70, 72, 73–74, 130, 135–36, 148, 268; Delphi as politically valuable, 201–2; democracy in Greece, 98, 109, 133; instability after Peloponnesian War, 139–48; international interaction, 76–77, 97–98; military events as context for reforms, 110; oracle and (see political roles of oracle); rivalry between Athens and Sparta, 111, 134–35; Solon and reshaping of Athenian social contract, 81; Spartan constitution, 56–57; tyranny, 54, 57–59, 63–64, 83, 328n39

Polycrates of Samos, 97

Polydeucion, 230, 242

Polygnota, 198, 206

Polygnotes, 128, 192

Polyzalus of Gela, 123

Pompeii, 252

Pompey, 200

Pomtow, Hans, 265–66, 273, 275

Poppaeus Sabinus, 207

Poseidon, 35

pottery. See ceramics

Pouilloux, Jean, 277

Praxias, 153

Praxo, 189

preservation of site, 275; environmental degradation and, 283; research and, 284

Price, Simon, 24

Priestess of Delphi (Collier), 22, Plate IV

priests, 18–19, 27–28, 312n25

processions: during Pythaïs festival, 204; routes for, 136, 157

prohedria, 85

promanteia, 15, 85, 147; Aetolia and, 165, 169; Athens and, 131, 155; of the Chians, 173, 294; Cyrene and, 160; Philip II of

Macedon and, 155; revoked, 155; Sparta and, 131; Thebes and, 148

Prometheus Unbound (Aeschylus), 277, 371n16

prophetes, 19

protection of site: legal, 257–58

proxenia, 165–66, 179, 183; Athens and, 178; and decline of Delphic influence, 193; as political tool, 344n6; as reflection of Delphi's attitude toward recipient, 172; Rome and, 185; Spartans and, 199

Prusias II of Bithynia, 251n17

prytaneum, 143

Psi figurines, 44

Ptolemies of Egypt, 173, 176, 184, 347n32, 348n48; control of Greek territories by, 184

Punic Wars, 175, 179–80, 184

purification, 20, 63; of Apollo, 35; springs at Delphi and ritual, 13, 15

Pydna, battle of, 190, 193; dedication commemorating victory, 299–300

Pylaioi, 174

Pyrrhus of Epirus, 173, 175

Pythaïs festival, 194–95, 204, 299; hymn inscription, 299; procession, 204

Pythia: access to, 90, 135, 136; and arbitration of disputes, 58, 135–36, 138, 140, 174; as authority on ritual practices, 86, 155–56; and competition among oracles, 39–40; decline of influence, 336n19; discover of "lost" oracles, 145; establishment of, 48, 53–54; "forced" prophecy, 20–21, 311n13; as fraud, 22–23, 27–28; in literature, 285–86; longevity and, 39, 41–42, 132; "madness" of the, 21–22, 312n34; as "management consultant," 30, 55, 57; myths linked to, 319n8; operation during reconstruction, 96–97; "peristyle house" as residence of, 214; political roles of (see political roles of oracle; politics); as religious authority, 364n33; reputation of, 26–27, 30, 39–42, 61, 63, 127–28, 132, 142, 145, 210, 285, 336n19; selection of, 12, 312n26, 315n14; "vapors" and inspiration of, 20–24, 211, 284, 357n18. See also consultation of the Pythia

Pythian, meaning of epithet, 32

Pythian games, 73, 75, 79–80, 123–24, 142, 174; 20th century revival of, 277; access to, 169; agonothetes, role of, 213; boycotted by Athens, 155; canceled during Sulla's campaign, 198; commemoration of victories at, 174; decline in attendance, 237; as economic enterprise, 236–37; "export" of, 236–38; funding of, 72; gymnasium and stadium built for, 157–59, **158**; Jason of Pherai and intent to preside over, 145; Nero as competitor in, 209–10; as Pan-Greek occasion, 76; Perseus and, 189; Philip II of Macedon and, 155; popularity of, 183–84, 197; returned to Greek control, 213; as Soteria festival, 175–76; theater constructed for, 295–926; victors list compiled, 159; women as competitors in, 209

Pythian Odes, 73

pythioi, 56

Pytho (serpent), 35, 36, 121, 316n30

quarries, 95, 235, 285

Quintus Fabius Pictor, 179

Raikes, Henry, 255

"Red house" (maison rouge), 64, 74

Regilla (wife of Herodes Atticus), 230

Replat, Joseph, 274–75

Revett, Nicholas, 252

Rhegion, 123

Rhodes, 184; border dispute arbitrated by, 188; sculpture of Helios dedicated by, 160 (another one collect)

Rhodopis, 87–88, 219

Robertson, Noel, 72

rock of the Sibyl: discovery and excavation of, 272

Romaia festival, 187, 220, 350n14

Rome, 173; Achean War, 193; consultation of Delphi by, 168–69, 179–80; control and management of Delphi, 194–96, 213, 226; dedications by, 168, 175, 179, 184–85, 190, 193, 203–4, 223; defeat of Antiochus and allies, 185–86; defeat of Carthage, 193; as enemy of Greece, 180; and "liberation" of Delphi, 186, 190; and "liberation" of Greece, 184–85, 209, 211; occupation of Delphi by, 189–90; and Perseus of Macedon, 189–90; Philip V of Macedon as enemy or ally of, 185; and Punic Wars, 179–80; relationship with Delphi, 168–69, 201–2, 203–14; Romaia festival at Delphi, 187; unified Greece as part of empire, 205–6; "unipolar" domination of Mediterranean by, 190–91, 193

roofing styles, 86–87, 329n50

Ross, Ludwig, 257

running track, 213, 224–26

sacred space: activities prohibited in sanctuary, 348n45; adyton as restricted space, 18; agriculture on sacred land, 183, 226; boundary markers and definition of, 66; cultivation of sacred land, 71–72, 73, 75, 80, 151, 161, 169; dedicators attempts to monopolize, 127; definition of boundaries for, 196; entryways into, 66, 103, 242, 246, 294, 347n28; land belonging to Apollo, 210; manipulation of dedicatory landscape within sanctuary, 167; monopolization of, 176, 293; paths and movement within, 103; placement of dedications and rivalry among dedicators, 166; reorganization and repositioning of dedications, 173; structures and definition of, 74–75, 87; visibility and domination of, 87; walls and definition of, 177

Sacred War, 72; First, 71–74, 144–45; Second, 130–32; Third, 149–51; Fourth, 161–62; Alcmaeonids and, 131–32; Amphictyony and, 144–45; in literature, 72–73, 160; and status of Delphi, 286

"sacred way," 103, 246, 293, 299; 331n23, 299

sacrifice, 15, 17–21, 26, 47, 67–68, 364n33; altars for, 94; and consultation of the Pythia, 15, 17–21, 364n33; Croesus and human, 84

sacrilege: accusations of, 148–49; theft and, 148–49, 199

Salamis, 81; battle at, 117, 120

Salamis Apollo, 120, 295; location of, 16

Samnite Wars, 168–69

Samos, 46–47; sanctuaries at, 173

Samos, sanctuary at, 47

Sarapion, 217

Sarcophagus of Meleager, 231–32, **232**, 257, 296

Sardinia, 132

Sardis, 179, 229

Satyrus of Samos, 184, 349n3

scandals, 114–16, 195–96; bribes, 25, 100–101, 111–12, 114–16, 134, 141; during Persian invasion, 114–16

Sciathus, inscription of, 17, 141, 311n16

Scipio Africanus (P. Cornelius Scipion), 350n12

Scordisci, 199

sculpture: Aetolian monument style at Delphi, 176; cultural homogeneity and, 77; as dedications, 87–88; and definition of community identity, 133; Elgin and Parthenon marbles, 256; kouroi statues, 110; kouros/kore style, 77; on metope panels, 82; paint and metal embellishment of, 107; pedimental sculptures, 102, 103, 298; reconstruction depicting placement of, **129**; Roman copies of Greek works, 362n15. *See also Specific dedications*

Scylla and Hydra group, 210–11

Scyros, 126

Sebasta festival, 220

Second Punic War, 179–80

Second Sacred War, 130–32

Seleucids, 173, 185

Seleucius II, 347n32

Septerion festival, 221

Septimus Severus, 235

serpent column. *See* Plataean serpent column

serpent of Delphi, 35, 36, 121; and Christian myth of St. George, 248

Seven Sages, 138, 184, 362n13

shields: as dedications, 67–68, 111, 113, 128, 160, 171–72, 185, 332n39, 346n25; in Museum, 296

Sibyls, 35–36

Sicily: Athenian expedition to, 136–37; colonization and, 60–63; dedications, **16**, 122–23, 142, 151, 295

Sicyon, 75, 105, 179; conflict with Corinth, 325n13; dedications of, 75, 82–83, 105, 272, 297, **Plate II**; and purification of Apollo, 35; Sicyonian treasury, 105, 272, 297, **Plate II**; tholos and monopteros dedications by, 82, 105; treasury at Olympia, 332n31; and war against Crisa, 71–72, 75

Sicyonian treasury: discovery and excavation of, 272

Sikélianos, Angelos, 277

silver: bull, 88, **89**, 297; mines of Siphnos, 105–6; vessels, 83, 84, 93, 151, 198

Sinope, 238

Siphnos,: Gigantomachy frieze, 107; reconstruction, **106**; Siphinian Treasury at Delphi, 105–8, 147, 293

slavery: manumissions at Delphi, 200, 355n58, 355n59

Smyrna, 176

Snodgrass, Anthony, 62

Society of Dilettanti, 252, 255–56

Society of Friends of the Muses, 254

Socrates, 139–40

Solon, 71, 81

Sophists, 229

Sosius Senecio, 215

Soteria (festival of "the saving" of Delphi), 173, 175–76, 220, 348n41, 354n52

space: dedications designed for Delphic, 107; Delphi as neutral, 134; domination of sanctuary, 87, 130, 162, 176; sanctuary space as undefined, 64–66, 68, 74; spatial politics of Delphi, 288; walls and definition of, 74–75, 89, 93

Sparta, 56–57, 70, 109; Aegospotamoi, dedication to victory at, **129**, 137, 147, 156, 219; Athens as political/military rival of, 100–102, 111, 130–32, 134–35, 134–37, 139–40; constitution and government of, 141; consultation of the Pythia by, 56–57, 114, 126, 137, 232; control of Delphi, 130–31, 134–37, 142; decline of, 140; dedications by, **129**, 131–32, 137, 141, 146, 199; defeat at Leuctra, 145–46; Delphi and, 134, 140–41; Great Rhetra constitution, 56–57; and Messenia, 57, 320n17; and Peristratid/

Sparta (continued)
Alcmaeonid rivalry, 98–101, 130–32;
preeminence in Delphi, 142; promanteia
granted to, 131; proxenia granted to, 199;
reconstruction depicting dedications at
entrance to Apollo sanctuary, **129**
Spartan stoa, 128, 129, 137
spatial politics. *See* sacred space
Speusippos, 72
Sphinx, Naxian, 87, **88**, 147, 278, 297, **Plate II**
Sphinx of Delphi, 87, **88**, 147
Spon, Jacob, 251
springs, sacred: dragon of Delphi and, 32
Spurius Postumius Albinus, 197
stadium, 157–59, 158, 197, **231**; completion
of, 173; Herodes Atticus and, 231, 235;
inscriptions on, 157–58, 296; location of,
3, **Plate I**; used for target practice during
W.W.II, 281
statuary. *See* sculpture
Stewart, Iain, 295
Stoa of Attalus, **Plate II**; converted to cistern
for baths, 365n43; dedication of, 177;
location of, 16
stoas: converted to house, 246; Spartan, 128,
129, 137; the West Stoa, 171–72, 347n28,
Plate II. *See also* Stoa of Attalus
Strabo, 6, 21, 35, 60, 72
Stuart, James, 252
Sturtzenbecker, A. F., 253
Sulla, 197–98, 206
Syngros, Iphigenia, 273
Syracuse, 86, 122–23, 137, 144–45

Tarantines, 127–28
Tarquinius Superbus, 168
Temple of Apollo, 295, **Plate II**; Amphictyony and construction of, 75, 113; archaeological excavation of, 258; Domitian and
refurbishment of, 211–12; fourth century
construction, 295; inscriptions on, 208,
211–12, 215; location of, 16; pedimental
sculptures, 153, **153**, 153–54, 298; photo-
graph of, **157**; rebuilding of columns, 278;
restoration during Roman period, 235;

sixth century, reconstruction, 101; temple
terrace, **16**, 102, 295, **Plate II**
Tenos, 176
terracing of site, 45, 87, 94, 102–3, 156, 287;
and destruction of previous structures,
102, 105, 156; polygonal wall and, 102;
during renovation of sanctuary, 156; for
stoa of Attalus, 177; Temple Terrace, **16,**
102, 295, **Plate II**; for West Stoa, 171–72
Thasos, 136
theater, 295–926, **Plate II**; civic use of,
326n23; constructed at Delphi, 188;
Delphi as theatron, 6; Delphi in Greek
tragedies, 126–27, 135, 136; plays staged at
Delphi, 136, 277, 371n16
Thebes, 110, 145; as ally of Athens, 161;
dedications commemorating victories
by, 160; defeated at Chaeroneia, 161–62;
as Persian ally, 160; Phocians accused of
sacrilege by, 149; rebellion and destruction
of, 165; rivalry with Athens, 148; sanctuary
of Dionysus at, 178
theft: accusations of, 85, 148–49; appropri-
ation of dedications, 195; bandit attacks
on pilgrims, 73; Brennus the Gaul and
looting of Delphi, 170–71; northern tribes
looting of Delphi, 199; tripod stolen by
Heracles, 74
Themis, 132
Themistocles, 117, 122, 335n8
Theocles, 207
Theodosius II, Emperor, 244–45
Theogony (Hesiod), 38–39
Theopompus, 219
Theoxenia, 220
Thermon, sanctuary at, 346n27
Thermopylae, 78, 117, 120; Roman defeat of
Antiochus and allies at, 185–86; sanctuary
at, 164
Theseus, 113, 126, 198, 298–99, 316n27
Thessalonike, games at, 237
Thessaly, 43, 45, 52, 70, 75, 132, 145; Aetolians
and control of, 178; as Amphictyony
member, 82, 210, 227, 342n44; dedications
from, 239, 323n56; dedications from Da-
ochus of, 163; and purification of Apollo,

35; relationship with Delphi, 82, 323n56, 342n44; as Roman province, 238–39; and war against Crisa, 71–72

Thiersch, Friedrich, 257

Third Sacred War, 149–51

tholos, 82; in Athena sanctuary, 149, 220, 278, 292; dedicated by Sicyonians, 82, 105; reconstruction of, 278

Thrace, 199

Thucydides, 59, 63, 121, 135, 136

Thurii, 132–33

Thyades, 152, 220–21

Tiberius, 207

Tiberius Flavius Soclarus, 213

Timon, 116–17

tin, inscribed sheets used in oracle consultation, 151–52

Titus, emperor of Rome: as archon of Delphi, 211

Titus Quinctius Flamininus, 184–85

tourism: 18th century, 252–53; 19th Century, 253–54; Plutarch on, 218–19; sights in modern city of Delphi, 300–301; tour of Museum, 296–300; tour of site, 291–96; visitors per year, 283

Tournaire, Albert: drawing by, 296

trade, 46–48, 52–53; trade networks and provenance of dedications, 68

Trajan, 214–15

treasuries at Delphi, 66, 68, 81, 86–87; Athenian, 112–13, **115**, 128, 194, 274–75, 293–94, **Plate II**; Cnidian, 212, 272, **Plate II**; converted to mundane use, 239, 246; Corinthian (Cypselus's), 66, 108, 327n32, **Plate II**; Cyrenean, 160, **Plate II**; Massalian, 105, **Plate III**; repurposing of Athena sanctuary, 159; Sicyonian, **Plate II**; Siphinian, 105–8, 147, 293, **Plate II**; Sulla and raid of, 197–98, 206; Theban, **Plate II**

treaties, 111, 136, 189, 346n20; between Philip II of Macedon and Athens, 155, 160

Tricoupis, Charilos, 265, 266, 267, 268

tripods, 45, 49, 53, 64, 66, 69; Heracles' theft of Delphic tripod, 74; and Platean serpent, 121; as symbol of Pythia, 121

Troizen, 117

Trojan War, 75

Trophonius, 32

Troy: discovery and excavation of, 263

Tryphosa, 209

tyranny: and consultation of the Pythia, 25, 57–59, 63–64; Delphi as antityrannical, 83, 328n39

Valens, 244

Valentinian, 244

Valerian, 238

vapors as source of prophetic inspiration, 20–24, 211, 284, 357n18

Vernon, Francis, 251

verse: dedications honoring poets, 197, 362n15; oracle's responses in, 27–28, 200, 218, 312n26

Vespasian, 209, 211

vessels: cauldrons, 67–68, 151, 296; craters, **125**, 157; melted down to finance war, 151; Minoan rhyton, 42; mixing bowls, 83, 84, 93, 151, 175, 198. *See also* ceramics

virginity or chastity, 12–13, 312n26

visibility, 110, 141, 146–47; Cnidian lesche and view of sanctuary, 128; omphalos as optical device, 315n19; placement of dedications, 105; terracing and, 87

von Pückler Muskau, Prince Hermann, 258

von Wilamovitz Moellendorff, 233–34

Walker, W: painting by, **Plate VII**

walls, 252; archaeological excavation of, 258; collapse during earthquakes, 145, 177; construction of boundary, 93–96; for defense of Delphi, 150, 249, 367n14; and definition of sacred space, 177; as foundation for treasuries, 105; inscriptions on, 157–58, 200, **201**, 252; interpretation of "wooden wall" oracle, 117; perimeter wall of Apollo sanctuary, 74–75, 87; polygonal wall, 102

Walpole, Horace, 252

war in Greek culture: Apollo's association with war, 40; community self-definition and warfare, 54, 59; dedications commemorating military victories, 16, 120–23,

war in Greek culture (continued)
127–29, 133, 137, 147, 156, 160, 167, 178, 190, **191,** 193, 210–11, 219, 238–39, 293–95, 299–300; destruction of dedications to finance war, 151; maritime power, 117, 120; oracle consultation and military advice, 57, 59, 110, 112–17, 314n58; supernatural heroes as warriors, 112, 116, 120, 170; war as context for civic reforms, 109–10. *See also Specific battles, wars*

War of the Allies, 179

water: site engineering and run-off channels, 156. *See also* baths, Roman; Castalian fountain

wedding at Delphi, conflict and, 148–49

West Stoa, 171–72, 347n28, **Plate II**

Wheler, George, 251, 253

Winckelmann, Johann Joachim, 252–53

wolf statue, 131

World Heritage Site, Delphi as, 373n3

World War I, 275

World War II, 278–82

Wormell, Donald, 11–12, 22, 140, 164, 167–68, 183

Xenocrates of Agrigentum, 125

Xenophon, 25, 139–40

Xerxes, 116

"Yellow house" *(maison jaune),* 64, 74